Eberhard Bohne, Charlie Karlsson (Eds.)

Repositioning Europe and America for Growth

Transatlantic Public Policy Series

edited by

Eberhard Bohne
Professor of Public Administration
German University of Administrative Sciences Speyer and
German Research Institute for Public Administration

Charles F. Bonser
Dean Emeritus
Indiana University
School of Public and Environmental Affairs, Bloomington

Tony Bovaird
Professor of Public Management and Policy
University of Birmingham
School of Public Policy

Suzanne J. Piotrowski
Associate Professor of Public Affairs and Administration
Rutgers University-Newark
School of Public Affairs and Administration

Volume 5

LIT

Repositioning Europe and America for Growth

The Role of Governments and Private Actors in Key Policy Areas

edited by

Eberhard Bohne and Charlie Karlsson

LIT

Bibliographic information published by the Deutsche Nationalbibliothek
The Deutsche Nationalbibliothek lists this publication in the Deutsche Nationalbibliografie; detailed bibliographic data are available in the Internet at http://dnb.d-nb.de.

ISBN 978-3-643-10776-3

A catalogue record for this book is available from the British Library

Fresnostr. 2 D-48159 Münster
Tel. +49 (0) 2 51-620 320 Fax +49 (0) 2 51-922 60 99
e-Mail: lit@lit-verlag.de http://www.lit-verlag.de

Distribution:
In Germany: LIT Verlag Fresnostr. 2, D-48159 Münster
Tel. +49 (0) 2 51-620 32 22, Fax +49 (0) 2 51-922 60 99, e-mail: vertrieb@lit-verlag.de

In Austria: Medienlogistik Pichler-ÖBZ, e-mail: mlo@medien-logistik.at

In Switzerland: B + M Buch- und Medienvertrieb, e-mail: order@buch-medien.ch

In the UK: Global Book Marketing, e-mail: mo@centralbooks.com

In North America by:

Transaction Publishers
New Brunswick (U.S.A.) and London (U.K.)

Transaction Publishers
Rutgers University
35 Berrue Circle
Piscataway, NJ 08854

Phone: +1 (732) 445 - 2280
Fax: + 1 (732) 445 - 3138
for orders (U. S. only):
toll free (888) 999 - 6778
e-mail: orders@transactionpub.com

Preface

This book presents the revised and updated contributions to the annual colloquium of the Transatlantic Policy Consortium (TPC) which was held on the general theme of "Repositioning Europe and America for Growth: The Role of Governments and Private Actors in Key Policy Areas" on May 28-30, 2009 at Jönköping International Business School (JIBS), Jönköping University, Sweden.

The TPC is a network of over 30 North-American and European universities and research institutions in the field of public policy and public administration.

The contributions analyze policy performance in key areas which seem particularly relevant for growth in the US and Europe: technology and innovation, energy, financial systems, and health and retirement systems. The focus of these analyses is on describing and comparing two different governance strategies in the policy areas under investigation: command and control and collaborative approaches. A specific form of collaborative governance, i.e. co-production of public service users and communities, is subject of the introductory essay.

Collaborative governance is high on the agenda of the international debate on governance. Its impetus comes from the United States. In the European context similar concepts have been discussed for a while using terms like cooperative/consensual governance/management, shared responsibility between governments and citizens, ensuring state etc. However, there seems to be a corporatist touch to the European debate, while the US concept of collaborative governance emphasizes transparency and inclusion of all stakeholders.

The contributions display a great variety of hierarchical and collaborative approaches. The general message is that hierarchical governance cannot be fully replaced by collaboration but should be complemented by collaborative approaches. There is no "one size fits all" solution for all policy areas. For each problem area one has to find the right mix of hierarchical and collaborative governance elements.

The TPC appreciates the financial support of Jönköping International Business School which made the colloquium and this publication possible.

The TPC is also indebted to the Bosch Foundation which funded three young German and three young American scholars to participate in the colloquium and to contribute to this volume.

Our special thanks go to Kerstin Ferroukhi whose organizational skills and good humour were essential for the success of the colloquium. The preparation of the camera-ready copy of the manuscript was in the hands of Andrea Langlotz; her diligence and patience are much appreciated.

Speyer/Jönköping *Eberhard Bohne* *Charlie Karlsson*
August 2010

Table of Contents

"Repositioning Europe and America for Growth: The Role of Governments and Private Actors in Key Policy Areas"

Liberalization of Energy Markets: the Role of Governments and Private Actors

Policy Framework for Technology and Innovation Through Markets or Regulation

The Future of Public and Private Health Systems and Retirement Systems in Aging Societies

Lessons from the Colloquium: Observations on Governance Approaches

Co-Production of Public Services and Collaborative Governance

1

Collaborative Governance Between the Public Sector, Service Users, and their Communities*

Tony Bovaird and Jörgen Tholstrup

Introduction

This chapter explores one of the most discussed topics in public governance in the last few years – user and community co-production of public value. In the UK, for example, there have recently been discussion papers by the Prime Minister's Strategy Unit (Horne and Shirley 2009), the new economics foundation (nef 2008), the Social Market Foundation (Griffiths *et al* 2009, Harris and Boyle 2009), Compass (Gannon and Lawson 2008), the Social Care Institute for Excellence (Needham and Carr 2009), and LARCI (Griffiths and Foley 2009; Löffler 2009; Löffler and Watt 2009 and Needham 2009). Internationally, studies have recently been published by Pestoff and Branson 2006), Alford (2007), Löffler et al (2008), Pestoff (2009) and

* The authors wish to thank the various organizations which have supported the research that has shaped the ideas presented here. Tony Bovaird wishes to thank, in particular, the Department of Communities and Local Government and Birmingham City Council, which have funded recent research projects into the issue of user and community co-production. Thanks are also due to the graphics department of Birmingham City Council for drawing my original version of Figure 1, which has been further adapted here.

Dunston *et al.* (2009). Most empirical research looks at specific forms of co-production such as co-commissioning (individual budgets, participatory budgeting), co-design of public services (Bradwell and Marr 2008) co-managing (e.g. the Quirk Review of community ownership and management of public assets (CLG 2007)), co-delivery (e.g. through peer support (Department of Health 2007)) and co-evaluation (e.g. Keast and Waterhouse (2006) and Hasenfeld et al. (no date)).

The chapter locates this discussion in the wider debate about collaborative governance, and shows how co-production links the public domain and civil society in a very specific way – through the *contributions* of users and communities, rather than through their *needs*. It also locates the concept of co-production in the recent debate around public value and shows how co-production contributes to public value through a number of different routes. One of these routes – the contribution of user co-production to greater user and social value, is explored through a case study, which also demonstrates that user co-production has the potential to deliver significant cost savings to the public sector, without simply transferring these costs to service users or to associations in civil society. The paper concludes with a discussion of the wider governance implications of user co-production for the public sector.

The Role of Service Users and their Communities in Collaborative Governance

In Figure 1, we set out a model for considering how outcomes are produced through collaborative governance. This model has a number of additions to the traditional 'inputs – outputs – outcomes' model.

In particular, it brings in:

- user and community co-production as well as public agency co-production
- citizen self-help and self-organization
- 'wider value added' to citizens other than direct users
- 'social value added', including equity achievements, which are usually treated as external to the conventional model, supplied by

a political reading of the various dimensions of society values (Mildinhall and Langridge 2006: 7)

- 'environmental value added' (e.g. reduction of carbon footprint, improvement of environmental attractiveness)
- 'political value added' (e.g. as measured by 'public confidence')
- 'financial value added' (e.g. cost savings achieved)
- 'social environment', 'economy', 'political environment' and 'physical environment' as important contextual factors which affect the other relationships in the model, particularly the outcomes.

In this section, we explain the importance of the first two additions to the traditional "inputs-outputs-outcomes" model – the role of user and community co-production and the role of self-help and self-organizing activities in civil society.

Figure 1: Model of Creating Outcomes in Local Governance

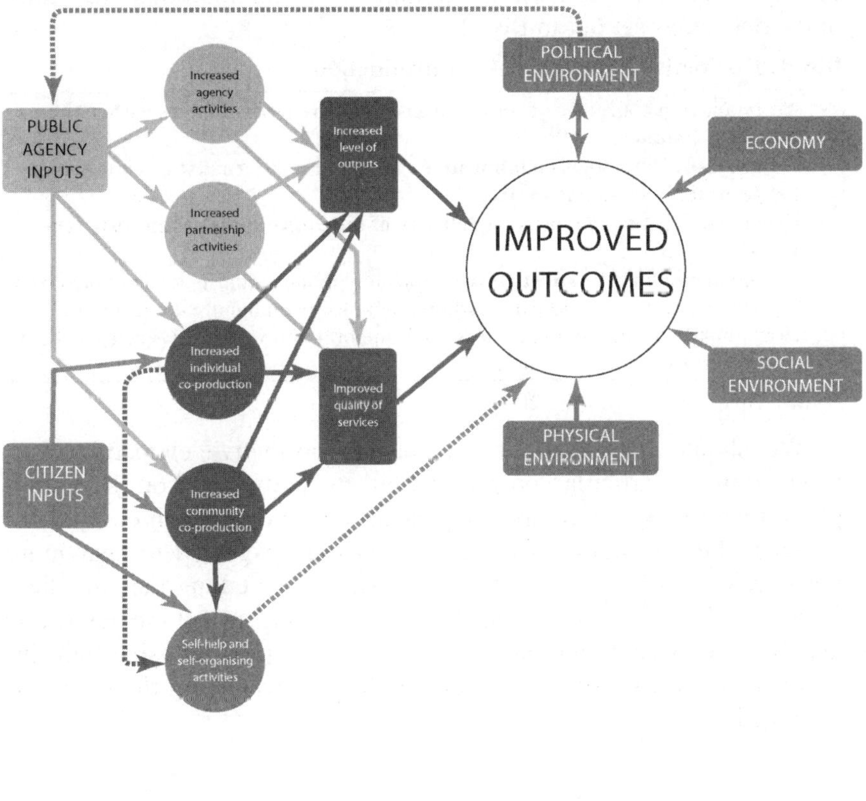

The model in Figure 1 explicitly highlights the inputs which citizens make to outcomes. In civil society, they consist of the self-help initiatives which individuals undertake and the self-organizing activities of communities, both of which contribute to societal outcomes – e.g. citizens discipline themselves to keep to appropriate diets and fitness regimes, in order to ensure that they maintain their health. These activities are usually (but not always) entirely independent of activities with and in the public sector.

However, there are many other activities which citizens undertake which do rely on an interaction with the public sector – this is the realm of "co-production". The literature on co-production of public and private services is already longstanding (Sharp 1980; Parks et al. 1981; Brudney 1984 and Normann 1984). While there is lively disagreement on the definition of and full implications of user and community co-production, there are a number of 'common denominators' in the debate, as set out in Box 1.

Box 1: Distinctive Principles of Co-production

- Co-production conceives of **service users as active asset-holders rather than passive consumers**.
- Co-production promotes **collaborative rather than paternalistic relationships** between staff and service users.
- Co-production puts the focus on **delivery of outcomes rather than just 'services'**.
- Co-production may be **substitutive** (replacing public sector inputs by inputs from users/communities) **or additive** (adding more user/community inputs to professional inputs or introducing professional support to previous individual self-help or community self-organizing).

Source: Adapted from (Löffler 2009)

We should note that there is also a normative element to co-production. In particular, co-production is usually based on the principle of reciprocity – in return for greater control over resources and decision making in public services, citizens are expected to bear more responsibility (e.g. for recycling their waste, for taking their medication according to prescription, for not behaving in anti-social ways) and not to expose public budget holders to risk (e.g. by using their individual social care budgets to take holidays away from their support network).

From a different normative perspective, some have argued that it is unfair that vulnerable and disadvantaged service users should have to put their resources into the co-production effort (Taylor 2003). Others have argued that, in practice, it is unlikely that those stakeholders who currently possess power will allow it to be shared, so that the promise of co-production is likely to be misleading and will eventually result in disillusion on the part of service users and communities.

Clearly, Figure 1 offers a very different conception of the relative roles of the public sector and civil society from that which has dominated the European welfare state since the 1940s. The inputs which produce important societal outcomes come not only from the state but also from citizens. Furthermore, the self-organizing and co-production activities of citizens are vital to the public sector achieving its overall goals and targets for improvements in societal outcomes. Consequently, the public sector must engage in collaborative governance mechanisms to influence and 'nudge' these self-organizing and co-production activities.

Creating Public Value – a Collaborative Enterprise

The traditional discussion of value added in services has focused on user value, which was taken to indicate the benefit of a good or service to its users. How can the benefit of a service to users be determined? Increasingly the economist's consumer sovereignty model has been adopted to identify the benefits of a service, with the user or citizens' views of what they want taking primacy – user satisfaction studies have become very common in public management. In order to achieve comparable figures between services and between agencies, there has been a search for ways of placing a value on the benefit produced by the service output, that is to say, on the satisfaction experienced by the users. In private services, evidence of the benefit of the output of a service is provided by its market price but such evidence is not usually available for public services, which are generally not sold, or when they are, may be sold at below market price. Of course, a consumer of a private service makes purchase not strictly because she values the service *per se,* but because it produces a stream of *outcomes* in the form of net benefits from the characteristics of that service (Bovaird and Watt 2009). The value of the service can thus ultimately be seen as being determined by the quantity and value of future net benefits from the characteristics of which it is made up. In the same way, in the public sector it is not the output of the service that is ultimately of interest to the local resident, but the outcome which that service produces.

However, the concept of value in public services tends to be even more heterogeneous than this implies, as is increasingly being recognized in the debate about the meaning of 'public value', a concept made popular by Mark Moore (1995). Moore argues that managers of public sector enterprises can create value, in the sense of satisfying the desires of citizens and clients (Moore 1995: 53), both through public sector production and through establishing and operating properly ordered and productive institutions, which are publicly accountable. Therefore, strategies which attempt to achieve public value have to be more complex than typical private sector strategies.

Consequently, it is necessary to extend the concept of value in the public sector beyond 'user value' to a further set of dimensions, as shown in Box 2.

Box 2: Ways in which Activities in the Public Sector can add Value

- *user value*
- *value to wider groups* (such as family or friends of service users)
- *political value* (support to democratic process, e.g. through co-planning of services with users and other stakeholders)
- *social value* (creation of greater equity, social cohesion or supporting of social interaction)
- *environmental value* (ensuring sustainability of all service provision)
- *financial value (achieving cheaper or more efficient service provision)*

The analysis in Box 2 takes Moore's concept of public value further by disaggregating it into six elements, each of which represents some increase in the satisfaction of citizens and clients but which avoids the crude distinction between 'what is produced' and 'how it is produced', which marks Moore's analysis. These different elements of public value are represented in the 'outcomes' in Figure 1.

The approach developed here is also more operational than Moore's, as it is possible to devise ways of assessing achievements in each of these five elements of public value, whereas the two categories used by Moore are at such an aggregate level that it is difficult for him – and for those who have subsequently sought to apply his approach to the concept of public value – to find a plausible way of assessing achievement of public value.

Moreover, this approach emphasises that 'public value' is not a technical or managerial concept, which can be managed in a non-political environment. Indeed, the itemisation of a portfolio of value-added" categories makes it immediately clear that aggregating the different categories of 'value-added' will involve making judgements of relative worth – both between types of value-added and between stakeholders experiencing value-added – which are at the very heart of political decision making. As John Benington (2009) has argued:

"The concept of public value allows for contest, and for diversities of values and identities, within a negotiated understanding of what it means to be part of the wider 'public' sphere, at that time and place".

Moore's approach is not uncontroversial – it has been attacked by Rhodes and Wanna (2009):

"Public officials are encouraged initially to by-pass the conventions of democratic politics and seek to interpolate the public interest as a means of enhancing their significance and self-worth."

However, our approach explicitly avoids this trap by making it clear that the calculation of individual elements of public value, and their aggregation are explicitly political acts, for which political authorisation is required in a democratic decision making system.

The approach suggested here therefore provides a way to operationalize the concept of public value by making it clear that it is a collaborative enterprise on the part of all stakeholders. It does not simply seek improvements in user value (as is sometimes thought to be the case in the private sector), nor does it appeal to some generic (and unfathomable) 'public interest', as has often been the case in public management.

A Model of the Production of Outcomes Through Collaborative Governance

In Figure 1, we demonstrate that user and community co-production potentially contribute to all outcomes, including those which can be categorised as 'user value', 'value to wider groups', 'social value', 'political value' and 'environmental value'.

From Table 1 it becomes clear that there is a wide range of behaviors which service users and their communities can undertake, either with public services or in a purely self-organizing way, which can have major consequences on all the dimensions of public value. Each of these will contribute to outcomes in different ways.

Table 1: Examples of User and Community Co-production Contributing to Public Value

Type of public value added	Self-help or self-organizing activity	User co-production	Community co-production
User value	Keeping to diet or fitness regime	Users monitoring own health condition	Experienced mothers helping new mothers with breast-feeding
Value to wider groups	Running sports clubs or music groups	Users participating in drug trials	Neighbourhood watch schemes to monitor crime or anti-social behaviour
Social value	Street parties to increase social interaction	After-school social activities run by parents of schoolchildren	Campaigning on behalf of community centres in neighbourhood
Political value	Not applicable	Users raising consciousness of other users about rights, duties, etc. of users	'Community chest' schemes of participatory budgeting
Environmental value	Switching off unnecessary lights in own house	Not dropping litter on streets	Street recycling scheme
Financial value	Not applicable	Users helping to reduce service costs	Volunteering to reduce service costs

For the public sector, the key difference is that it will normally be able to influence the volume and impact of the co-production activities more easily than for the self-help and self-organizing activities.

However, this is not to suggest that the latter are not a concern of the public sector. Where the institutions of civil society are poorly developed, so that self-help and self-organizing are correspondingly weak, it may be entirely appropriate for the public sector to engage in capacity building in the third sector (just as it may be seek to engage in market development in the private sector, in order to promote a mixed economy of provision).

The relationship between these different types of outcomes needs to be explored – it is likely that there will be substantial correlation between them, which needs to be identified. This is a good thing in terms of public policy, as it means that many policy initiatives have effects on several outcomes at the same time but it presents a problem from the modelling point of view, as it means it is hard to distinguish clearly what is leading to what.

In the case study in the next section, we demonstrate in detail how user co-production can result in three of the types of value added outlined in Table 1 – user value, social value and financial value.

Empowering Patients to Need Less Care and Do Better: A Case Study

In 2001, the unit of gastroenterology in the Highland Hospital in Eksjoe (in the South-Swedish Highland with 115.000 inhabitants) had long waiting lists – patients referred to the unit had to wait two to three months – and unprioritized scheduled revisits were done up to one year after the planned time. The unit looked carefully at the values behind its work and came up with a set of innovative approaches to involve patients more intensively in their own care, both improving the treatment of patients and lowering the demand on beds in the unit. Moreover, there was a dramatic improvement in the health of the patients.

Objectives of the Patient Involvement Initiative

The initiative was designed to rebalance the work of the unit, reducing the frustration of doing work which was rather fruitless and not being able to focus on the really important tasks. In addition, there was a desire to diminish waiting lists through providing more appropriate and cost-effective medical treatment.

Designing the Co-production Initiative

Given the waiting lists in 2001, the staff decided to undertake a fundamental review of the values behind the relations between its patients and the healthcare system. In particular, it analysed its service from a patient's perspective This analysis suggested that staff needed to redefine their roles, so that patients had greater personal responsibility for their health. As the unit was redesigned, it also had to find a way to monitor quality in a convincing way, as it was unacceptable to both patients and the hospital that quality should deteriorate.

It was recognized that the problems were deepset in the system – indeed, physicians and other involved staff were just as frustrated as patients themselves, who were understandably dissatisfied at having to wait for treatment. Moreover, making patients wait probably had adverse effects on their health, sometimes resulting in detoriation of their condition and causing worse flare-ups and longer hospital stays than would have occurred if care could be delivered at proper time. Furthermore, staff felt that some of the procedures being used did not have any particular value for the patients and, in some cases, might actually be harming their health.

The first thing that came out of the analysis was that it was possible to change the patient monitoring system. The underlying principle had previously been that the healthcare system forced patients into its way of doing things, instead of adapting the system to meet the patients' actual needs. It was realized that the unit was actually doing too much for some patients, and doing too little for others. At the same time, it was unable to guess when was the right time to intervene – this was when the unit realized that patients actually knew better than the staff when their disease was getting worse. The unit was therefore redesigned to set up a team-based healthcare delivery system in which all participants, including the patients, put their individual competences to use in a proper way. This immediately helped to cut out some of the inappropriate work which had previously been done, even though it had not produced any real value for the patient.

It was also realised that, traditionally, meetings between the physician and the patient, were, by their very nature, repressive. The physician was the 'top dog', his/her views were considered to be the central element of the process. Both the patient and the other staff were simply seen as being supportive to this central process, see Figure 2.

Figure 2: The Role of the Patient in Hospital Care, from the Hospital's Perspective

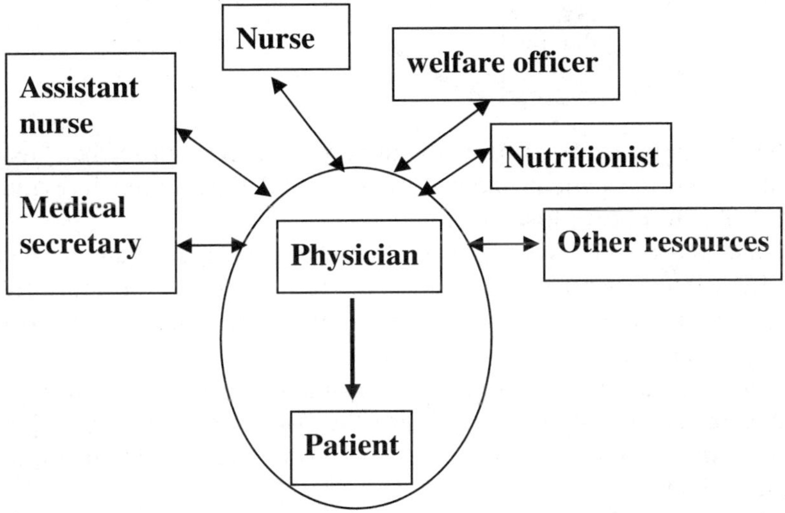

It was decided that this had to be changed – a setting had to be created where the team and the patients would actually negotiate what would be the proper treatment for each patient. So a team was designed in which all participants, including the patient, would be involved, using their individual competences. Each participant should feel in charge of at least part of the process. The patient is actually in the middle of two teams – the 'community team' of their family and friends and support system, and the 'medical team' here in the hospital, see Figure 3.

Figure 3: The Patient's View of the Team Involved in Hospital Care

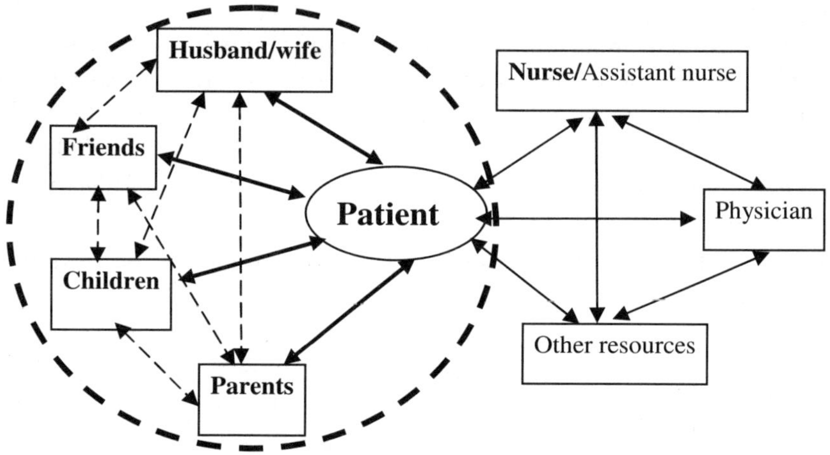

The hospital team's role is to support the patient in his/her "real" team, where the patient expects to be a well functioning individual with full control over his/her life.

First, the contact system was completely changed. Patients were stratified into several groups, each of which would be treated differently, rather than forcing all of them into the same system, as had been done previously.

The unit was aware that many of the annual visits were of little use – they revealed nothing wrong with the patient but took up a great deal of time on the ward and, of course, were stressful and disruptive to the patients.

Moreover, most of the flare-ups of the disease took place during the rest of the year – patients should therefore have contacted the unit at those times but appropriate routines were not in place to encourage that (nor was there the time to deal with such contacts, given that the unit was constantly dealing with the well patients who had come in for their regular check-ups). Consequently, patients' flare-ups were often more serious than they would have been if they had been picked up in time. The worst case is where a flare-up occurs when the patient has already made an appointment for some time in the future and decides to wait for that appointment, rather than making contact – this will often allow the flare-up to become worse – i.e. having a scheduled appointment will actually harm the patient.

Consequently, the unit moved to offering the group of patients with stable inflammatory bowel disease a phone contact with a nurse and asked them to contact the surgery whenever they felt they wanted to discuss their condition. Instead of coming in to the ward once a year for a check-up, patients are asked once a year to send in a blood test and to fill in a short form asking quality-of-life questions (using the SHS – Short Health Scale).

Then a nurse contacts them on the phone for a detailed conversation, covering their overall health condition, any troubles since the last contact, potential need for prescriptions, and any other issues the patient wants to discuss. They are offered a visit to the doctor, if they want it. However, they are encouraged to get in touch with the unit immediately any signs appear that the disease is getting worse or if they become worried for any other reason. When patients make these unscheduled calls, the nurse can recommend self-care, where suitable, or offer an appointment to see the physician at the hospital within three days. (Patients can also contact the clinic via e-mail, if they prefer).

Of course, this approach is not appropriate for all patients – it applies to about half – those patients whose disease is in a stable condition but not to patients who are receiving treatment for an unstable condition with immunosuppressive drugs or for patients who can not be considered responsible for their own actions – these are asked to make their traditional follow-up visits to the physician.

A further change we made was in the way the unit worked with in-patients. It realised that it seemed to apply a different set of values to the treatment of in-patients compared to out-patients. Instead of the medical team 'doing the rounds' every morning, and inspecting each patient in their bed, discussing their case 'over their heads', the procedure was reversed. Each patient is invited to come to the team room for a planning meeting, where the relevant charts, X-rays, etc. relevant to their case are displayed. Here they can interview the staff about what has changed since the last discussion, how they feel, what they are worried about and what the medical team suggests might be done.

The basic model has become one of team-working with the patient, who actively participates in the team and even 'chairs' the discussion about their own case. This then gives them a feeling of responsibility for and control over their health and their disease, which is necessary if they are to keep the disease under better control and it gives them the confidence to recognize when to contact the unit in future if they have concerns.

The unit also realized that it was holding daily discussions on cases where it really was not appropriate – e.g.where there was an ongoing course of treatment with no sign of any problems. To monitor the patient's progress more appropriately, the unit started to use a "process control chart" – a white board with coloured magnetic dots, indicating where patients were in the treatment process and showing where it would be appropriate to have a planning meeting.

Outcomes of the Co-production Initiative

In order to ensure that this approach to treatment did not decrease the quality of care or the patient's health outcomes, an extensive performance measurement system was used, covering the medical results, the patients' health and illness experiences, waiting times for referral visits and waiting time for endoscopic procedures. These involved questionnaire investigations of the patients' experience of care (both at home and as inpatients), and, in order to monitor medical results, use of the computerized medical register of diagnoses, simple biochemical markers and the patient's experience of health. Simple, one-off investigations were also undertaken, e.g. analysis of pharmacy records to assess patients' adherence to recommended drug treatment.

Overall, the outcomes can be summarised as better access to information and treatment for all patients, high quality care for those patients in need of immediate treatment, lower morbidity for patients with flare-ups in their disease, satisfied patients, satisfied staff, and lower use of health care system resources. In many ways, these outcomes were unplanned – the original intentions were simply to treat patients more in line with the values of the unit and to give them a greater role in their care, while also reducing waiting lists. The unit believed that it could achieve these things while maintaining the quality of patients' care. In practice, quality has improved considerably, a much better result than expected.

Health condition: The patients self-assess their health on the Short Health Scale form, reflecting four aspects of their health – symptom burden, function, experience of anxiety and general condition. Positive results are reported by the following proportions of patients:

- Symptom burden: 98 % for ulcerative colitis, 96 % for Crohns disease.
- Functionality in daily life: 96 % for ulcerative colitis, 86 % for Crohns disease
- Anxiety: 94 % for ulcerative colitis, 90 % for Crohns disease.
- General health condition: 95 % for ulcerative colitis, 95 % for Crohns disease.

Satisfaction: Patient and staff satisfaction are measured by questionnaires. Both groups have reported high levels of satisfaction with the current care system.

Utilization of in-patient care: The number of patients with inflammatory bowel disease, needing in-patient care at Highland Hospital (at the Medical as well as the Surgical Department) decreased 48 % during the period 1998-2005, compared to the nationwide decrease of 4 % reported by the National Board of Health. The clinic has moved from above the national average of in-patients per 100,000 residents to being almost half the national average during this period.

The number of unscheduled visits of patients with flare-ups in their condition decreased from 2 a day in 2001 to 2 a week by 2005, mainly, the unit believes, because patients were taking more responsibility for their own care and therefore were making contact much earlier when there was a flare-up in their condition, before they became really ill.

Availability: Referrals are registered in a computerized system and the number of patients coming for revisits in the ward are recorded manually – all data is presented once a week at the clinic review meeting. The goal is to have no waiting lists for re-visits, less than 14 days waiting time for referral patients, less than 3 days waiting time for urgent visits and immediate availability for all phone contacts. In practice, there is now no waiting list for planned revisits nor for urgent visits. Telephone availability is good – 93 % of incoming calls are answered within 3 minutes. For referral visits, the average waiting time for non-prioritized referrals in 2006 was 23.5 days. (The first seven days is taken up in handling the referral before it is passed to the clinic, so the actual time taken from when the referral is made to the clinic until the patient actually visits the unit is only 16.7 days on average).

Adherence to drug treatment: Available international studies show that adherence to recommended treatment with 5-ASA-preparations (an important maintenance treatment) is as low as 30-50 %. The patients in the unit have done much better than this – records show 68 % of patients with total ulcerative colitis have taken out from the pharmacy more than 70 % of their prescribed dose, and for left-sided colitis the figure is 58 %.

Figure 4: Number of Unique in-Patients per 100,000 Population

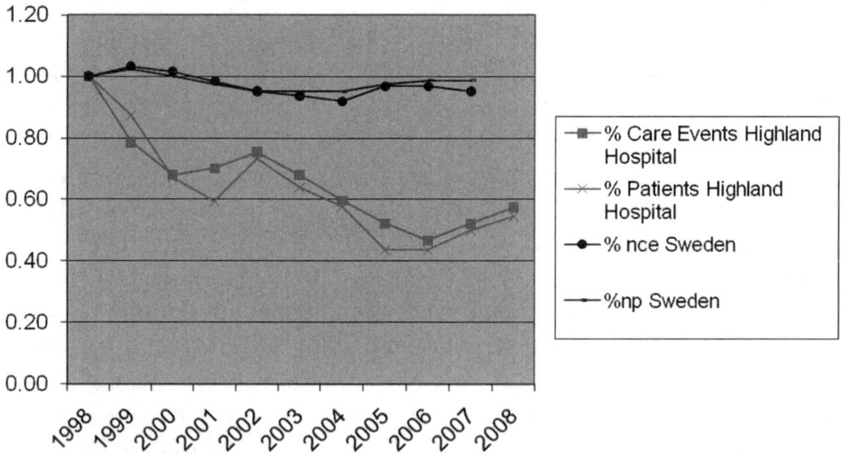

Medical quality: The unit use as an important medical target that 95 % of the patients should have a Hb > 120 – this has been achieved for 97 % of patients with ulcerative colitis and for 94 % of patients with Crohns disease. The use of haemoglobin levels as a quality indicator is not widely accepted; however, it is known from several studies that anaemia frequently follows on from IBD – indeed, in some studies 30 % of patients are anaemic. The number of patients with anaemia should therefore be an indicator of the unit's ability to discover and treat anaemia, so that being able to keep this number low is probably an indicator of quality.

Costs and Savings from Co-production

The key determinant of the cost of the unit is the size of the ward – the number of beds for in-patients. In the years after 2000, it seemed likely that the increasing number of in-patients would mean that the ward would have to be increased substantially in size. However, this new way of working has made that unnecessary. In fact, the number of hospitalizations of patients with inflammatory bowel disease decreased 48 % during the period 1998-2005. In consequence, the unit has been able to remain within budget since that time. Not only has this saved the costs of expanding the ward but the unit has been able to devote far more staff time to helping those patients with chronic but non-acute conditions, so that their quality of life is substantially improved and the risk of flare-ups of their condition are reduced.

Learning Points

The unit believes that what has made the project particularly successful is the fact that it has been able to improve care both from the perspective of the patients and from that of the staff. In doing this, user co-production brought clear improvements to user value in the system, through both the users monitoring of their own condition and their co-planning of their own treatment, and also improvements to the financial value added, as the new system demonstrated major financial savings.

Ensuring that this is the case has mean continuous monitoring of how the system is working. Every week, staff meet to plan the schedule for the coming weeks and to sort out any problems identified – this ensures that all staff are in a regular, systematic fashion, assuring the process and demonstrating their commitment to the philosophy underpinning it.

Basically the unit changed the way it delivered healthcare to a model which was consistent with its views on how anyone should behave toward a fellow human being. To avoid "dropping back" into the traditional repressive way of behaving, the unit had to discuss and agree the basic values shared by the staff. It also had to discuss with its patients how it wanted to change the "rules of engagement" – although, in practice, this proved to be a minor problem, as it turned out that patients were very keen to work with staff in this way. Consequently, the co-planning of their own treatment by patients has added 'social value' by demonstrating not only the feasibility but the functionality of different power relationships between patients and the medical team in the hospital.

The most important lesson to the unit, in the end, was that patients did not cause the healthcare system to "overflow", when they were put in charge. On the contrary, patients are rational people, so they don't seek health care when their needs have been met. Basically, they have used the system responsibly to improve their own health, and in so doing they have decreased unnecessary calls on the time of physicians and nurses. Actually, the results seem to be better, now that the patients are in charge, than when the healthcare system tried to force patients to do what it thought they should.

Wider Governance Implications of User Co-production for the Public Sector

This case study of increasing orientation towards the needs of patients and recognition of the contribution which patients can make to the better working of a complex medical system has demonstrated that:

- healthcare systems are often designed in ways which hugely undervalue the contributions which patients can make to service effectiveness;
- user co-production can be integral to service improvement;
- user co-production can bring system cost savings;

– users can behave responsibly when given the information and the tools to take more responsibility for their own health

While the most headline-grabbing implications of this case for health care administrators may be the improvements in health outcomes, together with the cost reductions achieved, for public managers more generally the most important lesson may be that the current system of governance of key public services is not designed to give adequate weight to the contributions which service users can make.

In particular, the mantra "To everyone according to their needs" has dominated in the resource allocation decisions of public services for most of the period of the welfare state. The decisions as to 'Which needs?' and 'Whose needs?' have been left largely in the hands of managers and professionals, with some (very arms-length) steering from politicians. However, this approach is now coming under increased attack from a number of fronts. The public is no longer content to assume that public sector managers and professionals are serving only the public interest when they make resource allocation decisions, while the role of politicians has become increasingly difficult, as the public has become more aware of who gains and who loses from the choices behind public services prioritization.

The growing interest in user and community co-production provides an extra layer of complexity in the debate about public services. Users who co-produce services are likely to expect that their view of their own needs are given more weight than the views expressed by managers, professionals and politicians. Users who refuse to co-produce may be seen less sympathetically by politicians and the media, especially where their refusal imposes significantly higher costs on public service systems. Yet both the willingness and ability to co-produce may be very unequally spread across the spectrum of service users and potential users, so that some method of protecting the non-co-producers may become essential, as the co-production tendency gathers momentum. Mechanisms to ensure that those who don't want to – or can't – take more responsibility for their own welfare may have to be introduced, as in the Highlands Hospital case. On the other hand, those who can and do participate in co-production may, almost inevitably, get more out of the processes of public services than those who can't and don't.

Conclusions

This chapter has explored the topic of user and community co-production, which is subject of fast growing interest in public services in Europe, the US and across the world. It has provided a number of different perspectives from which to view the contribution of co-production to public value and the achievement of outcomes valued by citizens. It has also demonstrated that the results of co-production in a specific healthcare case study can be dramatic. The paper cautions, however, that the co-production tendency may not be appropriate for all situations in which public services are provided and that mechanisms will need to be kept in place to ensure that those who cannot or will not take advantage of co-production possibilities do not suffer an inappropriate disadvantage.

References

Alford, J. (2009). *Engaging Public Sector Clients. From Service-Delivery to Co-production.* Houndsmill, Basingstoke: Palgrave: Macmillan.

Benington, J. (2009). "From private choice to public value?" in: John Benington and Mark Moore (eds.), *In Search of Public Value: Beyond Private Choice*. Houndmills, Basingstoke: Palgrave Macmillan.

Bovaird, T. (2007). "Beyond engagement and participation – user and community co-production of public services", *Public Administration Review,* 67 (5): 846-860.

Bovaird, T. and Downe J. (2008). *Innovation in Public Engagement and Co-Production of Services.* Policy Paper to Department of Communities and Local Government. Cardiff: Cardiff Business School.

Bovaird T. and Watt P. (2009). *Understanding Value for Money in Local Authority Led Public Services: Scoping a Research Programme*. Birmingham: INLOGOV.

Bradwell, P. and Marr S. in: co-operation with PricewaterhouseCoopers (2008): *Making the most of collaboration. An international survey of public service co-design.* Demos Report No. 23, London.

Brudney, J. L. (1984). 'Local Coproduction of Services and the Analysis of Municipal Productivity', *Urban Affairs Quarterly*, 19: 4: 465-484.

Cabinet Office (2009). *Power in People's Hands: Learning from the World's Best Public Services.* London: Cabinet Office.

CLG (2007). *Making assets work: The Quirk Review*, London.

COI (2009). *Communications and Behaviour Change*. London: Central Office of Information.

Department of Health (2007). *Research Evidence on the Effectiveness of Self-Care Support* (Work in Progress 2005-2007).

Dunston, R.; Lee A.; Boud D.; Brodie P. and Chiarella M. (2009). Co-Production and Health System Reform – From Re-Imagining to Re-Making, *Australian Journal of Public Administration*, 68 (1): 39-52.

Gannon, Z. and Lawson N. (2008). *Co-production: the modernisation of public services by staff and users*, London: Compass.

Griffiths, S. and Foley B. (2009). *Collective co-production: working together to improve public services*. Swindon: Local Authorities Research Council Initiative (LARCI).

Griffiths, S., Foley B. and Prendergrast J. (2009). *Assertive Citizens: New Relationships in the Public Services*. London: Social Market Foundation.

Harris, M. and Boyle D. (2009). *The Challenge of Co-production*, London: NESTA and new economics foundation.

Hasenfeld, Y., Hill K. and Weaver D. (No Date). *A Participatory Model For Evaluating Social Programs*. San Francisco: The James Irvine Foundation.

Horne, M. and Shirley T. (2009). *Co-production in Public Services: a new partnership with citizens*, London: Prime Minister's Strategy Unit.

Keast, R. and Waterhouse J. (2006). "Participatory evaluation: a missing component in the sustainable social change equation for public services", *Strategic Change*, 15(1): 23-35.

Löffler, E.; Bovaird T.; Parrado S. and van Ryzin G. (ed.) (2008): "*If you want to go fast, walk alone. If you want to go far, walk together": citizens and the co-production of public services*, published in www.5qualiconference.eu.

Löffler, E. (2009). A *future research agenda for co-production: Overview paper.* Swindon: Local Authorities Research Council Initiative (LARCI).

Löffler, E. and Watt P. (2009). *Understanding the efficiency implications of co-production.* Swindon: Local Authorities Research Council Initiative (LARCI).

Mildinhall, J. and Langridge C. (2009). *Literature Review: Value for Money in Public Services*, Department for Communities and Local Government.

Moore, M. H. (1995). *Creating Public Value: Strategic Management in Government*. Cambridge, MA: Harvard University Press.

Needham, C. (2009). *Personal co-production.* Swindon: Local Authorities Research Council Initiative (LARCI).

Needham, C. and Carr S. (2009). *Co-production: an emerging evidence base for adult social care transformation,* Research briefing 31, London: Social Care Institute for Excellence.

nef (2008). *Co-production: A manifesto for growing the core economy,* London: new economics foundation.

Normann, R. (1984). *Service management. Strategy and leadership in service business*. Chichester, New York, Brisbane, Toronto, Singapore: John Wiley and Sons.

OECD (2009). *Rethinking e-Government Services: User-centred Approaches.* OECD, Paris.

Parks, R. B.; Baker P. C.; Kiser L.; Oakerson R.; Ostrom E.; Ostrom V.; Percy S. L.; Vandivort M. B.; Whitaker G. P. and Wilson R. (1981). "Consumers as Coproducers of Public Services: Some Economic and Institutional Considerations", *Policy Studies Journal,* 9 (7): 1001-1011.

Pestoff, V. (2009). *A Democratic Architecture for the Welfare State. Promoting Citizen Participation, the Third Sector and Co-production.* London: Routledge.

Pestoff, V. and Brandsen T. (eds) (2006). *Co-production. The Third Sector & the Delivery of Public Services.* London: Routledge.

Rhodes, R. and Wanna J. (2009). "Bringing the politics back in" in John Benington and Mark Moore (eds.), *In Search of Public Value: Beyond Private Choice*. Houndmills, Basingstoke: Palgrave Macmillan.

Sharp, E (1980). 'Toward a New Understanding of Urban Services and Citizen Participation: The Co-production Concept', *Midwest Review of Public Administration,* 14: 105-118.

Taylor. M. (2003). *Public Policy in the Community*. Houndmills, Basingstoke: Palgrave.

Preventing and Resolving International Financial Crises through Regulation and Collaborative Arrangements

2

Responses to the Financial Crisis by the European Union and the Member States

José Ramón Salelles

Introduction

Identifying the Causes of the Crisis

A better understanding of the response given from a legal perspective to reduce the impact of the financial crisis requires a prior review of its causes, at least in broad terms. It seems reasonable to assume that the information that has been gathered about the crisis and its circumstances has greatly influenced the type of response chosen to minimize its effects, and some of its particularities. A look at the analysis* carried out shows a high degree of consensus concerning the main causes of the financial turmoil. It is now quite apparent that the enormous growth of credit in the period preceding the crisis strongly facilitated it. The implications of this process for the real economy cannot be missed if the inflationary trend in asset prices and the restrictions of lending are taken into account. This growth has had specific consequences for the financial sector, by restricting funding liquidity and reducing market liquidity[1]. On the one hand, there was the intense development of activities defined as "shadow" banking, as a parallel way for the banks to conduct business in the financial sector, off the accounting records, and for other financial institutions to undertake activities similar in their implications to those typically performed by banks, with the regulatory requirements avoided in both cases. The spread of investment banks and the success of investment banking compared with more traditional commercial activity can be presented as being part of these causes. On the other hand, and closely related with this dimension, was the growth of the market for derivatives, their increasing complexity and sophistication, with the emergence and consolidation in these years of financial euphoria of a formula of creating financial products merely to distribute them, as a way of facilitating capital inflows[2]. These developments cannot be accurately explained without taking into account the role that the rating agencies played, giving ratings to those products that did not properly reflect their financial status, and being the only reliable source of valuation because of the complexity and sophistication referred to above. Finally, and to a certain extent determined by these practices, there was an excess of risks in the financial sector, diluting the legal requirements concerning the adequacy of capital of the financial institutions.

What these facts reveal quite clearly is the limited role that the "rational" investor model can play in ensuring the proper functioning of the financial markets. The consequences linked to the search for liquidity through the markets (liquidity through marketability), the effects produced by the remuneration policies of managers and directors, or the role that the economic cycles should play when considering financial activities, are some good examples of those limitations.

A factor closely related to these limitations which has to be considered finally is the impact of the lack of a proper supervision on the development of the crisis. This is not only because of the nature of the financial activity performed by different entities or institutions, or the peculiarities of the financial products. What the crisis has revealed is that there has not been a proper identification and management of the systemic risk that might affect the financial sector, considering an aggregate picture of the whole system, or at least of the most important participants, and of the international nature of their activities and their interconnections.

Legitimation of the Response

Once the causes of the crisis were identified, a specific concern was raised in order to legitimate the response that it deserves. It cannot be overlooked that the financial sector was presented in recent years as a market whose participants were capable of self regulation, and not essentially different from other markets. The idea that financial stability constitutes a public good, clearly stated by the IMF in its *Global Financial Stability Report* of April 2009[3], identifies a common interest that private institutions are not always able to appreciate in its proper terms. It shows that a certain degree of public intervention is required, thus supporting the public response to the crisis. There is no doubt that the financial sector is strongly linked to economic development and growth, and plays a central role in the performance of the economic agents. Helping the financial sector has been perceived as a necessary requirement to reignite and promote economic development. A relationship between the type of crisis and the resolution technique can also be traced, in the sense that as they are systemic, public policies become more relevant[4].

Within the financial sector, particular attention has been paid, and has to be paid, to the position and performance of banks. Their singularity within the financial markets has not been overlooked. Their inherent instability, with illiquid assets facing liquid liabilities[5], determined the unavoidability of helping banks in order to help the financial sector. Reliance on short-term funding of long-term assets with potentially very low market liquidity, as the practice of the shadow banking system has showed, has been in fact a main source of fragility in the financial system[6]. Political pressure to rescue failing banks is a common feature at international level[7], notwithstanding the incentives that it creates in terms of dimension and interconnection[8].

Characteristics of the Response

It is possible to look at the response to the financial crisis from various perspectives, because there have been different levels of response. If we consider their nature, paying attention to the sphere in which the effects will take place, it is possible to distinguish between an international response, the G-20 meeting in London in April 2008, and the commitments made there, is probably the best example of the need for a global response to a problem that has a global dimension, a regional response, such as the response given by the European Union, taking into account the implications of the crisis for an area where different economies interact, and finally, a national response, determined by what national states have done in order to deal with the implications of the crisis for their own economies.

In terms of the scope of the response, it is possible to distinguish between short-term responses, basically by national states focused on preserving the stability of their financial system with an immediate intervention, and a long-term response as a result of a wider analysis, designing policies to prevent and deal with future financial crisis, based on the experience of the actual crisis.

Something that has been stressed at international level is the need for coherent response, as a feature linked to the international impact and consequences of the crisis[9]. The need for coherence is presented as being consistent with the globalization of the financial services and of the economy. The way the necessary degree of coherence can be reached will depend on the circumstances surrounding the required decision making process, and has some technical implications[10]. The existing institutional architecture can undoubtedly be used to that end. The role of the ECOFIN and of the Commission in the European Union are good examples of the efforts made to ensure coordinated action by Member States when dealing with the financial crisis. However, if there is no institutional support framework, coherence can be achieved by a comparative approach[11]. What is important to note is that coherence requires a collaborative attitude by various participants in the financial sector: between governments and regulators, central banks, entities and financial institutions. Agreements are deemed to play an important role in the way the implications of the crisis are to be faced and eventually prevented, and consensus tends to replace dominance. This is particularly true of the new functions that financial supervisors will have to assume regarding the control and prevention of systemic risks. However, it is also true if the position of single entities and institutions is examined: the process of concentration that is currently taking place, through mergers and acquisitions, reveals the importance of collaboration in achieving better adjustment of risks and capital requirements in the financial sector, thus contributing to its stabilization.

Some additional consequences arise from this perception. Probably the one with the most intense impact on the way the response has to be given refers to the need for simplification. The simplification of the response process, ranging from the agents involved to the formal procedures that have to be fulfilled, is deemed to guarantee a more coherent approach to the financial situation. In fact, one of the causes of the development of the crisis in the USA was the complexity of financial supervision, with different authorities sharing a common area of concern.

To complete this brief characterization, the importance of legal intervention must be stressed, and the importance of the legal system in orienting the performance of the markets. Legal rules are passed, and have to be passed, to deal with some of the effects of the financial crisis, and to prevent them. If it is accepted that because of the crisis the system of international financial governance can be expected to provide the basis for a more formalized approach[12], the importance of legal rules to that end has to be assumed. Various issues of liquidity, capitalization, or "toxic" assets of banks and financial institutions have led to the enactment of specific legislation, most frequently in the form of general programs or schemes, and legislation will be enacted in order to reorganize the institutional framework of the financial sector, from capital requirements to corporate governance issues, with particular attention paid to the structure of supervision.

The European Response

Legitimation and Control of Public Intervention

The European banking sector has not escaped the crisis, although it has affected some countries more intensively than others. At its meeting on 7 October 2008, the ECOFIN Council stressed the importance of public intervention in enhancing the soundness and stability of the banking system, and the need to establish a coordinated framework based on common principles[13]. The European Commission has tried to establish this framework, which was indeed designed to ensure a coherent response by the Member States, passing different Communications, including a general one concerning the application of state aid rules to measures taken in relation to financial institutions in the context of the current global financial crisis (hereinafter, Banking Communication)[14], and two Communications dealing with specific issues requiring immediate intervention by Member States. One covered the recapitalization of financial institutions, limitation of aid to the minimum necessary and safeguards against undue distortions of competition (hereinafter, Recapitalization Communication)[15], and the other covered the treatment of impaired assets in the Community banking sector (hereinafter, Impaired Assets Communication)[16]. This approach was completed by a recent Communication on the return to viability and the assessment of restructuring measures in the financial sector in the current crisis under state aid rules (hereinafter, Assessment of Restructuring Communication)[17], which explained how the Commission will examine aid for the restructuring of banks in the current crisis, with a view to ensuring a coherent approach. Other Recommendations and Communications have been passed concerning particular policy issues, and these will be considered in the light of the specific actions taken by the European Union, and specifically in terms of the reorganization of supervision.

A specific concern about the legitimation of public intervention in the financial sector has been raised as well by the European Union. This has to be regarded while taking into account the precise understanding of the role that the state can play in the economy under European legislation, and the importance attributed to the existence of competition for the proper performance of the markets[18]. This leads to an evident conflict between two goods: financial stability and (free) competition. In its Banking Communication, the Commission considers that article 87 (3) (b) of the Treaty[19], which gives the Commission the power to allow state aid to "remedy a serious disturbance in the economy of a Member State", is available as a legal basis for aid measures undertaken to address the systemic crisis. The general principles underlying the state aid rules are applicable in this context. The support measures therefore have to be well targeted in order to achieve the objective of remedying a serious disturbance in the economy, proportionate to the challenge that is faced, and designed to minimize negative spill-over effects on competitors, other sectors and other Member States.

In the Banking Communication mentioned above, the European Commission considered various techniques that Member States can use to minimize the impact of the crisis, and established common principles that have to be taken into account, as part of general schemes as well as on an individual basis. Specific attention is paid in this Communication to (a) guarantee schemes, protecting retail deposits and going beyond them, to cover debts and liabilities of financial institutions, (b) the recapitalization of financial institutions, in schemes targeted to support financial institutions that are fundamentally sound but may experience distress because of the conditions in the financial markets[20], (c) controlled winding up of financial institutions, stressing the importance that certain sales conditions will be respected[21], (d) provision of other forms of liquidity assistance, noting that general measures available to all comparable market players in the market are often outside the state aid rules, and establishing the conditions under which particular support to a specific financial institution may also be found not to constitute aid according to European legislation[22]. Additionally, a specific Communication has been passed taking into account the relevance of the valuation and location of assets in order to promote the flow of credit to the economy (Impaired Assets Communication). Asset relief is considered state aid because it frees the beneficiary bank from the need to register a loss, or a reserve for a possible loss. This qualification allows the same principles already given in the Banking and Recapitalization Communications to be applied, in an attempt to ensure the effectiveness of the measures of relief adopted, based on necessity, proportionality and minimization of competition distortions. In order to coordinate the intervention of Member States, some rules are given on the eligibility of assets, their valuation and management.

It is important to stress the guidelines that these different Communications have in common in order to accept the public intervention by Member States, as they permit a basic characterization of the type of response the European Union is willing to permit. (1) The beneficiaries have to participate in the risks that have been created, sharing the burdens of the intervention, as a way of avoiding perverse incentives. This means that the intervention has to take into account the beneficiary's profile and ultimately implies that financial entities and institutions that are not viable should not be helped. From this perspective, it has to be understood that the intervention has to be remunerated. (2) In no way should the intervention create competitive advantages that beneficiaries can use in order to implement a strategy to the detriment of their competitors. Proper mechanisms should be established in order to avoid distortions in competition. (3) Public intervention has to be functionally oriented: the financial system does not *per se* justify the intervention. The ultimate aim of the intervention is economic: to restore the conditions that facilitate lending to the real economy, promoting the increase in the demand for products and services. (4) Public intervention has been presented as being temporary in nature. This explains the reference to specific periods of time in public intervention programs, and the proposal for redemption mechanisms.

In a recent Communication, the Commission explained how it will assess the compatibility of restructuring the aid granted by Member States to financial institutions (Assessment of Restructuring Communication). This explanation is basically given to deal with the obligation of Member States to submit a restructuring plan[23], but it is also applicable to those cases where Member States are required to demonstrate the viability of a beneficiary bank, and it does not essentially differ from what has been already established. The assessment is structured considering four aspects: (1) restoration of the long term viability, (2) the beneficiary's own contribution, (3) the impact on competition and (4) procedural issues. Viability appears then as a condition to legitimate the intervention, ranking even above financial stability requirements: in the event the bank cannot be restored, the restructuring plan should indicate how it should be wound up. On the other hand, the bank and its capital holders should contribute to the restructuring as much as possible with their own resources. This premise limits the possibility of offsetting losses in order to guarantee the payment of dividends: banks should not use state aid to remunerate their own funds when those activities do not generate sufficient profits. In order to verify whether the measures adopted to limit distortions of competition are correct, the factors to be taken into account will be the amount of aid and the conditions and circumstances under which it was granted, the characteristics of the market or markets in which the beneficiary will operate, and the openness and contestability of national markets after the intervention (the extent the beneficiary bank will respect lending targets in Member States is regarded as a positive effect of the aid). Finally, in order to verify that the restructuring plan is being implemented, the Commission will request regular detailed reports.

Following the principles mentioned above, the activity of the European Commission has been quite intense. In the period between October 2008 and mid-July 2009, the Commission approved 11 guarantee schemes, 6 recapitalization schemes and 5 schemes providing for both guarantees and recapitalization. In addition, 40 state aid measures were approved outside the schemes, and a revision process of the different schemes is now being undertaken[24].

However, there are though certain limits that affect the coordination efforts. The basic limitation arises from the nature of financial information, and the relevance of the financial sector for the economic structure of Member States, as a central factor of their economic health. This explains to a certain extent the fact that it is not yet possible to have complete information on the real situation of some financial institutions in the European Union, as well as the reluctance to apply a stress-test to their own financial system shown by some Member States. In any event, it must be noted that this reluctance must be overcome in order to develop and implement a restructuring plan, according to European legislation. One of the conditions set by the Commission in order to assess the conformity of the state aid to the legal rules is that it must include a diagnosis of the bank's problems: banks will therefore be required to stress test their business[25]. Common parameters based on appropriate methodologies agreed at Community level will have to be established.

Specific Responses Given by the European Union

In addition to the general principles established to orient Member States' actions when dealing with the crisis, basically with regard to questions concerning state intervention, the European Union has adopted specific measures on issues that require particular attention according to the analysis of the crisis and of its circumstances, thereby implementing lessons from the crisis aimed at restoring confidence in the financial markets and preventing another failure as much as possible.

Remuneration Policies

It has been generally noted that there is a close relationship between the remuneration policies of managers and directors of financial institutions and risk taking in the financial services industry. Although this cannot be presented as a main cause of the financial crisis, there is no doubt that certain practices have created the wrong incentives, by promoting the assumption of excessive risks that have facilitated the development of the crisis. In fact, there is broad consensus that the reward of short term profits has affected the long-term position of the financial institutions, because potential losses in that timeframe were not taken into account[26].

The Commission has issued a Communication in order to improve risk management in financial firms and to align pay incentives with sustainable performance in a coordinated manner throughout the European Union (hereinafter, Remuneration Communication)[27]. The Communication deals with the structure of remuneration and its disclosure, and introduces supervisory concerns. The basic principle is that remuneration policies should be consistent with sound managerial practices, giving an institutional character to an approach that has oriented the recent review of these questions in general corporate law. It stresses the importance of the fixed components of remuneration and of adjusting the variable components for periods of time, as well as of taking performance in a multiyear framework into account, and of non-financial criteria for measuring individual performance. Specific consideration is also given to the way in which remuneration policy is designed and implemented. It insists, in accordance with good corporate governance practices, on the significant role that expertise and independence should play in that task. Transparency is also considered, not only from an internal perspective, but also from the stakeholders' point of view. The relevant stakeholders should at least have access in an easy and understandable way to the relevant information on remuneration policy. Finally, the way the proposed principles are implemented by the financial institutions should be controlled by the competent authorities, which must have specific powers to that end.

Credit Rating Agencies

There has been also a widespread perception that rating agencies contributed significantly to the financial crisis, because they did not properly estimate the risks posed by the financial products, and that self-regulation no longer offers the reliability required for their performance[28]. The European proposal for a regulation of Credit Rating Agencies in 2008[29] has been finally passed into law in 2009[30]. It tries to give a specific response to the need for an external and, to a great extent, imperative regulation of their activities. Again, the importance of a common approach to this need is stressed, taking into account the importance of the role that these agencies play in the functioning of the internal market.

The regulation is based around the legal statute of the rating agency and its activity. It establishes a registration procedure that the agency has to follow in order to ensure that its credit ratings can be used by participants in the market for regulatory purposes (only ratings given by registered agencies could be used for regulatory purposes). On the other hand, as regards the issuing of credit ratings, particular attention is paid to the agencies' independence and avoidance of conflicts of interest, with organizational implications, the abilities and conduct of their employees, the rating methodologies that have to be disclosed, ensuring that the information is reliable, and the disclosure and presentation of credit ratings. It is additionally required to disclose information that refers to the corporate structure of the agency and to its internal mechanisms of control, among other circumstances. Finally there is a specific concern with the supervision of the agency: Member States have to designate competent authorities that will supervise their performance. The importance of cooperation between Member States to that end is stated, giving specific competences to a college of supervisors and paying particular attention to the competences of the authorities of the host Member States to supervise their activities.

Risk Management and Capital Requirements

The complexity of some financial products, and the difficulties that this sophistication has created in valuing risks, has also been presented as a key factor in the origin of the crisis. The European Union has tried to deal with this issue by introducing a specific amendment to the technical regulations concerning risk management in European legislation. The Directive 2009/83 of 27 July 2009[31] amends the annexes of Directive 2006/48 as regards technical provisions concerning risk management to that end.

As a general principle, the economic implications of the financial transaction concerning derivatives where the financial institution invests or creates the product must be properly reflected in the risk assessment and in the managerial decisions taken. Policies and procedures implemented by the financial institutions have to be accurate to ensure this projection.

Additional legislation has been recently passed to deal with regulatory capital requirements, establishing criteria for their integration, and paying attention to the degree of concentration of risks, as part of their supervision (Directive 2009/111, of 16 September 2009, amending Directives 2006/48, 2006/49 and 200/64[32]).

European Financial Supervision

The fact that the crisis has been so extreme due to a failure in the supervision of the financial system is something that is now widely accepted. This is the case not only from a macroeconomic perspective, taking into account the systemic risks faced by the economy, but also from a microeconomic perspective considering the position of single institutions. The deterioration of their situation, which considerably limits any scope for their restoration, and the increase at the same time in the risks for the economy, has to a great extent been allowed by a weak system of financial supervision. The reform of the supervision system is therefore a necessary step in preventing and mitigating the effects of a financial crisis. Once again, the importance of having a coordinated approach is stressed, and collaboration between governments and supervisors is requested at an international level[33]. To that end, the European Commission, following the recommendations given in the *de Larosière Report*[34], has proposed a new architecture for the supervision system in its Communication on European financial supervision (hereinafter, the Supervision Communication)[35].

This proposal leads to a system consisting of two basic parts for the type of risk that is faced in each case. First, there is the creation of a

European Systemic Risk Council (ESRC). This Council will be in charge of macro-prudential supervision, and deal with risks that the financial system as a whole faces because of its interconnection and complexity[36]. Second, a *European System of Financial Supervisors* (ESFS) will be established, which will be in charge of micro-prudential supervision, looking at the position of individual firms and consumers of financial services.

Note that the legal design of the ESRC attempts to reinforce the efficacy of its role, seeking representation in the decision making process of different interests. The influence of its warnings and recommendations is in fact based on the quality of the participants, with specific emphasis given to the position of central bank governors, and the participation of micro-prudential supervisors of Member States considered to be indispensable (at least, the chairpersons of the three European Supervisory Authorities[37]). This is certainly a way of dealing with the interdependence of macro and micro prudential risks, while allowing collaborative arrangements to take place within this institutional framework. Additional requirements concerning the composition of the ESRC reinforce this perspective. A member of the Commission will be a member of the ESRC, and the Economic and Financial Committee chairperson would represent the finance ministries by participating as an observer. It is important to stress that when performing its duties, the ESRC is recommended to seek the advice of private-sector stakeholders, including consumer representatives, and they are attributed a consultative role[38].

From a micro-prudential perspective, the difficulties experienced in undertaking coordinated action have been decisive in the response that has been given. The ESFS is based on the creation of three new authorities that will replace the existing Committees of Supervisors: the European Banking Authority, the European Securities Authority, and the European Insurance and Occupational Pensions Authority[39]. A policy of collaboration comes across strongly in the European Commission's proposal. First, because the European Supervisory Authorities are to participate in meetings of the colleges of supervisors as observers, as a way of contributing to the creation of a common supervisory culture and of fostering consistent supervisory practices. This is a way of allowing the overall perspective of the Authorities to complete the local perspective that characterizes the position and expertise of national supervisory bodies. Second, because the roles attributed to the ESFS are substantially designed to ensure harmonization of the legislation process, its enactment and application, concerning the supervision of financial institutions, as well as coordination of the response to crisis situations, facilitating cooperation and exchange of information between competent authorities, and coordination between the supervised sectors. To that end, the creation of a Steering Committee is proposed, with representatives of the three Authorities, to ensure consistency in approaches when dealing with cross-sectoral issues. Finally, the corporative structure of each Authority continues to facilitate the participation of the chairperson of the competent national authority, and the participation of a representative of the ESRC as an observer is also required, meaning the competences of the ESFS will be exercised taking the various interests represented into account.

Finally, institutional collaboration between the ESRC and the ESFS is required. This collaboration will be established particularly through the transfer of information: the ESRC will receive relevant micro-prudential data, especially on large and complex cross-border groups, and also give powers to the ESRC in order to have direct input on particular issues from national supervisors.

This proposal has led to a significant legislative response by the European institutions, and various regulations are to be enacted in the near future. As regards the ESRC, a proposal has been made for the establishment of a European Systemic Risk Board[40]. This is in addition to a proposal for a Council Decision entrusting the European Central Bank with specific tasks concerning the functioning of the European Systemic Risk Board[41]. As regards the ESFS, there has been a proposal to establish a European Securities and Markets Authority[42], a European Insurance and Occupational Pensions Authority[43], and a European Banking Authority[44]. On the other hand, legislation has been enacted to coordinate the supervision of groups of banks by a college of supervisors (Directive 2009/111, of 16 September 2009, amending Directive 2006/48[45]).

Response Given by Member States

Access to Liquidity

One of the main effects of the crisis has been the lack of liquidity in the financial markets: as the position of the financial institutions is uncertain, access to credit has become very difficult, which has an immediate impact on its performance[46] and, as a consequence, on the real economy. This is the main reason why Member States tried to deal with this problem as early as possible, and focused on maintaining liquidity in the markets[47]. However, the response has taken various forms.

Member States have provided guarantees in order to facilitate access to credit in the financial market by financial institutions. This has affected single entities, following a specific intervention. This is true of Dexia, in Belgium, France and Luxembourg, for example[48]. Nonetheless, as a general rule, the intervention is conducted through a particular scheme. In fact the first plans authorized by the Commission are typically those enacted by Member States to provide guarantees[49]. This has usually been the case for the issuance of debt in the financial markets[50]. In other cases, it was established that Member States could subscribe the issuance of debt, thereby providing financial institutions with immediate liquidity[51]. The acquisition of assets has also been deemed an appropriate measure to directly inject liquidity into the financial system. This acquisition differs from that provided for "toxic" assets, and has different implications. In this case, the assets to be acquired have some degree of quality, so the acquisition is not designed as an instrument to reduce the existing uncertainty of the financial situation of a determined bank or institution, but rather to provide resources that will be used by the beneficiary according to its liquidity requirements[52]. The possibility of raising funds from the market through a specific vehicle in order to lend them to the financial institutions has also been considered[53]. These policies have to be implemented while taking into account the general efforts of Member States to increase the guarantee provided for deposits in financial institutions, which is in some cases a guarantee for the total amount of the deposits[54].

Even taking the European Commission's efforts at coordination into account, some differences have led to the implementation of the different guarantee schemes, which basically concern pricing issues[55]. This is due firstly to the relevance given to the guarantor's position. As the financial institutions are located in different Member States, the total cost of a guarantee issued by entities is determined by the rating of the government that provides the guarantee, which affects the position of financial institutions in the same situation. Meanwhile, in order to encourage the restoration of financial stability, the current pricing model does not take into account the different positions of banks after 31 August 2008, which has affected the position of banks without CDS spread. Finally, there has been asymmetry in the remuneration of debt; as it is less costly to obtain a guarantee for short-term debt, there has been an incentive to move away from long term debt, which seems nevertheless preferable for securing the maturity transformation role.

Recapitalization of Financial Institutions

Recapitalization of financial institutions as a response to the financial crisis involves the injection of resources by means of equity, taking into account that this might vary in quality: ordinary shares, non-core Tier 1 capital, or Tier 2 capital[56]. Recapitalization is not necessarily determined by failures in the solvency of the financial institutions. There is in fact evidence for the interaction between liquidity and solvency: problems of liquidity have often affected the solvency of the financial institutions[57]. Something that the crisis has clearly revealed is that higher capital ratios are necessary, taking into account the underestimation of risk and considering the increase of the cost of funding. These circumstances basically explain how recapitalization measures have been used by Member States as a way to restore financial stability, and the confidence required for the proper functioning of the interbank market and for lending to the economy[58]. More specifically, they also explain that recapitalization as a response to the crisis can also be targeted towards fundamentally sound financial institutions[59]. This situation has warranted priority treatment from the European Commission.

Intervention by Member states has taken various forms. There have been cases where these measures have been taken individually, providing a specific response to a particular situation in order to avoid further implications for the entire financial system. This is the case, for example, with the ING Group in the Netherlands, the JSC Parex Banka, in Latvia[60], or KBC in Belgium[61]. Specific programs have also been designed to offer a general and institutionalized framework that allows financial institutions to receive capital injections from Member States[62]. Recapitalization is in any case perceived as being a response of an exceptional nature, as clearly shown by the measures approved in the European Union, which have a relatively small impact on GDP compared with other measures. The approved injections represented 2.6 % of the GDP compared to the figure of 24.8 % for the impact of the guarantees on bank liabilities[63]. However, it is important to stress that the use of recapitalization measures has been relatively widespread, with a high ratio of take-up: 53.8 % for recapitalization and 32.8 % for state guarantees[64]. This reflects improved adaptation of the proposed measures to the financial needs of adequate capitalization.

Toxic Assets

Relief for impaired bank assets has been used as a complementary measure by Member States to avoid the effects of the crisis. As a general rule, this relief has been established after realizing that uncertainty over the level of credit losses could continue, even after programs aimed at reinforcing the liquidity and solvency of banks have been enacted. This measure is considered from a technical perspective on the good bank-bad bank strategy[65]. It basically divides the financial institutions into two parts: the good bank retains performing assets, while non-performing assets are transferred to a bad-bank shell. In this way a certain degree of functional specialization is achieved: the good bank can operate more efficiently and raise capital, once possible doubts about its solvency and the soundness of its financial status disappear, and the bad bank can concentrate its efforts on loan recovery and liquidation. However, the bad bank structure does not necessarily imply the creation of a new entity. The same effect can be achieved through insurance schemes; in this way banks retain the assets on their balance sheet, but are indemnified against losses by the state[66]. It must be stressed that the measure is aimed at poor quality assets, raising relevant issues in terms of the way this quality is evaluated and the relief is financed. The implications of these measures from an aggregate perspective also seem quite clear: a main reason identified for the insufficient flow of credit has been the uncertainty about the valuation and location of impaired assets. Making the situation more certain should help to avoid the risk of a continuous process of recapitalization; a significant part of the funds invested in banks has been used to create provisions against future asset impairments[67].

It is possible to find also different examples of this form of intervention by Member States. The German legislation covers the transfer of risk (§ 8 FMStG 2008) in order to allow a specific fund (*Finanzmarktstabiliesierungsfonds,* hereinafter, *SoFFin*) to acquire financial instruments that imply an assumption of risk by the financial institutions, or to put it another way, to insure the risks they assume. The German program was approved by the European Commission, which imposed the purchase of any risk position from the fund within three years, and the compensation of the fund for any loss incurred. Specific legislation to provide instruments to develop this strategy, called "bad-bank legislation" (*Gesetzes zur Fortentwicklung der Finanzmarktstabilisierung*, 23.7.2009) has been enacted. This provides the opportunity to create a vehicle company that will receive risky securities, giving debt guaranteed by the fund as consideration (*Zweckgesellschaftsmodell*). It also offers the opportunity to transfer positions of risk to a specific entity created at federal or regional level in order to liquidate them (*Konsolidierungsmodell*). The enactment in the United Kingdom of the *Asset Protection Scheme* (2009) is a specific response with a similar objective, although the toxic assets remain on the balance sheet of the financial institutions. In this scheme, the government provides protection against future losses on certain assets in exchange for a fee, with a first loss remaining within the institution (10 %). This consequence puts into effect the idea that institutions should participate in the measures adopted. The Government protection will cover 90 % of the credit losses exceeding the amount mentioned[68]. Furthermore, participants must assume certain obligations concerning the management of the institution, which include reporting duties.

Nationalization

Nationalization has been perceived as a measure of the last resort, and as such there is no substantial modification of its role as a legal technique for dealing with a financial crisis, as previous experience has already shown[69]. If the situation of the financial institution is so severe that none of the previous solutions can help prevent it, nationalization of the institution has been presented as a satisfactory outcome. It has to be noted in any case that one of the main arguments that has prevented Member States from using this technique involves the difficulty of privatizing the institution after the intervention[70], which thus makes its temporary nature less feasible, and thereby more intensively distorts the structure of the financial market. Valuation concerns also arise; although the difficulties posed by the bad bank strategy are not directly dealt with, the value of the shares transferred to the state has to be determined, which in fact implies taking into account the assets and liabilities of the institution[71]. Once the financial institution has gone into public ownership, the final outcome depends on its viability, not excluding *per se* its liquidation[72]. It must be noted that the fact of going into public ownership has not prevented the need for using additional techniques to avoid financial difficulties, such as those involving toxic assets[73].

This measure has been adopted in practice by some Member States, to deal with the problems posed by individual institutions, while trying to ensure that these problems did not spread through the entire banking system. This occurred in the United Kingdom with Northern Rock, which was taken into temporary public ownership in February 2008 by means of the Banking Act 2008, after experiencing severe funding problems, and with Bradford and Bingley, where after the retail deposits and branches were transferred to Abbey, the remainder was taken into public ownership. The weakened funding position and the damage to the Anglo Irish Bank's reputation in Ireland arising from unacceptable practices meant that recapitalization was no longer the appropriate and effective way to secure its continued viability, and also led to the decision to bring it into full public ownership in January 2009[74]. In some cases, nationalization has been the final stage in a long process of recapitalizations: this was true of the Hypo Real

Estate Group in Germany. In that group, the share capital of the public fund *SoFFin* reached 90 % in two months.

Lessons from the Crisis

The de Larosière Report

A group of experts was designated in the European Union in 2008, with a specific mandate to consider how supervision should best be organised to ensure the prudential soundness of institutions and after the weaknesses of the supervisory framework had been ascertained, and to strengthen European cooperation on financial stability oversight and cooperation with other jurisdictions, in order to safeguard financial stability at global level. It is important to note that cooperation is regarded by the European Union in its mandate as essential when dealing with the financial crisis at regional and international level, and covers one of the aspects that was particularly affected by the crisis: supervision. Based on this mandate, the expert group chaired by Jacques de Larosière presented a report in 2009 (the *de Larosière Report*) which basically focused on three questions: regulation, supervision[75] and management procedures in the crisis. For the IMF, the report is a good start for discussing intra-European Union coordination and cooperation[76].

From a regulatory perspective, the importance of overall cooperation between monetary and regulatory authorities has been stressed, in that the definition and implementation of a monetary policy should not be isolated from credit developments. A deeper involvement of the ECB in macro-prudential supervision is therefore regarded as essential for introducing regulatory tools which could help to meet countercyclical objectives. The various proposals concentrate on the role of capital within the financial structure in financial institutions, management of risks, accounting standards and on the extension and scope of regulation, while introducing some issues concerning corporate governance and management of the crisis. The importance of capital requirements as a regulatory tool is stressed. This implies obtaining a common definition on regulatory capital (rec. 2), recommending a general increase in the minimum requirements, and the reduction of pro-cyclicality (rec. 1). This measure has been proposed taking into account the Spanish experience, where dynamic provisioning was introduced in order to build buffers, which arose during expansions and could be drawn down in recessions, and which have proved to be an effective mechanism in dealing with the consequences of a recession[77]. Management of risks refers to the importance of taking into account liquidity risks, internal controls and auditing, while considering the complexity of the instruments and methods that can be used (rec. 1). Closely related to this recommendation is the importance of accurate measurement of risks, and the role that credit rating agencies should play to that effect. Regulation, as the European Union has attempted, should ensure the independence of the agency and the quality of the reports: to that end, a recommendation is that rating for structured products should be more product-oriented (rec. 3). From an accounting perspective, off-balance vehicles should be considered in very strict terms (rec. 3), as well as the convenience of a more flexible approach to the "mark-to-market principle", with emphasis on long term economic value being central to any valuation method (rec. 4)[78]. The proposals on this latter issue have stressed the relevance of the governance structure of the International Accounting Standard Board (IASB), requiring a more open approach to the views of the regulatory, supervisory and business communities.

Particular attention has been paid to extending the role of regulation. This was determined particularly by the fact that some financial institutions with no deposit base have been very vulnerable to the decrease in liquidity, leading to a major impact in the real economy. It has therefore been proposed that regulation should be extended to all firms or entities conducting financial activities of a potentially systemic nature, no matter what their own characterization as financial institutions, even if they do not have deposits (rec. 7). The importance of improving transparency in all financial markets has also been stressed, with particular consideration of the functioning of hedge and investment funds, and the provision of more information to the markets (rec. 7), and increasing simplification. This mainly affects the markets for securitized products and derivatives, because their complexity has affected the management of risks in the financial institutions a great deal (rec. 8). Finally, the importance of having a higher level of harmonization was stressed, in order to avoid the existing divergences in national legislation regulating financial markets. This implies a unification of the European position at international meetings and, furthermore, the identification of a core of rules that should be harmonised at the deepest level, with the use of regulations preferred to that end (rec. 10).

Finally the *de Larosière Report* dealt with corporate governance issues and crisis management from a regulatory perspective. Corporate governance issues basically refer to remuneration and risk management. The report deals with the remuneration problems arising from the conflict emerging between the position of shareholders and of managers in the financial institutions. The basic idea, followed by the European Union, is that compensation schemes should be better aligned with shareholder interests and long term firm wide profitability (rec. 11). Meanwhile, the importance that risk management should have as good practice of corporate governance is stressed, by reinforcing the internal controls of financial institutions to that end (rec. 12). Management of the crisis is considered from various perspectives, with a policy approach stated and specific issues covered. It includes a proposal to give priority to private sector solutions. The difficulty of creating a general framework that could help to articulate the response to the management of the crisis is accepted due to the national nature of the financial institutions, and the development of crisis prevention and intervention mechanisms are recommended (rec. 13). Transparency and certainty should in any event orient the public intervention. Specific consideration is given to the role that Deposit Guarantee Schemes (DGS) should play in a financial crisis, and there is a recommendation that they should be pre-funded by the private sector, providing equal protection to all bank customers (rec. 14), and the need to give more detailed criteria on burden sharing when the crisis affects more than one Member State (rec. 15).

Supervision received particular attention in the *de Larosière Report* and as mentioned above, its recommendations have been substantially followed by the European Union. Supervision is perceived as being a complementary tool for regulation in order to ensure financial stability. The report basically distinguishes between two levels of supervision, while taking into account the implications of the risks considered. The first is macro-prudential supervision, considering the financial system as a whole, and is focused in protecting the economy from significant losses in real output. To do so, the creation of a European Systemic Risk Council is proposed (rec. 16 and 17). The second is micro-prudential supervision, involving a European System of Financial Supervision, designed to coordinate the network of European financial supervisors (rec. 18). However, coordination is part of the role of national supervisors, because supervision *per se* is not considered collaborative in nature, and the importance of its independence and technical nature are stressed. Supervisory independence is in fact defined as a situation in which the supervisor is able to exercise his judgement and powers without being improperly influenced by the parties under supervision, the government, the Parliament or any other interested party. Collaboration must be referred to the control mechanisms that should be established; their performance is then limited in scope, to determining the legal framework, setting strategic goals, and monitoring the way supervision is exercised. A two-stage process is proposed to achieve this supervisory architecture: improvement of the quality of national supervision and the creation of a European culture of supervision (2009-2010, rec. 19-21), and the establishment of a European system for financial supervision, based on the work of three different Authorities: a European Banking Authority, a European Insurance Authority and a European Securities Authority (2011-2012, rec. 22-23), while leaving open the possibility of moving to a system which could rely on two Authorities (rec. 24).

Finally, some recommendations in the *de Larosière Report* consider questions arising from the need to provide a global response to the financial crisis. It stresses the importance of regulatory consistency, by means of an international standard setting process, that should be led by the Financial Stability Forum (now the Financial Stability Board, *FSB*)[79], and of cooperation between supervisors, ensuring a comprehensive risk assessment (recs. 25 and 26). It also identifies the lack of policy action as a key failure highlighted by the crisis: the development of crisis prevention mechanisms and of the quality of macroeconomic and macroprudential surveillance at international level are seen as necessary tools to remedy the situation (rec. 27). The lack of cooperative jurisdictions involves special duties for supervisors, with emphasis on the performance of institutions where standards are not comparable to those established at international level (rec. 28). Finally, it recommends the reinforcement of the IMF's role as a major macroeconomic supervisor (rec. 29). These recommendations take into account the international role of the EU, and stress the importance of the coherence of its representation, and of developing relations with the major financial powers (recs. 30 and 31)

The Turner Review

In 2008, the Chancellor of Exchequer asked Lord Turner to review the causes of the crisis, and to make recommendations on the changes in regulation and supervisory approach needed to create a more robust banking system for the future. The *Turner Review* was published in March 2009, as a regulatory response to the global banking crisis. After a description of what went wrong, with a diagnosis of the causes of the crisis which does not differ substantially from the *de Larosière Report*, and the challenges posed about the self-correcting nature of financial markets, the report proposes moves for the creation of a stable and effective banking system, stressing two lines of action that basically coincide with the analysis in the *de Larosière Report*: reinforcement of the role and scope of regulation and of supervision in the financial markets.

From a regulatory perspective, the focus is on capital adequacy, accounting and liquidity, and also deals with issues relating to the extension and scope of regulation, and finally introduces some proposals on corporate governance and management of the crisis. The report insists on the importance of capital as a regulatory tool, and also proposes the introduction of counter-cyclical mechanisms which could anticipate potential future losses, such as an "Economic Cycle Reserve". An increase in capital requirements is perceived as essential to create a more robust banking system, contributing to constrain the role of commercial banks in risky trading activities, and a review of the market's risk capital regime is also proposed. As for the management of risks, the report stresses as well the importance of credit rating agencies, and of paying attention to their governance and to the conflicts of interests that might affect them. It also highlights the need to supervise them. It establishes that a more accurate management of risks would require the development of clearing and central counter-party systems to cover the standardized contracts. Finally, the report stresses the importance of increasing the independence of risk management functions and of performing effective oversight of risks. The *Turner Review* also considers that legislation should be broader in scope in order to avoid shadow banking: regulation (and supervision) should cover the principle of economic substance, rather than form. Corporate governance issues are dealt from the perspective of remuneration policies: remuneration policies should be designed to avoid incentives for undue risk taking. Finally, as regards bank failures under the new Banking Act (2009) facilitating the orderly winding down of failed banks, the report recommends that retail deposit insurance should be generous enough to protect against the impact of bank failure.

From a supervisory perspective, the *Turner Review* also identifies the importance of a macroprudential analysis: to that end the Bank of England and the Financial Services Authority (FSA) should be extensively and collaboratively involved and the necessary capabilities should be developed. Supervision should therefore basically consider three issues: an individual bank's liquidity positions, bank balance sheet analysis and oversight of accounting judgements, while paying special attention to cross-border activities. It proposes an enhancement of international coordination between supervisors, which could help to anticipate the type of response. At European level, it recommends the creation of an independent authority with regulatory powers, setting standards and overseeing in the area of supervision, to replace the Lamfalussy Committees. Finally, it recommends a shift in the FSA's supervisory approach, broadening its scope, identifying key risks, and paying particular attention to high impact firms and to large and complex banks.

Concluding Remarks

The responses of the European Union and its Member States to the financial crisis are consistent with international developments and have basically stressed the importance of regulation and supervision of the financial markets. In that respect they reinforce their institutional dimension, and point towards a model that tends to reduce the role of markets as rule makers. A procedural and material approach to the response is helpful in considering its characteristics in more depth.

From a procedural perspective, the European Union has provided a response through its institutional architecture, and proposed some changes in its configuration. This framework, which is basically established around the state aid regime, has enabled the coordination of the response. The role of the European Commission has been very relevant, with various Communications designed to provide coherence to the type of response given by Member States. Member States have acted specifically to deal with the situation of a particular institution, or have enacted more general programs or schemes, which have been authorized in both cases by the Commission, taking into account the principles established. The response has also been institutional, in the sense that the Commission, or the competent organs of the Member States, state departments or regulators, have acted without involving other actors in the decision making process. However, in some cases regulators have performed their tasks while working closely with the economic agents. Proposed changes in the institutional architecture of the European Union focus on supervision of the markets, paying particular attention to systemic risks and reinforcing European supervision at microprudential level. The new architecture is designed to foster coordination between institutions, at European and national level, without considering the direct intervention of different actors in the decision making process. Collaborative processes will take place at institutional level, with an evident public dimension, so as a general rule it is not possible to say that governance is collaborative in this area.

From a material perspective, the responses reveal the importance of legislation in dealing with some of the problems posed by the crisis. The legal order is taken into account to play its more classical role regarding the functioning of the financial markets. The European Union has enacted legislation on specific issues revealed by the crisis, such as the condition and performance of the credit rating agencies, the management of risks, or the category of regulatory capital of financial institutions, and an important legislative reform will affect the structure of supervision at European level. Member States have enacted legislation to enable public intervention using different techniques, with the most common being those involving the provision of guarantees, recapitalization of financial institutions, and the acquisition or insurance of toxic assets. At an international level, the Financial Stability Board has been designed to guide the legislative response, and specific organizations will also affect this process, such as the Basel Committee on Banking Supervision, or the International Accounting Standards Board. The influence that these developments will have on the future performance and legislation of the European Union and of its Member States has to be taken into account considering that participation of different actors in those processes is very much on a consultative basis.

Endnotes

* Literature hade been reviewed until the end of November 2009.

1 *See* Marcus Brunnermeier, *Financial Crisis: Mechanisms, Prevention and Management*, *in* Macroeconomic Stability and Financial Regulation: Key Issues for the G20, 92 (Mahias Dewatripont, Xavier Freixas and Richard Portes, eds., 2009).

2 In the USA, the total amount of Asset Backed Securities (*ABS*), Collateralized Debt Obligations (*CDO*) and Mortgage Backed Securities (*MBS*) increased from 400,000 million dollars in 2000 to 2.2 billion in 2006, and 1.8 billion dollars in 2007. In Europe the increase for the same financial products was from 120,000 million dollars in 2000 to 1 billion dollars in 2007. *See* Guillermo de la Dehesa, *Regulación y supervisión financieras tras la crisis*, 21 Actualidad Jurídica Uría Menéndez, 7, 11-12 (2008).

3 IMF, *Global Financial Stability Report. Responding to the financial crisis and measuring systemic risk*, April, 2009, Executive Summary, at xxii, (www.imf.org) (hereinafter, *IMF April report 2009*).

4 *See* Glenn Hoggarth and Jack Reidhill, *Resolution of banking crises: a review*, Financial Stability Review, 109, 116 (2003).

5 This is widely accepted. *See* Anthony M. Santomero and Paul Hoffman, *Problem Bank Resolution: Evaluating the Options*, The Wharton School, 1, 3-5 (1998).

6 *See* Marcus Brunnermeier, *supra* note 1, at 92, 99.

7 *See* Glenn Hoggarth and Jack Reidhill, *supra* note 4, at 123.

8 *See* Marcus Brunnermeier, *supra* note 1, at 97.

9 *See*, for example, *Communiqué from the G 20 London summit*, at Statement 14 (www.londonsummit.gov.uk, hereinafter, *G 20 London summit*).

[10] Three basic approaches are commonly identified in coherent public sector regulation in the international financial markets: (1) harmonization of rules, (2) mutual recognition and (3) the creation of unregulated spaces: *See*, Julia Black and David Rouch, *The development of the global markets as rule-makers: engagement and legitimacy*, Law and Financial Markets Review, 218, 220 (2008).

[11] *See IMF April report 2009*, *supra* note 3, at xviii.

[12] *See* Julia Black and David Rouch, *supra* note 10, at 233. For Glenn Hoggarth and Jack Reidhill, *supra* note 4, at 112, a clear legal framework can have an important bearing on both the range and effectiveness of the policy options in resolving crisis.

[13] The ECOFIN Council conclusions enumerate the following principles: interventions should be timely and the support should in principle be temporary, Member States should be vigilant regarding the interests of taxpayers, existing shareholders should bear the due consequences of the intervention, Member States should be in a position to bring about a change of management, management should not retain undue benefits, legitimate interests of competitors must be protected, and negative spill-over effects should be avoided.

[14] OJC 270, 25.10.2008, 8-14.

[15] OJC 10, 15.1.2009, 2-10.

[16] OJC 72, 26.3.2009, 1-22.

[17] OJC 195, 19.8.2009, 9-20.

[18] The centrality of this question within the European Union has been generally accepted. *See*, Didier Martin, Olivier Saba, and Forrest G. Alogna, *European Responses to the Financial Crisis*, La Semaine Juridique, 39, 42 (2009).

[19] After the Lisbon Treaty entered into force on 1 December 2009, it is now Art. 107 (3) (b) of the Treaty on the Functioning of the European Union.

[20] This technique was specifically considered by the Recapitaliszation Communication, which stressed the importance of paying particular attention to the risk profile of beneficiaries, taking the market situation of each institution into account, keeping a level playing field by not providing a large subsidy to current market alternatives, proposing a methodology to determine the price of recapitalizations, and creating the proper incentives for redemption. Following the recommendations of the Eurosystem of 20 November 2008, a price corridor will be defined (1) by the required rate of return of subordinated debt representing a lower bound and (2) the required rate of return on ordinary shares representing an upper bound, taking into account the average values of the relevant parameters, which could lead to a rate of return of 7 %

on preferred shares with features similar to those of subordinated debt, and of 9.3 % on ordinary shares [*see* the Recapitalization Communication, *supra* note 16, at (27)].

[21] The sales process should be open and non-discriminatory, the sale should take place on market terms, the financial institution or the government should maximize the sales price for the assets and liabilities involved, and if it is necessary to grant an aid to the economic activity to be sold, this would lead to an individual examination according to the Community Guidelines on state aid for rescuing and restructuring firms in difficulty [*see* Banking Communication, *supra* note 15, at (49)].

[22] Conditions such as the financial institution being solvent at the time of the liquidity provision, and the latter not being part of a larger aid package, the facility being fully secured by collateral to which haircuts are applied according to its quality and market value, the central bank charging penal interest to the beneficiary, and the measure being taken at the central bank's own initiative, and not being backed by any counter-guarantee of the state, would legitimate the intervention under state aid rules [*see* Banking Communication, *supra* note 15, at (51)].

[23] This is particularly the case in situations where a distressed bank has been recapitalized by the state, or where a bank benefiting from asset relief has already received state aid in whatever form that contributes to coverage or avoidance of losses which altogether exceed 2 % of the bank's total risk weighted assets (*see*, for example, Impaired Assets Communication, *supra* note 17, at 55).

[24] *See* DG Competition's review of guarantee and recapitalization schemes in the financial sector in the current crisis, 7 August 2009, (hereinafter, DG Competition's review 2009), at 2.

[25] *See*, Assessment of Restructuring Communication, *supra* note 18, at 7.

[26] This explains the assertion of the *G20 London summit* to endorse and implement the Financial Stability Forum, (hereinafter, FSF) tough new principles on pay and compensation, and to support sustainable compensation schemes and the corporate social responsibility of all firms, *supra* note 9, at Statement 15. These principles basically refer to the effective alignment of compensation with prudent risk taking and to the efective supervisory oversight and engagement by stakeholders [*see*, FSF Principles for sound compensation practices, 2 april 2009 (www.financialstabilityboard.org)].

[27] OJC 120, 15.05.2009, 22-27.

[28] In fact, at an international level the *G20 London summit* made the commitment to extend regulatory oversight and registration to Credit Rating Agencies to ensure they meet the international code of good practice, and

particularly to prevent unacceptable conflicts of interest, see *supra* note 9, at Statement 15.

[29] COM (2008) 704 final.

[30] Regulation 1060/2009 on Credit Rating Agencies, 17.11.2009, OJ L 302, 16.09.2009.

[31] OJL 196, 28.7.2009, 14-21.

[32] OJL 302, 17.11.2009, 97-119.

[33] The *G 20 London summit* agreed that the Financial Stability Board (hereinafter, FSB) should collaborate with the IMF to provide early warning of macroeconomic and financial risks and the actions needed to address them, see *supra* note 9, at Statement 14. To that end, the establishment of a new FSB with a strengthened mandate was accepted as a successor to the FSF, including all G20 countries, FSF members, Spain, and the European Commission.

[34] An expert group chaired by Jacques de Larosière presented a report in 2009 on the financial crisis. *See infra* at 27.

[35] COM (2009) 252 final.

[36] In a recent report issued by the IMF, the Bank for International Settlements (BIS) and the FSB, Report to G 20 Finance Ministers and Governors: Guidance to Assess the Systemic Importance of Financial Institutions, Markets and Instruments: Initial Considerations, October 2009 (www.financialstabilityboard.org), it has been provided an analytical device to structure the assessment of the systemic importance, looking at size, substitutability and interconnectedness of institutions, and at complementary indicators, such as leverage, liquidity and maturity mismatches, and complexity.

[37] Each central bank governor should be accompanied by one senior representative of the national supervisory authorities as an observer.

[38] *See* Supervision Communication, *supra* note 35, at 3.3.

[39] The European proposal follows the classical model for organizing supervision by means of a vertical distribution of sectors, with each sector supervised by a different agency (the silos model). This conservative approach is consistent with the involvement of central banks in supervision in some Member States, giving continuity to the previous structure of Committees at European level. The structural implications of the central banks' involvement in financial supervision have been generally stressed, *see*, for example, Donato Masciandaro and Marc Quintyn, *Reforming financial supervision and the role of central banks: a review of global trends, causes and effects (1998-2008)*, 30 CEPR POL. INS., 1-9 (2009). Note that in other Member States in which supervision has been centralized in one agency, which supervises the

entire financial system in the pursuit of public goals, the functions of the agency are being reviewed because of the crisis, as has occurred with the Financial Services Authority in the United Kingdom, for example.

40 Brussels, 23.9.2009, COM (2009) 499 final. It is proposed that the following persons will have voting rights in the General Board: the President and Vice-President of the ECB; the Governors of the national central banks; a member of the European Commission; the chairperson of the European Banking Authority; the chairperson of the European Insurance and Occupational Pensions Authority; the chairperson of the European Securities and Markets Authority. Membership without voting rights of one high level representative per Member State of the competent national supervisory authorities, and of the President of the Economic and Financial Committee is proposed (art. 6).

41 Brussels, 23.9.2009, COM (2009) 500 final. The ECB is called on to provide analytical, statistical, logistical and administrative support to the ERSB.

42 Brussels, 23.9.2009, COM (2009) 503 final.

43 Brussels, 23.9.2009, COM (2009) 502 final.

44 Brussels, 23.9.2009, COM (2009) 501 final.

45 OJL 302, 17.11.2009, 97-119.

46 A relevant factor in the crisis in the United Kingdom has indeed been a number of specific banks, i.e. Northern Rock, Bradford & Bingley, Alliance and Leicester and HBOS rapidly becoming increasingly reliant on the permanent availability of large-scale interbank funding combined with the ability to securitize and sell down rapidly accumulating credit assets. *See The Turner Review. A regulatory response to the global banking crisis*, 2009, 35, (hereinafter, *Turner Review*).

47 *See* Didier Martin, Olivier Saba, and Forrest G. Alogna, *supra* note 19, at 43.

48 The guarantee was authorized by the Commission on 19.11.2008. *See* state aid: Overview of national measures adopted measures adopted as a response to the financial/economic crisis (Brussels, 13.10.2009, http://ec.europa.edu/competition/index_es.html, hereinafter, *state aid memo*).

49 *See state aid memo*, *supra* note 47. Various schemes to provide guarantees have been authorized by the Commission, as an initial first institutional response to the crisis: for Austria, 9.12.2008, Denmark, 10.10.2008, Finland, 14.11.2008, leading to guarantees provided for Kaupthing Bank, Germany, 27.10.2008, leading to guarantees provided for Bayern LB, IKB, or SdB, Greece, 19.11.2008, Hungary, 12.2.2009, Ireland, 13.10.2008, Italy, 14.11.2008, Latvia, 22.12.2008, Netherlands, 30.10.2008, Poland, 25.9.2009,

Portugal, 29.10.2008, leading to State guarantees provided for Banco Privado Portugues, Slovenia, 12.12.2008, Spain, 22.12.2008, and the United Kingdom, 13.10.2008.

[50] For example, this is true of Germany (§ 6 Finanzmarktstabilisierungsgesetz 2008, hereinafter, FMStG), Italy (DL n. 155, 2008), the United Kingdom (Credit *Guarantee Scheme*, 2008: over £100 billion of debt has been guaranteed under the Scheme) and Spain (RDL 7/2008).

[51] Such as Italy, for example (DL n. 155, 2008).

[52] This is true of the Special *Liquidity Scheme*, 2008, and the *Asset Purchase Facility*, 2009, in the United Kingdom, and a similar response can be seen in Germany (§ 8 FMStG), and Spain (RDL 6/2008).

[53] This is the main purpose of the creation of the *Caisse de Refinancement des Establisments de Credit* in France in 2008 (now the *Societé de Refinancement de l'Economie Française*) as a special-purpose financing entity, owned by the French state, which seeks financing on the international credit markets, issuing debt guaranteed by the government. *See* Didier Martin, Olivier Saba, and Forrest G. Alogna, *supra* note 19, at 45.

[54] Germany, Denmark and Italy have guaranteed all the deposits in financial institutions.

[55] *See* the DG Competition review 2009, *supra* note 35, at 5-6.

[56] *See* Recapitalization Communication, *supra* note 16, at (28) a).

[57] This is true of HBOS in the United Kingdom, for example: as it was affected by funding availability, the bank approved its recapitalization by means of the government recapitalization scheme, and the government invested £17 billion in what is now Lloyds Banking Group (created following the merger of Lloyds TSB and HBOS in January 2009).

[58] In order to justify the enactment of a recapitalization scheme, the Governor of the Central Bank of Ireland clearly stated that it was not acceptable to the authorities that banks would attempt to achieve higher ratios by curtailing credit to the real economy (*Opening Statement to the Joint Oireachtas Committee on Finance and the Public Service*, 21.1.2009, www.centralbank.ie, at 6). The ability of this type of measure to reignite lending is not accepted without reservations. *See* Marcus Brunnermeier, *supra* note 1, at 101.

[59] The French situation illustrates this situation very well: an initial 10.5 billion euros were distributed under the recapitalization scheme in December 2008 to Crédit Agricole (3 billion), BNP Paribas (2.55 billion), Société Générale (1.7 billion), Crédit Mutuel (1.2 billion), Caisses d'Epargne (1.1 billion), and Banques Populaires (0.95 billion). A second recapitalization tranche of 10.5 billion Euros has so far been distributed to BNP Paribas (5.1

billion), and Sociéte Générale (1.7 billion). *See* Didier Martin, Olivier Saba, and Forrest G. Alogna, *supra* note 19, at 48.

60 Recapitalization measure authorized by the Commission, 24.11.2008, (*see state aid memo* supra note 48).

61 Recapitalization measure authorized by the Commission, 18.12.2008 (*see state aid memo supra* note 48).

62 It is possible to find different examples: the United Kingdom, the Recapitalization Scheme 2008, leading to public investment in the Royal Bank of Scotland (RBS) and Lloyds Banking Group, Germany, (§ 7 FMStG) leading to the recapitalization of HSH Nordbank, and of Bayern LB, Spain (RDL 7/2008), Italy (DL 155/2008 for financial institutions with solvency problems and DL 185/2008 for fundamentally sound financial institutions), Austria, the aid scheme for the Austrian financial sector, leading to the recapitalization of Hypo Tirol. Portugal, Denmark, Finland, France and Sweden have also enacted bank recapitalization schemes (*see state aid memo supra* note 48).

63 *See* DG Competition's review 2009, *supra* note 24, at Annex 2.

64 *See* DG Competition's review 2009, *supra* note 24, at 4.

65 *See* Anthony M. Santomero and Paul Hoffman, *supra* note 5, at 14.

66 This has been the case, for example, for Dexia in Belgium, where the government opted for an insurance scheme to rebuild investors' confidence in their capacity to withstand severe further losses.

67 In Ireland, the need to create provisions concerning bad and doubtful debts has been presented as a main cause of the negative trends in the development of private sector credit (*see* Central Bank and Financial Services Authority of Ireland, June 2009).

68 On 26 February 2009, RBS announced its intention to participate in the *Asset Protection Scheme*, in order to protect £325 billion of eligible assets: RBS would pay a fee of £ 6.5 billion in B shares, and would bear a first loss of £42.2 billion in protected assets. On 7 March 2009, Lloyds also announced its intention to participate in the Scheme, to protecting £260 billion of eligible assets. Lloyds would pay a fee of £15.6 billion to participate in the Scheme by the issuance of B shares, bearing a first loss amount of £35.2 billion in protected assets.

69 *See* Anthony M. Santomero and Paul Hoffman, *supra* note 5, at 13.

70 *See* Anthony M. Santomero and Paul Hoffman, *supra* note 5, at 13.

71 The claims of the shareholders of the Northern Rock bank in United Kingdom due to the valuation of the shares in order for them to be transferred to the Treasury reveal that type of conflict. *See* Didier Martin, Olivier Saba, and Forrest G. Alogna, *supra* note 19, at 50.

[72] This was true of Bradford and Bingley in the United Kingdom. After becoming a public bank, a business plan for the wind-down was formulated: the Treasury provided Bradford and Bingley with a capital facility in order to enable an orderly liquidation of the remaining assets and liabilities, with its overriding objectives being to repay the capital and the statutory debt related to the transfer of deposits and branches to Abbey, to the Financial Services Compensation Scheme, and to the Treasury (*see* Business Plan, March 2009, www.bbg.co.uk).

[73] The case of the Hypo Real Estate Group in Germany illustrates this situation well. After going into public ownership, the group is considering the use of the instruments offered by German legislation in order to deal with non strategic portfolios (*see* Interim Report, 2009, www.hyporealstate.com).

[74] *See* the Governor of the Central Bank of Ireland, *Opening statement, supra* note 58, at 7.

[75] Emphasis on regulation and supervision has been presented as a key issue in the solution of the problems posed by the financial crisis at international level: *G 20 London summit, see supra* note 9, at Statement 14, and *IMF April report 2009, see supra* note 3, at xxii. The consistency of this approach with market economies has also been stressed by economists; *see* Daron Acemoglu, *The crisis of 2008: structural lessons for and from economics*, 28 CEPR POL. INS., 1, 5 (2009).

[76] *See IMF April report 2009*, *supra* note 3, at xx.

[77] One of *the* statements of the *G20 London summit* is based on the idea that supervision and regulation must dampen rather than amplify the financial and economic cycle, *see supra* note 9, at Statement 14. A similar approach can be found in the *IMF April report 2009*, *supra* note 3, at xxiii, in the sense that capital regulation and accounting standards should include incentives and guidance that permit the accumulation of additional capital buffers during upswings, when risks tend to accumulate and are typically underestimated. The Spanish experience has been widely presented as a relevant example of this type of practice. The Spanish legislation on dynamic provisioning was established by *Circular* 9/1999 of 17 December, by the Bank of Spain, amending *Circular* 4/1991, of 14 June, on accounting standards and models of financial statements (*Boletín Oficial del Estado* – Spanish official journal – 23 December 1999), in order to consider the latent risks faced by the financial institutions and to provide a mechanism for stabilization based on the past experience of institutions in the form of accounting provisions. *See* the lecture by Raimundo Poveda, La *reforma del sistema de provisiones de insolvencia*, 18.1.2000, www.bde.es. The importance of such an approach has been given widespread emphasis. *See*, Avinash Persaud, *The inappropri-*

ateness of financial regulation, *in* The First Global Financial Crisis of the 21ST Century, 157 (Centre for Economic Policy Research, ed., 2008), or Axel Leijonhufuvd, *Two systemic problems*, 29 CEPR POL. INS., 1, 4 (2009).

[78] Some proposals to that end have been made by economists. For example, *see* Marcus Brunnermeier, *supra* note 1, at 99, on introducing a "mark to funding" principle, designed to provide an incentive for long-term funding.

[79] When in performing its tasks, the FSF should take different interests into account, from a consultative perspective. The FSB Charter states when developing its medium and long term strategic plans, principles, standards and guidance, the FSB will consult widely among its members and with other stakeholders, including private sector and non-member authorities, in a process that will include regional outreach activities to broaden the circle of countries engaged in work to promote international financial stability (Art. 3) (www.financialstabilityboard.org). This can be presented as a way of building legitimacy (*see* Julia Black and Davied Rouch, *supra* note 11, at 228), rather than an expression of collaborative governance.

3

The Failure of the Guardians: Central Banking Reform and the Financial Crisis

Alasdair S. Roberts

The era of liberalization began in 1978-1980, with the advent of market reforms in China, led by Deng Xiaoping; the election of British Prime Minister Margaret Thatcher, and her subsequent assault on the British planned economy; and the election of US President Ronald Reagan, and his own program of economic deregulation. Economic liberalization was at first a revolutionary doctrine, but after three decades it became an orthodoxy, promoted by center-left politicians as well as those on the right. This epoch ended in 2007-2009, as the consequence of a global financial crisis that threatened to plunge the world into depression.

This era is typically regarded as one in which governmental functions were reduced or eliminated so that markets could flourish. However, governmental reform often consisted of more than a simple exercise in downsizing. In many critical areas, policymakers invented new ways of performing basic governmental functions. Sometimes they were looking for institutional arrangements that would promote key parts of the pro-market creed, such as the need for sound money and fiscal discipline. And sometimes policymakers were responding to the pressures of the new globalized economy – by expanding ports so that they could handle the boom in trade, improving other forms of infrastructure to keep pace with growth, or modifying regulatory and judicial systems to reassure investors.

A common mode of thinking influenced reform in the parts of government that were critical to the operation of a globalized economy. It is a design philosophy that I will call the *logic of discipline* (Roberts 2010). This approach to reform is deeply skeptical about conventional methods of democratic governance, which are alleged to produce policies that are short-sighted, unstable, or tailored to suit special interests, rather than the overall public interest. The aim, therefore, is to impose constraints on democratic processes, often by transferring power to technocrat-guardians who will make the difficult decisions that voters and legislators appear to be incapable of making otherwise. The archetype for this way of thinking about governmental reform is the independent central bank. Over the last three decades, there has been a "quiet revolution" in this field (Blinder 2004). Dozens of central banks – including all of the major banks – have acquired formal independence from the elected officials who once influenced their policies.

However, the global financial crisis of 2007-2009 has badly shaken faith in the value of central bank independence. There are two reasons for this. The first is that technocrats within major banks did a poor job of anticipating the crisis and taking measures to avert it. The second is that the model of independence was compromised in important ways during the management of the crisis. Technocratic governance has thus proved to be flawed, and also contingent on the state of the economy: when the financial sector was faced with collapse, doctrine about the appropriate role of central banks was quickly abandoned.

The logic of discipline, as it applies to central banking, is thus discredited by the financial crisis. This approach to reform has also been undermined in the other areas in which it was applied during the era of liberalization. The years following crises are likely to be ones in which voters and legislators are much more skeptical of claims about the virtues of technocratic governance, and thus more inclined to reassert political control over areas once protected by the logic of discipline.

The Logic of Discipline

It might seem peculiar to claim that a major theme of governmental reform across the last three decades was built on skepticism about democratic processes, and the desire to transfer authority to new groups of technocrat-guardians. This seems to be at odds with the widely accepted view that the era of liberalization was also one of democratization – that is, a time in which principle of popular sovereignty was firmly entrenched.

Indeed, it is possible to marshal a considerable amount of evidence in favor of this view. The past three decades have witnessed the collapse of authoritarian regimes in Latin America, South Korea, the Philippines and Indonesia; the end of apartheid government in South Africa and one-party rule in Mexico; and the collapse of the Soviet Union, and the integration of many of its former satellite states into the European Union. The 1990s were hailed as a decade in which democracy enjoyed an "unabashed victory" over rival forms of government (Fukuyama 1989). Pollsters reported a global surge in popular support for democracy as the ideal form of government (Klingemann 1999: 42-46). Governments around the world adopted a broad range of institutional reforms – new electoral systems, political decentralization, transparency and accountability laws – designed to entrench democratic values.

But the era was marked by contradictions. While many policymakers and civil society leaders campaigned for greater democracy, others raised questions about the stability of democratic systems, and pressed for reforms which they believed were necessary to preserve social and economic order.

This second and more skeptical camp of reformers were motivated by their memory of the troubles experienced by the major liberal democracies in the 1970s. In that decade, all of the major democracies were struggling unsuccessfully to revive stagnant economies. Several were also confronting the demands of newly enfranchised groups, pressures for the devolution of power to minority populations, and problems of domestic and international terrorism. The United States itself had been traumatized by a string of political assassinations, a sharp rise in domestic terrorism and crime, and a constitutional crisis that ended with the resignation of its President.

"Liberal democracy is in serious trouble," Scotty Reston wrote in 1975. Reston was an editor and columnist for the *New York Times*, and one of the most influential journalists in the world in the early 1970s. "We are living in a time of widespread doubt about the capacity of free societies to deal with the economic, political, and philosophical problems of the age . . . There is a kind of counter-revolution against liberal democracy now going on in the world" (Reston 1975).

This was a grim assessment of the state of liberal democracy. But it was affirmed in the same year in an expansive report by three prominent political scientists – Samuel Huntington, Michel Crozier and Joji Watanuki. "The crisis of democracy," as they called it, was in an odd way the product of its success. Traditionally, the effective operation of democratic political systems depended on "apathy and non-involvement" on the part of many individuals and groups. In the preceding decades, however, a resurgence of faith in democratic and egalitarian ideals had stirred many of these marginalized individuals and groups to action. "The democratic expansion of political participation," Huntington and his co-authors said, "generated a breakdown of traditional means of social control, a delegitimation of political and other forms of authority, and an overload of demands on government, exceeding its capacity to respond" (Crozier, Huntington et al. 1975: 8, 114-115, 161-164). The overload thesis, as it came to be known, gained popularity among conservative thinkers as an explanation of the malaise of the 1970s (King 1975; Rose 1980; Huntington 1981; Birch 1984).

While conservative political scientists such as Huntington led an assault on one flank of the liberal democratic state, conservative economists mounted a charge on another. Their method consisted largely of asking what sort of behavior would be expected if individuals in the public sector – politicians, bureaucrats, interest groups and voters – were assumed to behave just like individuals in the market place – that is, with an acute sense of their own self-interest and a sharp understanding of how the game should be played to improve their position (Mueller 2003: 1-2). The body of academic work that applied economists' tools to problems of governance became known as Public Choice theory, and it gained a wide readership in the 1970s and early 1980s.

The Public Choice perspective on political action was not flattering. Politicians, it was assumed, are fixated narrowly on maximizing votes in the next election, rather than the pursuit of broad programs or ideologies. To win elections, politicians must cater to voters who are themselves fixated on their material interests, but vary in their ability to protect those interests. The result is that politicians give disproportionate aid to the well-organized few. To deliver on their promises, politicians must rely on government agencies. But the bureaucrats who lead these agencies are themselves preoccupied with maximizing their budgets and perquisites, and often collude with their agency's clients to pressure politicians for more money than they really need (Buchanan and Tullock 1962; Niskanen 1968; Olson 1971; Becker 1983).

The Public Choice diagnosis proceeded from different premises than that of conservative political scientists – looking at the motivations of players within the system, rather than broad societal transformations – but in the end produced a similarly bleak view of the predicament of liberal democracies. The governmental system was myopic – largely because of the fixation of politicians on elections. It was biased towards constant expansion, because of pressure from organized interests and pandering by elected leaders. And it was ossified, because of resistance from powerful bureaucrats and the political influence of their clients. Public Choice theorists were not inclined to use the political scientists' terms, but their view was also one in which liberal democracies wrestled with problems of overload and declining "governability."

The two camps also agreed that the best way of restoring the health of liberal democracy was to impose firm checks against the destructive tendencies that were inherent within it. If Huntington and his colleagues were right in concluding that "an excess of democracy means a deficit in governability," then the survival of the political order clearly required "more self-restraint on the part of all groups" – or, in the alternative, the establishment of "limits to the indefinite extension of political democracy" (Crozier, Huntington et al. 1975: 113-115). Public Choice theorists, meanwhile, also favored similar constraints – such as new laws to limit spending and taxing, so that government budgets would not be left "adrift in the sea of democratic politics" (Buchanan and Wagner 1977: 125-126). Constraints were also needed to control self-aggrandizement by bureaucrats and public service unions, and minimize "political micro-management" aimed at distributing patronage to powerful constituencies (Schwartz 1994: 56).

It is clear, therefore, that enthusiasm for popular sovereignty during the era of liberalization was hardly unabashed. There was, at the same time, a sharp appreciation of the perceived dangers of unconstrained sovereignty – of what we might call the "systemic risks" inherent in the liberal democratic system of governance. The collision of these two viewpoints produced a new understanding of how liberal democracies should be constructed if they were to avoid problems of ungovernability. It was still possible, therefore, to say (as the US Department did in 2000), that democracy had "triumphed" in the last quarter of the twentieth century. But our understanding of what democracy *meant* also shifted significantly in those years. The clash of ideas seemed to produce a result that we might describe as enhanced sovereignty within a more limited space. Mechanisms for participation and oversight of the state would be improved, but at the same time the sphere within which public opinion had a direct effect on the content of policy would be reduced.

Central Banking as an Archetype

Central banking was the field in which the logic of discipline was most rigorously applied. Three decades ago, most central banks were agents of their national finance ministries. In 1967 John Kenneth Galbraith, then one of the world's best-known economists, dismissed the idea of central bank independence as an eccentricity (Galbraith 1967: 283-284). He took it to be self-evident that political leaders must retain control over monetary policy. Central bank independence, Australia's finance minister agreed, was "completely at odds with our traditions requiring public officials to be in the end accountable" (Keating 1989).

By the end of the era of liberalization, the conventional wisdom had been completely reversed. It was now taken as axiomatic that central banks should be organized so that they enjoyed a high degree of independence from elected leaders.

Figure 1: Number of Independent Central Banks, 1962-2002

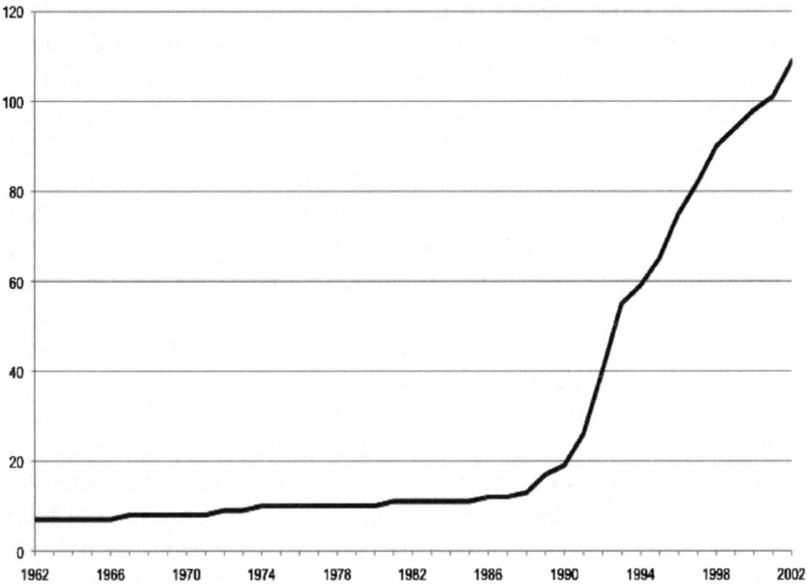

Data provided to the author by Professor Martin Marcussen, Centre for European Politics, University of Copenhagen

The European Central Bank, created as a result of the 1992 Treaty on European Union, was designed to be carefully sheltered from the influence of elected officials. In 1997, the Japanese government granted formal autonomy to the Bank of Japan, which had previously been "subject to the general directions of the government" (Cargill, Hutchison et al. 2000: 92 and 112). In the same year the United Kingdom's newly-elected Labour finance minister, Gordon Brown, startled observers with a surprise announcement that the law governing the Bank of England would also be overhauled to assure its formal independence (Seldon 2005: 280-281). A wave of similar reforms was undertaken in other countries as well (Fig. 1). By the end of 1990s, central banks had gone through a "global process of institutional transformation" (Marcussen 2007: 136).

This broad transformation was a direct result of the tumult of the 1970s. It came to be broadly accepted that the years of economic turmoil had been aggravated because central banks had been prevented from taking the firm and painful measures necessary to curb inflation and create the stable conditions that were a prerequisite for economic growth. The implication was that governments should assure the independence of their central banks, so that they are free to maintain firm anti-inflationary policies without regard to the political reaction that might be generated by their decisions. A central bank that is not "subservient to central government", and preferably led by conservative elements of the financial community, would serve as a "commitment device" – in the sense that it committed a country to a consistent and rigorously anti-inflationary path (Bade and Parkin 1985; Rogoff 1985; Alesina and Summers 1993).

Advocates of central bank independence went further, by defining exactly what independence meant in practice. These definitions typically emphasized the laws that defined the relationship between elected leaders and a central bank. (This was known as the degree of *de jure* independence.) For example, a central bank was more likely to be counted as independent if the law contained a guarantee that bank heads would be appointed for fixed terms, with removal only for serious misconduct; a proscription against government directions to the bank on monetary policy; and a mandate to focus on inflation control, to the exclusion of other objectives. Statutory restrictions on the capacity of governments to finance deficits by selling bonds to the central banks (who would then pay for them with newly created currency) were also taken as an important sign of bank autonomy (Arnone, Laurens et al. 2006: 8-20).

Scholarly research initially seemed to confirm a connection between the *de jure* independence of a country's central bank and its record on inflation control. In 1988, economist Alberto Alesina found a significant relationship between the formal bank independence and the inflation rate in twelve advanced economies, but was careful to note that the correlation did not imply that independence itself had led to lower inflation (Alesina 1988). A 1991 study of eighteen advanced economies was bolder, concluding that independence did contribute to lower inflation (Grilli, Masciandaro et al. 1991). In 1992, a study of seventy-two countries supported by the World Bank also concluded that the *de jure* independence contributed to low inflation in advanced economies, although evidence was equivocal for developing countries (Cukierman, Webb et al. 1992). And in 1993 Alesina and his co-author Lawrence Summers found a "near perfect negative correlation between inflation and central bank independence" in sixteen advanced economies. Alesina and Summers were now bolder about the policy implications, saying their research showed "the economic performance merits" of central bank independence (Alesina and Summers 1993).

A large body of later work challenged these early findings, arguing that the formal definition of independence was too simplistic. For example, a 1997 study that included rough measures of other potential factors – such as public "distaste for inflation" caused by episodes of high inflation – concluded that central bank independence was a "relatively unimportant" determinant of inflation performance in high-income states (Campillo and Miron 1997). Evidence about the relationship between independence and inflation in developing countries also remained ambiguous. A 2006 IMF study of seventy-one developed and developing countries simply concluded that formal independence "does not play an important role" in deterring inflation (Kwon, McFarlane et al. 2006: 11).

These studies came too late to influence elite opinion. By the early 1990s it was settled wisdom that formal bank independence was a prerequisite for achieving price stability. Charts showing the simple correlation between formal independence and inflation rates in advanced economies were often published in the popular press in the early 1990s (Posen 1993: 41). The academic evidence was "unequivocal," a columnist in Britain's *Independent* newspaper said in 1993 (Davies 1993). "The intellectual case for central bank independence," *The Economist* declared at the same time, "is more or less won" (The Economist 1993).

Development of a New Central Banking Regime

The transformation in central banking during the era of liberalization consisted of more than legal changes. For example, there was also significant change in the method of staffing senior positions within central banks. There is good evidence that central banks are more likely to pursue stringent anti-inflationary policies if their top ranks are dominated by former private sector bankers or businessmen, economists, or central bank careerists; and less likely to pursue such policies if there is heavy representation of former trade unionists and politicians. The anti-inflationary professions have historically dominated the leadership of central banks, but their hold weakened during the 1960s and early 1970s. Their dominance was reestablished during the era of liberalization. In most advanced economies, central banks were once again controlled by individuals whose professional background predisposes them to firmer anti-inflationary policies (Adolph 2005, Göhlmann and Vaubel 2005).

Central banks also shifted internal procedures for making decisions about monetary policy. A tradition in many central banks of concentrating authority in the hands of a single individual has given way to a practice of decision making on key issues by committee. As Alan Blinder observed in 2004, decision making by committee "has now become the rule" (Blinder 2004: 35). In a sense, there has been a double delegation: first to the independent central bank, and then *within the bank* to a collective body. "We are entering a time," agrees Robert Shiller, "when central bankers administer policies that come not just from their own individual minds but instead from the interaction of many minds" (Blinder 2004: xiii). This procedural change has the effect of anchoring monetary policy because of the inertial tendencies of group decision making.

There is a third significant change in internal structure. Throughout the 1990s, banks in the advanced economies increased their spending on internal research departments staffed by PhD economists. In 1990, these banks employed roughly three hundred researchers; by 2003, they employed seven hundred (St-Amant, Tkacz et al. 2005: Table 1a). (This growth occurred at a time when governments facing budget deficits were mainly concerned with *reducing* public payrolls.) For advanced-economy central banks, it was increasingly important to have internal research capabilities that could rival the economics faculty of a well-established university. Research departments insisted that the main measure of their effectiveness was set externally, by the number of papers accepted in highly regarded academic journals. In fact, the research departments of central banks were frequently scorecarded according to their productivity, defined in this narrow way (Eijffinger, De Haan et al. 2002; Jondeau and Pagés 2003: 1; Goodfriend, König et al. 2004: 2).

The expansion of research capabilities within central banks was undertaken with the expectation that it would improve the quality of bank decision making. But it also had the incidental effect of bolstering central bank independence. It contributed to the "scientization" of central banking – that is, to the perception that the field of monetary policy was one where finding the right course of action required the application of scientific, rather than practical, knowledge (Marcussen 2006: 199). Direction on monetary policy by elected officials became doubly problematic – not only because they were judged to have incentives to skew policy in the wrong direction, but also because they were judged to be unskilled in scholarly economics.

In addition to these internal changes, there were shifts in relationships *among* central banks. Mechanisms for inter-bank coordination became much more complex during the era of liberalization. More than ten multilateral forums for discussion among central banks have been created in the last two decades. Martin Marcussen suggests that we have seen the emergence of a "transgovernmental governance network" of central bankers – a "more or less formalized institutional framework" for development of central bank policy whose core is "small, coherent, and tightly interconnected" (Marcussen 2006: 181, 201 and Table 9.4). Anne Marie Slaughter agrees, arguing that central banks have constructed a "dense web of relations" that serve as a conduit for policy deliberations and also for information about central bankers' "reputations . . . concerning competence, quality, integrity, and professionalism" (Slaughter 2004: 54).

The development of this transnational network of central bankers was made easier by the extraordinary degree of continuity and conformity within the community of central bank governors. A 2001 study found that the average tenure for the world's central bank governors was seven years; to put it another way, the community loses only 14 % of its numbers in an average year. In 2001, the population of governors was almost exclusively male. Four-fifths had degrees in economics or finance, and well over half attended university in the United States or the United Kingdom. One third had once worked with the International Monetary Fund or the World Bank. "Central bankers in the global central bank network look like each other in objective terms," says Marcussen, who concludes that "they will probably also look at and analyze the world in very similar ways" (Marcussen 2006: 191).

Not only are central banks more tightly connected to one another; they are also linked more closely to the community of scholarly economists. Of course, we have already seen evidence of this in the growth of research capabilities within central banks. This was matched by an explosion of scholarly writing on central banking within academia itself (Blinder 2004: 1). Academics also became more likely candidates for the leadership of central banks. Ben Bernanke, chairman of the Federal Reserve after 2006, was previously a professor of economics at Princeton University; Mervyn King, governor of the Bank of England after 2003, had been a professor at the London School of Economics.

The economists Paul Bowles and Gordon White argued in 1994 that the contemporary central bank is "a modern embodiment of the Platonic guardian . . . [B]y virtue of its "independence" and "apolitical" character, it is deemed to be above and outside the normal political pressures and requirements of democratic societies" (Bowles and White 1994: 243). We can now see the truth of this statement. By the turn of the millennium, central banking had become a domain dominated by a tightly interwoven network of experts, similar in outlook and training, self-assured, and confident in asserting their prerogatives in the field of monetary policy. On the eve of the financial crisis, this community credited itself for a dramatic lowering of inflation rates around the world. "The global taming of inflation," IMF economist Kenneth Rogoff said in 2003, was a "huge success. . . Inflation has dropped to levels that, only two decades ago, seemed frustratingly unattainable." Independent central banks, Rogoff concluded, "[have] unquestionably played a central role in the overall reduction of inflation" (Rogoff 2003). Indeed, some central bankers were so impressed with their own success that they enthusiastically recommended the same model of technocratic governance in other policy domains (Blinder 1997).

The Regime in Crisis

The credibility of the central banking regime was badly damaged by the financial crisis, largely because of the perception that leading central banks – the Federal Reserve in particular – had contributed to the onset of the crisis. Three charges could be made against the Federal Reserve (Kaufman 2009). The first was that it had simply failed to acknowledge evidence of a housing bubble or anticipate the damage that would be done to the financial system and economy when the bubble inevitably burst. The second was that it had failed to use its regulatory powers to control mortgage lending and the booming market for complex financial instruments. The third was that the central bank had failed to use its influence over interest rates to deflate the bubble, or at least slow its growth, by raising the cost of borrowing by homeowners.

In the popular press, blame for these errors was often put on the shoulders of Alan Greenspan, chairman of the Federal Reserve from 1987 to 2006. Greenspan, one writer said, "is the leading villain in this story" (Baker 2008: 140). But it is simplistic to explain a massive policy failure only as the result of one man's errors in judgment. We have already established that the system for crafting monetary policy was radically transformed in the era of liberalization. Advanced economies built an elaborate new regime for determining monetary policy. It is reasonable to ask whether this complex system contributed to the failure as well.

This is not an unusual question to ask. On the contrary, the question has been routinely posed in the wake of other policy debacles of the last decade – such as the failure to anticipate the 9/11 attacks, the decision to invade Iraq, the destruction of the space shuttle Columbia, and the response to Hurricane Katrina. Common themes connected the reports produced after each of these debacles. One theme is the tendency of complex systems to remain fixated on the crisis that led to their emergence, rather than new threats. A related difficulty is the inability to respond intelligently to new threats, either because evidence about the serious of those threats is discounted, or because an appropriate response would require heavy investment in new capabilities. These are variations on the same central point: complex systems can remain preoccupied with old dangers, and oblivious to new ones.

The renovated system of central banking suffered from the same vulnerability. Once the financial crisis was underway, it became commonplace to say that one of the central functions of any central bank is to maintain the overall stability of the financial system as a whole. But this function was largely subordinated in importance during the preceding three decades. Central bank independence was not justified as a technique for protecting systemic stability. The renovated system of central banking was, above all, an *anti-inflation* regime, constructed to avoid a reprise of the trauma that had afflicted the advanced democracies during the 1970's. The regime was not built to anticipate the new threats to economic order that would arise when the primary goal – a long period of price stability – had been achieved, and businesses and households felt emboldened to take greater financial risks.

The central banking system suffered from doctrinal blindness. Throughout the system there was a "near-consensus view" that the main task of central bankers was to focus primarily on inflation control (Wright and Smithers 2002: 20). Systemic stability was not regarded as the core function. A related difficulty was the unwillingness to acknowledge mounting evidence of a bubble in the housing market or concede that central bankers could do anything to anything to discourage a bubble, if it existed. The "intellectual assumptions" dominant within the central banking system assumed that markets were rational and efficient; that for this reason bubbles could not persist; and that attempts at intervention would be counterproductive (Financial Services Authority 2009: 39-42).

A correlate of doctrinal blindness was hostility to dissenting points of view. Economist Barry Eichengreen says that the "pressure of social conformity" within the economics profession was intense, discouraging attention to scholarship that warned of potential disaster (Eichengreen 2009). Fellow economist Robert Shiller – one of the world's most influential economists – described his own experience with "groupthink" within the system:

> "From my own experience on expert panels, I know firsthand the pressures that people may feel when questioning the group consensus. . . . While I warned about the bubbles I believed were developing in the stock and housing markets, I did so very

gently, and felt vulnerable expressing such quirky views. Deviating too far from consensus leaves one feely potentially ostracized from the group (Shiller 2008)".

IMF research director Raghuram Rajan encountered this problem in 2005 when he warned of a "low probability" of financial catastrophe because of irrational market behavior (Rajan 2005). Rajan was excoriated by leading economists and central bankers (including former Treasury secretary Lawrence Summers) for a "lead-eyed" analysis that would encourage "misguided policy impulses in many countries" (Federal Reserve Bank of Kansas City 2005: 374, 387-389, 394). In 2006 William R. White, chief economist for the Bank of International Settlements, also warned that central banks were fixated on price stability and ignoring risks posed by asset bubbles (White 2006). White, too, was ignored. He said later that he struggled with an "acceptance problem . . . The signs were perfectly clear [but] people didn't want to respond to the warnings . . . [T]he analytic framework that you use is crucial and the vast majority of people were not prepared to accept [the danger]" (The Spectator 2009).

Major central banks were moved to more radical action as the financial crisis deepened. Their reaction was often spasmodic, but this was a natural consequence of the blindness that afflicted the central banking system before the collapse. Willem Buiter, a former member of the Bank of England's monetary policy committee, laid part of the blame on scholarly economists who now played a key role within many central banks. "The strong representation of academic economists and other professional economists . . . turned out to be a serious handicap," Buiter said in 2009. "The economics profession was caught unprepared when the crisis struck" (Buiter 2009).

In many ways, the banks' response to crisis up-ended the orthodoxy about how central banks were supposed to behave. Refined calculations about the long-run inflationary effect of bank decisions on monetary policy were put aside in an urgent effort to avoid a slide into depression. "Inflation," one critic complained in 2008, was now "almost an afterthought" (Grant 2008). As conventional tools for reducing interest rates lost their effectiveness, the major central banks resorted to the purchase of government-issued debt with newly-created money, a tactic described as "quantitative easing". Only a few months earlier, this tactic had been regarded as one of the traits of a central bank that lacked real independence from government. Indeed, an August 2009 IMF research paper conceded that quantitative easing "exposes the central bank to a possible perception of capture by the fiscal authority . . . especially during times of high deficits" (Meier 2009).

Central banks were also compelled to work closely with Treasury officials in crafting a response to the crisis. The image of independence was blurred as the Federal Reserve coordinated statements with the Treasury and collaborated in implementing programs to rescue failing financial institutions and maintain liquidity in key markets. Critics complained that the Federal Reserve had become an instrument for making risky and politically sensitive commitments to the financial sector that should have been made by the Treasury directly. "Independent central banks don't do what this Fed has done," economist Allan Meltzer said in 2009 (Meltzer 2009).

This tension between the demands of crisis management, and orthodox ideas about central bank independence, had been seen before. The Bank of Japan encountered a "serious problem" a decade earlier because it was granted *de jure* independence just at the moment that the Asian financial crisis required it to coordinate closely with the Japanese finance ministry. "Inevitably," Bank of England head Mervyn King observed in 2004, "the desire to respect the newly won independence of the [Japanese] central bank came into conflict" with the reality that it was "no longer possible to identify clear and distinct responsibilities for the two institutions" (King 2004: 11). Ironically, this became King's own predicament – and also the Federal Reserve's – five years later.

The shift in behavior by the US, British and Japanese central banks showed that conventional wisdom about the role of central banks was not inviolable after all: it could be bent in moments of crisis. In the words of business journalist David Wessel, the Federal Reserve would do "whatever it takes" to avoid calamity (Wessel 2009). For Anglo-American policymakers in particular, the ultimate consideration was pragmatism, not doctrinal rigor. This was manifest in the charges made against the European Central Bank as the financial crisis deepened. The ECB was broadly recognized as the best example of the rigorous application of *de jure* independence. The ECB was less willing to lower interest rates, because its mandate required strict attention to long-term price stability. It also hesitated to undertake quantitative easing, arguing that this might violate treaty requirements and jeopardize the ECB's autonomy. The ECB's position earned it the sort of criticism that is always made by pragmatists: that it was rigid, inflexible, and orthodox in its response.

By 2009, the argument for central bank independence had been discredited in several ways. The most obvious difficulty was the failure of leading central bankers to anticipate and avoid the crisis of 2007-2009. The sophisticated anti-inflation regime built in the preceding three decades may well have proved effective in avoiding a reprise of the Great Inflation, but this particular virtue was accompanied by a glaring weakness. The regime also institutionalized a vulnerability – a blindness to the new risks engendered by careless liberalization and a long period of growth and price stability. The newly empowered class of technocrat-guardians had proved unable to manage those risks properly.

This manifest failure of performance made it possible for critics to challenge to central bank power. U.S. Senator Bernie Sanders criticized the Federal Reserve for wielding power "with absolutely no accountability, no transparency, and no honest reckoning with the American people." By August 2009, two-thirds of the U.S. House of Representatives had co-signed Rep. Ron Paul's bill to give the Government Accountability Office the power to scrutinize Federal Reserve activities. Other legislators threatened to strip the Federal Reserve of important regulatory functions.

The argument for central bank independence was also shown to hinge on important but previously undeclared assumptions about the state of the world – principally, that the risks of systemic instability were not substantial. When this assumption collapsed after 2007, elite opinion about appropriate bank behavior shifted rapidly, to countenance activities that had previously been regarded as suspect.

The fact that the case for central bank independence was revealed to be contingent on these undeclared assumptions about prevailing conditions caused it to lose a significant amount of its rhetorical force. It provided reluctant policy makers in many countries with the opportunity to argue that the model might not fit their own circumstances either. Anglo-American proponents of bank independence might claim that the crisis of 2007-2009 was truly exceptional, but this was not so clear. In fact, financial crises were endemic during the age of liberalization (Duménil and Lévy 2004: 86; Wolf 2008: 31-34). There was ample opportunity for other governments to argue that they, too, confronted "unusual and exigent" conditions. And if leading economies were permitted to deviate from the orthodoxy in such circumstances, why were others precluded from doing the same?

The Future of Discipline

The "quiet revolution" in central banking during the era of liberalization was built upon a mode of reasoning, which I earlier called the logic of discipline. Deeply skeptical about the capacity of democratic processes to pursue appropriate policies, this logic favors the imposition of constraints on democratic choice, and often the transfer of authority to technocrat-guardians who wield that authority in the public interest. The same logic was applied in many other areas of government, often with the apparent success of independent central banks in mind. But in these other areas, the case for reform has also been tainted by the financial crisis.

For example, regulatory authority in many countries was transferred from government ministries to new autonomous regulatory authorities, often given the same sort of *de jure* independence that was granted to central banks. And the rationale was the same: that some check was necessary against the tendency of politicians "to behave in a shortsighted and populist manner that reduces welfare summed over a medium to long-term period" (Cubbin 2005: 5). In the era of liberalization, independent regulation also became "an hegemonic institution grounded in a new convention in economic governance" (Jordana and Levi-Faur 2006: 336). But the competence of financial regulators was quickly called into question as the financial crisis revealed the frailty of major financial institutions.

Finance ministries also consolidated their hold on power during the era of liberalization. Finance officials were intended to serve as fiscal guardians, just as central bankers served as guardians of monetary policy; the presumption was that they would be "driven less by particularistic spending interests" than other ministries (Poterba and von Hagen 1999: 10). The entrenchment of finance ministry power was expected to create "a commitment device for fiscal discipline" (von Hagen and Harden 1995: 779). But the financial crisis weakened this argument as well. Finance ministries themselves became major spending departments, committing billions of dollars to sustain failing financial institutions and provide economic stimulus. Skeptics questioned whether finance officials, with their close ties to the financial sector, might not also be captured "particularistic spending interests." In the United States, many legislators rebelled against attempts by the U.S. Treasury to consolidate its legislative authority in the early phases of the financial crisis (Newsweek 2008).

Throughout the era of liberalization, reformers also promoted technocratic governance for ports, airports, and other elements of infrastructure that were necessary to support globalized production systems. Ports and airports went through "an unprecedented transformation on a global scale," with power again being transferred from government ministries to newly autonomized bodies (Aaronson 2005: 345). Meanwhile private investors were invited to take over major components of infrastructure, on the theory that this would "remove undue political influence in service provision" (Commonwealth Business Council 2006: 2). But global trade experienced its worst decline in modern history during the financial crisis, undermining arguments about the need for mainport expansion; while private investors fled to safe havens, causing the delay or cancellation of infrastructure projects.

The financial crisis raised two broad questions about the logic that had guided reform in all of these areas. The first was whether the competence of experts had been badly overestimated. The second was whether the problem of discipline was limited to democratic processes alone. Markets also had proved to be unruly. Leaders of major financial institutions conceded that they did not know what their subordinates were doing. Financial markets proved to be susceptible to wild swings, driven by short term profit seeking and herd behavior. The global economy was more prone to crisis than it had been in the three decades that preceded the era of liberalization. The financial crisis encouraged the belief that it was markets, and not democratic processes, that were in need of stricter discipline.

In August 2009 the editors of the *Financial Times* concluded: "The era of economic theocracy, in which unelected experts ran the global economy, is over" (Financial Times 2009). This is an overstatement. There is no evidence that the crisis will result in the complete overthrow of the bastions of technocratic power. It is unlikely, for example, that the *de jure* independence of central banks or regulators will be wholly reversed. But it seems probable that skepticism about technocratic governance and about the trustworthiness of markets will encourage the reassertion of political influence in policy domains that were, in the heyday of liberalization, the preserve of technocrat-guardians.

References

Aaronson, R. (2005). Forces Driving Industry Change. *Strategic Managment in the Aviation Industry*. W. Delfmann, H. Baum, S. Auerbach and S. Albers, Eds., Ashgate: 345-361.

Adolph, Ch. (2005). The Dilemma of Discretion: Career Ambitions and the Politics of Central Banking, Harvard University. PhD: Pages.

Alesina, A. (1988). "Macroeconomics and Politics." *NBER Macroeconomics Annual* 3: 13-52.

Alesina, A. and Summers L. (1993). "Central Bank Independence and Macroeconomic Performance. " *Journal of Money, Credit and Banking* 25(2): 151-162.

Arnone, M., Laurens B. and Segalotto J. F. (2006). *The Measurement of Central Bank Autonomy: Survey of Models, Indicators, and Empirical Evidence.* Washington, DC, International Monetary Fund. October.

Bade, R. and Parkin M. (1985). *Central Bank Laws and Monetary Policy.* London, Canada, University of Western Ontario.

Baker, D. (2008). Plunder and Blunder: The Rise and Fall of the Bubble Economy. Sausalito, CA, PoliPointPress.

Becker, G. S. (1983). "A Theory of Competition among Pressure Groups for Political Support. " Quarterly Journal of Economics 98(3): 371-400.

Birch, A. (1984). "Overload, Ungovernability and Delegitimation." *British Journal of Political Science* 14(2): 135-160.

Blinder, A. (1997). "Is Government Too Political? " *Foreign Affairs* 76(6): 115-126.

Blinder, A. S. (2004). *The Quiet Revolution: Central Banking Goes Modern.* New Haven, CT, Yale University Press.

Bowles, P. and White G. (1994). "Central Bank Independence: A Political Economy Approach." *Journal of Development Studies* 31(2): 235-264.

Buchanan, J. M. and Tullock G. (1962). *The Calculus of Consent: Logical Foundations of Constitutional Democracy.* Ann Arbor, MI, University of Michigan Press.

Buchanan, J. M. and Wagner R. E. (1977). Democracy in Deficit: The Political Legacy of Lord Keynes. New York, Academic Press.

Buiter, W. (2009, March 3). "The Unfortunate Uselessness of Most 'State of the Art' Academic Monetary Economics. " Retrieved May 5, 2009, from http://blogs.ft.com/maverecon/2009/03/the-unfortunate-uselessness-of-most-state-of-the-art-academic-monetary-economics/.

Campillo, M. and Miron J. (1997). Why Does Inflation Differ across Countries? Cambridge, MA, National Bureau for Economic Research.

Cargill, Th. F., Hutchison M. M. and Ito T. (2000). Financial Policy and Central Banking in Japan. Cambridge, MA, MIT Press.

Commonwealth Business Council (2006). An Agenda for Growth and Livelihoods: Public-Private Partnerships for Infrastructure. London, Commonwealth Secretariat.

Crozier, M., Huntington S. P. and Watanuki J. (1975). *The Crisis of Democracy: Report on the Governability of Democracies to the Trilateral Commission.* New York, NY, New York University Press.

Cubbin, J. (2005). Regulatory Effectiveness and the Empirical Impact of Variations in Regulatory Governance. Washington, DC, World Bank. March.

Cukierman, A., Webb St. B. and Neyapti B. (1992). "Measuring the Independence of Central Banks and Its Effect on Policy Outcomes. " *The World Bank Economic Review* 6(3): 353-398.

Davies, G. (1993). The Arguments for an Independent Old Lady. *The Independent:* 29.

Duménil, G. and Lévy D. (2004). *Capital Resurgent: Roots of the Neoliberal Revolution.* Cambridge, MA, Harvard University Press.

Eichengreen, B. J. (2009). "The Last Temptation of Risk. " *The National Interest.*

Eijffinger, S., De Haan J. and Koedijk K. (2002). "Small Is Beautiful: Measuring the Research Input and Output of European Central Banks. " *European Journal of Political Economy* 18(2): 365-374.

Federal Reserve Bank of Kansas City (2005). *The Greenspan Era: Lessons for the Future.* Kansas City, MO, Federal Reserve Bank of Kansas City.

Financial Services Authority (2009). *The Turner Review: A Regulatory Response to the Global Financial Crisis.* London, Financial Services Authority. March.

Financial Times (2009). The Value of Bank Independence. *Financial Times.* August 2.

Fukuyama, F. (1989). "The End of History? " *National Interest* 16(3): 3-16.

Galbraith, J. K. (1967). *The New Industrial State.* Boston, MA, Houghton Mifflin.

Göhlmann, S. and Vaubel R. (2005). The Educational and Professional Background of Central Bankers and Its Effect on Inflation – an Empirical Analysis, RWI Essen.

Goodfriend, M., König R. and Repullo R. (2004). *External Evaluation of the Economic Research Activities of the European Central Bank.* Frankfurt, Germany, European Central Bank.

Grant, J. (2008). Paying the Price for the Fed's Success. *New York Times.* January 27.

Grilli, V.; Masciandaro D.; Tabellini G.; Malinvaud E. and Pagano M. (1991). "Political and Monetary Institutions and Public Financial Policies in the Industrial Countries. " *Economic Policy* 6(13): 342-392.

Huntington, S. P. (1981). *American Politics: The Promise of Disharmony.* Cambridge, MA, Belknap Press.

Jondeau, E. and Pagés H. (2003). *Benchmarking Research in European Central Banks.* Paris, Banque de France. May.

Jordana, J. and Levi-Faur D. (2006). "Toward a Latin American Regulatory State? The Diffusion of Autonomous Agencies across Countries and Sectors." *International Journal of Public Administration* 29(4-6): 335-366.

Kaufman, H. (2009). How Libertarian Dogma Led the Fed Astray. *Financial Times*. April 28: 11.

Keating, P. (1989). The Reserve Bank: Let the Parliament Rule. *Sydney Morning Herald*. September 22: 11.

King, A. (1975). "Overload: Problems of Governing in the 1970s." *Political Studies* 23: 284-96.

King, M. (2004). "The Institutions of Monetary Policy." *American Economic Review* 94(2): 1-13.

Klingemann, H. D. (1999). Mapping Political Support in the 1990s: A Global Analysis. *Critical Citizens: Global Support for Democratic Governance*. P. Norris, Ed. New York, Oxford University Press: 31-56.

Kwon, G., McFarlane L. and Robinson W. (2006). *Public Debt, Money Supply and Inflation: A Cross-Country Study and Its Application to Jamaica*. Washington, DC, International Monetary Fund. May.

Marcussen, M. (2006). The Transnational Governance Network of Central Bankers. *Transnational Governance*. M.-L. Djelic and K. Sahlin-Andersson, Eds. New York, Cambridge University Press: 180-204.

Marcussen, M. (2007). Central Banking Reform around the World: Only by Night Are All Cats Grey. *Transcending New Public Management*. T. Christensen and P. Laegreid, Eds. Aldershot, UK, Ashgate Publishing: 135-154.

Meier, A. (2009). Panacea, Curse, or Nonevent? Unconventional Monetary Policy in the United Kingdom. Washington, DC, International Monetary Fund. August 1.

Meltzer, A. (2009). Inflation Nation. *New York Times*. May 4: A19.

Mueller, D. (2003). *Public Choice III*. New York, Cambridge University Press.

Newsweek (2008). Taking Stock of Henry Paulson. *Newsweek*. 152: 21: 14.

Niskanen, W.(1968). "The Peculiar Economics of Bureaucracy". *American Economic Review* 58(2): 293-305.

Olson, M. (1971). The Logic of Collective Action: Public Goods and the Theory of Groups. Cambridge, MA, Harvard University Press.

Posen, A. (1993). Why Central Bank Independence Does Not Cause Low Inflation: There Is No Institutional Fix for Politics. *Finance and the International Economy: 7*. R. O'Brien, Ed. Oxford, United Kingdom, Oxford University Press: 40-65.

Poterba, J. and von Hagen J. (eds.) (1999). *Fiscal Institutions and Fiscal Performance*. Chicago, IL, University of Chicago Press.

Rajan, R. (2005). *Has Financial Development Made the World Riskier?* Washington, DC, International Monetary Fund. September.

Reston, J. (1975). The Crisis of Democracy. *New York Times*. June 29.

Roberts, A. (2010). The Logic of Discipline: Global Capitalism and the New Architecture of Government. New York, Oxford University Press.

Rogoff, K. (1985). "The Optimal Degree of Commitment to an Intermediate Monetary Target. " *Quarterly Journal of Economics* 100(4): 1169-1189.

Rogoff, K. (2003). *Globalization and Global Disinflation*. Washington, DC, International Monetary Fund.

Rose, R. (1980). *Challenge to Governance: Studies in Overloaded Polities*. Beverly Hills, Sage Publications.

Schwartz, H. (1994). "Public Choice Theory and Public Choices: Bureaucrats and State Reorganization in Australia, Denmark, New Zealand and Sweden. " *Administration and Society* 26(1): 48-77.

Seldon, A. (2005). *Blair*. London, Free Press.

Shiller, R. (2008). Challenging the Crowd in Whispers, Not Shouts. *New York Times*. November 2.

Slaughter, A.-M. (2004). *A New World Order*. Princeton, NJ, Princeton University Press.

St-Amant, P., Tkacz G., Guérard-Langlois A. and Morel L. (2005). *Quantity, Quality, and Relevance: Central Bank Research, 1990-2003*. Ottawa, Canada, Bank of Canada.

The Economist (1993). Narrow Money. *The Economist* (August 28): 16.

The Spectator. (2009). "Transcript of Interview with William R. White." Retrieved May 3, 2009, from http://spectatorinquiry.pbworks.com/William-White-transcript.

von Hagen, J. and Harden I. (1995). "Budget Processes and Commitment to Fiscal Discipline." *European Economic Review* 39(3-4): 771-779.

Wessel, D. (2009). In Fed We Trust: Ben Bernanke's War on the Great Panic. New York, Crown Business.

White, W. R. (2006). *Is Price Stability Enough?* Basel, Switzerland, Bank for International Settlements.

Wolf, M. (2008). *Fixing Global Finance.* Baltimore, MD, Johns Hopkins University Press.

Wright, St. and Smithers A. (2002). *Stock Markets and Central Bankers: The Economic Consequences of Alan Greenspan.* London, Birkbeck College, University of London.

4

Reforming the International Financial System by Regulation and Collaborative Arrangements

Hubert Fromlet

Financial Markets, Economic Growth, and Lessons from History

Literature has given us a great number of contributions to the importance of well-working or well-developing financial markets on economic growth – from Raymond Goldsmith in the late 1960s to Andrei Shleifer and Ross Levine more recently.

In reality, the whole globe gradually became aware of what a major financial crisis can mean to the real economy. In 2008, a severe global recession became unavoidable. Such a bad development was simply not on the cards two years ago when the first signs of more concrete troubles in the American financial sector became visible. Despite the fact that most of us then understood that global financial markets had become much more integrated in the past decades, there were only a few experts like Nouriel Roubini and James Hamilton who at least roughly foresaw the degree of global contagion in the real economy.

However, there have been enough financial crises in the past that were caused by excesses in money supply and credit growth. I still wonder why bank executives have such short memories. In Sweden, we had a severe banking crisis in the early 1990s. Only a few years later, the world was confronted with the dot.com crisis. And when that crisis more or less had passed by, American and Swedish financial officers "prepared" for another bubble, i. e. what was to become the subprime bubble in the U.S. and the credit bubble in the Baltic states. Bounded rationality – using the great Herbert Simon's words – must have penetrated the minds of many executives at some point as well.

I tend to reject the opinion that economic theory and research did not give warning signals for preventing the current global financial crisis. Sure, we still do not have a comprehensive theory for global financial markets, and we still do not know how to model or calculate global multiplier effects from certain financial events or trends. However, a couple of hints – though from different angles – on a forthcoming major financial crisis could be found already around 2004/2005, for example, from

- *economic history:* (Charles Kindleberger, John K. Galbraith, Ben Bernanke, etc.)
- *psychology*: behavioral finance (Robert Shiller; herd mentality, overconfidence, control illusion)
- *institutional economics:* (Douglass North, Oliver Williamson, etc)
- *incentives* (Bo Holmström, Jean Tirole, etc.)
- *liquidity, micro and macro* (Jean Tirole, Axel Leijonhufvud, Otmar Issing, etc.)

However, some research areas were highly underdeveloped before the financial meltdown in 2007, such as

- *modeling bounded rationality (psychology)*
- *behavior and skills of financial managers and investors*
- *links between global financial markets and global macroeconomics*
- *systemic financial risks*
- *global contagion (modeling global multiplier effects)*
- *links between financial products (micro) and their aggregated markets/volumes.*

In order to find remedies for avoiding future bursting bubbles, one has to look at the background of the still ongoing global financial and economic crisis. The following summary does not cover every single reason for the current financial and growth disaster.

Reasons for the Ongoing Global and Financial Crisis (without Ranking):

Failures / shortcomings	**Institutions for improvement**
Monetary policy (too low rates for too long time)	Central banks
Asset prices in monetary policy	Central banks
Liquidity (too high, yield hunger, increasing risk)	Central banks / *banks*
Modeling (global aggregates/multipliers, etc)	Central banks / research
Co-operation central bank/supervision (insufficient)	Central banks / supervision
Capital reserves in banks (insufficient)	Supervision (X) / BIS
Banks' capital requirements (procyclical)	Supervision (X) / BIS
Risk leverage in banks' activities (too high)	Supervision (X)
SIV (mismatched balance sheets, capital shortage)	Supervision (X), *banks*
Incentives for new credits (too little risk-oriented)	Supervision (X), *banks*
Cross-border supervision (totally insufficient)	Supervision (X) / BIS (X)
Supervision itself (analysis methods, competence)	Supervision (X), gvmnt. (X)
Resources to supervision (too limited financially, in skills)	Government
Rating agencies (weak models, dependence on banks)	Supervision (X)
Financial literacy (too weak, private households)	Supervision (X), *banks*
Financial literacy (too weak, bank officers/leaders)	Supervision (X), *banks*
Consumer protection	Supervision (X)/law(X), *banks*
Greed of investors	Supervision (?), *banks*
Banks' risk models (too static, insufficiently global)	Supervision (X), *banks*
Banks' bonuses (wrong incentives)	Law, supervision (X), *banks*
Financial products (too complicated, low transparency)	Supervision (?), *banks*
Research (too national, too much "homo oeconomicus")	Governments, *banks*

* (X) = improvements that can be achieved by regulation – if handled carefully

But the list shown on the previous page should be long enough to make readers understand that there were many factors behind the first big global financial explosion during the ongoing crisis in August 2007 and behind the extremely dangerous acceleration of the crisis in early fall 2008 when Lehman Brothers crashed. From September 2008 onward, rapid global contagion from the financial sector to the real part of the economy – i.e. corporate and private households – can be observed. This happened because the financial crisis was attacked too reluctantly and wrongly. Too little emphasis was put on lost confidence within the banking sector. John Taylor pointed out this fatal mistake and I share his opinion (Taylor 2009).

Even a quick look at this list shows that there is quite a substantial number of areas that cannot be improved by the banks directly. Only half of about 20 areas can be left to the banks themselves to find more sophisticated solutions. However, this conclusion does not guarantee that the banks will stick to such a commitment forever or even at all. In this context, I am easily reminded of some words coined by Wall Street's greatest guru ever – Henry Kaufman from Salomon Brothers – in the mid 1980s when he commented so briefly and sharply then on financial deregulation: "Some re-regulation will be unavoidable in the future" (Kaufman, 1986).

Responsibility and Regulation

When looking at the reasons for the global financial crisis as mentioned above, five institutions with major responsibility for the still ongoing financial earthquake can be found. They are

- central banks
- supervision
- governments
- rating agencies
- banks.

In other words, there are further institutions and groups of interest that can be partly blamed for the expanding and bursting financial bubble, with the U.S. as the causal and geographic origin. Thus, harder regulation of banks, of other financial institutions and financial products cannot do the job alone to prevent the world from financial crises or to limit future damage. There is also a great need of changing behavior and governance. But how can bad financial behavior be addressed when we still know by far too little about how to explain, measure, model and combat all those major shortcomings on financial markets?

Obviously, experts agree worldwide these days that necessary regulation on deregulated financial markets proved to be insufficient or lagging. Again, I ask myself why so many financial leaders did not listen to criticism from experts, sometimes not even when coming from their own organization. I personally remember written and verbal warnings concerning the procyclicality of the Basel II-capital requirements and the insufficiencies of rating agencies by the professors and central bank leaders Charles Goodhart (previously Bank of England) and Hans-Helmut Kotz (previously Deutsche Bundesbank). Claudio Borio (BIS) has been concerned about rising asset prices for a long time. Some other professors such as Robert Shiller, Raghuram Rajam and James Hamilton also sent their early warnings to the general public – though from different research angles.

Unfortunately, too few influential people listened to them. We simply had – and still have – too much flock mentality on global financial markets, analysts included. This phenomenon cannot disappear or be diminished decisively by regulation. The issue is rather a better understanding of markets – which again underscores the importance of behavioral finance, deepened global financial research and information.

On the other hand, certain financial areas cannot work without ef fective regulation. This takes us to another keyword – efficacy. Regulations must function well under all circumstances, even the most dramatic ones. I usually make a distinction between

- necessary and well-working regulations
- necessary and improvable regulations
- unnecessary regulations.

Samuelson's and Nordhaus' (2005) definition is still the one I usually apply. They write that "regulations consist of government rules or laws issued to control the prices, sales, or production decisions of firms... (and there is) in addition a newer form of regulation, known as social regulation".

Social regulations in the aftermath of this ongoing crisis should be implemented ambitiously in order to more consequently protect bank customers – both households and corporates – but also to better protect the banks themselves and their employees. The social aspects of meaningful regulations should not be overlooked. This is why I have been pleading for a long time so strongly for improved financial literacy. Improved financial literacy should be achieved mainly by regulation – but also by giving financial support to voluntary organizations, directly or indirectly by tax reductions (Fromlet 2008).

Financial literacy may serve as a good example of combining regulations and private initiatives – as an area where the future probably would not be changed markedly by co-operation only. More examples will be addressed in the next section.

Looking at my list of reasons for the current global financial crisis, takes us "easily" to the conclusion that most areas with regulatory problems already had their regulations before the eruption of the acute crisis – but that many of these existing regulations did not work properly and/or allowed for loopholes. In other words: Regulations must be efficient which is not always easy to recognize during their design or preparation. Thus, regulations need their own stress tests.

What we need are not only stress tests for banks but also for regulations. This assumes, however, much better macroprudential research, better models and practical application. Even extreme scenarios should not be ruled out. Apparently, the development of the current crisis must be considered as a very unique event.

However, some obvious major risks in this current regulation cycle should not be neglected, such as

- too strong general belief in regulation
- the risk of overregulation
- the risk of insufficiently functioning financial markets
- lagging efficiency
- overlooked future loopholes and shortcomings.

To summarize: certain regulations are without doubt unavoidable on globalized financial markets. This assumes improved institutions. Or as Dani Rodrik puts it: "The market economy is necessarily embedded in a set of nonmarket institutions" (Rodrik 2007). This means that certain public intervention must happen in a market economy for special protective measures.

Rodrik's term "institutions" could easily be substituted by the term "regulations" in our financial market perspective – but only if the two objectives of welfare gains and/or risk reduction are favored by regulations.

Responsibility and Collaborative Agreements

I have already tried to point out that regulations alone cannot prevent future financial crises. Regulations can only partly counteract irrational psychological behavior. Since the second part of this topic refers to collaborative arrangements, some comments must be made on this angle as well.

First. Who should be partners in collaborative agreements? In our case, it could be single financial institutions with their branch organization, financial institutions with public agencies or branch organizations with public organizations.

Second. Collaborative agreements need a common objective. Looking at my list of failures and shortcomings by the banks that contributed to the current global financial crisis, most of these factors are counteracting pure commercial profit-making. In our case, the avoidance of a future financial turmoil or crisis must be regarded as the real common denominator of collaborative agreements between financial institutions and, for example, supervisory authorities. However, this mentioned common denominator is too long-term oriented for ensuring the effectiveness of collaborative agreements. This long time horizon may mean that there are incentives for short-term and profit oriented banks to eventually be rather lax about certain collaborative agreements.

Third. Many financial issues are nowadays international or global. It seems to be very doubtful whether collaborative agreements can be achieved on a broad geographical basis. Positive exceptions, however, could be developed by creating enlarged formal co-operation between supervisory authorities, both nationally and internationally. Particularly EMU countries need much more cross-border supervision – and more far-reaching than the de Larosière plan is pointing at. However, one single European/EMU supervisory authority does not seem to be attainable in the forthcoming years – despite the urgency of the issue. In the meanwhile, collaborative supervisory agreements within the Euro area may be the right method. Non-Euro EU countries joining these agreements could be an option.

Consequently, collaborative agreements could be a way forward in certain, special cases.

Conclusions and Some New Thoughts

Generally speaking, the main impediments to well-working regulations and collaborative agreements come from human behavior (psychology). The current global financial and economic crisis can to a great extent be attributed to phenomena like greed, abuse of incentives, performance pressure ("angst"), overconfidence, neglect of historical experience, etc. Without improved research / interest for behavioral finance and understanding of this exciting scientific orientation, financial regulations will be continually limited in their efficiency. The "homo oeconomicus" has disappeared from global financial markets.

Another important step forward is the recognition that regulations should be completely designed for giving the right incentives to players on financial markets. "Perverse incentive structures"– as Rajan calls one of the main characteristics of the current crisis – should not exist anymore in the future regulatory framework (Rajan 2006).

Collaborative agreements make sense in certain cases, for example, on an international basis between public institutions. History of financial markets, however, has demonstrated many times that collaborative agreements between banks and public institutions – according to their design – many times cannot work as a powerful instrument for a long time.

Instead, it would make sense to raise the status of collaborative agreements. This could be achieved by including certain agreements as conditions for "good corporate governance". Such a change could be made efficient by demanding comments from banks on certain collaborative rules they should follow carefully on a regularly basis in their quarterly or annual reports. In other words: Much more pressure should be put on banks' performance in corporate governance. And the press should write more about it.

Whatever regulatory or collaborative changes we are talking about, one extremely important precondition for – hopefully – (somewhat) declining future financial risks should be mentioned particularly: increased transparency, demanded by regulators and central banks. This need cannot be stressed sufficiently. Innovations in the past such as Structured Investment Vehicles (SIVs) and conduits must be made much more transparent than has been the case in recent years – but the quality of credits must also be made more transparent. Supervision should become much more active in this respect. By the way China should join the path to increased financial transparency as well – as it underwrote in spring 2009 in the communiqué of the London G20-summit.

I would finally like to quote Axel Leijonhufvud who recently said: "If we could eliminate the next crisis, we would not discuss these things so much." (Leijonhufvud 2009).

He may be right. But isn't it worthwhile to try to postpone the next crisis or to make it milder than the current financial earthquake?

References

Fromlet, H. (2008). Financial Literacy and its Benefits on a Household, Corporate and Wealth Management Level. Discussion paper presented at a SUERF Conference in Munich, June 14.

Kaufman, H. (1986). Interest Rates: The Markets and the New Financial World. London Tauris&Co.

Leijonhufvud, A. (2009). Curbing Instability, Policy and Regulation. OeNBs Economics Conference, May 14-15.

Rajan, R. (2006). Has Finance Made the World Riskier? European Financial Management. No 4, pp 499-533. September.

Rodrik, D. (2007). One Economics, Many Recipes. Globalization, Institutions, and Economic Growth .Princeton University Press.

Samuelson, P. A. and Nordhaus W. D. (2005). Economics, 19th edition, Boston: McGraw-Hill.

Taylor, J. (2009). How Government Created the Financial Crisis. Wall Street Journal. February 9.

5

Conclusions on Hierarchical versus Collaborative Governance in the Finance Sector

Jörg R. Werner (discussant)

Introduction

The aim of this paper is twofold: first, it tries to derive some conclusions on the relative merits and shortcomings of hierarchical versus collaborative modes of governance in the finance sector, particularly in light of the recent financial crisis. Second, it aims at discussing this book's chapters on hierarchical versus collaborative arrangements in the finance sectors and to put the respective contributions into perspective.

Inquiring into the relative merits and shortcomings of hierarchical versus collaborative governance first requires recalling what is meant by both concepts. To begin with, *hierarchical governance* can be understood as a traditional mode of regulation where agents such as parliaments or ministerial bureaucracies create binding rules by means of law. It is characterized by legislated policy design elements and mandated administrative procedures and exerted by administrative units (Hill and Lynn 2005: 181). The main advantage of hierarchical governance – at least in democracies – is that rules created under this regulatory scheme display high levels of legitimacy as they are enacted by elected agents. However, hierarchical governance has some serious disadvantages that mainly have become visible in an increasingly globalized world: first, the process of rule setting is relatively inflexible and time-consuming, what is particularly a problem in fast-changing, complex environments. Second, there is probably a lack of technical knowledge by those creating the rules (i.e., parliaments and ministerial bureaucracies). Third, this lack of technical knowledge might be compensated by involving lobbyists what is usually done in an intransparent process. Fourth, hierarchical governance, so far, relies on nation states implying that nationally set rules typically do not have global outreach.

Globalization has challenged hierarchical governance (Cope et al. 1997). As a consequence, collaborative modes of governance have emerged in many policy fields. The concept of *collaborative governance* refers to coordination efforts exerted by institutionalized arrangements or organizations in which public and private actors jointly participate. In this vein, collaborative governance "brings public and private stakeholders together in collective forums with public agencies to engage in consensus-oriented decision making" (Ansell and Gash 2008: 543). Broadly understood, collaborative governance also covers the concepts of co-regulation and "regulated-self-regulation" which are sometimes summarized in the role models of the enabling and/or ensuring state (Gilbert and Gilbert 1989, Schuppert 2003). Collaborative governance heals most of the outlined problems of hierarchical governance, but has some serious disadvantages as well. Most notably, the authorization of collaborative actors and, even more important, the legitimatization of their decisions are at stake (Freeman 1997). Additionally, it is not always clear whether regulatory solutions developed under collaborative governance are effective and efficient – an issue particularly debated in the recent financial crisis.

A Move Towards Collaborative Governance in the Finance Sector (Before the Crisis)

Since the 1990s, there is strong evidence that transformations of the nation state are taking place (Zürn and Leibfried 2005, Hurrelmann et al. 2007). These changes are observable in many policy fields and have led to the emergence of (more) collaborative modes of regulation (Genschel and Zangl 2008, Volmer et al. 2007). A key question is whether this trend can also be observed in the finance sector. The finance sector consists of economic actors – mainly intermediaries like banks, insurance companies and pension funds – that use financial markets. In general, governance of financial markets would include organizing money, capital and debt markets and regulating behavior and entry in such markets. However, traditionally, there has not been so much regulation of the financial sector. The finance sector thus is sometimes characterized as an autonomous social system, strongly relying on self-referential, transintentional, and emergent properties (Hessling and Pahl 2006). Even though it would be beyond the scope of this paper (and also hardly be possible) to provide a full overview, there is indeed evidence for an increasing involvement of collaborative actors and arrangements in the finance sector (being in line with its autonomous character). This might be illustrated by the following examples:

– The regulation of *money markets* is to a large extent under the scrutiny of central banks. In his contribution to this book, Alasdair Roberts gives a good overview of increasing central bank independence all over the world. Central bank independence implies that central banks and their officers are exempted from political pressures and controls. Hence, elected politicians cannot exert an influence on central bank's policies. Independence is justified by the argument that central banking requires technical expertise and independent actors that can withstand political pressures to, for example, increase inflation. Indeed, some studies find that higher levels of independence have positive economic consequences – a point that is critically discussed in Roberts' contribution. Of course, independent central banks can be regarded as collaborative actors: they act as independent private actors, but they are also supposed to act in the public interest and are therefore furnished by nation states.
– In regard to the regulation of *capital markets*, collaborative actors also play an increasingly important role. A good example is the emergence of the International Accounting Standards Board (IASB), an organization under private law that develops and issues

the International Financial Reporting Standards (IFRS). In recent years, many countries have decided to require listed firms to prepare their financial reports following IFRS (as the application of these standards is supposed to lead to financial reports that contain high quality and decision relevant information for investors). While the IASB is a purely private organization, the regulatory solution to transfer accounting standard setting from national parliaments or authorities to this international organization is collaborative in nature: national laws require national firms to comply with the IASB's standards; moreover, arenas have been introduced that assure – at least to some extent – institutionalized contacts between national regulators and the IASB in order to guarantee that the IASB's standards are in the public interest (Zimmermann et al. 2008).

- In regard to the *regulation of intermediaries* such as banks, also collaborative actors entered the stage. A good example is the Basel Committee on Banking Supervision. Founded in 1974 under the umbrella of the Bank of International Settlements, the committee provides a forum for regular cooperation on banking supervisory matters and aims at developing guidelines and supervisory standards in areas where they are considered to be desirable. Most prominently, the Basel Committee issues international standards on capital adequacy. The committee can be labeled a collaborative actor at least for two reasons: first, it is an international organization in which countries are represented by their central banks. Second, its pronouncements were never intended to have legal force. Thus, the committee cannot take advantage of hierarchical solutions but has to rely on national regulators for implementation of its standards and recommendations or on firms voluntarily adopting them (Herring 2007).

The three examples point to the fact that collaborative arrangements in the finance sector indeed gained importance in recent decades. However, this trend does not necessarily imply that collaborative actors simply took over responsibilities that were formerly organized in a hierarchical fashion. In many cases, the involvement of collaborative actors can be seen as an attempt to achieve any regulation of the autonomous financial system, or at least as an answer to new regulatory challenges that particularly can be traced back to the globalization of financial markets. In this vein, collaborative solutions are sometimes not a substitute for national regulations – as there was no regulation before. But more commonly, collaborative solutions are an "add on", complementing the traditional hierarchical solutions that failed in coping with new regulatory challenges (Hill and Lynn 2005). Of course, establishing a parallelism between hierarchical and collaborative arrangements (the former mainly on the national, the latter mainly on the international level) can create tensions, an increasingly important topic.

Drivers of the Emergence of Collaborative Governance in the Finance Sector

One of the most prominent and most cited drivers for the retreat of the state and the emergence of collaborative arrangements is, without doubt, globalization (Levitt 1983). An important outcome of globalization is that political and economic spaces fall apart (Zürn and Leibfried 2005). The key problem of globalization – from a governance point of view – thus is: the emergence of globalized markets did not go in hand with a globalization of the political system. While markets are increasingly international and open for private actors, the political system could not keep up with this process. In other words: while globalization has led to the emergence of globally integrated capital markets, there is no political authority, no "world state", that would be responsible for regulating such markets. The emergence of collaborative arrangements can be seen as one answer to this problem. Indeed, national regulation of globalized markets must fail. Simply consider that one state creates tighter rules for financial markets (e.g. prohibiting specific transactions) while another offers weaker standards (allowing them). An expectable outcome is that business will anyway occur in the country offering weaker standards what, from a regulatory point of view, makes a race to the bottom in regards to financial regulation a very likely outcome (Bebchuk 1992). Thus, cooperation of national regulators on the international level, very often including cooperation with private actors, is the only means to the end of achieving global regulatory minimum standards. To summarize, globalization hardly challenged hierarchical (national) modes of governance as it increased the demand for international solutions and also contributed to quicker changing environmental conditions with which regulation has to deal.

However, globalization is not a natural disaster. In fact, globalization is a process that was deliberately started by (national) political actors. Not surprisingly, it was triggered in a period that Alasdair Roberts in this book calls "the era of liberalization". Given that economic liberalization might sometimes indeed have been a "revolutionary doctrine" or an "orthodoxy", as Roberts states, liberalization itself can be identified as a potential driver of the emergence of collaborative modes of governance (without taking the loop way of globalization). Roberts does a great job in making this point, taking central banking as an intuitive example: liberal reformers stressed that the political system might be incapable to regulate certain areas of financial markets, mainly due to problems of public choice. Hence, regulation should better be performed by independent institutions consisting of technical experts who are, in exerting their work, not affected or constraint by political pressures. Roberts calls this the "logic of discipline". Central banks are indeed a good example, but similar arrangements can also be found in a lot of further cases including accounting standard setting or even market oversight (wherefore the UK is a good example). However, Roberts keeps silent on what he suspects to be a better (or alternative) solution to the "logic of discipline" in those cases where national solutions cannot be an answer to global problems. Moreover, even though triggering globalization might be traced to liberalization efforts, it seems not very plausible that the consequences of this process have been fully anticipated: while globalization might indeed have been triggered by liberal reformers, it gained momentum and is now a self-energizing process that challenges and constrains national regulatory solutions in many policy fields. Globalization thus has contributed to the emergence of an international and quick-changing environment that necessitates collaborative solutions at least in those cases where regulation is supposed to be in the public interest. This implies that collaborative solutions are not necessarily an outcome of the "logic of discipline" but probably the only means to achieve any regulation on global financial markets. However, the latter argument might have been proven wrong with the occurrence of the recent financial crisis. In the following, thus, the financial crisis will quickly be described, also pointing to some reasons for its emergence. This allows discussing whether hierarchical and/or collaborative governance have contributed to the emergence of the crisis and whether they, respectively, are discredited in resolving it.

The Financial Crisis and its Causes

The banking and financial market crisis mainly originated from the United States and has its roots in banks' practice to confer mortgage loans to borrowers with a low degree of creditworthiness (Sanders 2008). As the houses bought by the borrowers used to massively increase in value over time (which was, as proven later, due to a market bubble), the case of a mortgage default would have been no problem: banks would simply have to sell the houses, what could be done above their historical costs. Of course, founding credit businesses on a market bubble is risky and highly speculative – however, to be fair, it has to be kept in mind that the market bubble was not identified as such until it burst in 2007 (Barrell and Davis 2008). This event led to rapidly decreasing house prices and first created a problem for the lending banks: the conferred credits proved as being uncollectible and houses potentially had to be sold with a loss. Interestingly, not only those banks that directly conferred the loans were affected by the crisis but also a large number of other institutes. The reason lies in the practice that the risky mortgage loans had been bundled (securitized) to so-called asset-backed-securities (ABS) and sold to other banks and institutional investors all over the world. The buying banks usually refinanced such purchases by issuing revolving bonds with short maturities. Such businesses were usually designed as off-balance-sheet transactions (hence, there was not much transparency on these transactions and the risk incurred). When the real estate market crisis in the United States revealed that the underlying loans were uncollectable, also the issued bonds lost in value. As maturities were short, the respective banks faced massive liquidity problems: with the bond market collapsing, banks were no longer able to refinance the redemption of the matured bonds by issuing new bonds. With many banks facing similar liquidity problems, it got almost impossible to obtain funds –

not even from the interbank market as the banks were mistrusting themselves. Securitization of mortgages thus made a regional crisis in the US real estate sector to a global crisis of the financial system, also affecting the real economy.

However, the discussion so far remains on the surface. More important questions are: why did banks take such immense risks? Why did anybody discover what was going on? Quick answers to these questions include that there was a lot of short-term thinking and selfish acting – bankers were rather interested in their next bonuses than in long-term stability. However, it has to be mentioned that there are basically two – probably simplistic – systemic explanations for the emergence of the crisis (Hellwig 2009).

According to the first explanation, the crisis is the result of *market failure*, particularly caused by excessive risk taking and compensation, yield mania and short-term thinking (Sinn 2008). In broader terms, the crisis then can also be regarded as an outcome of liberalization and probably also of the collaborative governance mechanisms at place (Daniel and Jones 2007). Salelles and Alasdair both seem to agree that the crisis has proven that the financial sector's capability of autonomous self-regulation is constrained and that the crisis marks the end of an era of liberalization. In other words: a strong – or at least stronger – role of the state seems thus be plausible as an outcome of the crisis. Alasdair Roberts particularly points to the US Federal Reserve having contributed to the onset of the crisis, particularly in three ways: first, it failed to acknowledge the evidence of the housing bubble as believing in market efficiency made the Federal Reserve blind for detecting bubbles. Second, it did not make use of its regulatory powers to control mortgage lending and the market for complex financial instruments evolving with securitization (probably due to capture). Third, it contributed to the emergence of bubbles by a politic of low interest rates (that formerly also contributed to the emergence of the new economy bubble). Besides central banking, other examples for collaborative actors having contributed to the emergence of the crisis can be found. For instance, the capital adequacy rules of the Basel Committee have been criticized for creating procyclicity in the financial sector. Accounting standard setters, particularly the IASB, have been blamed for their reliance on fair value accounting which makes both positive and negative market "overreactions" more likely (Hellwig 2009; Sinn 2008).

The second explanation points to a state or *regulatory failure* contributing to the emergence of the crisis. One lapse – also identified in Salelles' and Fromlet's contributions – is nation state's failure to install proper and sufficiently funded (hierarchical) oversight and enforcement mechanisms. This indeed might be a failure of nation states, as the effectiveness of regulations – probably emerging under collaborative arrangements – depends on efficient enforcement, usually necessitating public authority (Zimmermann et al. 2008). However, this is not the only problem of public policy. It is noteworthy that the expansion of home ownership was an important political goal in the US and that politicians also benefited from economic growth driven by low interest rates (Sinn 2009). A further issue, interestingly only seldom addressed, is concentration in the banking sector. Indeed, there is empirical evidence for an increasing concentration in the banking sector in the last decades (Nissan and Niroornand 2006). In fact, ongoing concentration in the banking sector was usually appreciated by national politicians. For instance, the recent merger of *Commerzbank* und *Dresdner Bank* in Germany was highly welcomed by the German federal government (Schnabel and Hakenes 2006). In a lot of countries, particularly in Europe, it was for a long time at least an implicit political goal to create "national champions" which were supposed to be able to compete in the global financial system (Carbó Valverde et al. 2007). Concentration in the national banking sector thus has been welcomed or at least tolerated by national political actors as a means to the end of strengthening the national financial market place. However, concentration usually goes in hand with a *too big to fail* problem: if banks cannot fail, why should they prevent from excessive risk-taking and why should they be engaged in creating efficient governance structures? It should be noted that the functioning of markets require effective competition policies: liberalization thus cannot be held responsible for the lack of such policies. The lack of maintaining and strengthening competition in the national banking markets is also not caused by collaborative governance – it is simply a failure of traditional modes of regulation.

As outlined, both explanations are simplistic in nature. Instead of looking at them as alternative explanations, one should rather assume that both apply contemporaneously. Of course, private actors' behavior on markets was fundamental to the crisis. However, also regulation failed in shaping private actors' incentives. The discussion points to the fact that not only collaborative arrangements did a bad job in this respect, but also traditional hierarchical modes of regulation. Thus, expecting a return to hierarchical solutions to be an efficient answer to the crisis is not convincing, a point also mentioned in Hubert Fromlet's analysis. He argues that too strong general beliefs in regulation and overregulation are potential risks in the current efforts to reform governance of financial markets. The question thus is: how can a reasonable solution look like?

A Path for Reforms

In this book, Salelles gives a good overview over the crisis management measures and reforms both on the European and the member states level. In a way, the regulatory measures taken on the European and national levels seem to be indicative for a return of the strong nation state (to the detriment of collaborative solutions). However, such a conclusion might be overhasty. As Fromlet puts it, "… harder regulation of banks, of other financial institutions and financial products cannot do the job alone to prevent the world from financial crises or to limit future damage." This very much fits to the discussion above, revealing that neither hierarchical nor collaborative governance per se contributed to the emergence of the crisis, but that both types of regulation in their given form failed to prevent it. Both types of regulation seem to have their relative merits and shortcomings. Thus, neither hierarchical nor collaborative governance per se are totally discredited by the crisis. Contrarily, it seems likely that efficient regulation has to rely on both mechanisms: on collaborative arrangements to cope with the need of international solutions and to allow for flexible and technically-sound reactions to a quickly changing environment, and on hierarchical solutions – particularly in enforcement and oversight – to take advantage of the state's authority and sanctioning power to complement the collaborative solutions. Hence, the question is how to improve both mechanisms. Therefore, their relative shortcomings have to be identified. First, national (hierarchical) solutions still cannot cope with issues of global regulation while collaborative arrangements can be an answer to such problems. Second, collaborative solutions tend to suffer from too narrow focusing on specific issues (such as inflation in central banking) and to fail to consider a macroeconomic perspective and to strive for stability. Thus, collaborative arrangements are not necessarily efficient regulatory solutions. Third, regulatory capture is not restricted to public (hierarchical) regulation, but can also extent to collaborative modes of governance. Fourth, there might be expectation gaps in regard to the power of regulation – irrespective of stemming from hierarchical or collaborative settings.

The latter issue points to the need to influence market participants' behavior, because it is an ex ante, not an ex post measure of regulation (like supervision). Such an approach implies that regulation must assure that economic agents do not behave in a detrimental manner (macro view) because such behavior would also not be in the interest of the individual actors themselves (micro view). This assertion implies that even though there might have been an era of liberalization, market mechanisms did not fully work, pointing to a need of enhancing them. This can particularly be done by four measures: the first is to improve corporate governance mechanisms, the second to increase transparency, the third to strengthen competition policies and the fourth to increase litigation risk (by means of both increasing legal sanctions and the likelihood of detecting detrimental actions). Corporate governance practices should particularly assure that there is efficient risk sharing between economic actors. Transparency refers to enhancing disclosures on risk and particularly risky off-balance-sheet transactions. Strict competition policies shall assure that there are no too big to fail problems. Increasing litigation risk, finally, decreases the expected utility of fraud from a manager's point of view. Such measures would also account for the autonomous character of the financial system.

Summary

In recent years, several transformations of the nation state have taken place. These changes had been triggered by globalization and the integration of financial markets and probably also by liberal reformers. The increasingly global financial system challenged national modes of regulation, and particularly the traditional approach of hierarchical governance. As a consequence, collaborative arrangements have emerged that can be observed in the financial sector but also in many other policy fields. However, the recent financial crisis raised the question whether the move towards more liberal, self-regulating markets and collaborative governance was a failure and even contributed to the emergence of the crisis. Without doubt, the financial crisis has led to massive interventions and new regulations by the public sector. To conclude that the strong nation state with its reliance on hierarchical modes of regulation will return might even though be overhasty. The reason is that national hierarchical solutions have their own shortcomings: they do not cope with global markets, they tend to be inflexible and they suffer from a lack of technical knowledge in regards to the subject of regulation. Thus, the lesson to learn from the financial crisis is neither that hierarchical is better than collaborative governance nor that collaborative governance is better than hierarchical solutions. The lesson rather is that both mechanisms should be combined, taking their respective merits and shortcomings into account. Further, it should also be kept in mind that regulation of markets also includes setting up strong ex ante measures like corporate governance, transparency, litigation risk and competition.

References

Ansell, Ch. and Gash A. (2008). "Collaborative Governance in Theory and Practice." *Journal of Public Administration Research & Theory*, *18*(4), 543-571.

Barrell, R. and Davis E. P. (2008). "The Evolution of the Financial Crisis of 2007-8." *National Institute Economic Review*, 206, 5-14.

Bebchuk, L. A. (1992). "Federalism and the Corporation: The Desirable Limits on State Competition in Corporate Law." *Harvard Law Review*, *105*(7), 1437-1510.

Carbó Valverde, S., Humphrey D. B. and López del Paso R. (2007). "Do cross-country differences in bank efficiency support a policy of "national champions"?" *Journal of Banking & Finance*, *31*(7), 2173-2188.

Cope, St., Leishman F. and Starie P. (1997). "Globalization, new public management and the enabling State." *International Journal of Public Sector Management*, *10*(6), 444-461.

Daniel, Betty C. and Jones J. B. (2007). "Financial liberalization and banking crises in emerging economies." *Journal of International Economics*, *72*(1), 202-222.

Freeman, J. (1997). "Collaborative governance in the administrative state." *UCLA Law Review*, *45*(1), 98-99.

Genschel, Ph. and Zangl B. (2008). "Transformations of the State – From Monopolist to Manager of Political Authority." TranState Working Papers, No. 76, University of Bremen.

Gilbert, N. and Gilbert B. (1989). *The enabling state: modern welfare capitalism in America*. New York: Oxford University Press.

Hellwig, M. (2009). "Systemic Risk in the Financial Sector: An Analysis of the Subprime-Mortgage Financial Crisis." *De Economist*, *157*(2), 129-207.

Herring, R. J. (2007). "The Rocky Road to Implementation of Basel II in the United States." *Atlantic Economic Journal*, *35*(4), 411-429.

Hessling, A. and Pahl H. (2006). "The Global System of Finance - Scanning Talcott Parsons and Niklas Luhmann for Theoretical Keystones." *American Journal of Economics and Sociology*, *65*(1), 189-218.

Hill, C. J. and Lynn L. E. (2005). "Is hierarchical governance in decline? Evidence from empirical research." *Journal of Public Administration Research & Theory*, *15*(2), 173-195.

Hurrelmann, A., Leibfried St., Martens K. and Mayer P. (2007). "The Transformation of the Golden-Age Nation State: Findings and Perspectives". Basingstoke: Palgrave.

Levitt, Th. (1983). "The Globalization of Markets." *Harvard Business Review*, *61*(3), 92-102.

Nissan, E. and Niroornand F. (2006). "Banking Bigness: Concentration of the World's 50 Largest Banks." *Multinational Business Review*, *14*(1), 59-78.

Sanders, A. (2008). "The subprime crisis and its role in the financial crisis." *Journal of Housing Economics*, *17*(4), 254-261.

Schnabel, I. and Hakenes H. (2006). "Braucht Deutschland eine 'starke private deutsche Bank'? Über die Notwendigkeit nationaler Champions im Bankwesen. (Is There a Need for a 'Strong Private

German Bank'? On the Desirability of National Champions in the Banking Sector)." *Kredit und Kapital*, *39*(2), 163-181.

Schuppert, G. F. (2003). The Ensuring State, in: Giddens, A. (ed), The Progressive Manifesto, Cambridge: Polity Press, 54-72.

Sinn, H.-W. (2008). "Why Banking Crises Happen: The role of bad accounting and moral hazard missteps.!" *The International Economy*, *2008*(Summer), 60-61.

Sinn, H.-W. (2009). Kasino-Kapitalismus: Wie es zur Finanzkrise kam, und was jetzt zu tun ist. Berlin: Econ.

Volmer, Ph. B., Werner J. and Zimmermann J. (2007). "New governance modes for Germany's financial reporting system: another retreat for the nation state?" *Socio-Economic Review*, *5*(3), 437-465.

Zimmermann, J., Werner J. and Volmer Ph. B. (2008). *Global governance in accounting: rebalancing public power and private commitment*. Basingstoke et al.: Palgrave Macmillan.

Zürn, M. and Leibfried St. (2005). "Reconfiguring the national constellation." *European Review*, *13*(Supplement 1), 1-36.

Liberalization of Energy Markets: the Role of Governments and Private Actors

6

Energy Regulation in Great Britain: Lessons Learned for Collaborative Governance*

Richard Green

Introduction

This chapter describes how collaborative governance – decision making split between companies, the government and its agencies – has worked in the energy utilities of gas and electricity in Great Britain. Originally founded by a mix of private and municipal companies, these industries were nationalized in the 1940s, and privatized in 1986 and 1990-1, respectively. Since that time, the structure of each industry has changed dramatically, and the way in which those changes were brought about, by pressure from government agencies (regulators and competition authorities) and by company decisions, is the first major topic of the chapter. Second, it discusses the way in which the regulators' own behavior and governance has changed over the years, and powers originally vested in individuals have now been passed to a board. The third major topic is the way in which the industries' trading rules have evolved, and with them the arrangements for

* I would like to thank participants at the Transatlantic Policy Consortium meeting at Jönköping International Business School, Sweden, for helpful comments

making changes, a process in which cooperation between experts employed by different companies is essential.

To understand the energy utilities, we must consider their different vertical stages. In the electricity industry, these consist of generation at the power station, high voltage transmission over a country-scale grid, the system operation that coordinates generation and transmission, local distribution to customers and retailing. In gas, the analogous stages are production or importing, high pressure transmission (sometimes called transportation), system operation, distribution at lower pressures, and retailing. There is an additional stage in the gas industry, however, which is storage. Electricity cannot be stored, but must be produced at the moment of consumption, whereas gas can be injected into depleted fields, salt caverns or (most expensively) liquefied natural gas facilities when it is relatively abundant in summer, and withdrawn at times of higher prices in the winter.

Transmission, distribution and system operation are natural monopolies, in that it is most efficient for a single body to be responsible for each activity within each area. This avoids duplicating facilities, which would be the result if two different companies were to build lines to offer competing connections to the same consumer. The area actually covered by a given company often depends on accidents of history, but may also depend on the economies of scale available. These are greatest for transmission system operation – the benefits of coordination over a wide area imply that it can be most effective to have a single operator covering a whole country (or significant part of a large country). Distribution can be successfully carried out at a much smaller scale – in some countries, there are numerous systems serving no more than a few thousand customers – although there are economies of scale which imply that these systems would be more efficient if they were to merge with their neighbors.

Traditionally, the natural monopolies in transmission and distribution were taken to mean that the entire industries were natural monopolies, although it was quite common to split transmission (and its associated generation or production) from distribution (and its associated retailing). From the 1980s onwards, however, a number of experiments have shown that it was for the network to deliver energy on behalf of competing companies, and so this has led to the widespread adoption of liberalization measures around the world.

Some History

The energy utilities have their roots in the nineteenth century. Town gas, made from coal, was used for lighting from the early nineteenth century onwards. The enterprises involved were mostly local, as there were no gains from operating on a national scale, and many were in fact municipal.[1] Electricity followed from the 1880s, again with a mix of municipal and private undertakings. The latter were established under a law which allowed the local municipality to buy them out after 40 years. Many of the undertakings were small, failing to achieve economies of scale, but municipal boundaries were fixed and cross-border collaboration seems to have been rare. A notable exception was in the north-east, where the private-sector Newcastle-upon-Tyne Electricity Supply Company was able to achieve economies of scale, expanding to cover a wide area with an efficient system of transmission and distribution (Hannah 1979).

By the 1920s, the benefits of coordinating generation on a national scale had become apparent, since this would allow operations to be concentrated on the most efficient stations. A publicly-owned Central Electricity Board was established to build a national transmission system and coordinate the operation of the selected stations, at first on a regional scale, but moving to nationwide operation shortly before the Second World War. This produced significant economies (Foreman-Peck and Hammond 1997).

After the war, in 1948, the Labour government nationalized the industry. This followed its philosophy of nationalizing the commanding heights of the economy, but also finally brought together the many local undertakings with incompatible systems, and prevented municipalities from taking over additional companies as their 40-year franchises expired. The industry invested significantly in the 1950s, to meet rapid demand growth, bring electricity to rural areas, replace worn-out assets and convert systems running on non-standard voltages. The Electricity Act 1947 had created 14 regional Area Boards in England, Wales and the south of Scotland – the North of Scotland Hydro-Electric Board had been created in 1943. A Central Authority was responsible for coordination between the boards. Further reorganization took place in the 1950s – the two Scottish Area Boards were amalgamated (with their generation assets) into the South of

Scotland Electricity Board in 1954, and generation and transmission in the rest of the country were given to the Central Electricity Generating Board in 1958.

The gas industry was also nationalized, in 1949, but its operations remained largely local – 12 Area Boards reported to a Council, but there was no national transmission system, nor any need for one. This changed in the 1960s, when natural gas was discovered under the North Sea. The government decided to convert every appliance in the country to burn natural gas (rather than coal gas) and to build a national transmission system to bring this to consumers. The Area Boards were amalgamated into the British Gas Corporation in 1973. The post-war period can thus be seen as one of increasing centralization in the energy utilities.

In a parallel trend, their governance changed over this period, with more government control. One of the architects of nationalization, Herbert Morrison, had hoped that public corporations would do the right things from a sense of public duty – their boards should see themselves as the "high custodians of the public interest" (Morrison 1933: 157). Morrison was concerned that ministers should not interfere with the day-to-day running of the industries, contenting themselves with occasional general directions. In practice, ministers quite often interfered in detailed issues, particularly the choice of fuel and size of the power station building program. The pricing policies followed by the industries were also a source of concern to the Treasury. The nationalization statutes had obliged the boards to break even, taking one year with another, which meant that they had to cover interest payments on the money they had borrowed from the government, but allowed them to earn a very low rate of return on the overall capital invested. This was economically inefficient, if it encouraged too much consumption of under-priced goods and services, and hence required too much investment to provide them. It also deprived the Treasury of money.

A White Paper in 1961 laid down the principle that the nationalized industries should earn a minimum rate of return (varying by corporation) on the capital invested (Treasury 1961). A second paper (Treasury 1967) set forth an elaborate, and consistent, scheme which required the public corporations to use a specified test discount rate when assessing the costs and benefits of their capital investments, relate their prices to marginal costs, and make a specified rate of return on their capital stock. (If set correctly, this return could be consistent with the other targets.) The inflation of the early 1970s destroyed this system, however, for several of the nationalized industries were required to keep their prices down to fight inflation, regardless of the impact on their financial targets. In the second half of the decade, two further White Papers (Treasury 1976, 1978) attempted to return to a formal system of control, but with the emphasis mainly on the rate of return that the corporations were expected to earn, and the amount of money they would be allowed to borrow, or required to return to the Treasury. There was thus a trend for greater central government control of the nationalized industries, particularly over their financial policies. Government ministers were also heavily involved in the often troubled labor relations of the public sector, although there were very few strikes in the energy utilities – their importance to the country ensured that their workers were generally well-treated without the need for industrial action.

To some extent, ministers found it easier (and perhaps more necessary) to intervene in the affairs of public corporations which were seen to be doing badly. This put British Gas in a strong position, since the conversion to natural gas was seen as a great technical and economic success. The record of the nationalized electricity industry was far more patchy. Commentators such as Pryke (1982) attacked the nationalized industries for their record on productivity, and the industry's rate of return was generally low, although this partly reflected government instructions about the level of prices. Most serious, however, was the industry's record on investment. British power stations took longer to build, and cost more, than those in other countries, and the industry's nuclear programs were disastrous. The first, expanded under political pressure, produced a set of "Magnox" stations that were known to be obsolescent even as they were being built. The second program ordered five advanced gas-cooled reactors in the late 1960s, three of which were not completed until the late 1980s. With a degree of criticism unusual for one public body describing another, the Monopolies and Mergers Commission said that the CEGB's investment appraisals were "seriously defective and liable to mislead" (1981: 13, 14).

By this time, Mrs. Thatcher's Conservative government had been elected (in 1979), and gradually started to privatize state-owned assets. The policy was extended to British Telecommunications in 1984 (to allow it to invest in upgrading its network without falling foul of Treasury attempts to cut public spending) and became politically popular when large numbers of private investors saw their shares increase dramatically in value on flotation. (The sale was marketed to individuals because the sums involved were too large for institutional investors to absorb, and the normal first-day price increase was magnified (in percentage terms) because small investors could pay for their shares in installments.)

British Gas was soon chosen as the next large privatization. The White Paper announcing the sale was issued in April 1985, and the sale took place in December 1986. This timetable did not allow for any restructuring of the industry, even if the government had wished it. The Gas Act 1986 allowed competition to sell gas to consumers taking more than 25,000 therms (733 MWh) a year, requiring British Gas to deliver this gas and to publish information on the payment it would charge for doing so. In practice, no entry took place, because the barriers to it were overwhelming. North Sea gas producers would be reluctant to help entrants competing with the company that was still bound to be their main customer. British Gas supplied its customers through individual, confidential, contracts that would allow it to offer discounts to any companies likely to defect to a rival, and published too little information for a competitor to estimate transmission costs in advance. Less than a year after the privatization, the company was referred to the Monopolies and Mergers Commission, which ordered a series of measures to remove these obstacles (MMC 1988).

Partly in response to emerging dissatisfaction with the state of the gas industry, the plans for electricity privatization announced in 1988 were far more radical. The Central Electricity Generating Board was to be split into two competing generating companies and a transmission company, with the vertical separation ensuring that the latter had no incentive to favor one generator over another. There would be free entry into generation. The White Paper mentioned the possibility of giving customers a choice of retailer, but as the plans evolved, a decision was made to allow competition for all customers, opening the market in stages between 1990 and 1998. The costs of the nuclear stations proved too high for a successful privatization at that time, and so a third generating company was created, but the Area Boards, renamed Regional Electricity Companies were privatized in December 1990, and the two non-nuclear generating companies in March 1991. The Regional Electricity Companies collectively owned the National Grid Company, responsible for transmission and system operation, but this was separately floated in December 1995. The two integrated companies in Scotland were privatized in June 1991. The last privatization was of the more modern nuclear stations, owned by British Energy, in 1996.

The Governance of Regulation

When the energy utilities were privatized, it was recognized that, even though the government wished to create as much competition as possible, some parts of each industry would remain natural monopolies for the foreseeable future, and others would have little competition at first. It was therefore necessary to create some form of regulation, in order to protect customers from exploitation. However, there was a second reason for ensuring that this regulation was independent of the government, and that was to protect the privatized company and its shareholders. The first large-scale privatization was that of British Telecommunications, as described above, in 1984. The privatization had been announced in 1982, and bitterly opposed by the opposition Labour party. Following its defeat in 1979, the party had moved towards the left wing in its policies, and lost heavily in the 1983 general election, in part because the non-Conservative vote was split between Labour and the centrist Liberal-Social Democratic Party Alliance. The Conservatives were returned with another large majority in 1987, and with a small one in 1992. In 1984, however, the government had to plan on the basis that the Labour party might return to government at the next election, and carry out its announced policies. These included a promise to renationalize British Telecommunications, without paying compensation.

There was nothing that the government could do in the regulatory system to counter the risk of a future government carrying out this threat – a British parliament is unable to bind its successors – but the government did need to consider the possibility that the regulatory system might be used to penalize the company without renationalizing it. It therefore needed a regulatory model that would protect the company, effectively making the regulation independent of government.

The model chosen was to issue British Telecommunications with a license, which allowed the company to offer telecommunications services of various kinds, set out the conditions which it had to observe, and the rights that it thereby acquired (such as the right to dig up the streets to install cables). It became illegal to offer telecommunications services without an appropriate license, which allowed the government to restrict entry into fixed-line services – it had announced in 1983 that it would only grant one other license (to Mercury) at that time, and that this policy would not be revisited until 1990.[2] The license set out a control on the prices that the company could charge for some of its services, the famous RPI-X rule (Littlechild 1983). The aim of this control was to limit the prices which the company could charge for those services where its monopoly would last the longest, for line rentals and for calls within the UK, while minimizing the burden of regulation. The company had to ensure that a weighted average of the regulated prices rose by less than the rate of inflation, less an efficiency factor initially set at 3 %, each year. A subsidiary rule prevented line rentals (where competition would be least) from rising by more than 2 % a year in real terms. Littlechild wanted to directly protect consumers by concentrating on the matters of most concern to them, while giving the company the maximum freedom to operate efficiently and to innovate. Littlechild viewed the control as a way of "holding the fort" until competition arrived, and not as a long-term substitute for competition.

The regulatory system had to be able to cope if competition did take time to arrive, however, as turned out to be the case. The answer, perhaps counter-intuitively, was to allow the price control to lapse after four years, unless steps were taken to renew it. This provided the trigger to ensure that the situation was regularly reviewed, and action was taken in the light of the review.

Somebody had to carry out that review, and the Telecommunications Act 1983 established the office of Director General of Telecommunications, the industry's regulator. In giving formal powers over the industry to a single individual, the government was following the model of the Fair Trading Act of 1973, which created the Director General of Fair Trading (DGFT), responsible for consumer protection and for the initial investigations needed to carry out competition policy. There were further parallels, in that when the DGFT found a potential problem in an industry, or with a proposed merger, he would refer the matter to the Monopolies and Mergers Commission (MMC), now the Competition Commission, for further investigation. At that time, the MMC would issue a recommendation to the Secretary of State, the relevant government minister, who would make the final decision. The secretary of state could not block a merger that the MMC deemed acceptable, but he could permit a merger which the MMC believed likely to act against the public interest. Alternatively, the MMC might recommend that the merger be allowed to proceed only if the companies accepted some remedies (such as partial divestitures or constraints on their behavior), and the secretary of state might impose these or a different set of remedies. Both the DGFT and the new Director General of Telecommunications (DGT) were appointed for fixed terms, renewable, and could only be removed in case of incapacity or gross misconduct. This gave them independence from government. (Some individual office-holders have reinforced their independence by stating, early in their terms, that they are not interested in seeking reappointment, removing the government's remaining source of leverage.)

The DGT was therefore responsible for ensuring that the company behaved in accordance with its license, for dealing with consumer complaints, and for recommending changes to the license. He could also issue new licenses, where government policy permitted. To assist in these tasks, he had a staff of civil servants at the Office of Telecommunications (later absorbed into Ofcom).

The procedures for changing British Telecommunications' license also had a parallel with the Fair Trading Act 1973. If the regulator and the company could agree on a set of changes, then the license could be amended by agreement. If they could not agree, however, then the regulator would need to refer the matter to the MMC, just as the DGFT would refer a competition case to the Commission. The MMC would then take three months (usually) to make a decision. Formally, it was required to decide whether leaving the license unchanged (that is, without a price control in operation, since the clause would normally be about to expire) could be expected to act "against the public interest." For the MMC, the public interest was a broad concept, occasionally expanded to include considerations that might not seem central to competition policy, but the key concerns were the prices charged for goods and services, and their availability. The most important thing about it, however, was that it was well understood by professionals who had dealings with the MMC (including professional investors and fund managers). The MMC also had a good reputation for independence from the government.

This meant that investors could have confidence that the MMC would not recommend changes to British Telecommunications' license that made it unprofitable for the company to carry out its activities. Furthermore, the Telecommunications Act 1983 set out the regulator's legal duties, primary amongst which was the need to promote the availability of telecommunications services, and ensure that the companies providing them could finance themselves. Protecting consumers was secondary to these concerns. The final protection was in the terms of the license itself – this was a contract which could only be revoked after 10 years' notice, which could not be given within the first 15 years of the contract's life. These terms were not intended to imply that the contract would have a fixed life of 25 years, but that its life was to be very long. Levy and Spiller (1996) contrast the protection offered to British Telecommunications under these arrangements with the situation in a number of other countries, where a lack of regulatory commitment made it impossible to retain a private company in the face of political pressure for unsustainably low prices.

When British Gas was privatized, the same basic model was applied. There were minor differences to fit the industry's circumstances, together with one major shortcoming. The Director General of Gas Supply (based at Ofgas) was not given any powers over the non-franchise market, those gas consumers large enough to be offered a choice of supplier. This meant that when British Gas was referred to the MMC, in 1987, the reference was made by the DGFT rather than by the company's own regulator. For the next few years, the task of monitoring the development of competition in the gas industry was carried out by the Office of Fair Trading (the DGFT's department) rather than by Ofgas. In 1992, the tensions involved in trying to increase competition in this way became too great, and British Gas was again referred to the MMC, at the company's own request. In this case, there were two references, one made by the DGFT under the Competition Act 1980, and one made by the Director General of Gas Supply under the Gas Act 1986. The MMC had to produce two separate reports, one considering the matters that fell under the Gas Act (regulation of the pipelines; MMC (1993a)) and one the matters that fell under the Fair Trading Act (the development of competition and of the industry's structure; MMC (1993b)). Fortunately, the evidence (in two thick volumes) was common to both of the inquiries and did not need to be published twice. The government's response to the reports, which included opening the entire gas market to competition, required a new Act of Parliament, and the Gas Act 1995 extended the regulator's powers to the whole industry.

Regulation in the electricity industry followed the same basic model as in telecommunications and in gas, again with minor variations. The Director General of Electricity Supply was responsible for regulating the industry, supported by the Office of Electricity Regulation (Offer). The regulator had to deal with fourteen separate companies owning distribution networks, and therefore established local offices, one in each region, to liaise with the companies and handle customer complaints in that region. A consumer consultative committee was established for each region, and supported by the regulator's staff. This contrasted with the situation in the gas industry, where there was a single national committee, independent of the regulator, employing its own staff.

Unlike the gas regulator, the electricity regulator had powers over both the competitive and the monopoly part of the industry from the start. One of his most important early tasks was to reset the price controls on the distribution businesses, which had turned out to be relatively generous after privatization – the companies' charges had mostly been allowed to rise in real terms, and the companies' profits rose dramatically, even though the economy was in recession. In August 1994, the regulator announced price reductions averaging 14 % in real terms, to take effect the following spring. Unfortunately, leaks earlier in the process had created expectations of still tougher cuts, and the companies' share prices rose on the announcement. A few months later, one of the companies, fighting off a take-over bid, promised to give shareholders special dividends, and shares in the National Grid

Company (soon to be floated), which together were worth over £5 a share, and to increase dividends in real terms after that, even though it was only just over four years since the company had been floated at a price of 240 pence a share. The reaction to this was understandably unfavorable, and in March 1995 the regulator unexpectedly announced that a (pre-planned) consultation process on the legal form of the license amendments needed to put the proposed price controls into effect would be extended to look at the substance of the decision. The outcome was that the regulator decided to implement a further sharp reduction in the companies' prices for the following year, although the announcement of this decision was controversial, when companies given forewarning of the decision leaked the information.

While the English distribution price controls were proving controversial, one of the Scottish Companies, Scottish Hydro-Electric, had appealed against its own price control proposal, and the case went to the MMC. The Commission already had to recommend a price control for British Gas' pipelines, as part of its 1992-3 inquiry, but had done so without setting out detailed calculations. In the Hydro case (MMC 1995), the Commission calculated what it believed to be an appropriate control, and reported in detail on its calculations and thinking. This was important, in that while the MMC is not strictly bound by precedent, and a different group of Commission members is responsible for each report, the Commission does aim to be consistent over time. Once a methodology for price control calculations becomes established, it will be possible for regulators, companies and commentators to predict the outcome, should a company appeal against the regulator's proposal. This would constrain a regulator from being significantly tougher than the MMC methodology would imply, and the prospect of unfavorable comment from analysts who spot an unduly generous price control (coupled with sharp increases in share prices as the companies do better than expected) should discourage leniency. In other words, the existence of a formal, published, methodology made the process more predictable.

Regulators also reacted to the experience with the distribution price controls by publishing much more information as the process of resetting a control unfolded. This meant that no single announcement should carry too much weight, or provoke too great a share price movement, for the companies would have an opportunity to provide extra information if the regulator appeared too harsh. This has led to a much more transparent process, with an improvement in its governance.

The appeals process has also been clarified. Legally, the MMC was required to decide whether it would be against the public interest to continue with an existing price control, or without any price control. In the same way as the Secretary of State was not bound to follow the MMC's recommendation as to his reaction to a finding (except that if a merger was not against the public interest, it had to be allowed unhindered), the privatization acts did not explicitly require the regulator to adopt the Commission's recommendations as to the price control that should be set. It was implicit that the regulator would do so, but in 1996, the electricity regulator for Northern Ireland referred a disputed price control to the Commission, accepted its finding that it would be against the public interest for there to be no control at all, and then attempted to impose his original decision, rather than the (significantly different) control that the Commission had recommended. The company asked for a judicial review of this decision, arguing that the regulator had not followed due process, and won its case. Amazingly, the Court of Appeal overturned that decision, but it was reinstated by the House of Lords (acting as the highest court in the UK). This confirmed the principle that the MMC's task was to recommend a price control that the regulator would then implement, and subsequent Acts of Parliament have codified this principle. To avoid any doubt, the Commission's reports now even include recommended wording for the license amendments needed to put the control into practice.

The regulators have also changed. The original model, of a single Director General, led to some very personalized disputes, particularly in industries where an individual regulator was confronting the head of a single company. There was also the problem that the actions of a single individual could be less predictable than those of a group, even though, in practice, regulators had taken advice from their senior staff. The electricity regulator appointed a group of senior outsiders, including former senior executives from the electricity industry, to provide additional advice. The logical conclusion of this process, however, would be to replace individual regulators with a group. In the UK case, regulatory commissions follow the model of a company board, with a separate chair and chief executive (the latter being responsible for running the regulatory office), and a mix of full- and part-time members. In the case of the energy utilities, the regulators have also merged. During the 1990s, gas became an important fuel for electricity generation, and companies started to sell both fuels in the part of the markets that had been opened up for competition. It was therefore logical to combine the regulation of both fuels. A Director General of Gas Supply was appointed on the basis that he would soon also become the Director General of Electricity Supply, with the previous incumbent standing down a few months early to facilitate this. Regulatory documents started to appear with the logos of both Offer and Ofgas on them, before the Utilities Act 2000 formally created the Gas and Electricity Markets Authority as the first board-type regulator, and the Office of Gas and Electricity Markets (Ofgem) to support it.

One final collaborative aspect to the price controls is that the regulator now allows the companies to choose some of the key variables. The price control is set so that an efficient company can recover its operating costs, necessary investment, and a return on its capital, and the companies supply the regulator with information on what these costs have been in the past. The essence of the regulatory problem has always been to predict what these costs might be in the future, were the company to respond to appropriate incentives. In the past, the regulator used expert consultants to adjust each company's prediction, and then based the price control for each company on this revised prediction. Where there are several companies involved in the same activity, comparing their performance and predictions can also be useful. One branch of the economic literature on regulation has come up with the idea of implementing a theoretically optimal regulatory rule by allowing the company to choose between a menu of regulatory contracts (Sappington 1982, Laffont and Tirol 1993). Companies can choose to base their price control on a higher or a lower level of investment than the regulator forecasts, and will be able to retain some of the benefits if the out-turn level is below their chosen target. The scheme is calibrated so that companies earn more (relative to their out-turn cost) if these costs and the forecast are low (giving an incentive to keep costs down) and if the forecast is accurate (giving an incentive for truthful revelation) (Pollitt and Bialek 2008).

Changing Industry Structure

As already described, when British Gas was privatized, the market for large customers was formally opened to competition, but the company faced no competitors. The immediate barriers to this were removed by the first MMC inquiry, of 1987-8, and some large industrial customers were able to switch to competing suppliers. In the early 1990s, however, a new market for gas appeared, as gas-fired power stations were built in response to electricity privatization. This reduced the amount of gas available for more traditional customers, since most of the supplies from existing fields had been bought by British Gas on long-term contracts. The company and the Office of Fair Trading had agreed targets for the proportion of customers who would buy from its competitors, and British Gas started to release bulk supplies to facilitate this. (At first, the company simply swapped gas with entrants, providing supplies immediately in return for gas from new fields (contracted by the entrant) that would become available in a few years time; later, straightforward sales were made.) As competition developed more slowly than the OFT had hoped, it attempted to place more restrictions on British Gas. As the proportion of gas passing through the company's pipes on behalf of rivals grew, its transportation charges became more financially important, and the regulator started to develop a separate price control for these. When Ofgas and British Gas failed to agree on the cost of capital to be used in this price control, the matter had to be referred to the MMC, but British Gas actually asked for the entire industry to be referred, in an attempt to clarify the company's situation.

The MMC (1993a, 1993b) recommended that British Gas should be divided into its pipeline business and its supply business, and that competition should, at a later stage, be extended to all consumers. The logic for the separation was that the owner of a network will often have some ability to frustrate competition over that network, and although British Gas had introduced a system of separate businesses with Chinese Walls between them, this had proved cumbersome in practice. The logic of introducing competition for all consumers was partly based on the idea that small consumers would also benefit directly from a choice, and partly to improve the degree of choice available to the very largest interruptible customers. These customers were willing to have their supplies cut off at times of peak demand, in return for a significant reduction in their bills, but creating such an interruption was more valuable to a supplier, the more peaky the supplier's remaining customers were (and hence, the greater the need to flatten those peaks). Since domestic customers generally had the peakiest demands, the domestic monopoly enjoyed by British Gas meant that it had far more to gain from offsetting those demands with customer interruptions, and so could offer a much better deal to interruptible customers than any of its rivals. Opening the domestic market to competition would create other companies with a need to balance domestic customers with interruptible ones, and hence better deals for both large and small customers. British Gas naturally lobbied hard against the suggestion that it should be broken up, and won the argument.

The government decided to introduce competition for all gas consumers by the same deadline as for the electricity industry, 1998, and accepted the argument that it would not be possible to do this while simultaneously imposing a significant structural change on British Gas. The government therefore rejected the MMC's recommendations about the structure of the gas industry. Ironically, while preparing for the introduction of competition (and achieving it on schedule), British Gas itself decided that the company should be broken up, and split itself into BG plc (pipelines, and most of the exploration and production business) and Centrica (the British Gas retail brand) in 1997. Three years later, BG split off its pipelines, and these then merged with National Grid in 2002. Given the links between gas and electricity, it is logical to have a single company that can coordinate the national transmission systems for both industries, even though the consequences of that company failing would naturally be severe. In 2006, several of the regional gas distribution networks were spun off, again voluntarily, in a move that generated significant amounts of cash for National Grid. The regulator did not require these divestitures, but it has allowed Ofgem to compare the performance of different networks owned by independent companies. As this can put the less efficient companies under pressure to improve their performance, and lead to lower prices for consumers, the regulator welcomed the change.

Competition in the electricity wholesale market in England and Wales also proved to be inadequate. The legacy of the failed attempt to privatize nuclear power was two large conventional generators, National Power and PowerGen, with the ability and incentive to raise prices well above competitive levels. To some extent, their behavior was constrained by the presence of a regulator, but spot market prices gradually rose (from low levels) over the first three and a quarter years following the industry's restructuring, and a series of reports set out the regulator's concerns (Green 2006). In July 1993, he announced that he would refer the companies to the MMC unless he was able to agree acceptable remedies with them, using the threat of a reference to gain voluntary concessions. This paralleled the process of resetting a price control, in which a company might agree to limits on its prices because it fears that the MMC would impose a tighter control if it were to appeal. In February 1994, the companies agreed to use all reasonable endeavors to sell (or otherwise dispose of) 6 GW of plant to competitors (about 15 % of their capacity) and to keep prices down for a two-year period while they were doing so.

The negotiations over these disposals involved the regulator, the selling companies and potential acquirers. The regulator had made it clear that more competition was most needed in the mid-merit part of the market, for power stations that operated for a significant part, but not all, of the year – there had already been significant entry by baseload plants that aimed to run continuously. National Power and PowerGen were nervous that if they were to sell stations which had been operating in mid-merit without any constraints on the way that they were operated, the new owner would attempt to increase their load factors, and would succeed. This would mean that the selling companies lost more market share than they had bargained for, and could lead to further regulatory pressure if they were still perceived to dominate the mid-merit part of the market. The selling companies and potential acquirers tried to find mechanisms that would keep the stations operating at mid-merit, while the regulator did not want these to unduly limit their ability to compete. In the end, the regulator agreed that National Power and PowerGen could charge an "earn-out" of £6/MWh generated by each station, alongside annual lease fees, thus making base load operation uneconomic.

While these disposals were being negotiated, in September 1995, both National Power and PowerGen announced a merger with a Regional Electricity Company. Given the level of competition in the industry, these were referred to the MMC, which reported the following spring. The report was actually leaked a few weeks before it was published, and proved to recommend that the mergers be allowed, albeit with some conditions. As with the decision on the gas industry, the secretary of state[3] chose a different course, and prohibited them altogether, on the basis that the industry was still insufficiently competitive.

This conclusion was borne out by the events of the following years. The regulator continued to monitor the wholesale market, and to find that some companies were abusing their market positions. This led to changes in the market rules, described below, but it also led to pressure for more divestitures. In the end, National Power and PowerGen each accepted the divestiture of a further 4 GW of capacity, in return for permission to make vertical mergers. PowerGen merged with one of the RECs, East Midlands, and subsequently acquired the neighboring network and two other retail supply businesses. National Power ended up as the owner of three supply businesses, one of which was effectively swapped for the only network that it acquired.[4] Both companies continued to sell power stations, however, going beyond the divestitures required by the regulator – they found buyers willing to pay prices that the sellers believed to be attractive. They were also taken over by larger German groups – RWE bought the successor company to National Power, and E.ON bought PowerGen. Electricité de France had earlier bought London Electricity, and acquired several power stations, distribution networks and retailing businesses, rebranding the overall group as EdF Energy. Both of the (vertically integrated) Scottish companies had merged with English RECs. Centrica, the company that trades in the UK as British Gas, has also acquired a number of power stations. Most recently, at the start of 2009, EdF Energy acquired the nuclear generator, British Energy, and sold 20 % of it to Centrica.

The upshot of these corporate moves is that the electricity industry now has a very high degree of vertical integration, and is also quite concentrated. The figure shows that six companies were responsible for the bulk of retail supply in 2007, and also for a high proportion of generation. Much of the remainder was produced by British Energy, which has now been acquired by two of the big six. The big six are also the dominant sellers of gas, at least for domestic customers. The regulator is now attacking the companies for what it portrays as an inadequate level of competition to serve these customers – the ex-incumbents are typically uncompetitive in their local market for their "traditional" product, even though they will usually offer a competitive price for the "dual fuel" combination of gas and electricity.

Figure 1: Electricity Market Shares in Great Britain, 2007

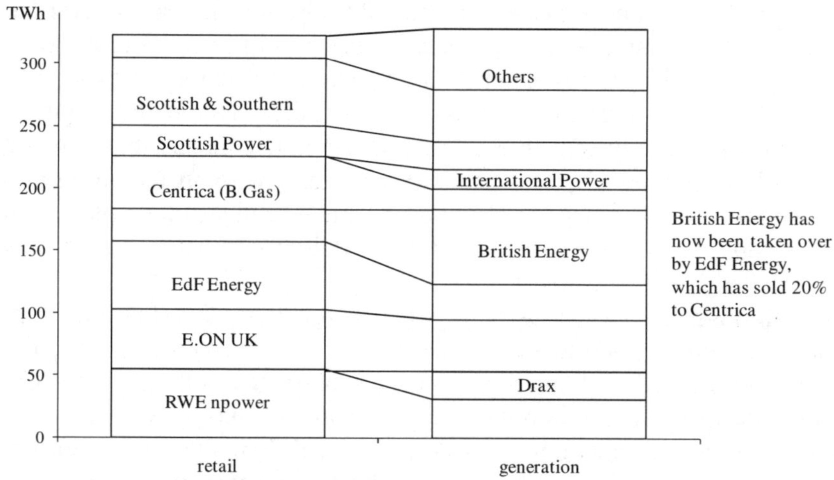

Source: E.ON UK, Evidence to Business and Enterprise Committee, HC 293 of 2007-8

Nonetheless, the vertical integration is the result of trends started in order to increase competition. Regional electricity companies were allowed to build power stations in order to compete with the major generators, and the major generators were allowed to sell electricity to compete with the RECs in retailing to large customers. British Gas proved the most effective entrant to sell electricity to domestic customers, just as each local electricity company was the strongest competitor faced by British Gas in that region. Since the generators voluntarily went beyond the divestitures forced upon them by the regulator, we can conclude that this industry structure is one that has been chosen by the companies themselves, and allowed by the competition authorities. However, it is certainly possible that if no divestitures at all had been required, one or other of the major generators would have chosen a strategy that rejected vertical integration (as was largely the case with British Energy). Furthermore, the incentives to be vertically integrated were perceived to have risen during the late 1990s as a direct result of changes to the electricity wholesale market rules that were being imposed by the regulator and the government.

Governing Energy Markets

Many goods and services can be sold without the use of a formal market. Buyers and sellers can agree a price, a quantity, and a means of delivery, without any need to coordinate their actions with anyone else. This is not the case for gas and electricity. The need to operate the transmission system in a coordinated manner means that it is not possible to deliver physical gas and electricity without having regard to technical constraints. Purely bilateral trades can still take place, but there must be some way in which their delivery is assured – or they are cashed out financially.

Although the gas industry was privatized first, the slow development of competition meant that the electricity industry was first to develop centralized trading arrangements. Companies selling gas to consumers had to secure supplies of gas from the North Sea (or some other gas field), arrange its transportation with British Gas, and ensure that the amount of gas they put into the system was the same as the amount their customers took out. If there was a difference, the transportation contract set out what would happen – the supplier would effectively have to buy top-up supplies from British Gas if it was short, and would sell back any surplus if it had put too much gas into the system. The task of dealing with these imbalances was eased by the fact that gas can easily be stored within the transmission system, simply by changing the pressure that it is working at, and so it was not necessary to keep track of inflows and outflows over short time periods.

Electricity cannot be stored, and its value changes significantly over the day. This made it essential to keep track of power flows over a relatively short period – the British system chose half-hours, although many other countries run their markets on an hourly basis. Furthermore, there are significant short-term fluctuations in demand, and in the amount of power some stations may be able to generate, so that it is very unlikely that a company's actual trades will equal those that it planned to make in advance. This means that even if most trades are carried out bilaterally well in advance, some mechanism will be needed to deal with the unanticipated deviations, keeping track of the amounts of power each company is liable for, and setting the prices at which these can be settled.

When the arrangements for electricity privatization were first discussed, it was suggested that most trading should be bilateral, but that generators should then "pool" their contracts to ensure that the cheapest available stations were actually called on to generate. Similarly, the buyers should create a separate pool of their purchase contracts to ensure that they could buy from the companies offering the lowest prices. It was quickly realized that this system would be far too unwieldy, and a single, unified, Pool was created instead.

The Electricity Pool of England and Wales was based upon the procedures that the CEGB had used to dispatch its plant before privatization. Each generating company submitted offers for each of its units, one day before real time, consisting of technical parameters and several prices for different kinds of operation (starting up, running without any load, and generating power). These prices corresponded exactly to the items of cost information that the CEGB had fed into its optimization program to derive the cost-minimizing generation schedule, subject to the same technical constraints. The Pool continued to use the same program, with minor amendments. The key difference was that the companies were now allowed to submit any price offers that they wished in order to try to maximize their profits, and sometimes also changed their technical parameters with the same objective.

The Pool was established by a contract, the Pooling and Settlement Agreement, had a chief executive with a small staff, and subcontracted most of its operations to various subsidiaries of the National Grid Company. The contract foresaw the need for its own amendment, and set out governance procedures for this. The most important consideration seems to have been to prevent one group of companies from changing the rules to the disadvantage of another group. The main decision making body was thus a Pool Executive Committee of ten members, five generators and five retailer representatives. Four of the retailers represented the regional incumbents (the posts rotating within four groups of three companies each), and the three largest generators also had a seat apiece. Simple "generator versus retailer" proposals would therefore be deadlocked. If the Pool Executive Committee agreed a rule change that some members disliked, they could call for a meeting of all Pool Members, and a vote, followed by a postal vote in which votes were weighted by the companies' shares of market activity. The final stage was for a decision to be appealed to the regulator, who was represented as an observer on all the Pool's bodies. His role in deciding appeals meant that the regulator's staff was reluctant to give opinions on the desirability of any given rule change, in case this was to prejudice a later appeal. This made it difficult for the regulator to influence the direction or speed of any changes.

The Pool was able to take some decisions, dealing with obvious anomalies in its rules, in a timely and efficient manner. Company representatives would work with the National Grid Company on various committees to analyze the impact of proposed changes (which were always proposed by a company). This analysis was essential, given the complexity of the market's operations and of its rules. However, the procedures designed to protect minorities also made it very easy for dissenting companies to block changes that they believed would be against their financial interests.

The most egregious case of this was an attempt to introduce regional differentials into the payments for transmission losses. When the Pool was set up, these losses were shared among all generators and all retailers, scaling down the metered generation of each power station, and scaling up the metered demand for each retailer until the quantities were equal. This did not reflect the reality that more of the power from northern generators than from southern stations was lost in the transmission system, or that losses rose by more when a southern customer increased demand than when a northern customer did. This had been listed as an issue that needed to be resolved (in a cost-reflective direction) at the time of the restructuring, in a schedule of items that could not be sorted out before the deadline for the market to start operations. Before the restructuring, there had been (in principle) a chance that the issue could be resolved through some process of log-rolling, in which the companies which stood to lose from regional transmission losses could have traded this off against progress with an issue that would benefit them. After privatization, each issue was handled separately.

In 1994, a decision by the Pool Executive Committee to introduce a regional transmission losses scheme was appealed, and the regulator ruled in favor of the decision. The Executive Committee than had to approve the work program to design the detailed rule change. Their decision to do so was also appealed. The regulator again turned down the appeal, pointing out that the issue of transmission losses had been discussed for many years, and that he had already approved the principles underlying the proposed scheme. The losing companies then took the process to judicial review, and succeeded in delaying it until imminent changes to the whole trading system made the process irrelevant.

The gas industry started to develop more formal trading arrangements during the 1990s. Once British Gas had finally decided to embrace competition, the company took active steps to facilitate it, balancing its rivals' inputs and outflows of gas as required. As more companies started to sell gas to consumers, the volume of adjustments required grew, and it was frequently the case that some companies would have a surplus of gas while others had a shortage. This meant that trading amongst themselves could be a better option than automatically cashing out an imbalance with British Gas. The On-the-day Commodity Market (OCM) was established to give them a chance to do so. It is a screen-based market where companies trade anonymously, with the market operator (now APX Group) acting as a counterpart to all trades. It opens eighteen hours before the 24-hour window for delivery, and closes just under two and a half hours before that window closes. Companies can trade with each other to balance their physical and contractual positions, while the system operator (now National Grid) also trades to bring injections and withdrawals into line. Companies with an imbalance between their physical and contractual positions have to cash these out at prices based on the cost of the trades that the system operator had to make.

Because the gas industry faces fewer technical problems in matching demand and supply, the OCM is a relatively simple market. The technical problems facing the electricity industry are much more significant, but the OCM still offered an attractive model as criticisms of the Pool mounted. The Pool was attacked as being slow to change its rules (which was true), and for facilitating the exercise of market power (which was basically untrue (Newbery 1998)). Nonetheless, the attacks enjoyed political support, in part because reforming the Pool was seen as a way of reducing electricity prices and of supporting the coal industry – a political imperative for the new Labour government.[5] In 1998, the regulator recommended replacing the Pool with New Electricity Trading Arrangements, and these came into force in 2001. An Act of Parliament gave the Secretary of State the power to override companies' objections to the changes, abolishing the Pool and requiring them to follow the new rules.

The New Electricity Trading Arrangements (known since 2005 as the British Electricity Transmission and Trading Arrangements) abolished the centralized day-ahead auction run by the Pool. Instead, companies could trade bilaterally (or internally – there was a significant amount of vertical integration by this time) until shortly before real time. At Gate Closure, companies had to notify the system operator of their bilateral trades and operating intentions, and the system operator had to work out how to reconcile these with the need to match demand and generation, and keep the system stable. This required National Grid to buy and sell power from some stations – trading after Gate Closure is only allowed where National Grid is the counter-party.

In practice, very few companies will be able to match their actual operations with their contracted positions, and will have imbalances that need to be cashed out. The trading arrangements contain the rules for calculating the prices at which this will happen. The underlying principle has been to give companies an incentive to contract accurately in advance, with the result that the imbalance prices are intended to be unattractive. In a chapter focussing on governance, the details of how (or whether) this is achieved are not important.

In terms of governance, the key difference from the Pool is that it has become much easier to change the market rules. In the central question of how the imbalance prices are set, there have been two major changes since the market was introduced, changes that would almost certainly have been resisted successfully under the Pool's governance arrangements. As with the Pool, there is a contract at the heart of the market, the Balancing and Settlement Code. A panel, elected by the industry, is responsible for overseeing the Code, and recommending changes, with the difference that, even though elected by a particular group, each panel member is required to act in the interests of the industry as a whole, as set out in the Code's Objectives.

As with the Pool, when a company proposes a rule change, industry experts will collaborate to examine its implications, and produce a report to the BSC Panel. The Panel will decide whether to recommend that the change is accepted or not, but the formal decision is made by the Gas and Electricity Markets Authority, the regulator. At first, there was no appeal against the authority's decision, but the Energy Act 2004 made it possible for companies to appeal to the Competition Commission, if (and only if) the Authority's decision had differed from the Panel's recommendation (in either direction). This had the benefit of preventing frivolous appeals against decisions where the regulator agreed with the majority of the industry, but acting as a check against the arbitrary exercise of the regulator's powers.

Conclusions

This chapter has shown how the collaborative governance has worked in the energy utilities of Great Britain. The system has evolved significantly during the twenty or so years since privatization, just as there were changes during the period when the industry was in public ownership. However, some common themes can be identified.

The level of transparency in the industry's governance has risen. Regulators give far more information on their evolving thinking, aiming to avoid significant surprises. This is a good thing, as uncertainty is likely to lead to bad decisions, and less investment. The only cost is that the resources devoted to regulation have grown, but those are small in proportion to the importance of the industry.

The structure of the industries, set by the government at privatization, has changed. This has partly been in response to pressure by the regulators, enforced by the threat (and actual use) of references to the MMC. However, all three companies subject to these pressures have gone further with divestitures than the government and the regulators required. Horizontal competition has therefore improved significantly over time, but the quid pro quo (sometimes explicit, sometimes not) has been an overwhelming increase in vertical integration. This has clearly been at the companies' behest, while the government's role has been permissive. The nature of competition in the industries is now very different from that envisaged at privatization.

The competition would be impossible without formal markets and trading rules. These can only be set by experts, given the complexity of the industries. Most of those experts are, naturally, employed by the companies in the industry, and they have generally cooperated well with the regulator to devise and adjust the trading systems. There are inevitable conflicts of interest when some companies know that a particular change, however desirable from the point of view of economic efficiency, will disadvantage them, but the governance procedures are intended to rise above such conflicts. Companies now have the right of appeal if the regulator goes against the industry view in imposing, or refusing a rule change.

The roles of the government (setting overall policy), the regulator (overseeing the industry, and setting prices for the monopoly parts) and the companies (making profits, hopefully by giving customers what they want and need) are now clear. We have learned that it is possible to create competition, with collaboration in setting the necessary rules, but that some disagreements are inevitable, and that governance that promotes change where needed is essential. It has been much easier to make progress when the major companies in the industry have decided that it is in their interests to travel in the same direction as the regulator.

Endnotes

[1] The first Chancellor of the University of Birmingham, Joseph Chamberlain, rose to prominence as Mayor of Birmingham with civic reforms which included the creation of a municipal gas company for his city.

[2] That review led to the complete opening of the industry, from 1991 onwards.

[3] The two decisions were taken by different people; Michael Heseltine was President of the Board of Trade in 1993, and Ian Lang in 1995

[4] National Power bought Yorkshire Electricity, including distribution and retailing, but then sold the distribution network to the owners of (neighboring) Northern Electricity, simultaneously buying that company's retail business.

[5] The argument was that the Pool had allowed coal-fired generators to exercise market power, encouraging excessive entry by gas-fired generators, and hence reducing coal's share of the market. The argument was correct about the impact of market power, but not in ascribing this to the Pool's pricing rule.

References

Foreman-Peck, J. and Hammond C. (1997). "Variable Costs and the Visible Hand: the Re-regulation of electricity supply, 1932-37" *Economica* vol. 64, pp. 15-30

Green, R.J. (2006). "Market power mitigation in the UK power market" *Utilities Policy*, vol. 14, no. 2, pp. 76-89

Hannah, L. (1979). *Electricity before Nationalisation* London, MacMillan

Laffont, J.-J. and Tirole J. (1993). *A Theory of Incentives in Procurement and Regulation*, Cambridge, The MIT Press

Levy, B and Spiller P. (1996). Regulations, Institutions and Commitment: A Comparative Analysis of Telecommunications Regulation, Cambridge, Cambridge University Press

Littlechild, S. C. (1983). Regulation of British Telecommunications Profitability London, HMSO

Monopolies and Mergers Commission, (1981). Central Electricity Generating Board: A Report on the Operation by the Board of its System for the Generation and Supply of Electricity in Bulk, HC 315, HMSO, London

Monopolies and Mergers Commission (1988). Gas: A report on the matter of the existence or possible existence of a monopoly situation in relation to the supply of gas through pipes to persons other than tariff customers. Cm 500, London, HMSO

Monopolies and Mergers Commission (1993a). British Gas plc: Volume 1 of reports under the Gas Act 1986 on the conveyance and storage of gas and the fixing of tariffs for the supply of gas by British Gas plc. Cm 2315, London, HMSO

Monopolies and Mergers Commission (1993b). Gas: Volume 1 of reports under the Fair Trading Act 1973 on the supply within Great Britain of gas through pipes to tariff and non tariff customers, and the supply within Great Britain of the conveyance and storage of gas by public gas suppliers, Cm 2314, London, HMSO

Monopolies and Mergers Commission (1995). Hydro-Electric plc: A report on a reference under section 12 of the Electricity Act 1989, London, HMSO

Morrison, H. (1933). *Socialisation and Transport,* London, Constable

Newbery, D. M. (1998). "The Regulator's Review of the English Electricity Pool" *Utilities Policy*, vol. 7 no 3, pp.129-142

Pollitt, M. G. and Bialek J. (2008). "Electricity network investment and regulation for a low-carbon future" in Grubb M., Jamasb T. and Pollitt M. (eds.) *Delivering a Low Carbon Electricity System: Technologies, Economics and Policy*, pp. 183-206, Cambridge, Cambridge University Press

Pryke, R. (1982). The Nationalised Industries: Policies and performance since 1968 Oxford, Oxford University Press

Sappington, D. (1982). "Optimal Regulation of Research and Development under Imperfect Information" *The Bell Journal of Economics*, Vol. 13, No. 2, pp. 354-368

Treasury (1961). The Financial and Economic Obligations of the Nationalised Industries, Cmnd 1337, London, HMSO

Treasury (1967). Nationalised Industries: A Review of Economic and Financial Objectives, Cmnd 3437, London, HMSO

Treasury (1976). *Cash Limits on Public Expenditure,* Cmnd 6440, London, HMSO

Treasury (1978). *The Nationalised Industries,* Cmnd 7131, London, HMSO

7

Clash of Regulatory Cultures in the EU: The Liberalization of Energy Markets

Eberhard Bohne

The title of this essay is – as some readers may have noticed – an allusion to Samuel Huntington's book "The clash of civilizations and the remaking of world order" (1996). The choice of this slightly dramatic title for an essay on energy regulation is to highlight

– that EU policymaking and regulations are heavily influenced by political, administrative, and legal cultures of member states, and
– that, therefore, mono-disciplinary theoretical concepts – like neoclassical economic theory in the case of restructuring energy markets – are likely to fail in reality, because they do not survive the clash of regulatory cultures.

Ten years of EU command and control regulations aimed at liberalizing European energy markets have not resulted in truly competitive and integrated electricity and gas markets in Europe (European Commission 2009b). Incomplete implementation and enforcement of EU energy legislation by EU member states are held responsible for the shortcomings of the European liberalization efforts (European Commission 2009b, ibid.).

The question is whether and to what extent the dominant regulatory approach of command and control regulations based on neoclassical economic theory is a major cause for implementation and enforcement deficits, and should be replaced or, at least, complemented by reform measures based on the public administration concept of collaborative governance[1].

Main Characteristics and Conceptual Foundations of EU Energy Regulations

EU Directives and Regulations 1996- 2009

According to neoclassical market theory integrated competitive energy markets will emerge when the following requirements are met (Brunekreeft, 2003; 16 ff; Joskow 2008: 12 f.; Spanjer 2009: 3251):

- the abolition of closed service areas which involves the introduction of free generation, imports, supply, trade and consumer choice of energy,
- non-discriminatory third party access to transmission and distribution grids,
- unbundling of vertically integrated utilities,
- the establishment of regulatory authorities.

In the first regulatory phase of 1996/1998, the EU issued two directives[2] and established general principles for limited competition, third party access to the transmission and distribution grids, and unbundling. The establishment of regulatory authorities was left to EU member states. The directives were based on the assumption that competitive markets would emerge "naturally" once legal barriers to competition were removed.

In the second regulatory phase of 2003/2005, the EU replaced the 1996/1998 directives with two new directives[3] which contained detailed regulations for third party access to the energy networks, legal unbundling of vertically integrated utilities, and the requirement to establish national regulatory authorities. The EU also issued two regulations on access to the networks for cross-border exchanges in electricity[4], and on access to the gas transmission networks[5].

In the third regulatory phase of 2009, the EU further tightened the regulatory screws by replacing the 2003/2005 legislation with two new directives[6] and three new regulations[7]. The new law prescribes inter alia[8]

- ownership unbundling of transmission systems and the functions of electricity generation or gas production respectively and energy supply in vertically integrated utilities[9] with three complicated exceptions:
  - the Independent System Operator (ISO) model[10],
  - the Independent Transmission Operator (ITO) model[11]

  and
  - existing national arrangements which guarantee more effective independence of the transmission system operator than the ITO model[12],
- legal unbundling of distribution system operators in vertically integrated utilities[13],
- non-discriminatory third party access to the transmission and distribution networks[14],
- annual ten-year network development plans[15] for infrastructure investments,
- the establishment of a single regulatory authority with detailed and comprehensive duties and powers in each member state[16],
- the creation of two European Networks of Transmission Systems Operators (ENTSO) for electricity and gas through which all transmission system operators shall cooperate at Community level[17],
- the establishment of a European Agency for the Cooperation of Energy Regulators to assist national regulatory authorities[18].

This short overview of the three phases of regulating EU energy markets shows that the EU produced a large amount of detailed and complex regulations whose number increased in each regulatory phase. For instance, each of the two 2009 directives on the electricity and gas markets encompasses more than 20 additional articles as compared to its 2003 predecessor. The regulations consist of commands, prohibitions, permits, controls and sanctions which are addressed to utilities and other stakeholders of the energy markets. The rules must be implemented and enforced by public authorities. It seems that the uncritical belief in the market forces of the first EU liberalization directives has now been replaced by an equally uncritical belief in the capacity of government to impose market competition by command and control regulations.

Transfer of the British Regulatory Model to the EU Level

Conceptually, the EU regulations largely follow the UK model of restructuring energy markets (*Ranci* 2003:121, *Bulmer et al.* 2007: 2, 83, 91, 93 f; Thatcher 2007a:159). The British model[19] is characterized by command and control regulations providing for ownership unbundling of transmission systems from energy generation and supply, a price-cap regulation for tariffs on network services, and a central independent regulatory authority with far-reaching powers. In its annual report of 2008/2009, the British regulatory authority (Ofgem[20] 2009: 24/25) considered itself "the leading voice in Europe", and reported as "key achievements for 2008-2009", inter alia, that "Ofgem has provided the European Union with a strong steer in its bid to inject competition into its energy markets and its moves to consolidate the regulatory framework."

Neoclassical Economic Theory as Conceptual Base of Energy Regulations.

Conceptually, the British regulatory model and EU energy regulations are off-springs of neoclassical economic theory (Spanjer 2009: 3251). While there are many facets of neoclassical economics, their common foundation are the following basic assumptions (Weintraub 2002):

- "People have rational preferences among outcomes.
- Individuals maximize utility and firms maximize profits.
- People act independently on the basis of full and relevant information."

Consequently, competitive markets are the most efficient mechanism for the allocation of goods and services, and, thus, for achieving the common welfare. Since vertically integrated utilities whose network ownership constitutes a natural monopoly have plenty of opportunities to impede competition in the up-stream markets of electricity generation and gas production, and in the down-stream markets of energy supply, ownership unbundling is the neoclassical recipe for ensuring competition in these markets (Spanjer 2009: 3251). Similarly, price or revenue cap regulations of network charges simulate a market on the basis of efficiency benchmarking of network operators assuming that profit maximizing operators will increase network efficiency in order to keep network charges below the price or revenue cap. However, market activities are embedded in a context of regulations. The proper implementation of these regulations is often a prerequisite for the functioning of markets as is the case, for instance, in respect to the regulations on ownership unbundling. Neoclassical economics are not concerned with the effective implementation of regulations underlying the functioning of market concepts. In their models proper implementation is taken for granted. Implementation deficits are problems of politics and public authorities but not of (maybe ill conceived) market concepts. The neoclassical neglect of the impacts of regulations on market activities has led to the emergence of new institutional economics (Furubotn/ Richter 2005; Crouch 2007). Regulations are considered institutions whose effects are taken into account in market analyses, However, these analyses tend to be confined to transaction costs issues of institutions (Spanjer 2009: 3253), and do not (yet) focus on the political, administrative, personnel, legal, and other constraints of rulemaking and regulatory implementation. This is the realm of public administration research, and the topic of this essay.

Conflicts of Regulatory Cultures and Consequences for Energy Markets

Concepts of Regulatory Culture

The concept of regulatory culture is used to understand and explain the behavior of public authorities and private actors in regulatory arenas (Meidinger 1987: 356 f) like rulemaking and regulatory decisions in individual cases. The concept overlaps with notions of administrative and organizational culture. There is no generally accepted demarcation of these concepts. From a pragmatic perspective, the concept of regulatory culture can be considered narrower than the other two concepts because rulemaking constitutes a specific segment of administrative and organizational tasks. Common element of all concepts of culture is the notion of shared understandings, beliefs, values, principles and attitudes which are based on traditions, common historical experience and fundamental norms which influence the regulatory, administrative or organizational behavior of public and private actors (Meidinger 1987: 359, Kerandren 1996: 73 f, Anechiarico 1998: 17, Fisch 2008: 23 f, Hill and Lynn 2009: 52). Regulatory cultures are specifically characterized by

- shared values and beliefs concerning the relationship between government, markets, and the individual
- common legal and administrative traditions and principles,
- the extent to which public authorities enjoy regulatory discretion, and
- the distribution of regulatory competencies and related organizational structures.

National Regulatory Cultures and Energy Regulations in Great Britain, France and Germany

Shared values and beliefs concerning the relationship between government, markets, and the individual are reflected in three state models with corresponding market models which provide the conceptual base for the British, French and German regulatory systems. Table 1 presents the three state models with corresponding market models and ensuing characteristics of regulatory systems in British, French and German energy markets.

The British Regulatory System

The British government supports the concept of the "strategic and enabling state" (HM Government 2007: 4). The central idea of the enabling state is to "empower its citizens to develop their own lives" (Giddens 2003: 13), and – according to HM Government (2007: 4) –

"to hold public institutions to account" by "redistributing power to people".

Table 1: Characteristics of National Regulatory Cultures

Characteristics of regulatory cultures / country	Great Britain	France	Germany
State model	Enabling state	Providing state	Ensuring state
Market model	Regulated competitive market model	State-led model of market coordination	Corporatist model of market coordination (social market economy)
Regulatory system	Private ownership Central independent regulator Licence system with wide regulatory discretion	State ownership Central independent regulator with shared competencies Public service obligations	Private and government ownership Federal and Länder regulators Restricted regulatory discretion

The market model corresponding to this state vision is "a regulated competitive market"[21] where the government operates at arm's length from suppliers who are privately owned (Thatcher 2007a: 151 f). Regulations are supposed to ensure fair and effective competition. Independent regulatory agencies make and enforce rules for competition while suppliers seek maximization of profits and stock market value.

Private Ownership: Until the mid-1980s, the electricity industry (generation, transportation, supply) and the gas industry (transport, supply) were nationalized; only gas producers were private companies.[22]. The gas industry was privatized by the Gas Act 1986 (Dow 2007: no. 15.141). The privatization of the electricity industry followed suit on the basis of the Electricity Act 1989 (Dow 2007: no. 15.204). After various organizational modifications of the original privatization scheme, the British electricity and gas industries display in 2009 the following ownership pattern:

The transmission networks for electricity and gas are owned by the private National Grid Company (2008: 6). An exception is the electricity transmission grid in Scotland which is not owned but operated by National Grid.

There are 18 electricity distributors, and 20 gas distributors (Ofgem 2008: no. 60, 239, and 240). National Grid does not only own the gas transmission network but is also the largest gas distributor.

Electricity is generated and/or supplied by over 20 private companies.[23] Six companies are the most important generators and suppliers (European Commission 2007a: 164). They include the two large German utilities RWE and EON and the French state-owned utility Électricité de France (EDF) which hold together 43 % of the transmission entry capacity by generation owners (Ofgem 2009: no.87). EDF is now Britain's biggest producer of electricity[24] after its acquisition of British Energy in 2009 which operates all nuclear power plants.

The electricity transmission network is fully ownership unbundled. National Grid has no generation or supply assets (European Commission 2007a: 163). Most electricity suppliers, however, belong to company groups which own distribution networks (Ofgem 2008: no. 178). This means they are only legally unbundled. There are quite a few gas offshore producers and importers. In the gas downstream market, the six main electricity supply companies also have the bulk of customers (European Commission 2007a: 165). The largest market share is held by British Gas, the former gas monopoly supplier (Ofgem 2009: no. 230).

The gas transmission system is fully ownership unbundled. Also most gas distributors are not affiliated with production and supply companies (Ofgem 2008: no. 297).

Independent Central Regulator: The electricity and gas industries of England, Scotland and Wales are regulated by the Office of the Gas and Electricity Markets (Ofgem) under the Utilities Act 2000, the

Electricity Act 1989 and the Gas Act 1986. Ofgem is an independent central energy regulator and, in principle, free from political interference by the Department of Energy and Climate Change (DECC) and other government authorities. However, DECC has some indirect political influence on Ofgem (Dow 2007: no. 15.28 f), for instance, through its rights

- to veto any proposal by the regulator to modify licences[25,]
- to give non-binding guidance on social and environmental policies, and
- to appoint Ofgem's chief executive and the members of the Gas and Electricity Markets Authority (GEMA).

GEMA consists of executive and non-executive members, and governs Ofgem, inter alia by determining strategy, setting policy priorities, and taking decisions on a range of matters, including price controls and enforcement.[26] Ofgem's principal objective is to protect the interests of consumers by promoting competition in the gas and electricity markets. Ofgem's functions include[27]

- issuing, modifying, enforcing and revoking licences,
- setting price controls in the natural monopoly licensed sectors (transmission and distribution networks),
- investigating and penalizing those in breach of licence conditions.

Given Ofgem's independence from government, it is primarily held accountable by Parliament and the courts (Bremen 2005: no. 15: 121 f).

The electricity and gas industries remain subject to competition law which is implemented by the Office of Fair Trading (OFT), an independent, non-ministerial government department, and the Competition Commission (Dow 2007: no. 15.31; OFT 2009).

License System with Wide Regulatory Discretion: The generation/production, transmission, distribution and supply of gas and electricity require separate licences under the Gas Act 1986 and the Electricity Act 1989. The holder of a gas transmission licence must not be granted a gas supply licence and vice versa[28], while the same person may not be the holder of both electricity distribution licence and electricity supply licence[29]. The purpose of these provisions is to prevent cross-subsidization and discrimination of competitors.

The most important characteristic of the British licensing system which distinguishes it from the regulatory systems of other countries is the wide administrative discretion of the British regulator (Parker 1999: 119; Coen 2005: 378, 380; Dow 2007: no. 15.152, 15.227 ff; Littlechild 2009b: 3). This discretion is not unique to energy regulations but a fundamental characteristic of the British regulatory approach (Vogel 1986: 220 and Bell/McGillivray 2008: 237 ff). The content of the gas and electricity licences is largely determined by standard conditions which are issued by the Ministry. The standard conditions are very detailed, complex and voluminous. Ofgem has the competence to modify these conditions or to add special conditions when granting a licence in a given case[30] (Simmonds 2002: 55). However, subsequent modifications of conditions in existing licences require either the consent of the licence holder[31]or, in the case of disagreement, a directive by the Competition Commission[32] (Newbery 2006: 8). There are no substantive statutory criteria to guide or restrict Ofgem in exercising its regulatory discretion other than the general objectives of the Gas Act 1986[33] and the Electricity Act 1989[34] like consumer protection or energy security. Constitutional or other legal principles provide hardly any restrictions on the exercise of regulatory discretion (Sieckmann 1999: 132, Spreng 2005: 44-46). Finally, judicial review of regulatory decisions is very limited, and confined to procedural issues (Parker 1999: 119, Coen 2005: 378).

The French Regulatory System

In contrast to the concept of enabling state, the providing state is more of a producer of goods and services than an enabler of people to help themselves (Giddens 2003: 3). The providing state[35] seeks to actively[36] influence the economic and social well-being of its citizens, for instance, through publicly owned enterprises, plans and programs, regulations, and infrastructure projects. The market model corresponding to this state vision is the state-led model of market coordination[37] (Thatcher 2007a: 151). This model is characterized by

- dirigiste industrial government policies, and government coordination of mayor market actors,

- state ownership of enterprises which provide essential goods and services to the public, and which often have a monopoly over supply,
- the establishment of public service obligations which replace market competition.

State Ownership: The generation / production, transmission and distribution as well as the supply of electricity and gas are primarily in the hands of two large state-owned companies and their subsidiaries: EDF and Gaz de France (GDF) Suez. [38] Pursuant to Art. 24 of the law no. 2004-803[39], the state holds over 70 % of the EDF capital and over 33 % of the GDF Suez capital. The transmission network for electricity is owned and operated by the Réseau de transport d'électricité (RTE), a 100 % daughter company of EDF. EDF also owns most of the distribution networks for electricity supplying 95 % of customer sites. There are 169 local distribution companies [40] of which 160 companies supply the remaining 5 % of the market (CRE 2008: 38).The two transmission networks for gas are owned and operated by GRTgaz (88 %), a subsidiary of GDF Suez, and by TIGF (12 %), a subsidiary of Total (CRE 2008: 62). GDF Suez also operates some 96 % of the distribution networks for gas, while 23 local distribution companies[41], mainly in the hands of municipalities, operate the remaining distribution networks.

The transmission networks are legally unbundled from the generation/production and supply activities of EDF, GDF Suez, and Total. The process of legal unbundling had not been completed in 2008 at the level of distribution networks (CRE 2008: 30, 79).

There are three significant generating companies in the electricity market (CRE 2008: 32): EDF with 87 % of the installed generation capacity, Elactrabel-Suez, a subsidiary of GDF Suez with 4 %, and the private SNET with 2 % of the installed generation capacity. The remaining generation capacity belongs to a large number of small independent generation and distribution companies.

GDF Suez dominates the import and supply markets for gas, while some 22 local distribution companies account for about 4 % of gas supplies [42].

Independent Central Regulator with Shared Competencies: The Energy Regulatory Commission (Commission de régulation de l'energie – CRE) is the single central regulator of the electricity and gas markets (Thatcher 2007b, CRE 2008). The nine commissioners enjoy legally ensured independence. Part of CRE is the Dispute Settlement and Sanctions Committee (Comité de règlements des différends et des sanctions – CoRDIS) which is responsible for settling disputes between the operators and users of the electricity and gas transmission and distribution networks. CRE's main competencies include

- to propose access-tariffs for public electricity and gas networks,
- to regulate the terms and conditions for access to and use of the networks, and
- to approve the annual investment programs of the operators of the electricity and gas transmission networks.

However, CRE must share some of its functions with other authorities. For instance, CRE may only propose network-access tariffs to the Ministers for the Economy and Energy while the Ministers will accept or reject the proposals but cannot modify them (CRE 2008: 16).

The electricity and gas industries remain subject to competition law which is implemented by the Competition Council (Conseil de la concurrence), CRE (2008: 8) also has the power to stop any anticompetitive practices that are based on refusing network access.

Finally, CRE (2008: 8) monitors the electricity exchange in cooperation with the Financial Market Authority.

Public Service Obligations: The main and distinctive characteristic of the French regulatory system for energy is a comprehensive system of public service obligations imposed by law[43] on EDF, GDF Suez and other utilities. Public service obligations represent aspects of the common welfare which must be observed in operating the electricity and gas networks and in exercising the functions of energy production and supply. According to Art. 3(2) and (3) of the Electricity Directive 2009/72/EC and Art. 3 (2) and (3) of the Gas Directive 2009/73/EC, public service obligations relate, for instance, to energy security, regularity, quality and price of supply, environmental protection, energy efficiency, energy from renewable sources, climate protection, and consumer protection, in particular vulnerable customers. The practical consequences of public service obligations are, pursuant to Art. 106

(2) of the Treaty on the Functioning of the EU (TFEU), to exempt utilities from the rules of market competition in so far as the application of such rules obstructs the achievement of the particular tasks assigned to them. Public service obligations have a long tradition in the French political system. They are considered a symbol of "social-Colbertism", and of French interventionist industrial policies ("dirigisme") both representing constitutive elements of the providing state. EDF and GDF Suez are strongholds of this model, and preserves of the powerful technical "grands corps" controlling large segments of the French economy (Cole 1999: 173 f, Bauby/Varone 2007: 1052 f).

The German Regulatory System

The prevailing paradigm of the German regulatory system is the concept of the ensuring state. Its central idea is "shared responsibility" of state and citizens for the common good (Schuppert 2003: 55). State and private actors must take part in setting and implementing public policy. No one has a monopoly over this. Consequently, the concept of the ensuring state emphasizes the responsibility of the state in areas where private actors play a dominant role in the provision of public services (Schuppert 2003: 57). This means: the ensuring state should enable its citizens to develop their lives, but "after enabling" the ensuring state has the responsibility for the delivery of policy outcomes, and for the coordination of services many of which it does not directly provide (Giddens 2003: 13). Unlike the providing state, the ensuring state does not necessarily deliver public services but often leaves this to private actors. However, the ensuring state "guarantees"[44] that public services are delivered when their provision by private actors fails. Thus, the ensuring state can be ranked between the enabling and providing state.

A specifically German characteristic of the concept of the ensuring state is the notion of "Daseinsvorsorge" which includes all public services that are indispensable for ensuring a humane existence (Judgement of the Federal Constitutional Court of 20 March 1984, BVerfGE 66: 248, 258; Judgement of 10 September 2008 – 1 BvR 1914/02 –, no. 12). "Daseinsvorsorge" has been translated into English by the European Commission[45] as "services of general interest". A subcategory are "services of general economic interest" within the meaning of

Art. 14 and Art. 106 (2) TFEU. The German concept of "Daseinsvorsorge" and the EU concept of "services of general (economic) interest" overlap but are not identical (Ronellenfitsch 2009: 43). The main difference between these concepts relates to their legal consequences. Services of general economic interest may be exempted from market competition (Art. 106 (2) TFEU), whereas services of "Daseinsvorsorge" are subject to restrictions of public and constitutional law but they are not necessarily exempted from market competition (Ronellenfitsch 2009: 44). The market model corresponding to this state vision is the "social market economy". This is a corporatist model of market coordination[46] characterized by industry associations, labour unions, environmental and consumer organizations, and other societal groups having considerable influence on setting and implementing public policies including regulations. These organizations often enjoy the privilege of (regulated) self-regulation in certain, usually technical areas. Principles of "self-help, collaboration and self-organization" are said to make "for the marked difference between regulation in Germany and regulation in the Anglo-American politico-legal tradition" (Dyson 1992: 260).

Private and Government Ownership: The German electricity and gas markets have traditionally been characterized by decentralization with some 1600 utilities most of which were owned by municipal and county governments. At the same time, both energy markets have been dominated by a few large private companies. Länder and local governments held small shares of some of these companies.

These market structures have basically remained unchanged after liberalization.[47] However, market concentration of large utilities has increased since then, and foreign state-owned companies are now playing a major role on German electricity and gas markets.

There are four transmission networks for electricity. One network is owned by the Dutch company Tennet whose shares are held by the Dutch Government.[48]

60 % of the second transmission network is owned by the Belgian company Elia. Some 60 % of its shares are held by Belgian municipalities and by Electrabel, a subsidiary of the French state-owned GDF Suez.[49]

The third transmission network is owned by EnBW which is in the hands of German local governments (45 %) and the French state-owned EDF (45 %).

The fourth transmission network of RWE has primarily private owners but the largest share (16 %) is in the hands of local governments.

Most distribution networks for electricity are also owned by local governments although the two largest utilities EON and RWE which have private owners hold significant shares of over 200 local utilities.

In the gas market, private ownership of transmission networks prevails.[50] There are five big companies (EON-Ruhrgas, RWE-Thyssengas[51], Ontras-VNG, Wingas, BEB) which own and operate interregional gas transmission networks (European Commission 2007a: 32). The largest network is owned by EON-Ruhrgas, a private company. The other network companies have private owners, too, with the exception of Wingas Transport, where Gazprom, a Russian state-owned company, holds 50 % of the shares. Some ten other companies operate interregional or regional gas transmission networks (Bundeskartellamt 2009: 7 f, 32). Significant shares of some of these companies are held by foreign state-owned companies.[52]

Most gas distribution networks are owned by some 700 local governments.

In general, electricity and gas networks are part of vertically integrated utilities which are also active on the upstream generation/production markets and/or on the downstream supply markets. Larger companies are unbundled in legal and functional terms. However, distribution system operators are exempted from these unbundling obligations if they are serving less than 100 000 customers (European Commission 2007a: 30).

The market for electricity generation is dominated by four vertically integrated utilities (EON, RWE, Vattenfall, EnBW) whose accumulated market share amounts to 90 % of total net electricity generation (European Commission 2007a: 31). According to the Federal Cartel Office, EON and RWE with about 60 % of the market share represent a duopol (Monopolkommission 2007: no. 162).

Electricity supply is generally provided by some 800 municipal and county utilities. However, a great many of them are formally or informally controlled by the four big utilities.

Domestic gas production (18 % of total gas supply) and gas imports are in the hands of the large companies which own interregional transmission networks. Gas supply is generally provided by over 600 municipal and county utilities which are formally or informally controlled by EON-Ruhrgas and other big gas companies.

Federal and Länder Regulators: The Federal Network Agency is the main regulator for the access to grids, the approval of network access fees, and the implementation of the unbundling provisions (Theobald 2009: 275). The Agency is not an independent regulatory agency in the Anglo-Saxon sense but subject to general directives by the Federal Ministry of Economics and Technology.[53] It is an undecided legal issue whether the Agency is also subject to case-specific ministerial directives (Franke 2008: 1056 f).

Due to the principles of German federalism the Länder have retained some competencies of energy regulation. They regulate the networks and unbundling of utilities which serve less than 100 000 customers, and operate only in one Land.[54]

The Federal Cartel Office and the cartel authorities of the Länder are responsible for the implementation of anti-trust law concerning the control of mergers , and the abuse of market power if it is unrelated to grid access and grid connection, e.g. energy prices (Theobald 2009: 277).

Restricted Regulatory Discretion: The German regulatory system is characterized by constitutional constraints on the exercise of administrative and regulatory discretion (Dyson 1992: 260). Constitutional sources of these restrictions are

- the German version of the rule of law (principle of “Rechtsstaat”),
- the principle of the “social state” (Sozialstaat) which encompasses the notion of “Daseinsvorsorge” as outlined above (II.2 c, before aa), and
- human rights.

The concept of “Rechtsstaat” establishes legal restrictions on discretionary decision-making in terms of legal precision, consistency, predictability, proportionality, and judicial controls.

The concept of "Daseinsvorsorge" (services of general interest) imposes requirements of public interests, in particular consumer interests, on the exercise of administrative and regulatory discretion.

The constitutional provisions of human rights restrict discretionary decisions which entail negative consequences for individual rights. The constitutional protection of existing property rights (Bestandsschutz) tends to preserve the regulatory status quo.

Finally, regulatory decisions are subject to comprehensive judicial controls.

Given the many legal restrictions on the exercise of regulatory discretion, there is an ongoing debate on whether and to what extent regulatory discretion should be exempted from some of these restrictions (Oster 2009: 158 ff).

Differences and Conflicts Between National Regulatory Cultures and EU Energy Regulations

Differences Between National Regulatory Cultures

British energy regulations represent the lead model for the liberalization of EU energy markets. The British regulatory system is based on the state paradigm of the enabling state, and reflects a regulated competitive market model. Its main characteristics are

- private ownership of electricity and gas networks, and of generation/production and supply companies,
- an independent central regulatory agency, and
- a license system with wide regulatory discretion of the competent authority.

In contrast, the French regulatory system is based on the state paradigm of the providing state, and reflects a state-led model of market coordination.

State-ownership of the two largest electricity and gas utilities (EDF, GDF Suez), political influence over the central regulatory authority (CRE) and veto powers of the competent ministry concerning certain decisions of the regulatory authority as well as the extensive use of public service obligations – absent in both the British and German energy systems – constitute a dirigiste energy policy in the

French mercantilist tradition. These characteristics distinguish the French regulatory system significantly from the British and German regulatory systems.

The German regulatory system is based on the state paradigm of the ensuring state, and reflects a corporatist model of market coordination. The most visible difference between the German regulatory system and the British and French systems is the large number (app. 1600) of municipal and county utilities acting primarily on the energy supply markets. These activities represent the German version of services of general interest (Daseinsvorsorge) which – unlike the French public service obligations – are not exempted from market competition.

Another distinctive feature of the German regulatory system is the federal structure of regulatory authorities. Unlike Great Britain and France, Germany has no single central regulator but, in principle, 16 Länder regulators which are competent for utilities with less than 100.000 customers. However, six Länder have delegated their regulatory competencies to the Federal Network Agency. In sum, there are one federal and 10 Länder regulatory authorities.

Furthermore, German regulatory authorities are not independent regulatory agencies in the British sense which are not subject to ministerial oversight and directives. The exclusion of this oversight would contradict the German constitutional doctrine of democracy which requires an uninterrupted chain of political oversight and accountability from the administrative authorities up to the elected government and parliament. Finally, the regulatory decision powers of the German regulatory authorities are to a much greater extent subject to legal restrictions and detailed judicial controls than the decision powers of the British and French counterparts.

Conflicts Between National Regulatory Systems and EU Energy Regulations

Given these characteristics and differences of national regulatory systems, the question is whether and to what extent these systems are compatible with EU energy regulations.

There is no specific regulatory culture as defined above (II 1.) on the European level.[55] Terms like "acquis communautaire", community method or better regulation could suggest cultural aspects of regulation. However, they have a technical meaning in practice.

The “acquis communautaire” is simply the body of existing EU legislation (European Commission 2009a: 2).

The “community method” denotes the formal legislative and judicial procedures of the European institutions (European Commission 2001: 8).

“Better regulation” is a reform concept of the European Commission (2001: 18 ff, 2009a) for improving existing and future EU legislation.

European legislation has been shaped by national regulatory concepts. Member states compete on the EU level for political dominance of their national regulatory concepts in the legislative process (Young 2010: 58 f). As outlined above (I 2.) EU energy legislation follows the British regulatory model.

From a legal perspective, the wording of EU energy directives and regulations is generally broad enough to allow for certain national differences in the implementation.

From a practical perspective, though, EU liberalization of energy markets will only be successful, if the basic functional prerequisites of the British model are, at least in principle, met by national regulatory systems. These functional prerequisites are

(1) primarily private ownership of networks and utilities,
(2) existence of a central independent regulatory agency which is largely removed from ministerial oversight,
(3) decision powers of the regulatory authority for detailed market regulations as exemplified by the British licence system with wide regulatory discretion,
(4) a manageable number of companies to be regulated.

These functional prerequisites are not met in the French and German regulatory systems due to different regulatory cultures. Therefore, EU energy regulations conflict with the regulatory systems of these countries.

The French energy system does not fulfil the first three prerequisites. The system is dominated by two state-owned companies. This ownership enables close interactions and interdependencies between company and government executives, and ensures strong government influence on company policies, and company influence on government policies. State-ownership is the basis for French government interventions into energy markets, particularly through imposing public service obligations and energy tariffs (Thatcher 2007b: 1040). The ownership-based government influence is institutionally backed by the establishment of a central regulatory authority (CRE) which has to share decision powers with the competent ministry. The dirigiste energy policies are reinforced by a closely knit network of a technocratic and political elite produced by a few elite schools (grandes écoles) and belonging to the influential technical and administrative "grands corps" of the state. It has been observed that despite regulatory reforms under EU energy regulations, the old "complicity between political elites and EDF technocrats" continues to exist (Bauby/Varone 2007: 1056 f), and that regulatory authorities "have overwhelmingly been colonized by the 'grands serviteurs de l'Etat' (or more pejoratively, 'technocrats') drawn from the 'grandes écoles' and state 'grands corps'" (Thatcher 2007b, 1035).

The German energy system does not meet any of the aforementioned functional prerequisites of the British regulatory model underlying EU energy legislation.

Ownership of local distribution networks and energy supply companies lies primarily in the hands of municipal and county utilities. Their activities are motivated by providing services of general economic interest and less by market competition. Moreover, German corporatist culture values cooperation over competition.

There is no central independent regulatory authority in the British sense. Regulatory competencies are divided between the Federal Network Agency and Länder authorities. Administrative discretion of the regulatory authorities is restricted by law and detailed judicial controls. The German regulatory authorities do not have the British Ofgem's powers to impose and enforce competitive market structures. Last but not least, a system of detailed regulatory intervention like the British license system would not be manageable with over 1600 utilities on the German electricity and gas markets.

All in all, the heavy reliance of the EU on the British regulatory model (and neo-classic economic theory) has led to "clashes of regulatory cultures" in France and Germany (and in other countries with regulatory traditions different from the British model) which generate enormous bureaucratic burdens and impede the realization of an integrated European energy market.

National Implementation and Market Deficiencies

Implementation Deficiencies

Conflicts between national regulatory cultures and EU energy legislation generate a deficient implementation of EU regulations into national laws.

Since EU energy legislation is modelled on the British regulatory system, it does not come as a surprise that the European Commission (2007a: 166) considers the implementation of EU energy legislation in the UK to be flawless. However, the implementation of EU energy legislation in the other EU member states, particularly in France and Germany, has been slow and partly deficient. Germany, for instance, was dubbed "the heavy weight laggard of the EU reform process" (Newbery 2009: 49). The most prominent example of questionable government intervention into the French electricity and gas (retail) markets, is the introduction of regulated tariff-contracts which represent an alternative to market-price contracts (CRE 2008: 35, 85). Regulated tariff-contracts can be offered only by EDF, GDF Suez and other incumbent suppliers designated by the government. Beneficiaries of these contracts are all customers, and not only small businesses and private households. The tariffs are well below negotiated market prices, and financed by cross-subsidization of different tariffs and state taxes (European Commission 2007a: 65).[56] Consequently, the great majority of energy costumers opts for regulated tariff-contracts. These contracts clearly distort fair market competition. The European Commission has started an investigation into this practice[57], and observed[58] (European Commission 2007a: 65) that the tariff-contracts are neither justified as state aid under Art. 108 (2) TFEU (ex Art. 88 (2) TEC) nor as public service obligations under Art. 3 of the Electricity and Gas Directives (2009/72/EC and 2009/73/EC). The tariff-contracts reflect the French "providing state" and the country's traditional dirigiste industrial policies.

Germany has been slow to implement and enforce EU unbundling provisions. Ownership unbundling is generally viewed as an unjustified intrusion into constitutional property rights. However, the European Commission forced the large utilities EON and RWE in the context of anti-trust law proceedings to voluntarily sell the electricity transmission network (EON) and the gas transmission network (RWE) to third parties. While EU unbundling provisions have been properly transposed into German law (European Commission 2007a: 30), the enforcement of these regulations is deficient. In 2009, the Federal Network Agency (Bundesnetzagentur 2010: 173) has, therefore, started investigations into the unbundling practice of EON and its regional subsidiaries.

How can one explain that conflicts between national regulatory cultures and EU legislation lead to implementation deficits of EU directives and regulations in EU member states?

The theoretical concepts of political incrementalism are best suited to explain this relationship.[59] According to incremental theory (Braybrooke/Lindblom 1970; Hayes 2001 and 2006; Bohne 2002: 114-124 and 2006: 540-543), political decision making tends

- to be incremental under normal circumstances, i.e. to deviate only marginally from the existing political status quo, and
- to be caused by
    - cognitive and informational constraints on decision makers,
    - lack of resources and
    - the beneficiaries of the status quo who wish to preserve the existing power balance.

Non-incremental decision making, e.g. changes of existing political and regulatory structures, principles and traditions, only occur under exceptional circumstances. Necessary conditions for non-incremental changes are

- a decision situation which is characterized by political, economic, ecological or other crises,
- a public or strong interest groups which support a major departure from the status quo,
- a strong political leadership which pursues policy changes.

The implementation of EU energy regulations in Great Britain, France and Germany only brought about incremental changes of existing national market structures. Causal factors were the complexity of the regulatory problems with ensuing information and resource constraints on political and regulatory authorities as well as existing political power structures and power relations which benefited the main actors on the energy markets.

In Great Britain, incremental changes of national energy regulations sufficed to implement EU regulations, since the latter followed the British model.

In France and Germany, however, full implementation of EU energy regulations would have required a partial breach with existing regulatory cultures. The conditions for non-incremental changes of this sort were not met in these countries:

- there were no major political or economic crisis demanding non-incremental changes of energy markets.
- The public was, by and large, disinterested in the liberalization project, or several powerful interest groups opposed it.
- National political leadership only half-heartedly supported the reforms.

In sum, the deficits in the implementation of EU energy regulations were pre-programmed in France and Germany.

Market Deficiencies

The European Commission (2007a, 2009b, 2010) has frequently maintained that implementation shortcomings of EU energy legislation are the main causes for deficient market results like high market concentration, too high energy prices, and unsatisfactory competition.

However, there are no systematic empirical studies on the implementation of EU and national energy regulations restructuring the internal electricity and gas markets. The evidence on the relationship between implementation shortcomings and market deficiencies is only anecdotal.

At least in theory, the main causes for dissatisfactory market results could also stem from conceptual shortcomings of the regulatory model pursued by the EU. Even in Great Britain doubts are rising whether the neo-classic regulatory approach delivers the desired results. Some experts claim that British end consumers have been suffering from increasing energy prices in recent years (Harker and Waddams 2007, Wright 2007 and Waddams 2009).

Stephen Littlechild (2009 a and b), the architect of the British reform model (Bartle 2003), deplores the fact that price-cap regulations have led to over-regulation and enormous bureaucratic burdens, and, therefore, calls for replacing the present regulatory approach with negotiated settlements.

Other experts (Pollitt 2008) criticize that network regulations have prompted utilities to delay necessary infrastructure investments, and impaired the quality of British transmission and distribution networks.

In light of these concerns, Ofgem (2009: no. 13, 14) has launched a critical review of the present regulatory reform model.

While the final verdict on the adequacy of the EU (and British) regulatory model is not yet in, it can be said that the European Commission's (2010: 2) claim that the third legislative package makes the opening of energy markets effective, "in the interest of achieving the lowest possible energy prices, better energy security and sustainability" is empirically and theoretically arguable. Therefore, this essay will close with an alternative perspective on energy regulation.

A Collaborative Governance Perspective on Energy Regulation

Implementation Constraints on Command and Control Regulation

EU energy regulations fall, by and large[60], into the category of command and control regulations (Koch 2008: 1). This type of regulation is designed to make regulatees comply with the rules through commands and prohibitions which are backed by coercion, inspections, and sanctions. Command and control regulations have traditionally been and still are the most frequently used government instruments to achieve the objectives of public policies. However, these regulations suffer from three inherent weaknesses[61]:

- information asymmetries disadvantaging regulatory authorities,
- limited resources for controls,
- limited power to impose sanctions.

Issuing and implementing commands and prohibitions usually require detailed information on the given problem situation, possible solutions, and on the characteristics of the regulatees (Majone 1996: 9). In technically and economically complex problem situations regulatory authorities, by and large, lack sufficient information. These information lie with the regulatees. Since it is them and not the regulator who are operating energy networks, import gas, or supply customers with electricity, regulatees are familiar with cost structures, technological innovation, or development of markets, whereas regulatory authorities do not have this knowledge. The information asymmetries disadvantaging regulatory authorities are further increased by legal (constitutional) information requirements derived, for instance, from the principles of calculability, consistency, or proportionality which have to be met by regulatory decisions in order to survive judicial controls.

Even if all necessary information is available, regulations will only be complied with if the relevant activities of regulatees are subject to effective inspections and supervision by the competent authorities. In case of deficient controls, non-compliance cannot be punished. Consequently, regulations will be ignored.

Inspections and other control activities in complex sectors like energy markets are generally very resource-intensive in terms of personnel, funds, technical equipment, and time. In the past, the German Federal Network Agency, for instance, did not have sufficient personnel and time resources to fully control all relevant cost parameters when approving the network access fees of utilities (Monolpolkommission 2007: no 370).

Finally, economically powerful actors like large utilities and industry associations tend to have the political power to prevent or alleviate regulatory decisions and enforcement actions which would severely impair their economic interests.

In sum, the main problem of the implementation of command and control regulations is for national regulatory authorities to cope with information asymmetries (Coglianese, Zeckhauser and Parson 2004). These asymmetries do not only often prevent necessary regulatory decisions. They can also increase the detailedness and complexity of regulatory decisions in an attempt to find adequate case-specific solutions where technical and economic issues are often poorly understood, and where regulatory decisions, therefore, have an experimental character (Eberlein 2010: 65). The elusiveness of "the right solutions ... in the face of imperfect knowledge and uncertainty about the future" (Littlechild 2009a: 3) has been considered a major factor for the quantitative expansion of British energy regulations. The implementation constraints following from information asymmetries are aggravated by the regulatory authorities' scarce resources and (factual) limitations on the power to impose sanctions.

Collaborative Governance – Smart Regulations

Collaborative governance is a normative model of collective decision making (Freeman 1997: 21). The model has been proposed in general (Donahue and Zeckhauser 2006: 496, 506 and 511 f), and for the energy sector in particular (Koch 2008) to cope with the constraints of traditional command and control regulations. President Obama announced in a memo of 21 January 2009 on "Transparency and Open Government" that "Government should be collaborative".[62]

There is no generally accepted definition of collaborative governance. However, there are three basic elements of collaborative governance which can be found in almost all definitions of the concept (Freeman 1997: 22; Donahue and Zeckhauser 2006: 496; Thomson and Perry 2006: 23; Ansell and Gash 2008: 544; Bauer 2010):

- collaboration of public authorities and private actors in making or implementing public policies,
- shared discretion, and
- transparent decision processes.

Collaboration involves all private stakeholders (Freeman 1997: 22, Ansell/Gash 2008: 546).

Shared discretion means that public authorities and private stakeholders act consensus-oriented, and have some leeway in making their decisions. Shared discretion distinguishes collaborative governance from mere consultation processes (Ansell and Gash 2208: 544) on the one hand, and, on the other hand, from interactions between public authorities and private actors which are unilaterally dominated by one party (Donahue and Zeckhauser 2006: 509 f).

Transparent decision processes will usually require a certain degree of formalization; however, informal relationships are not excluded from collaborative governance (Donahue and Zeckhauser 2006: 509).[63]

The concept of collaborative governance resembles the state paradigm of the ensuring state. Both concepts are based on the notion of shared responsibility between government and citizens. However, the concept of collaborative governance emphasizes the requirements of transparency and participation of all stakeholders in the interactions between government and private actors while the German ensuring state has traditionally been characterized by a certain degree of corporatism of large societal groups.

The theoretical power of the concept of collaborative governance is limited to descriptive and normative functions; its explanatory power is questionable.[64] However, the concept of collaborative governance may help reconcile the divergent regulatory cultures of the enabling, providing, and ensuring state by forging a mix of regulatory instruments which is rooted in these state paradigms but enables regulators to move intelligently between different regulatory modes according to circumstance. This approach has been dubbed "the smart regulatory state" (Moran 2003: 24).

A "smart" set of regulatory instruments combines the regulatory modes of

- command and control,
- negotiation and self-regulation, and
- public controls.

The notion of shared responsibility between government and citizens underlying the concepts of collaborative governance and the ensuring state does not exclude command and control regulations. Even when sharing responsibility the government ultimately remains responsible for protecting the common good. This may require unilateral command and control decisions by public authorities when consensus with stakeholders cannot be reached (Ansell and Gash 2008: 546). Thus, command and control regulations are compatible with the concept of collaborative governance and the paradigms of the enabling, providing and ensuring state. In comparison to the paradigms of the enabling and providing state, the concepts of collaborative governance and the ensuring state add the requirement to seek consensus with stakeholders and to check options of collaboration or self-regulation before issuing command and control regulations. In Germany, the "Joint Rules of Procedure of the Federal Ministries" of 1 December 2006[65] have incorporated this requirement in the rulemaking process.

Instruments of collaborative governance are designed to overcome or mitigate the implementation constraints of command and control regulations caused by information deficits and asymmetries, lack of resources for controls, and limited power to impose sanctions. The basic form of collaboration are formal and/or informal negotiations between public authorities and private actors like regulatees, recipients of public services and other stakeholders. Negotiations are a way for public authorities to create incentives for private actors to disclose information needed by the authorities. Incentives include (Coglianese, Zeckhauser and Parson 2004: 35 ff, 49 ff)

- providing regulatees and other stakeholders with the opportunity to influence government decisions and to have their specific interests taking into account (e.g. by forestalling more stringent or costly regulations),
- offering reduced administrative burdens concerning monitoring and reporting obligations, enforcement scrutiny etc. in exchange for needed information and compliance with regulations,
- rewarding the disclosure of information and regulatory compliance with public recognition and positive publicity.

Informal negotiations are particularly well suited to provide regulatees and stakeholders with incentives which help mitigate implementations constraints (Coglianese, Zeckhauser and Parson 2004: 63 ff, 75 ff). This is because informal interactions allow private actors to provide information without being publicly exposed. The negative side of this is the intransparency of informal interactions and the risks of making decisions at the expense of stakeholders who are excluded from the interactions.

Consequently, the concept of collaborative governance seeks to strike a balance between the requirements of confidentiality and publicness of formal and informal negotiations. This means that basic "rules of the game" for informal interactions must be established concerning transparency and stakeholder participation. Violating these rules will generate negative publicity for authorities and private actors involved. However, industries and other private organizations fear negative publicity and tend to avoid it. Therefore, a certain degree of public controls must be built into a regulatory approach of collaborative governance.

The European Commission (2007b: 12) stressed in its communication of 20 November 2007 on "A Simple Market for the 21st Century Europe" its commitment "to using a 'smarter' mix of tools-instruments that are simple and take subsidiarity, proportionality and different national traditions fully into account" in carrying forward the single market. The Commission (2007b: 4) promised that "more attention will be paid to implementation and enforcement; further strengthening impact assessments and consultation of stakeholders; simplifying existing legislation where possible, cutting unnecessary red tape; and subjecting policies and laws to systematic evaluation."

In stark contrast to these promises, the third legislative package of energy regulations of 2009, in particular the Electricity Directive (2009/72/EC) and the Gas Directive (2009/73/EC) represent a bureaucratic monster of command and control regulations written in a meandering language, full of opaque provisions (for instance, the unbundling provisions), and totally oblivious of the needs of implementation and enforcement. The transposition of these directives into national laws will produce equally monstrous national regulations. This has been the experience with German regulations which transposed the similarly complex previous Electricity and Gas Directives into German law. Students of German energy law expressed the suspicion that the authors of the German regulations "had not always been in possession of full clarity about what and with which consequences they were regulating" (Britz 2006: 95).[66]

Consequences for Energy Regulation

A US scholar, Charles Koch (2008: 1, 18, 20) has characterized EU energy regulations and the third legislative package as "federalized command and control regulations". He observes that the US experience with restructuring energy markets suggests "that the EU is trying to 'do it the hard way'", while the US is trying to escape 'the command and control box' by moving to an organizational model of 'collaborative governance' known as the ISO/RTO[67] model.

The US ISO/RTO Model

This model is based on the notion of regulated self-regulation. An ISO/RTO is a non-profit organization which independently operates the grids of different utilities in a given region. The utilities are members of the ISO/RTO and transfer control of their transmission facilities to the ISO/RTO. This is comparable to legal unbundling (Koch 2008: 6) but ownership unbundling can be voluntarily established.[68] Other members of the ISO/RTO include private and public stakeholders, e.g. industries, consumers, other public authorities (Koch 2008: 9). There is no prescribed organizational form for ISO/RTOs.[69] A possible governance structure of ISO/RTOs could consist of a "Board of Managers", a Members Committee, various specialized committees and a Market Monitoring Unit guarding against the abuse of market power by any market member (Koch 2008: 11). ISO/RTOs engage in self-regulation by various members under the supervision of the competent regulatory authorities which must also approve of the establishment of ISO/RTOs.[70] In the US, some 67 %, and in Canada over 50 % of electricity customers are served by ISO/RTOs (Koch 2008: 8).

The key differences between ISO/RTOs and EU-type ISO/ITOs regulated in the 2009 Electricity and Gas Directives are the absence of profit motives, and the requirements of transparency and participation of all stakeholders in the ISO/RTO governance structure (Koch 2008: 7, 9). The ISO/RTO model is no panacea for all ills of the energy markets. Cost and effectiveness problems have been attributed to its non-profit and participatory features (APPA 2004, Kwoka 2008: 193). However, the collaborative design of the model is considered to be better suited for alleviating the negative effects of information asymmetries and lack of controls and sanctions than the adversarial approach of command and control regulations (Koch 2008: 9 f). Thus, the EU is advised to abandon its confrontational restructuring approach and replace it with a collaborative regulatory model (Koch 2008: 20 f).

Starting Points for Collaborative Governance in EU Energy Markets

A "smart" set of regulatory instruments following the concept of collaborative governance is based on the notion of shared responsibility between government and citizens, and combines command and control regulations, negotiations and self-regulation and transparent and participatory structures and procedures. Given the differences in European regulatory cultures, there is no uniform European-wide solution for the right mix of instruments. National solutions have to be developed, while EU regulations must be modified, where necessary, to allow for national collaborative solutions. In many instances, however, a (re-)interpretation of EU regulations in the spirit of collaborative governance is likely to suffice to accommodate the implementation of "smart" regulatory instruments.

In Great Britain, Ofgem has launched a critical review of the present regulatory system. Even its former architect (Littlechild 2009a and b) and other students of British energy regulations propose a new regulatory strategy which can be subsumed under the concept of collaborative governance. They call for replacing or complementing command and control regulations with negotiated settlements between utilities, consumer organizations, and other stakeholders in areas like network investments (Doucet and Littlechild 2006: 275 f and 2009: 22 ff; Pollitt 2008: 80), price controls and other issues (Littlechild 2008: 34). These agreements have to be approved by the regulatory authority which will apply command and control instruments in the event that a settlement is not reached. These proposals are expected to mitigate the problems of information asymmetries and to reduce over-regulations generated by the existing regulatory system (Littlechild 2009a: 9, 43).

In Germany, the notion of collaborative governance has some affinity to the consensus-oriented, corporatist regulatory culture of the country. Central to the implementation of the first Electricity and Gas Directives of the 1990s were association agreements of the electricity and gas industries which set rules, standards and methods for network operation, access, and fees. However, these agreements were legally non-binding, and the negotiation processes were intransparent and did not include all stakeholders. These agreements were replaced by detailed command and control regulations of the Federal Energy Management Act 2005 which implemented the second Electricity and Gas Directives of 2003. But the Act also provides for legally binding agreements of cooperation between the operators of gas networks designed to foster competition.[71]

However, a regulatory approach of collaborative governance would require additional steps. In the (unlikely) event that the owners of the electricity and/or gas transmission networks agree on establishing a national grid company, it would be reasonable to create a non-profit organization which includes all stakeholders. Given the large number of utilities in Germany, the model of a non-profit organization could also be used to alleviate the information and resource problems of the regulatory authorities.[72] To this end, the regulatory competencies of controlling grid access, fees and unbundling could be legally bestowed upon a non-profit organization[73] which includes stakeholders, and operates under the legal supervision of the Federal Network Agency. This private non-profit organization would have easier access to necessary information held by utilities and public authorities. Stakeholder participation and the supervision by the Federal Network Agency would minimize the risks for the non-profit organization to be captured by industries. Furthermore, independent private "energy verifiers"[74] could assist the new regulatory body in controlling network operators and utilities. This would considerably increase the control resources of the regulatory body, while, at the same time, private energy verifiers are likely to be more trusted by utilities than government inspectors.

In France, the introduction of transparent and participatory collaborative structures and procedures is probably more difficult than in Great Britain and Germany given the dirigiste tradition of the French providing state. However, the country is likely to be forced by the European Court of Justice to change its legally questionable tariff structure. This could provide an opportunity to introduce stakeholder participation and more transparent decision making processes of the state-owned EDF and GDF Suez.

"Smart" energy regulations of collaborative governance will probably not bring about market competition as prescribed in text books of energy economics. However, one can expect better market results than today which will be achieved at considerably lower regulatory costs than under existing command and control regulations.

Endnotes:

[1] The term "collaborative management" is often used synonymously with "collaborative governance" (see Bingham/ O'Leary/Carlson 2008: 3f). The latter term is preferred here, because it implies structural and procedural components of collaboration, and avoids the possible misunderstanding that collaboration is only an activity.

[2] Directive 96/92/EC of the European Parliament and of the Council of 19 December 1996 concerning common rules for the internal market in electricity; Directive 98/30/EC of the European Parliament and of the Council of 22 June 1998 concerning common rules for the internal market in natural gas

[3] Directive 2003/54/EC of the European Parliament and of the Council of 26 June 2003 concerning common rules for the internal market in electricity and repealing Directive 96/92/EC; Directive 2003/55/EC of the European Parliament and of the Council of 26 June 2003 concerning common rules for the internal market in natural gas and repealing Directive 98/30/EC

[4] Regulation (EC) No 1228/2003 of the European Parliament and of the Council of 26 June 2003 on conditions for access to the networks for cross-border exchanges in electricity

[5] Regulation (EC) No 1775/2005 of the European Parliament and of the Council of 28 September 2005 on conditions for access to the natural gas transmission networks

[6] Directive 2009/72/EC of the European Parliament and of the Council of 13 July 2009 concerning common rules for the internal market in electricity and repealing Directive 2003/54/EC; Directive 2009/73/EC of the European Parliament and of the Council of 13 July 2009 concerning common rules for the internal market in natural gas and repealing Directive 2003/55/EC

[7] Regulation (EC) No 713/2009 of the European Parliament and of the Council of 13 July 2009 establishing an Agency for the Cooperation of Energy Regulators; Regulation (EC) No 714/2009 of the European Parliament and of the Council of 13 July 2009 on conditions for access to the network for cross-border exchanges in electricity and repealing Regulation (EC) No 1228/2003; Regulation (EC) No 715/2009 of the European Parliament and of the Council of 13 July 2009 on conditions for access to the natural gas transmission networks and repealing Regulation (EC) No 1775/2005

[8] See the overviews of the 3rd legislative package by Lane 2009 and Gundel/ Germelmann 2009

[9] Art. 9 (1) of 2009/72/EC and 2009/73/EC

[10] Pursuant to Art. 13 of 2009/72/EC and Art. 14 of 2009/73/EC the ISO model enables vertically integrated utilities to retain the ownership of their transmission networks if they transfer the technical and commercial operation of the transmission networks to a separate body, called ISO, to be designated by member states and complying, inter alia, with the rules of independence as outlined in the scheme of ownership unbundling.

[11] Pursuant to Art. 17 of 2009/72/EC and 2009/73/EC the ITO model also allows vertically integrated utilities to retain ownership of their transmission networks if they transfer the technical and commercial operation of their transmission networks to a separate body, called ITO, to be designated by member states and complying, inter alia, with a set of special organizational provisions like the establishment of a supervisory board, and with detailed procedural rules ensuring its independence from the vertically integrated utility.

[12] Pursuant to Art. 9 (9) of 2009/72/EC and 2009/73/EC vertically integrated utilities can retain ownership of their transmission networks if national arrangements are in place which guarantee more effective independence of the transmission system operator than the ITO model.

[13] Art. 26 of 2009/72/EC and 2009/73/EC

[14] Art. 32 of 2009/72/EC and 2009/73/EC

[15] Art. 13 (2) lit. c, (4) and Art. 22 of 2009/72/EC; Art. 14 (2) lit. c, (4) and Art. 22 of 2009/73/EC

[16] Art. 35, 37 of 2009/72/EC and Art. 39, 41 of 2009/73/EC

[17] Art. 4 of Reg. 714/2009 and Reg. 715/2009

[18] Art. 1, 6-9 of Reg. 713/2009

[19] See Littlechild 1983 who is considered the architect of the UK model, and the contributions in Bartle 2003

[20] Office of Gas and Electricity Markets

[21] Some authors use the term “market capitalism” for the model, see Schmidt 2000: 39.

[22] For the history of the energy industries, see Green 2010: chapt.7, and Dow 2007: n. 15.144 (gas), no. 15.208 (electricity).

[23] For a list of British electricity and gas suppliers, see UK Power at <http://ukpower.co.uk/home_energy/suppliers>

[24] See British Energy at http://www.british-energy.com/

[25] See DECC, Regulation of GB energy markets at <http://www.decc.gov.uk/en/content/cms/what_we_do/uk_supply/markets/regulation/regulation.aspx>

[26] See Ofgem, The Gas and Electricity Markets Authority at <http://www.ofgem.gov.uk/About%20us/Authority/Pages/TheAuthority.aspx>

[27] See DECC, fn. 25

[28] s. 7 (3) and 7A (3) of the Gas Act 1986

[29] s. 6 (2) of the Electricity Act 1989

[30] s. 7B (4) and 8 (3) of the Gas Act 1986, s. 7 (1) and 8A (2) of the Electricity Act 1989

[31] s. 23 (6) of the Gas Act 1986, s. 11 (1A) of the Electricity Act 1989

[32] s. 26 (1) and 26A of the Gas Act 1986, s. 14 (1) of the Electricity Act

[33] s. 4 AA

[34] s. 3A

[35] Related concepts are the "état-providence" (Wikipedia at http://wikipedia.org/wiki/%C3%89tat-providence) and the welfare state which both focus on social aspects (e.g. social security) while the concept of providing state depicts an active mode rather than substantive policies of government.

[36] In the German debate the term "active state" (aktiver Staat) is used rather than providing state, see Jann/ Wegrich 2004: 195 ff.

[37] Some authors use the term "state capitalism" for the model, see Schmidt 2000: 41

[38] See the overview of the electricity and gas industries by the European Commission 2007: 62-69

[39] Loi no. 2004-803 du 9 août 2004 relative au service public de l'électricité et du gaz et aux entreprises électriques et gazières

[40] The figures are taken from table 8 in CRE 2008: 82

[41] See CRE, fn. 40

[42] See European Commission, France – Internal market fact sheet at <http://ec.europa.eu/energy/energy_policy/doc/factsheets/market/market_fr_en.pdf>

[43] See the overview by Lauriol 2007: no. 8.241 f., and Loi no. 2000-108 du 10 février 2000 relative à la modernisation et au développement du service public de l'électricité, Loi no. 2003-8 du 3 janvier 2003 relative aux marchés du gaz et de l'électricité et au service public de l'energie, Loi no. 2004-803 (fn. 39).

[44] The German term for these guarantees is "Gewährleistungsverantwortung".

[45] See Communication from the Commission, Services of general interest in Europe [Leistungen der Daseinsvorsorge in Europa], OJ C17/4 of 19 January 2001.

[46] Thatcher's (2007a: 150) term "industry model of coordination" is too narrow because labour unions and other societal groups have a great influence on market coordination, too.

[47] In 2007, there were about 700 gas companies and 900 electricity companies, see Schiffer 2009: 173, 210.

[48] See Tennet at <http://tennet.org/english/tennet/organisation/holding/index.aspx.>

[49] See Der Spiegel online of 12 March 2010: Vattenfall verkauft Stromnetz an Elia; see Elia at <http://elia.be/repository/pages/5013a27370d5347ad801a6b5cc3abd634.aspx>.

[50] For a geographic overview of gas networks see BDEW at <http://www.gasnetzkarte.de/index.html>.

[51] RWE plans to sell its transmission gas network owned by Thyssengas in fall of 2010; see:Dow Jones Deutschland of 23 March 2010 "Update: RWE verkauft Gasnetz später – Gasunie bietet nicht" at <http://www.finanzen.net/nachricht/aktien/UPDATE-RWE-verkauft-Gasnetz-spaeter-Gasunie-bietet-nicht-761516>

[52] Examples are: Dong Energy - Denmark, Statoil Deutschland - Norway, Gasunie Deutschland - Netherlands, GRTgaz Deutschland - France, Eni Gastransport - Italy.

[53] s. 61 of the Energiewirtschaftsgesetz (Federal Energy Management Act).

[54] s. 54 (2) of the Federal Energy Management Act. There is an exception to this rule for six smaller Länder, which have delegated the regulatory competencies under the Act to the Federal Network Agency (Franke 2008: 1049, Theobald 2009: 276).

[55] For instance, the European Commission announced in 2007 to "develop a European regulatory culture" as a mid-term objective for the electronic communications sector; see "Overview of the EU regulatory framework for the electronic communications sector" at <http://ec.europa.eu/information_society/policy/ecomm/todays_framework/overview/index_en.htm>.

[56] See also press release of the European Commission of 10 March 2009 at <http://europa.eu/rapid/pressReleasesAction.do?reference=IP/09/376>.

[57] See the Commission's decisions on state aid C17/07 of 13 June 2007 (2007/C164/05), OJ C164/9 of 18 July 2007, and of 10 March 2009 (2009/C96/08), OJ C96/18 of 25 April 2009.

[58] See the Commission's decision of 2009 (fn. 57), OJ C96/19/31f of 25 April 2009.

[59] The frequently used "misfit concept" (Knill 2001, Falkner et al. 2005) for explaining implementation deficits lacks operationalized criteria for determining misfits between national and EU structures and institutions, and does not explain why "misfits" cause implementation deficits. For a critique of this concept see Bohne 2006: 539 f.

[60] The 3rd EU legislative package contains a few collaborative elements. Art. 4 of Reg. 714/2009 and Reg. 715/2009 provide for the creation of two European Networks of Transmission Systems Operators (ENTSO) for electricity and gas through which all transmission system operators shall cooperate at Community level.

[61] See Moran's (2003: 22 f) critique of command law, though his contention is exaggerated that "command law is bound to be mired in failure through a combination of unintended consequences, subversion, circumvention, direct defiance, and the sheer impossibility of fitting general rules into particular circumstances" (ibid. 23). While this kind of criticism has become fashionable in recent years, it ignores the fact that command law ensures social security and stability in a political system.

[62] Federal Register 74, no. 15 of 26 January 2009: 4685

[63] Some authors confine the definition of collaborative governance to formal collaboration (Ansell/Gash 2008: 546). This restriction would render the concept of collaborative governance impracticable, because it excludes large parts of interactions between public authorities and private actors which have an informal character, and are relevant for reaching consensus.

[64] See the critical observations on the governance concept by Frederickson/Smith 2003: 225 f; Offe 2008: 61 ff.

[65] See s. 43(1) no. 3 and annex 7. The "Joint Rules of Procedure" or accessible at <http://www.bmi.bund.de/cln_174/SharedDocs/Downloads/DE/broschueren/EN/Joint_Rules_of_Procedure_of_the_Federal_Id_90695_en.html?nn=441658>

[66] Translation by the author

[67] ISO stands for "Independent Systems Operator" which is a non-profit organization and, therefore, "almost the exact opposite" from the EU ISO in the third legislative package (Koch 2008: 7).

RTO means "Regional Transmission Organization" and is a regional ISO (Koch, ibid.).

[68] See Federal Energy Regulatory Commission (FERC), Order No. 2000 of 20 December 1999, introduction, p. 6

[69] For the core characteristics and functions of the ISO/RTO model see Vince et al. 2006: 71 ff.

[70] See FERC, Order No. 2000 (fn. 67), p. 7

[71] s. 20 (1b) of the Federal Energy Management Act

[72] The following proposal is modeled on the implementation of the "Eco-Management and Auditing Scheme" (EMAS), Regulation (EC) No. 1221/2009 of 25 November 2009, through the German Environmental Auditing Act (Umweltauditgesetz).

[73] The German legal term for this concept is "Beleihung".

[74] Verifiers are licensed or accredited persons or organizations which carry out verification and validation within the meaning of Art. 2 no. 20 of Regulation (EC) No. 1221/2009. The concept could be applied analogously to control activities in the energy sector.

References:

Anechiarico, F. (1998). Administrative culture and civil society. A comparative perspective, Administration and Society 30, 1: 13-34.

Ansell, Ch. and Gash A. (2008). Collaborative Governance in Theory and Practice, Journal of Public Administration Research and Theory, 18: 543-571.

American Public Power Association (APPA) (2004). Restructuring at the crossroads. FERC electricity policy reconsidered, Washington, December 2004 at http://www.APPAnet.org.

Bartle, I. (ed.) (2003). The UK model of utility regulation, CRI proceedings 31, The University of Bath.

Bauby, P. and Varone F. (2007). Europeanization of the French electricity policy: four paradoxes, Journal of European Public Policy: 14: 1048-1060.

Bauer, Ch. (2010). "Collaborative Governance" – Ein neues Konzept für die Regulierung der europäischen Strom- und Gasmärkte?, FÖV Discussion Papers 56.

Bell, St. and McGillivray D. (2008). Environmental law, 7th ed., Oxford: Oxford University Press.

Bingham, L. Blomgreen, O'Leary R. and Carlson Ch. (2008). Frameshifting: Lateral thinking for collaborative public management, in: Bingham, L. Blomgreen, O'Leary, R. (eds.), Big ideas in collaborative public management, Armonk, N.Y.: M.E. Sharpe: 3-16.

Bohne, E. (2002). Muddling-through im Umweltrecht, in: Bohne, E. (ed.), Perspektiven für ein Umweltbesetzbuch, Berlin: Duncker & Humblot: 113-195.

Bohne, E. (2006). The quest for environmental regulatory integration in the European Union, Alphen aan den Rijn: Kluwer Law International.

Braybrooke, D. and Lindblom Ch. E. (1970). A strategy of decision, New York: The Free Press.

Bremen, J. (2005). The United Kingdom, in: Cameron, Peter D. (ed.), Legal aspects of EU energy regulation, Oxford: Oxford University Press: 345-372 (no. 15.01 ff).

Britz, G. (2006). "Selbstregulative Zusammenarbeit" und "Moderierende Regulierung" im EnWG Energienetz, CNER 2006, 91-96.

Brunekreeft, G. (2003). Regulation and competition policy in the electricity market, Baden-Baden: Nomos.

Bulmer, S., Dolowitz D., Humphreys P. and Padgett St. (2007). Policy transfer in European Union governance. Regulating the utilities, London: Routledge.

Bundeskartellamt (2009). Sektoruntersuchung Kapazitätssituation in den deutschen Gasfernleitungsnetzen, Dezember 2009.

Bundesnetzagentur (2010). Jahresbericht 2009, Redaktionsschluss 23.2.2010.

Coen, D. (2005). Business-regulatory relations: Learning to play regulatory games in European utility markets, Governance, 18: 375-398.

Coglianese, G., Zeckhauser R. and Parson E. A. (2004). Seeking truth for power: Informational strategy and regulatory policy making, University of Pennsylvania Law School, paper 111 at <http://lsr.nellco.org/upenn/wps/papers/111>

Cole, A. (1999). The service public under stress, West European Politics 22: 166-184.

Commission de Régulation de L'Enérgie (CRE) (2008). Report sent to DG Tren, July 2008 <http://www.energy-regulators.eu/portal/page/

portal/EER_HOME/EER_PUBLICATIONS/NATIONAL_REPORTS/National%20reporting%202008/NR_En/E08_NR_France-EN.pdf>

Crouch, C. (2007). Neoinstitutionalism: still no intellectual hegemony?, Regulation and Governance 1: 261-270.

Donahue, J. D. and Zeckhauser R. J. (2006). Public-private collaboration, in: Moran, M., Rein, M. and Goodin, R. E. (eds.), The Oxford handbook of public policy, Oxford: Oxford University Press: 496-525.

Dow, St. (2007). Energy law in the United Kingdom, in: Roggenkamp, M., Redgwell, C., del Guayo I. and Rønne, A. (eds.), Energy law in Europe, 2nd ed., Oxford: Oxford University Press: 1169-1261 (no. 15.01 ff).

Dyson, K. (1992). Regulatory culture and regulatory change: Some conclusions, in: Dyson, K. (ed.), The politics of German regulation, Dartmouth: Aldershot: 257-271.

Eberlein, B. (2010). Experimentalist governance in the European energy sector, in: Sabel, Ch. F. and Zeitlin, J. (eds.), Experimentalist governance in the European Union, Oxford: Oxford University Press: 61-77.

European Commission (2001). European Governance. A white paper, 25 July 2001, COM (2001): 428 final.

European Commission (2007a). Implementation Report, SEC (2006) 1709, 10 January 2007.

European Commission (2007b). A single market for 21st century Europe, communication of 20 November 2007, COM (2007): 724 final.

European Commission (2009a). Third strategic review of Better Regulation in the European Union, communication of 28 January 2009, COM (2009): 15 final.

European Commission (2009b). Report on Progress in creating the internal gas and electricity market, 11 March 2009, COM (2009): 115 final.

European Commission (2010). Report on progress in creating the internal gas and electricity market, communication of 11 March 2010, COM (2010): 84 final.

Federal Network Agency for Electricity, Gas, Telecommunications, Post and Railway: 2008 report by the Federal Network Agency for Electricity, Gas, Telecommunications, Post and Railway to the

European Commission on the German electricity and gas market at http://www.energy-regulators.eu/portal/page/portal/EER_HOME/EER_PUBLICATIONS/NATIONAL_REPORTS/National%20reporting%202008/NR_En/E08_NR_Germany-EN_Summary.pdf

Falkner, G., Treib O., Hartlapp M. and Leiber S. (2005). Complying with Europe, Cambridge: Cambridge University Press.

Fisch, S. (2008). Mechanisms creating a European administrative culture, in Beck, J. and Thedieck F. (eds.), The European dimension of administrative culture, Baden-Baden: Nomos, 23-30.

Franke, P. (2008). Energieregulierungsbehörden und behördliche Verfahren, in: Schneider, J.-P. and Theobald Ch. (eds.). Recht der Energiewirtschaft. Praxishandbuch, München: C.H. Beck: 1047-1093.

Frederickson, H. G. and Smith K. B. (2003). The public administration theory primer, Boulder, Col.: Westview Press.

Freeman, J. (1997). Collaborative governance in the administrative state UCLA Law Review 45, 1: 1-98.

Furubotn, E. G. and Richter L. (2005). Institutions and economic theory: the contribution of the new institutional economics, 2nd ed., Ann Arbor: University of Michigan Press.

Giddens, A. (2003): Introduction. Neoprogressivism. A new agenda for social democracy, in: Giddens, A. (ed.), The progressive manifesto, Cambridge. Polity Press, 1-34.

Green, R. (2010). Energy regulation in Great Britain: Lessons learned for collaborative governance, in: Bohne, E. and Karlsson, Ch. (eds.), Repositioning Europe and America for growth: The role of governments and private actors in key policy areas, Münster: LIT Verlag, chapter 7.

Gundel, J. and Germelmann C. F. (2009). Kein Schlussstein für die Liberalisierung der Energiemärkte: Das Dritte Binnenmarktpaket, EuZW 2009: 763-770.

Harker, M. and Waddams C. (2007). Introducing competition and deregulating the British domestic energy markets: A legal and economic discussion, Journal of Business Law (May 2007): 244-268.

Hayes, M. T. (2001). The limits of policy change: Incrementalism, world view, and the rule of law, Washington D.C.: Georgetown University Press.

Hayes, M. T. (2006). Incrementalism and public policy, Lanham, Md.: University Press of America.

Hill, C. J. and Lynn L. E. (2009). Public Management: A three-dimensional approach. Washington, D.C.: CQ Press.

HM Government. Policy Review. Building on progress: the role of the state, May 2007. http://archive.cabinetoffice.gov.uk/policy_review/documents/role_%20of_the_state_final.pdf

Jann, W. and Wegrich K. (2004). Governance und Verwaltungspolitik, in: Benz, Arthur (ed.),Governance – Regieren in komplexen Regelsystemen, Wiesbaden: VS Verlag: 193-214.

Joskow, P. L. (2008). Lessons learned from electricity market liberalization, The Energy Journal, special issue; The future of electricity: Papers in honour of David Newberry: 9-42.

Kerandren, P. (1996). In search of culture: Lessons from the past to find a role for the study of administrative culture, Governance 9,1: 71-98.

Knill, Ch. (2001). The Europeanization of national administrations, Cambridge: Cambridge University Press.

Koch, Ch. (2008). Collaborative governance: Lessons for Europe from US electricity restructuring, William and Mary Law School, Research paper no. 08-03: 1-36 at <http://ssr.com/abstract=1147160>

Kwoka, J. (2008): Restructuring the U.S. Electric Power Sector: A Review of Recent Studies, Review of Industrial Organization, 32: 165-196.

Lane, R. (2009). Energy third package published in the EU Official Journal. http://www.allbusiness.com/print/12736461-1-22eeq.html

Lauriol, T. (2007). Energy law in France, in: Roggenkamp, M., Redgwell, C., del Guayo, I. and Rønne, A. (eds.), Energy law in Europe, 2nd ed., Oxford: Oxford University Press: 529-621 (no. 8.01 ff.).

Littlechild, St. C. (1983). Regulation of British telecommunications' profitability, Report to the Secretary of State, February 1983, London: Department of Industry.

Littlechild, St. C. (2009a). Regulation, over-regulation and deregulation, Centre for the Study of Regulated Industries, University of Bath, School of Management, Occasional Lecture 22, January 2009 at <http://www.Ofgem.gov.uk/Networks/rpix20/forum/Documents1/4.pdf>

Littlechild, St. C. (2009b). RPI-X regulation: Ofgem's RPI-X@20 review and the scope for more customer involvement, Network, issue 34, December 2009 at http://www.ofgem.gov.uk/Networks/rpix20/forum/saap/Documents1/nework.pdf

Majone, G. (1996). Regulating Europe, London: Routledge.

Meidinger, E. (1987): Regulatory Culture: A theoretical outline, Law and Policy, 9, 4: 355-386.

Monopolkommission: Strom und Gas 2007. Wettbewerbsdefizite und zögerliche Regulierung, Baden-Baden.

Moran, M. (2003).The British regulatory state, Oxford: Oxford University Press.

National Grid Company (2008). Fiscal year 2007-2008 corporate responsibility summary report, at <http://www.nationalgrid.com/corporate/Our+responsibility/Publication+and+Speeches>

Newbery, D. (2006). The relationship between regulation and competition policy for network industries, March 2006, CWPE 0631 and EPRG 0611, at <http://www.eprg.group.cam.ac.uk/category/publications/working-paper-series/2006>

Newbery, D. (2009). Refining market design, in: Glachant, J.M. and Lévêque, F. (eds.), Electricity reform in Europe, Cheltenham: Edward Elgar: 35-64.

Offe, C. (2008). "Empty signifier" oder sozialwissenschaftliches Forschungsprogramm?, in: Schuppert, G. F. and Zürn, M. (eds.), Governance in einer sich wandelnden Welt, Politische Vierteljahresschrift, Sonderheft 41: 61-76.

Office of Fair Trading (OFT) (2009). Flexibility for changing markets. Annual report and resource accounts 2008-09 <http://www.oft.gov.uk/about/>

Ofgem (2008). Ofgem 2008 National Report to the European Commission, 31 July 2008, <http://www.energy-regulators.eu/portal/page/portal/EER_HOME/EER_PUBLICATIONS/NATIONAL_REPORTS/National%20reporting%202008/NR_En/OfgemNationalReport2008%20-%20FINAL%20V2.pdf>

Ofgem (2009). Ofgem 2009 National Report to the European Commission, 31 July 2009 at <http://www.ofgem.gov.uk/Europe/Pages/Europe.aspx>

Oster, J. (2009). Normative Ermächtigungen im Regulierungsrecht, Baden-Baden: Nomos

Parker, D. (1999). Regulating public utilities: lessons from the UK experience, International Review of Administrative Sciences, 65: 117-131.

Pollitt, M. (2008). The future of electricity (and gas) regulation in a low-carbon policy world, The Energy Journal, 29, 2: 63-94.

Ronellenfitsch, M. (2009). Daseinsvorsorge und service d'intérêt général im Interventionsstaat in: Magiera S. and Sommermann K.P. (eds.), Daseinsvorsorge und Infrastrukturgewährleistung, Berlin: Duncker & Humblot: 27-63.

Schiffer, H.-W. (2008). Energiemarkt Deutschland, 10th ed., Köln: TÜV Media.

Schmidt, V. (2000). Still three models of capitalism? The dynamics of economic adjustment in Britain, Germany, and France, in: Czada, R. and Lütz S. (eds.), Die politische Konstitution von Märkten, Wiesbaden: Westdeutscher Verlag: 38-72.

Schuppert, G. F. (2003): The ensuring state, in Anthony Giddens (ed.), The progressive manifesto, Cambridge: Polity Press: 54-72.

Sieckmann, J.-R. (1999). Zum verfassungsrechtlichen Eigentumsschutz im deutschen und britischen Recht, Baden-Baden: Nomos.

Simmonds, G. (2002). Regulation of the UK electricity industry, 2002 edition, CRI industry brief, The University of Bath.

Spanjer, A. R. (2009). Regulatory intervention on the dynamic European gas markets – neoclassical economics or transaction cost economics?, Energy Policy 37: 3250-3258.

Spreng, Nicole 2005. Netzzugang im deutschen und britischen Gasmarkt, München: C.H. Beck

Thatcher, M. (2007a). Reforming national regulatory institutions: the EU and cross-national variety in European network industries, in Hancké, B., Rhodes M. and Thatcher M. (eds.), Beyond varieties of capitalism, Oxford: Oxford University Press, 147-172.

Thatcher, M. (2007b). Regulatory agencies, the state and markets: a Franco-British comparison, Journal of European Public Policy, 14: 1028-1047.

Theobald, Ch. (2009). The transformation of German energy regulation: Struggling with policy legacy, in: Eberlein, B. and Doern G. B. (eds.), Governing the energy challenge. Canada and Germany in a multi-level regional and global context, Toronto: University of Toronto Press, 259-28.

Thomson, A. M. and Perry J. L. (2006). Collaborative processes: Inside the black box, Public Administration Review 66, special issue: 20-32.

Vince, C. A.; Quirk S. A.; Wolf St. P; Smith T. R.; Barbulescu S. and Berry M. (2006): What is happening and where in the world of RTOs and ISOs?, Energy Law Journal, 27: 65-145.

Vogel, D. (1986). National styles of regulation, Ithaca: Cornell University Press.

Weintraub, E. R. (2002). Neoclassical economics, in Henderson, D. A. (ed.), Concise encyclopedia of economics, 1st ed. at econlib <http://www.econlib.org/library/Enc1/NeoclassicalEconomics.html>

Wirtschaftsausschuss des Bundesrats: Empfehlung der Ausschüsse, 836. Sitzung des Bundesrates am 21. September 2007, Verordnung zum Erlass und zur Änderung von Rechtsvorschriften auf dem Gebiet der Energieregulierung, Bundesratsdrucksache 417/1/07.

Wright, P. (2007). Competition in gas and electricity: Companies profit, consumers pay, Consumer Policy Review, Vol. 17: 2-11.

Young, A. R. (2010). The European policy process in comparative perspective, in: Wallace, H., Pollack M. A. and Young A. R. (eds.), Policy-making in the European Union, 6th ed., Oxford: Oxford University Press: 45-68.

8

Liberalization of Energy Markets in the EU: Comments and Conclusions on Hierarchical versus Collaborative Governance

Sylvia Veit (discussant)

In accordance with the blossoming of neo-liberalism and ideas of a minimal or "lean" state in the Western world, in the 1980s and 1990s energy policy in the EU was dominated by a strong belief in market forces. In practice, the notion that liberalization and deregulation are two sides of the same coin, turned out to be wrong. Because of their dependence on transmission grids and distribution network services, energy markets show in part characteristics of natural monopolies. Therefore, and due to technical constraints (electricity can not be stored), liberalization efforts in the energy sector did not lead to less regulation but (to the contrary) to new governance demands and new regulations (re-regulation).

In his chapter on the liberalization of energy markets in the EU in this volume, Eberhard Bohne argues that in the EU the former uncritical belief in market forces has now been replaced by an equally uncritical belief in command and control regulation (CaC). The "third package" of EU energy regulation from 2009 calls for stronger and more intrusive Regulatory Agencies in the Member States and a larger role for a European Agency for the Cooperation of Energy Regulators.

Bohne states that the recent EU energy regulations are to a great extent modeled on the British example.

Energy liberalization in Britain is characterized by regulatory governance through a licence system and the existence of a strong independent regulatory authority (see Richard Green in this volume). All in all, the British liberalization process is considered as a success (Ilie et al. 2006) compared to other European Union member states, e.g. Germany and France. Both countries are considered to be laggards of the European liberalization process.

Despite the apparent advantages of the well-functioning of British CaC-regulation in energy liberalization, as Bohne argues, a transfer of the British role model to the whole EU is destined to fail because it does not account for the specific characteristics of different regulatory cultures in EU member states. Empirical studies in policy analysis have shown that the efficiency of CaC-regulation relies on administrative control capacities and capabilities as well as on the deterrence effects of sanctions. In this context, information asymmetries between regulator and the regulated industries are a crucial factor. Since perfect control and an optimal definition of sanctions are unrealistic assumptions, compliance with CaC-regulations very much depends on the social acceptance of rules, or more generally on the compatibility of formal rules and the rule-making processes within a country's regulatory culture.

To improve implementation of energy policy goals in the whole EU, a strengthening of CaC-regulation is highly risky. Inherent deficits (e.g. inflexibility with regard to different regulatory cultures) have to be compensated by more regulation, more bureaucracy and more control. Regulatory costs are high, efficiency is uncertain. According to Bohne, the existing implementation and enforcement deficits of energy policy in the EU as well as the high regulatory costs in countries like Germany or France could be diminished by fostering collaborative governance arrangements instead of CaC-regulation.

Collaborative governance is defined as "a governing arrangement where one or more public agencies directly engage non-state stakeholders in a collective decision making process that is formal, consensus oriented, and deliberative and that aims to make or implement public policy or manage public programmes or assets." (Ansell and

Gash 2007). Collaborative governance arrangements usually are set up for long-term duration (Donahue and Zeckhauser 2006).

Collaborative governance shows similarities to the concepts of "cooperative administration" (Benz 1994) and "network governance" (see e.g. Mayntz and Marin 1991), even if "cooperative administration" mostly refers to the implementation of regulations and to ad-hoc cooperation processes between public authorities and the regulated parties in order to improve implementation while the importance of policy networks has been proved for all stages of the policy cycle (problem definition, agenda setting, policy formulation, implementation, policy evaluation and termination).

All three concepts have in common that public and private actors cooperate "at eye level" (Benz 1994) or at least only "in the shadow of hierarchy" (Scharpf 1994) and that the arrangements are designed to meet specific shared concerns or challenges common to the collaborating parties. Contrary to "cooperative administration" and "network governance", collaborative governance emphasizes broad participation, inclusion of all stakeholders and transparency to assure public regarding performance (Koch 2009).

Collaborative governance can therefore be interpreted as an attempt to formalize and re-structure informal policy networks in policy formulation (e.g. the strong internal networks of private and state-owned utilities and their associations in Germany) and implementation (e.g. the creation of a more democratic mode of "cooperative administration"). This formalization process involves the chance to strengthen transparency and democratic legitimacy.

Collaborative governance approaches could improve the outcome of EU energy policy for the following reasons:

- Performance of collaborative governance schemes is less dependent on national regulatory cultures than CaC-regulation.
- Collaborative governance fosters reliance on expert decision making and is an adequate solution for problems resulting from information asymmetries between regulator and the addressees of regulation.
- Collaborative governance fosters stakeholder participation in decision making processes.
- Collaborative governance fosters legitimacy of policy measures.

- Collaborative governance diminishes implementation deficits and increases compliance.
- Collaborative governance causes lower regulatory costs than CaC-regulation.

Koch (2009) argues that the US model of electricity restructuring could serve as a model for the European Union. In the US, energy policy was dominated by CaC-regulation until the middle of the 1990s. Then, a strategic shift prevailed which was reflected by a new order, the so-called "open access regulation" from 1996. Subsequently, the Federal Energy Regulatory Commission (FERC) abandoned reform strategies based on CaC-regulation. The industry was charged with the task of working out a policy solution for the goals of unbundling (of generation, transmission and distribution/supply activities) and open access (to transmission grids).

Finally, the US industry advocated the so-called ISO/RTO solution which was also the preferred policy option for FERC. ISOs (independent systems operators) are non-profit organizations, who manage bulk transmission. RTOs are regional transmission organizations. They preside over a spatial area according to maximum efficient physical and economic organization and not according to state borders. ISO/RTOs, who today represent two thirds of electricity costumers in the US and more than half the customers in Canada, are typical collaborative governance arrangements which are characterized by decentralized decision making structures and an integration of all stakeholders, including consumers and various governments (Koch 2009, see also Eberhard Bohne in this volume).

In conclusion, the US example shows that collaborative governance arrangements in the energy sector are feasible to foster evidence-based policy making (see e.g. Sanderson 2006) and a good compliance. They optimize sectoral policy outputs ("better decisions") from a technical, professional point of view. But there are some risks, too:

- The optimization of sectoral policy solutions can lead to a stronger neglect of so-called "negative external effects" (unintended negative effects in other sub-systems of society or other policy sectors).

- It can also lead to a decrease in democratic participation when you look at the society as a whole and not only at a single policy subsystem like energy policy.
- Formalized and institutionalized policy networks as the ISO/RTO arrangements in the US can work very efficiently, but they can lead to less democratic control and to less "arguing" in terms of competing policy goals.

In general, division of labour and specialization are crucial elements of modern and complex societies. Sectoral collaborative governance arrangements can be seen as an adaptation of decision making processes to the needs of modern states. The challenge is to find a good balance between efficient, sector-specific modes of governance and the needs of the society as a whole. Transparency is therefore essential to avoid possible deficits of collaborative governance arrangements which are less democratic control, sectoral "tunnel vision" and – in the long term – sub-optimal policy solutions for the society as a whole.

References

Ansell, Ch. and Gash A. (2008). Collaborative Governance in Theory and Practice. *Journal of Public Administration Research and Theory*. 18: 543-571.

Benz, A. (1994). Kooperative Verwaltung. Funktionen, Voraussetzungen und Folgen. Baden-Baden: Nomos.

Donahue, J. D. and Zeckhauser R. (2006). Public-Private Collaboration. In: *Oxford Handbook of Public Policy*, edited by Moran M., Rein M. and Goodfin Robert E. Oxford: Oxford University Press: 496.

Ilie, L., Horobet A. and Popescu C. (2007). *Liberalization and Regulation in the EU energy market*. MPRA Paper No. 6419.

Koch, Charles H. Jr. (2009). *Collaborative Governance: Lessons for Europe from US Electricity Restructuring*. William & Mary Law School Research Paper No. 08-03.

Mayntz, R. and Marin B. (1991). Policy Networks: Empirical Evidence and Theoretical Considerations. Frankfurt a. M.: Campus.

Sanderson, I. (2006). Complexity, "practical rationality" and evidence-based policy making. *Policy & Politics*. 34: 115-132.

Scharpf, F. W. (1994). Games real actors could play: positive and negative coordination in embedded negotiations. *Journal of Theoretical Politics*. 6: 27-53.

Policy Framework for Technology and Innovation Through Markets or Regulation

9

The Structure of US R&D Policymaking: An Overview

Kingsley E. Haynes
Haifeng Qian

Overview of US R&D Policy

Research, development and innovation have been recognized as driving forces in long-term economic growth (Romer 1990). Science and technology (S&T) therefore have drawn much attention in the policy arena particularly in developed countries. According to Hill (2006), S&T policy involves both the impact of S&T on policy making (*science for policy* or *technology for policy*) and policy instruments to influence S&T development (*policy for science* or *policy for technology*). The primary focus of this paper is on the structure of US policymaking organized to influence research and development (R&D) activity.

Recognizing the important role of technology in national defense, the US federal government became the primary source for R&D investments after World War I, replacing philanthropists (Smith 1990). The foundation for R&D expansion after World War II and the basis of today's US R&D policy was laid by a 1945 report, *Science, the Endless Frontier* by Vannevar Bush, then the Director of the White House Office of Scientific Research and Development. This report elaborated the importance of scientific research to public health, national security and public welfare, and recommended the federal government support R&D activity. The Bush report led to the establishment of the National Science Foundation (NSF) in 1950. It also rationalized the significant increase in federally funded R&D activity. The federal share of US R&D expenditures grew from 20 % in 1939 to more than 50 % by 1962 (Mowery 1998). Those federal R&D funds focused primarily on defense related technologies and basic research particularly in biomedical sciences.

Federal R&D spending was boosted by the cold war "space race" and the establishment of science-driven mission agencies such as the National Aeronautics and Space Administration (NASA). This spurred the development of civilian technologies (e.g. semiconductors and computers) through defense and basic research "spillovers," leading to the rapid growth of high technology industries in the private sector in the 1960s and 1970s. Later, the enactments of the Bayh-Dole Patent and Trademark Amendments Act of 1980 and the federal Technology Transfer Act of 1986 (amended in 1989) paved the way for commercialization of federally funded research, amplifying the effects of federal R&D spending on private technology advancement in pursuit of economic efficiency. The two Acts echoed the earlier established linear model of innovation (Mowery 1998, see Figure 1).

Figure 1: The Linear Model of Innovation

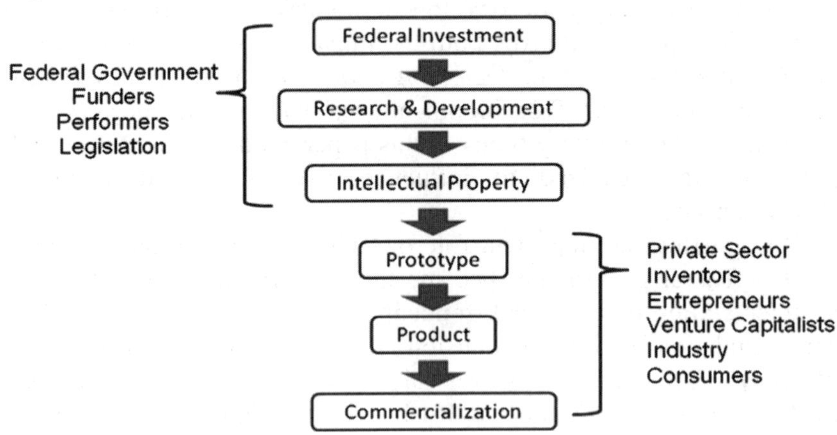

Source: Wang et al. (2003), cited by Stine (2009)

Today, the direct federal share of US R&D spending has been reduced, and there has been a growing concern over the level of federal R&D funding required for meeting societal needs in areas such as health, energy, environment, transportation, IT, agriculture, and homeland security. In 2006, federal government R&D funds reached 94 billion dollars, accounting for 27.7 % of total US R&D expenditure (Figure 2). National defense is still the key area where federal R&D spending flows, followed by health, space research and technology, and general science and basic research (Figure 3). Accordingly, the Department of Defense (DOD) is the largest recipient of federal R&D funds (Figure 4), followed by the Department of Health and Human Services (HHS, administrating the National Institutes of Health), the National Aeronautics and Space Administration (NASA), the Department of Energy (DOE) and the National Science Foundation (NSF). While defense R&D is dominated by development, other support to a large extent involves basic and applied research.[1]

Figure 2: US R&D Expenditures by Source of Funds (2006)

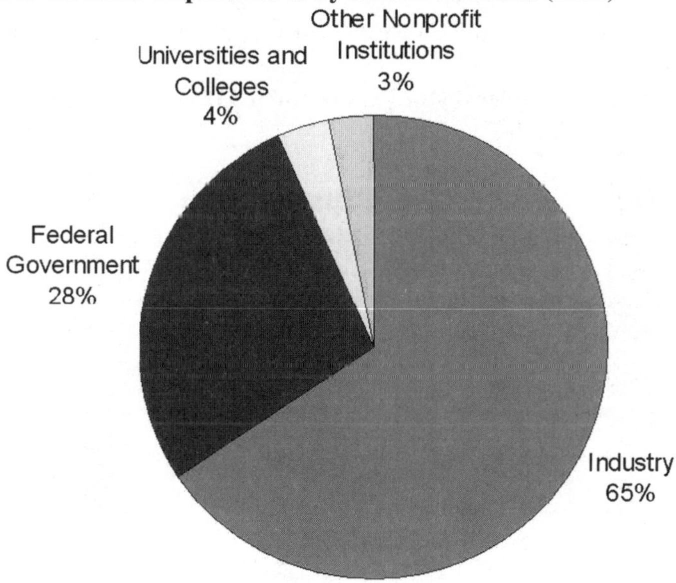

Source: National Science Board (2008)

Figure 3: Federal R&D Budget Authority by Function (2007)

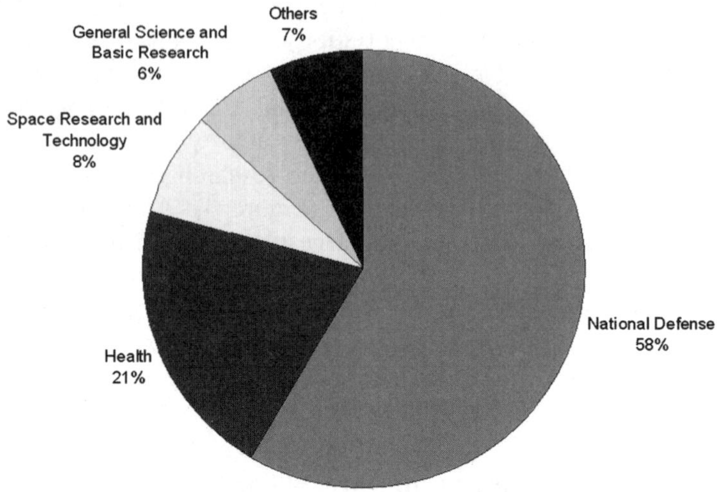

Source: NSF. Available at: http://www.nsf.gov/statistics/nsf08315/pdf/tab1.pdf, accessed March 14, 2009

Figure 4: Projected Federal Obligations for R&D by Agency and Character of Work (2007)

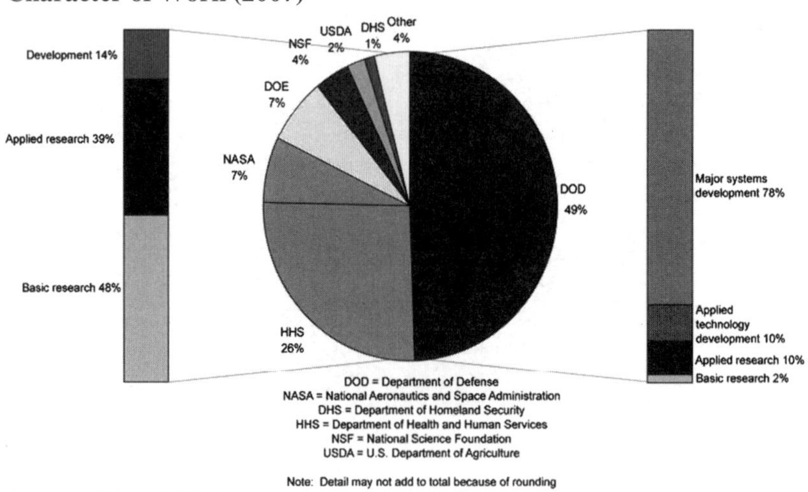

Source: Stine (2009)

This paper presents an overview of the structure of US R&D policymaking. It proceeds as follows. Section 1 briefly introduces the US R&D policy. Section 2 focuses on the federal structure of R&D policymaking, highlighting the roles of Congress, the executive branch and advisory groups. Section 3 features four examples of federal R&D policymaking structure. Section 4 shifts to the state level, exemplified by three influential state R&D initiatives. Section 5 concludes.

Federal Structure of R&D Policymaking

US R&D policymaking at the federal level involves both Congress and the White House. The judicial branch plays a role to a much lesser extent and often indirectly. In administrative terms this policy area has both formal and hierarchical structures blended with cooperation and coordination elements particularly as elements relate to budgetary cross-agency activity as well as extra-governmental inputs. While policymakers are primarily rooted in Congress and the executive branch, their decisions are influenced by advisory groups and institutions either associated with or independent of the federal government.

Congress in R&D Policymaking

In Congress, the power of R&D policymaking and appropriations is dispersed among several committees and subcommittees. The House Committee on Science and Technology and the Senate Committee on Commerce, Science, and Transportation play primary roles in non-defense R&D policymaking in areas such as energy, astronautical and civil aviation, environment, marine research, technology commercialization, development, etc. (Stine 2009). They are not involved in biomedical and defense research policymaking (Table 1). R&D appropriations as Table 1 shows are administrated by different subcommittees under the House and Senate Committees on Appropriations.

Besides those committees and subcommittees, R&D policy related caucuses allow for interactions among Members of Congress who are interested in or related to R&D policy. Examples of such caucuses in the 111th Congress (2009) are the Congressional Research and Development Caucus, the Congressional High Technology Caucus, the Biomedical Research Caucus, and the Congressional House Aerospace Caucus.[2]

Table 1: S&T Policy Decision Making Committees in US Congress

Policy Area	House Committee	Senate Committee
Decision Making:		
Most non-defense research activities	Committee on Science and Technology	Committee on Commerce, Science, and Transportation
Biomedical research	Committee on Energy and Commerce	Committee on Health, Education, Labor, and Pensions
Defense research	Committee on Armed Service	Committee on Armed Services
Appropriations:		
Funding for NSF, NASA, NIST and OSTP	Committee on Appropriations's Subcommittee on Commerce, Justice, Science, and Related Agencies	Committee on Appropriations's Subcommittee on Commerce, Justice, Science, and Related Agencies
Funding for NIH	Committee on Appropriations's Subcommittee on Labor, Health and Human Services	Committee on Appropriations's Subcommittee on Labor, Health and Human Services
Funding for energy research	Committee on Appropriations's Subcommittee on Energy and Water Development	Committee on Appropriations's Subcommittee on Energy and Water Development
Funding for DOD	Committee on Appropriations's Subcommittee on Defense	Committee on Appropriations's Subcommittee on Defense

Source: Compiled Based on Stine (2009)

Executive Branch in R&D Policymaking

Office of Science and Technology Policy

The President's Office of Science and Technology Policy (OSTP) is the central executive organization involved in R&D policymaking. The OSTP was established by Congress in 1976 through the National Science and Technology Policy, Organization, and Priorities Act. Since then, the role of this office has varied across different Administrations, depending on the views of both the President and the OSTP Director who also serves as the President's Science Advisor (Stine 2009). The 1976 Act authorizes the OSTP to be "a source of scientific and technological analysis and judgment for the President with respect to major policies, plans, and programs of the Federal Government."

The OSTP Director also co-chairs the President's Council of Advisors on Science and Technology (PCAST), a federal advisory committee consisting of members from industry, educational or research institutions and NGOs who provide advice to the President in S&T policymaking. In addition, the OSTP Director supports the President's National Science and Technology Council (NSTC), a cabinet-level council that "coordinates science and technology policy across the diverse entities that make up the federal research and development enterprise."[3] Figure 5 presents the latest organizational structure of the OSTP.

National Science and Technology Council

Chaired by the President, the National Science and Technology Council (NSTC) is also responsible for the establishment of national goals for federal science and technology investments. It consists of four committees focusing respectively on Environment and Natural Resources, Homeland and National Security, Science, and Technology. Committee members are officials from various cabinet-level agencies. At the next level, each committee has its own subcommittees (SC), interagency working groups (IWG) or task forces (TF). Committee on Technology as an example is shown in Figure 6. NSTC activities are co-managed by OSTP staff and federal agency staff. The OSTP and the NSTC act as the key coordinative and integrative processes for centralized policy decision making.

Figure 5: Organization of the President's Office of Science and Technology Policy

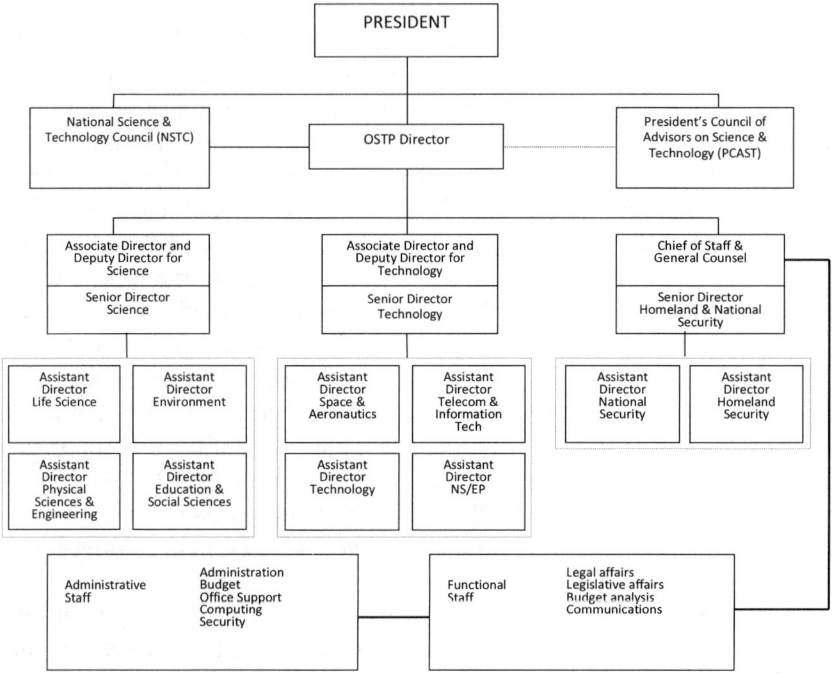

Source: OSTP. Available at: http://www.ostp.gov/galleries/default-file/OSTP %20org%20charts%2010-15- 08.pdf, accessed March, 14 2009

Figure 6: Committees of the National Science and Technology Council

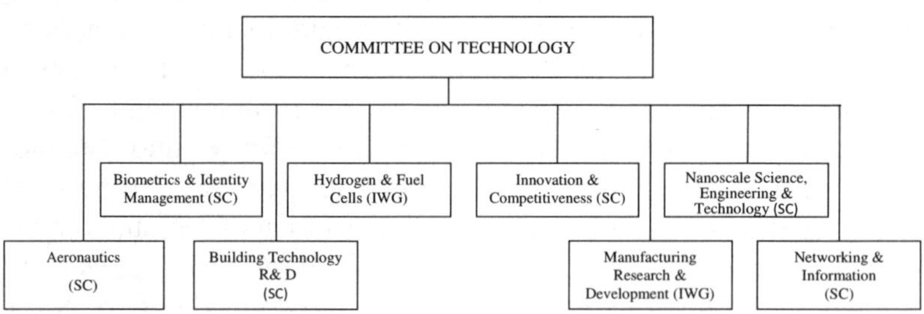

Source: OSTP. Available at:
http://www.ostp.gov/galleries/NSTC/NSTC%20org%20chart%20Portrait%20October.pdf, accessed March 14, 2009

Office of Management and Budget

Besides the OSTP and the NSTC, the President's Office of Management and Budget (OMB) plays a leading role in setting federal R&D budget priorities each year. The OMB works closely with the OSTP and the NSTC so that the proposed R&D budget reflects national priorities. This is a major control and enforcement point in the executive portion of the R&D policy process.

Federal Agencies

R&D policies are implemented through federal agencies, which report to the executive branch via the executive appointed cabinet but are funded through an executive recommended budget that must be legislatively appropriated. Those agencies focusing on conducting or funding research include (Stine 2009):

- National Science Foundation (NSF),
- National Institutes of Health (NIH),
- National Aeronautics and Space Administration (NASA),
- National Institute of Standards and Technology (NIST),
- National Oceanic and Atmospheric Administration (NOAA),
- U.S. Geological Survey (USGS).

Those federal research agencies are generally located within more general departments. For instance, the Department of Health and Human Services (HHS) supervises the NIH. Those departments closely related to R&D policy include (Stine 2009):

- Department of Defense (DOD),
- Department of Energy (DOE),
- Department of Health and Human Services (HHS),
- Department of Agriculture (USDA),
- Department of Homeland Security (DHS),
- Department of Transportation (DOT),
- Department of Veterans Affairs (VA),
- Department of Education (ED),
- Department of Justice (DOJ),
  Department of Interior (DOI),
- Department of Labor (DOL).

Advisory Groups or Institutions in R&D Policymaking

R&D policymaking process is influenced by advice from various groups and institutions. They can be government-associated or independent. According to a recent list by Stine (2009), government-associated advisory groups and institutions include:

- Federal Advisory Committees:
  - *President's Council of Advisors on Science and Technology (PCAST),*
  - *National Science Board (NSB).*
- Congressionally Chartered Honorific Organizations:
  - *National Academy of Sciences (NAS),*
  - *National Academy of Engineering (NAE),*
  - *Institute of Medicine,*
  - *National Academy of Public Administration (NAPA).*
- Federally Funded Research and Development Corporations (FFRDC), such as (38 as of May 2007):
  - *Los Alamos National Laboratory,*
  - *Lincoln Laboratory,*
  - *Oak Ridge National Laboratory,*
  - *Ernest Orlando Lawrence Berkeley National Laboratory.*

Other generic advisory groups and institutions include (Stine 2009):

- International Organizations,
- Think Tanks,
- Public and Individual Opinion Leaders,
- Universities,
- Interest Groups,
- Industry and Trade Associations,
- Labor Associations.

Synthesis

The US R&D policymaking process can be described as in Figure 7. Those in the White House and Congress are the primary policymakers, but their decisions are influenced by advisory groups and institutions. The judiciary branch plays a very limited role in this process through its interpretation of the legal system of rights, responsibility, intellectual property, etc. Figure 7 also suggests that states may influence federal R&D resources allocation, which will be explained later.

Figure 7: US R&D Policymaking

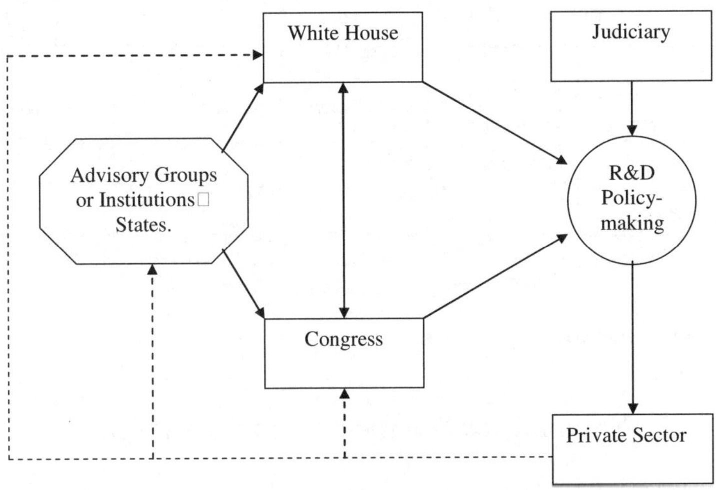

Source: Authors.

We have not discussed the role of the private sector in R&D policymaking. According to the linear model of innovation (Figure 1), federal R&D policy may have a major impact on the private sector which leads the commercialization of federally funded R&D outputs. Without feedback loops, this linear model suggests little influence of the private sector on policymaking. In practice, however, R&D policies at both federal and state levels are greatly affected by the private sector. At the federal level, for example, policy advisory groups are generally composed of leaders in the private sector. Moreover, federally supported scientific research is highly reliant on instruments, machines, tools, and procedures of technology that are produced by the private sector. This is consistent with the non-linear model of innovation (Kline & Rosenberg 1986, see Figure 8). In addition, the private sector may directly influence policymaking in the White House and Congress through industry lobbying groups. At the state level, the public-private relationship is even closer. This will be discussed later. The feedback effect from the private sector has been embedded in Figure 7.

Figure 8: The Non-linear Model of Innovation

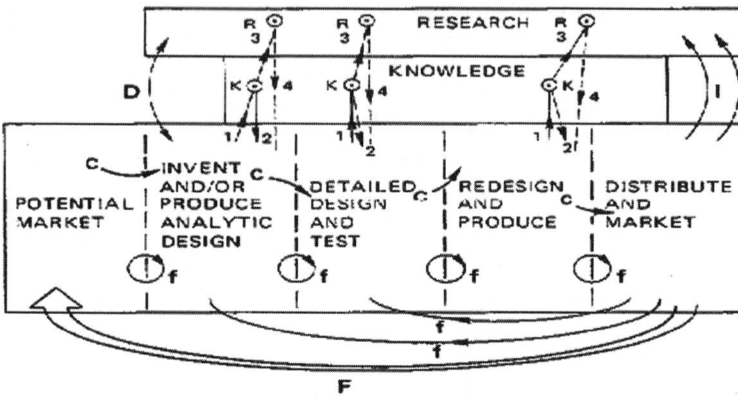

Source: Kline and Rosenberg (1986).

National R&D Policymaking: Examples

There are classic examples of R&D policy activity at the federal or nation level, such as the DOD's Defense Advanced Research Projects Agency program (DARPA), the NASA's remote sensing program and the NIH's infectious disease program including but not limited to the Centers for Disease Control and Prevention (CDC). Specifically these programs represent a combination of hierarchically and centrally directed decision making (e.g. DARPA), and collaborative decision making across units of government and across governments (e.g. infectious disease management) versus between government and the public at large (e.g. popularization of remote sensing by Google).

We have selected four alternative policy examples from the national perspective to give the reader some appreciation of the administrative complexity in the R&D area. It should be noted that each of them demonstrates different emphasis on cross-organizational interaction. The Networking and IT R&D policy case represents a typical

S&T policy example which highlights the role of the NSTC. The nuclear energy case describes how a general cabinet-level agency (the Department of Energy) gets involved in R&D policymaking. The biomedical research case exemplifies the loose but powerful relationships between a research-based federal agency (the National Institutes of Health), and its affiliating cabinet-level agency (the Department of Health and Human Services) as well as its affiliated institutes and centers and the private sector. The Small Business Innovation Research (SBIR) program is among the most successful federal initiatives with state partnerships and focuses on stimulating private sector activity.

Federal Example 1: Networking and IT R&D Policymaking

IT technology is one of the major research areas that the US government supports. The federal government funds networking and IT research primarily through the Networking and Information Technology Research and Development (NITRD) program that was established by the High-Performance Computing Act of 1991.[4] The proposed budget for this program reached $ 3.5 billion in Fiscal Year 2009.5

Figure 9 shows how the NITRD program is administrated in the executive branch. The interagency NITRD program is primarily coordinated by the Subcommittee on NITRD, whose umbrella committee – Committee on Technology – is one of the four committees of the cabinet-level NSTC. Members of Subcommittee on NITRD include representatives from 13 member agencies,[6] the OMB, the OSTP and the National Coordination Office (NCO) for NITRD. The major research areas of the NITRD program, called Program Component Areas (PCAs), are guided by an Interagency Working Group (IWG) or a Coordinating Group (CG) of agency program managers, which coordinates projects within its own area and reports to the Subcommittee. Seven groups (two IWGs and five CGs) plan and manage the NITRD program in eight PCAs: Cyber Security and Information Assurance (CSIA), High Confidence Software and Systems (HCSS), High End Computing Infrastructure and Applications (HEC I&A), High End Computing Research and Development (HEC R&D), Human Computer Interaction and Information Management (HCI&IM), Large

Scale Networking (LSN), Social, Economic, and Workforce Implications of IT and IT Workforce Development (SEW), and Software Design and Productivity (SDP).

Figure 9: Federal Networking and IT R&D Policymaking Structure at the Executive Branch

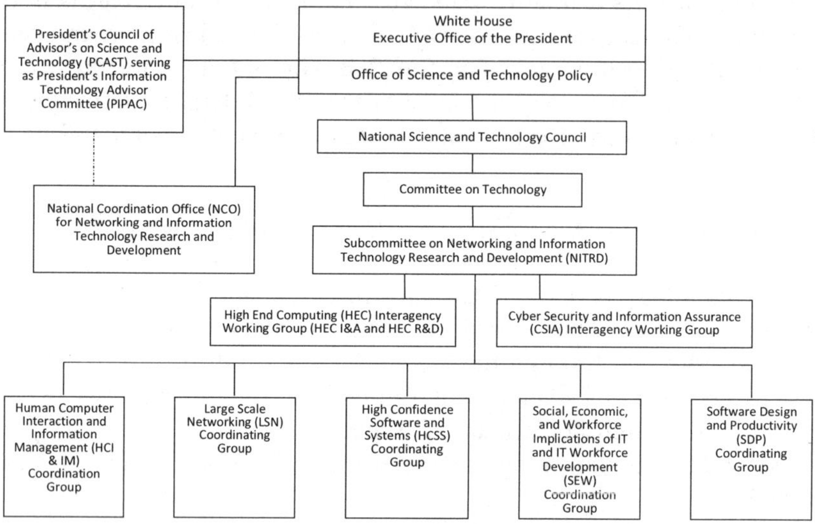

Source: National Coordination Office for NITRD
Available at http://www.nitrd.gov/about/ presentations_nco/2008/documents/McDuffie_Cyber_Security_Collab_031408.pdf, accessed March 28 2009

The President's Council of Advisors on Science and Technology (PCAST) is the key advisory group for networking and IT R&D policymaking. The PCAST consists of the Director of the OSTP and 45 expert members outside the federal government from academia, industry, and NGOs, and provides the President with independent advice on national S&T policies including NITRD policies. NITRD policymaking was originally advised by the President's Information Technology Advisory Committee (PITAC), which was dismissed by Present Bush in 2005 and whose functions were taken over by the PCAST.

The Subcommittee on NITRD and the PCAST are primarily supported by the National Coordination Office for Networking and Information Technology Research and Development (NCO/NITRD), whose Director is appointed by the Director of the OSTP. The NCO works closely with NITRD agencies, IWGs, CGs, the OSTP and the OMB in networking and IT R&D plans and budget issues. It also provides technical support to the PCAST.

Congress also plays a major role in networking and IT R&D policymaking. The House Committee on Science and Technology and the Senate Committee on Commerce, Science, and Transportation are committees in Congress which introduce or pass laws related to the NITRD program. They also oversee and hold hearings on the operation and budgeting of the NITRD program. The budget of the NITRD program must be approved by the House and Senate Committees on Appropriations.

Federal Example 2: Nuclear Energy (Civil) R&D Policymaking

Different from most S&T areas including networking and IT, nuclear energy R&D policymaking is primarily but not solely associated with the Department of Energy (DOE) at the cabinet level and has little to do with the OSTP and the NSTC.

Nuclear energy accounts for 20 % of total US electricity generation through over 100 nuclear plants. Although no new nuclear power plants have been ordered for the past 30 years, US policy programs, such as DOE's Nuclear Power 2010 Program, have been set to develop new nuclear technologies and build new reactors as a result of rising prices of oil and natural gas, sources of international oil dependence, and concerns over carbon dioxide emission. The Office of Nuclear Energy in DOE plays a leading role in national nuclear energy R&D policymaking, initiating nuclear energy R&D programs addressing advanced reactors, fuel cycle technology and facilities, nuclear hydrogen production, and infrastructure support (Holt 2008). For the Fiscal Year 2009, the Office of Nuclear Energy received $ 803 million funding from the Senate Appropriations Committee, supporting nuclear R&D programs such as Nuclear Power 2010, Generation IV Nuclear Energy Systems Initiative, Advanced Fuel Cycle Initiative, Nuclear Hydrogen Initiative, and Integrated University Program. Another nuclear R&D program with a budget of $ 487 million, Mixed Oxide Fuel Fabrication Facility, although proposed by DOE, was placed under the National Nuclear Security Administration's Office of

Defense Nuclear Nonproliferation by the Senate. The organizational structure of the Office of Nuclear Energy in DOE is shown in Figure 10.

Figure 10: Organizational Structure of the Office of Nuclear Energy at DOE

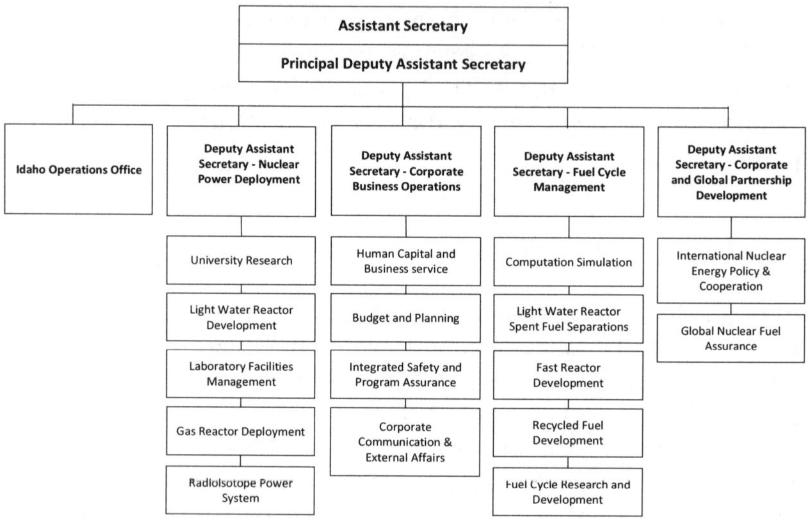

Source: DOE. Available at: http://www.ne.doe.gov/neOrganization2.html, accessed April 4, 2009

Congress determines funding for nuclear energy research based on the budget proposed by DOE. It also influences the organization of nuclear R&D, for instance, by transferring the Mixed Oxide Fuel Fabrication Facility program from DOE to the National Nuclear Security Administration as mentioned above.

National nuclear R&D policymaking is primarily advised by the Nuclear Energy Advisory Committee (NEAC), formerly known as the Nuclear Energy Research Advisory Committee (NEAC) which was established on October 1, 1998. It consists of representatives from universities, industry, foreign nationals, and national laboratories, and offers independent advice to the Office of Nuclear Energy on "complex science and technical issues that arise in the planning, managing, and implementation of the DOE's nuclear energy program."[7] In addition, several federally Funded Research and Development Corporations (FFRDCs) including Idaho National Laboratory (INL), Oak Ridge National Laboratory (ORNL), Los Alamos National Laboratory (LANL), and Brookhaven National Laboratory (BNL) host DOE's research programs and provide additional policy advice.

Federal Example 3: Biomedical Research Policymaking

Biomedical (or health) research constitutes the largest category of US federal nondefense R&D spending. For the Fiscal Year 2009, federal budget for health research reached $ 30.8 billion, accounting for almost 50 % of federal civilian R&D budget and roughly 20 % of the total federal R&D spending. Biomedical research focuses primarily on research rather than development, and represents the most visible federal efforts to advance science.

The National Institutes of Health (NIH), an agency within the Department of Health and Human Services (HHS), is the primary organization associated with federally funded biomedical research. The organizational structure of the NIH is presented in Figure 11. The NIH is composed of the Office of the Director and 27 other components (19 institutes, four research centers, the National Library of Medicine, and three other centers that provide central services). The Director supervises budgets and activities of the 27 components, coordinates cross-institute programs, and sets overall NIH policies. The NIH Director also leads several staff offices directly under the Office of the Director.

Research institutes and centers, which are located in a variety of US states, have different research focuses and run "independently" with a loose relationship with the Office of the Director. Those institutes and centers sponsor two types of research: *extramural research* and *intramural research*. The former category, representing over 80% of the NIH budget, supports biomedical research conducted by nonfederal scientists (generally in universities) through peer-review-based grants and contracts. The latter category supports research performed by NIH scientists. Leaders of those institutes and centers, together with the top NIH management, play a leading role in preparing the NIH budget, which is submitted to the OMB through the HHS.

Figure 11. Organizational Structure of National Institutes of Health at the HHS

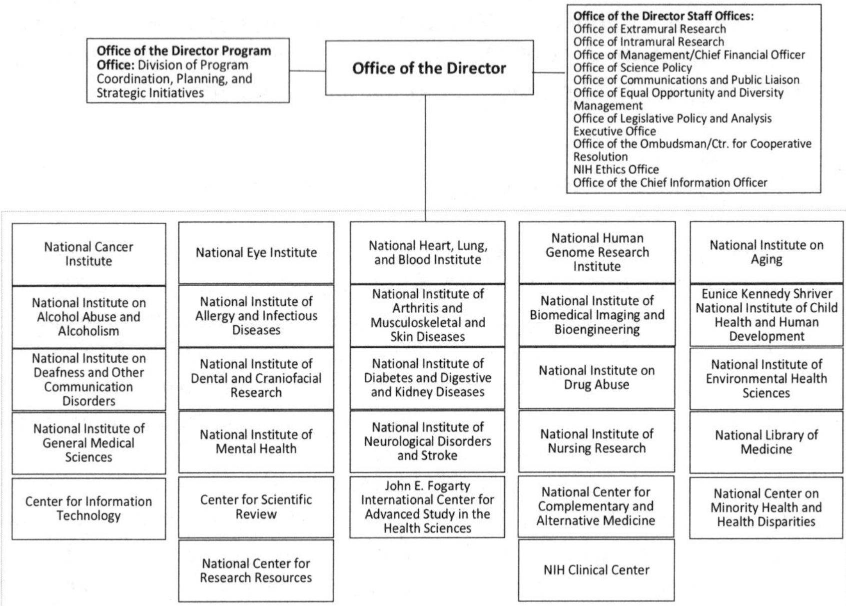

Source: NIH. Available at:
http://www1.od.nih.gov/oma/manualchapters/management/1123/nih.pdf, accessed April 7, 2009

Research funded by the NIH is not necessarily basic research. Among the member centers of the NIH, the National Center for Research Resources (NCRR) manages the General Clinical Research Centers (GCRCs) program which supports clinical research in those centers that are generally affiliated with medical schools. This program by providing a research infrastructure aims at accelerating the pace of developing or transferring basic research into practically useful clinical settings (Haynes et al. 2000).

The House and Senate Committees on Appropriations's Subcommittees on Labor, Health and Human Services are responsible for appropriations for the NIH, which generally draw bi-partisan support (Smith 2006). The NIH Office of the Director, 24 of the 27 components, and buildings and facilities are separately funded. Congress also plays an important role in setting priorities for biomedical research and organizational changes of the NIH through the House Committee on Energy and Commerce and the Senate Committee on Health, Education, Labor, and Pensions.

Policymaking at the NIH is advised by more than 150 federally charted groups or committees that are established by the Office of the Director, institutes or centers. Those advisory groups provide advice on research programs and health policies, and perform peer reviews for the NIH grant applications.

There are close relationships between NIH research, and experimentation and the private sector. A major controversy exists around how to best manage these interactions in order to maintain independence and objective analysis on the one hand and innovation transfer and commercialization on the other hand.

Federal Example 4: Small Business Innovation Research Program (SBIR)

The Small Business Innovation Research (SBIR) program was created by US Congress in 1982 to support research and innovation in small- and medium-sized enterprises (SMEs, less than 500 employees). It was reauthorized in 1992 and 2000. Congress through this program requires 11 federal agencies[8] to allocate at least 2.5 % of their R&D budget to fund SMEs for innovation projects. In 2000, the total budget for the SBIR program was over $ 1 billion, representing 60 % of all public SME finance programs (Audretsch et al. 2002). The SBIR program supports SMEs through three phases. Phase I studies the scientific and technical merit and feasibility of an idea proposed by an SME and the award is limited to $ 100,000 for six months. Phase II is a further development of Phase I and awards those promising Phase I projects with up to $ 750,000 for 2 years. Phase III focuses on commercialization of developed technologies and requires private or non-SBIR federal funding. The SBIR program has fostered entrepreneurial activity (Audretsch et al. 2002) and accelerated growth of awardee firms (Lerner 1999).

Participating federal agencies run the SBIR program individually. Each agency is responsible for selecting SBIR topics, releasing SBIR solicitations, evaluating SBIR proposals, and awarding SBIR funding agreements on a competitive basis.[9] The Small Business Administration (SBA) through its Office of Technology coordinates program activity, monitors program implementation, and reports program progress to Congress.

There has been a growing state level involvement in the SBIR program. Government agencies, quasi-government corporations, economic development entities or technology centers at the state or local level play important roles not only in helping SMEs compete for federal SBIR contracts but also in helping awardees to succeed. The 2000 congressional SBIR reauthorization featured the establishment of the Federal and State Technology Partnership (FAST) program. The states according to this program can receive SBA grants which are used to offer an array of services to support the SBIR program, for instance, covering the costs of SMEs to develop a SBIR proposal.

Discussion of Federal Examples

The NITRD program highlights an integrative structure of coordinative governance and hierarchical governance. On the one hand, the Subcommittee on NITRD is a collaborative entity whose members are from different federal agencies. Such a composition guarantees a relatively fair allocation of federal R&D for networking and IT among those agencies involved in such activity. On the other hand, the Subcommittee on NITRD supervises two IWGs and five CGs and must report to its umbrella Committee on Technology which further reports to the President and the OSTP through the cabinet-level NSTC. This vertical structure reflects hierarchical governance that is intended to enhance policymaking efficiency. The NITRD program represents a typical R&D policymaking process. Most S&T areas are associated with the NSTC and share similar policy structures.

The nuclear energy R&D activity represents a different type of governance structure from the NITRD program. Compared with the latter, the research portion of civil nuclear energy development is primarily concentrated within one government agency (DOE) rather than a committee with a joint representation. Policymaking in such a structure is more hierarchical than collaborative. It is however characterized by at least two collaborative elements. First, like all other R&D

policymaking cases, the advisory group has a wide representation from industry and academia, among others. Second, despite the leading role of DOE, US nuclear energy policy as a whole (part of which is R&D related) is simultaneously influenced by several government agencies. Sometimes the roles of those agencies are overlapping, bringing challenges to efficient policymaking. Those agencies which work collaboratively in this area include (Stine 2009):

- Nuclear Regulatory Commission – Safety and design,
- Federal Power Commission – Rate bases and authority,
- Occupational Safety & Health Administration – Worker safety,
- Environmental Protection Agency – Environmental impact studies,
- Department of Energy – Nuclear power research and development,
- Federal Emergency Management Agency – Nuclear power plant emergency,
- Department of Homeland Security, Federal Bureau of Investigation, Federal Aviation Administration, U.S. Coast Guard, and others – Nuclear power plant security,
- Department of Transportation – Shipment of radioactive materials.

Biomedical research policymaking organizationally features a loose relationship between the key federal policy agency (the NIH) and its umbrella cabinet-level agency (the HHS) as well as a loose relationship between the NIH Director and its member institutes and centers. As a basic research area, scientists and researchers play an important role in the policymaking process.

Different from the three aforementioned federal R&D initiatives, the SBIR program addresses conversion of R&D into business usage and new products rather than R&D itself, and recognizes SMEs as the best transfer vehicle. The private sector thus gets highly involved in this program. Structurally, although the SBA Office of Technology is responsible for the SBIR program, allocation of the SBIR budget is primarily performed by each individual participating agency but not the SBA, representing decentralization of R&D and innovation policy. The SBIR program also differs from other R&D policies with high level state participation. It is initiated by the federal government but can be best described as a federal state partnership.

State R&D Policymaking

The US system of government is characterized by federalism that addresses decentralization and the role of state governments in policymaking. Public support for R&D has been traditionally considered as national policy. Recently, there has been a growing state level concern over the role of R&D in building regional competitive advantages. More and more state initiatives are created to support R&D activity particularly in those sectors that underpin the state economy or state competitiveness. State governments however have different views on science and technology from the federal government. While the federal government recognizes the importance of basic research to national defense, public health, and competitiveness of the US in the long run, state governments focus primarily on regional economic development and local advantages. Compared with relatively independent R&D policy at the federal level, state level science and technology policy has not been "an autonomous dimension" (Rees & Bradley 1988) and this has not changed. Science and technology are considered as instruments for economic development by state governments. As a result, it is hard to distinguish high technology programs from general economic development efforts. For economic development purposes, state policies favor technology over science and development over research. When R&D activity at the state level is mostly funded by the federal budget, state governments have considerable interests in commercializing the fruits of such R&D as a way to facilitate local economic development.

Rees and Bradley (1988) categorize state high-technology development programs into three groups: those encouraging university-industry relationships, those encouraging startup businesses, and those encouraging the upgrading of a state's existing technology base (by establishing industrial extension-services and other types of technology-transfer mechanisms). Schmandt and Wilson (1988) establish a program/policy typology of science and technology initiatives based on cases in eight US states[10] (See Table 2). One aspect deserving attention in this table is the state funding for science and engineering education. State governments play an important role in both supporting basic and applied research albeit with strong federal direction and in generating the highly trained, high caliber research work force. The latter is realized primarily by funding state university, college and community college systems.

Table 2: Policy and Program Clusters in State Science and Technology Initiatives

Program clusters	Policy clusters			
	R&D	Entrepreneurship	Attracting high-tech firms	Development of human resources
Technology transfers between universities and industries	X	X		
Science and engineering education				X
Financial incen-tives for business	X	X	X	X
Job training		X	X	X
Direct funding of university research	X			

Source: Schmandt and Wilson (1988)

The increasingly important role of science and technology has pushed state governments forward in forming S&T advisors or S&T advisory boards (Berglund and Clark 2000). It has also led to many state S&T initiatives. This section examines the structure of R&D policymaking at the state level through the selective lens of some important state S&T initiatives. The previous section has introduced the SBIR program, a typical federal initiative with state support. These three examples in this section are typical state initiatives which also draw on federal resources.

State Example 1: Oklahoma Center for the Advancement of Science and Technology

The Oklahoma Center for the Advancement of Science and Technology (OCAST), legislatively established in 1987, has obtained national recognition in boosting economic development through S&T research, development and commercialization. It is the only state agency in Oklahoma that focuses exclusively on R&D-based economic development programs. The OCAST programs, as shown in Figure 12, support researchers, innovators, as well as entrepreneurs using state appropriations. The OCAST works closely with its partners including the Oklahoma Department of Commerce, i2E Inc.(a not-for-profit Oklahoma corporation assisting technology entrepreneurs), Oklahoma Manufacturing Alliance, Oklahoma State University and the private sector, advancing technologies in advanced materials, agriculture, aviation/aerospace, bioscience (human, animal & plant), energy and energy-related, IT and telecommunications, sensors and sensor-related, weather, and nanotechnology. By the Fiscal Year 2007, the $ 151.8 million state budget for the OCAST had resulted in the additional $ 2.6 billion in private and federal funding.

The OCAST is governed by the Oklahoma Science and Technology Research and Development Board, which consists of 21 members including the executive director of the Oklahoma Department of Commerce, the chancellor of the Oklahoma State Regents for Higher Education, the secretary of agriculture, the presidents of both the University of Oklahoma and Oklahoma State University, the president of a private university, the president of a regional university, 12 members appointed by the governor (with the consent of the senate), and two nonvoting legislators appointed by the leader of each house.[11] Daily management is performed by the Executive Director and program directors.

Several committees provide guidelines and advice to the OCAST, such as the Oklahoma Applied Research Advisory Committee, the Oklahoma Health Research Committee, the Oklahoma Nanotechnology Applications Project Advisory Committee, the Oklahoma Plant Science Research Advisory Committee, the Seed Capital Investment Committee, and the Small Business Research Assistance Committee. Members of those committees have a comprehensive representation, including experts of different disciplines from industry, academia, and NGOs.

Figure 12: The Model of the OCAST

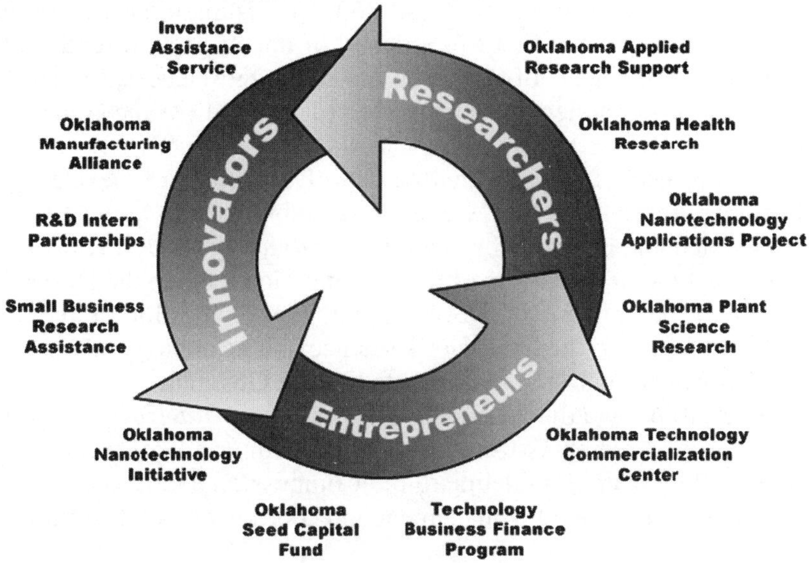

Source: OCAST. Available at http://www.ok.gov/ocast/Programs/index.html, accessed April 14 2009

State Example 2: Ohio Third Frontier Project

Ohio is among those states that address technology and innovation explicitly as one of the primary sources of economic development. Its impressive $ 6 billion R&D industry renders Ohio third in R&D testing nationwide.[12] The Ohio Governor's Office of Development has proposed many initiatives that facilitate technology development and commercialization, such as Technology Investment Tax Credit, Ohio Venture Capital Authority, and Edison Technology Incubator Program. The most aggressive one however is the *Ohio Third Frontier* project, which was initiated in 2002 and featured a 10-year $ 1.6 billion state R&D investment. The whole project was expected to attract federal and private money as well and eventually give rise to total

R&D investment of $ 6 billion. The purposes of this project are to "build world-class research capacity," "support early stage capital formation and the development of new products," and "finance advanced manufacturing technologies to help existing industries become more productive."[13] The 18 programs[14] of this project currently offers support in S&T areas of advanced materials, biosciences, information technology, instruments, controls, electronics, and advanced manufacturing.

This project is managed by the Ohio Department of Development. Funds appropriated by the General Assembly for this project are administrated and allocated through the legislatively created *Third Frontier Commission*. Members of this Commission include the Director of the Ohio Department of Development, the Chancellor of the Ohio Board of Regents, the Governor's science and technology advisor, and six regional commissioners appointed by the Governor.

The project is advised by the *Third Frontier Advisory Board* that consists of 16 members from industry, academia and government. The Board offers overall guideline to the Commission and advises on strategic planning, general management and coordination of programs.

State Example 3: Georgia Research Alliance

The Georgia Research Alliance initiative (GRA, created in 1990) represents more than 80 % of Georgia's state budget for technology-based economic development (Bozeman 2000). By the Fiscal Year 2005, the GRA had received $ 450 million in state appropriations, which had spurred $ 2 billion in private and federal investments. Compared with the OCAST and the Third Frontier project, the GRA has put university research at the center of technological and economic development. It features three programs: GRA Eminent Scholars which has attracted world-class scholars to lead research in Georgia universities, Centers of Research Excellence which has supported two dozen research centers in Georgia universities, and Commercialization (basically through the VentureLab program) which has brought commercially viable research produced in Georgia universities into the market. The GRA programs primarily address biomedical research. In 2007, the GRA launched the Next-Generation Vaccines and

Therapeutics Initiative, which was intended to position Georgia as a world leader in discovering new vaccines and therapeutics. Additional research areas include telecommunications, environment and energy.

The GRA is primarily a three-sector partnership between Georgia's six research universities,[15] the business community and the state government. Although its programs are funded by the state budget (part of the budget of the Office of the Governor and approved by the Georgia Legislature), the GRA is not a government agency but "a private, independent, nonprofit corporation governed by a Board of Trustees made up of prominent Georgia business and academic leaders."[16] The operational costs of the GRA are covered by private foundations or industry. Daily issues are managed by a President, the CEO, and the staff team.

Discussion of State Examples

The three examples discussed above represent different patterns of state level R&D policy, although all of them rely on state appropriations. The OCAST features a government agency that focuses exclusively on R&D related economic development policies, presenting deep and sustainable government involvements in R&D activity. The Ohio Third Frontier project also manifests itself in a large role of government, while the Ohio Department of Development leads the Third Frontier Commission. The project however is a temporary program that lasts for 10 years. The GRA by contrast operates with much lesser government intervention as a private, independent, nonprofit corporation, but is intended as a long-time project. The comparison of these three examples is presented in Table 3. The success of all these three projects suggests that there is no uniform model for state level R&D policy.

In addition, another R&D initiative organizationally similar to the GRA (both are three-sector partnerships and not-for-profit organizations) is the well known Triangle Research Park (RTP) in the state of North Carolina. While the GRA addresses state funding for research, the RTP emphasizes private research with public support in networking and infrastructure. This further demonstrates diversity of state R&D initiatives in the US.

Table 3: Different Patterns of State R&D Policy

		Sustainability	
		Long	**Short**
Government Involvement	High	OCAST	Ohio Third Frontier
	Low	GRA	N.A.

Source: Authors

The three examples are used to present R&D policymaking at the state level. They complement many programs based in economically large states such as California and New York, but they are more typical among US state level R&D initiatives. They provide different views into state strategic and administrative processes in initiating their own R&D policy in lesser complex contexts. Although already partially successful, it remains to be seen how they will develop in hard economic times and what their long term success will be in impacting national R&D issues and strategic trajectories.

Summary and Discussion

This paper provides an overview of the structure of the US R&D policymaking at both federal and state levels. The federal government and state governments have different views on the functions of R&D, which leads to differences in both policy orientation and policymaking structure at these two levels. The federal government recognizes the role of science and technology in long-term US competitiveness and the importance of R&D to national defense, public health, energy, and transportation, among others. Federal R&D policy is an independent policy dimension and involves institutionalized government agencies that are exclusively structured for the promotion of R&D activity (e.g. the OSTP and the NSTC). While a large proportion of the federal R&D budget is science-based, industry in many cases plays a relatively limited role in R&D policymaking compared with government and academia.

State governments, on the other hand, are more concerned with economic development than R&D itself. R&D policy presents no independence at the state level and is always associated with economic policy. In other words, state policymakers consider science and technology as a tool for economic development. As a result, the leading agency responsible for R&D-related policies in a state government is generally the economic development department (such as the Ohio Department of Development). Giving their concerns over economic impacts of R&D, it is not uncommon for state governments to place at least equal emphasis on commercialization to development of new technologies. Industry therefore can greatly influence R&D policymaking. The innovation system at the state level, particularly for the three examples we have discussed, can be best described as the Triple Helix Model of university-industry-government relations proposed by Etzkowitz and Leydesdorff (2000), in which those three parties interact with each other in the policymaking process. Even though, state R&D initiatives exhibit diversity in terms of government involvement as well as program sustainability. The states never deviate from their focus on commercialization and development as opposed to knowledge generation. However, in the science and technology labor force generation, state governments play a critical – often underappreciated – role through their state higher education systems (Haynes and Stough 1985, 1988; Bowen et al. 1990).

Federal state collaborations in R&D policy are commonly seen in the US. Due to different concerns over R&D, the federal government and state governments have complimentary policy focuses. While the federal government allocates its research money to different states (universities as primary recipients), the state government exhibits tremendous interests in local commercialization of those federally funded research. Among centrally funded agencies, congressional federalism drives state based distributive concerns in expenditures. It results in a natural tension between the highest quality R&D often concentrated in a few states and distributive opportunities to build up R&D capacity in other states. Some federal programs (e.g. NSF's Experimental Program to Stimulate Competitive Research program) guarantee that less competitive states receive at least a minimum amount of NSF's R&D money. For other federal state R&D links, the implementation of federal R&D initiatives may require cooperation of the state government (e.g. the SBIR program), and state R&D initiatives may also attract federal investments (e.g. the GRA program).

Broadly speaking, the US R&D policymaking represents an integrative process of hierarchical governance and collaborative governance. At the federal level, R&D policy agencies reveal a hierarchical organizational structure. For instance, in the NSTC, each subcommittee must report to their umbrella committee, and the umbrella committee report to the OSTP and the President. At the subcommittee level, however, members are from a variety of government agencies that get involved in that S&T area, presenting a collaborative approach to policymaking. Collaboration governance is reflected not only within the government, but also by the broad participation of academia, industry, not-for-profit organizations and other social components in the policymaking process especially through congressional hearings and advisory groups. It is the same at the state level. The state R&D policymaking particularly highlights collaborations and partnerships between government, university, and industry.

The phenomenon of collaborative governance implies that the innovative process at both federal and state levels is by no means a linear model as presented in Figure 1. The private sector and entrepreneurs play a role not only in commercializing new knowledge and introducing new products but also in allocating federal and state R&D resources. Government as a key R&D supporter on the other hand also actively spurs entrepreneurship and technological commercialization. In addition, both government and the private sector can be consumers of new products, suggesting another channel of feedbacks from the market end. The US innovation systems, to a large extent shaped by R&D policy, therefore show interactive and recursive characteristics, supporting a nonlinearity approach to innovation (Kline and Rosenberg 1986, Edquist 1997, Etzkowitz and Leydesdorff 2000).

Endnotes

[1] According to NSF (2008), Basic research is defined as systematic study directed toward fuller knowledge or understanding of the fundamental aspects of phenomena and of observable facts without specific applications toward processes or products. Applied research is defined as systematic study

to gain knowledge or understanding necessary to determine the means by which a recognized and specific need may be met. Development is defined as systematic application of knowledge or understanding, directed toward the production of useful materials, devices, and systems or methods, including design, development, and improvement of prototypes and new processes to meet specific requirements. It excludes quality control, routine product testing, and production.

[2] More S&T policy related caucuses can be found from the US House of Representatives. Available at: http://cha.house.gov/member_orgs111th.aspx, accessed March 14 2009.

[3] Source: OSTP. Available at: http://www.ostp.gov/cs/nstc/about, accessed March 14 2009.

[4] The Next Generation Internet Research Act of 1998 and the America COMPETES Act of 2007 are also related to the NITRD program.

[5] Source: National Coordination Office for NITRD. Available at http://www.nitrd.gov/about/presentations_nco/2008/documents/McDuffie_Cyber_Security_Collab_031408.pdf, accessed March 29 2009.

[6] The 13 member agencies of Subcommittee on NITRD by size of NITRD budget are: National Science Foundation (NSF), Office of the Secretary of Defense and Services research organizations (OSD), Defense Advanced Research Projects Agency (DARPA), National Institutes of Health (NIH), Department of Energy Office of Science (DOE/SC), National Security Agency (NSA), National Aeronautics and Space Administration (NASA), National Institute of Standards and Technology (NIST), Agency for Healthcare Research and Quality (AHRQ), Department of Energy National Nuclear Security Administration (DOE/NNSA), National Oceanic and Atmospheric Administration (NOAA), Environmental Protection Agency (EPA), and National Archives and Records Administration (NARA).

[7] Source: DOE. Available at http://www.ne.doe.gov/neac/neNeacOverview.html, accessed April 4 2009.

[8] Participant agencies are Department of Agriculture, Department of Commerce, Department of Defense, Department of Education, Department of Energy, Department of Health and Human Services, Department of Transportation, Environmental Protection Agency, National Aeronautics and Space Administration, National Science Foundation and Department of Homeland Security.

[9] Source: SBA. Available at http://www.sba.gov/aboutsba/sbaprograms/sbir/faq/sbir_sbir_faq.html, accessed April 10 2009.

[10] Those States are California, Florida Massachusetts, Minnesota, New York, North Carolina, Pennsylvania, and Texas.

[11] Source: OCAST. Available at: http://www.ok.gov/ocast/About_OCAST/Boards_Committees/index.html, accessed April 14 2009.

[12] Source: Business Xpansion Journal. Available at: http://www.bxjonline.com/bxj/article. asp?magarticle_id=444, accessed April 14 2009.

[13] Source: Ohio Channel. Available at: http://www.ohiochannel.org/your_State/third_frontier_project/ about.cfm, accessed April 14 2009.

[14] Details of these 18 programs can be found from Ohio Channel. Available at: http://www.ohiochannel.org/your_State/third_frontier_project/ programs.cfm, accessed April 14 2009.

[15] The six universities are Clark Atlanta University, Emory University, Georgia Institute of Technology, Georgia State University, Medical College of Georgia and the University of Georgia.

[16] Source: GRA. Available at: http://www.gra.org/AboutGRA/FAQs/tabid/355/Default.aspx, accessed April 15, 2009.

References

Audretsch, D. B., Weigand J. and Weigand C. (2002). The impact of the SBIR on creating entrepreneurial behavior. *Economic Development Quarterly,* 16(1), pp. 32-38.

Berglund, D. and Clark M. (2000). Using research and development to growth state economies. Washington, DC: National Governor's Association.

Bowen, W. M., Haynes K. E. and Stough R. R. (1990). Regional analysis and planning for educational program design. *Proceedings Modeling and Simulation*, 21(1), pp.147-52.

Bozeman, B. (2000). Technology and economic development for whom?: the prospects for "dual agenda" state programs. In Teich A. H., Nelson S. D., McEnaney C. and Lita S. J. (eds.), *AAAS science and technology policy yearbook.* [Online] Washington, DC: AAAS. Available at: http://www.aaas.org/spp/yearbook/2000/ch18.pdf [Accessed March 15, 2009].

Bush, V. (1945). Science: the endless frontier: a report to the President by Vannevar Bush, Director of the Office of Scientific Research and Development. [Online] Available at: http://www.nsf.gov/od/lpa/nsf50/vbush1945.htm [Accessed March 15 2009].

Edquist, C. (ed.) (1997). Systems of innovation: technologies, institutions and organizations. London: Pinter.

Etzkowitz, H. and Leydesdorff L. (2000). The dynamics of innovation: from national systems and "Mode 2" to a triple helix of university-industry-government relations. *Research Policy*, 29, pp. 109-23.

Haynes, K. E., Philogene G. S.and Dinc M. (2000). The relative efficiency of the general clinical research centres – an application of data envelopment analysis to medical research infrastructure. *International Journal of Healthcare Technology and Management*, 2, pp. 403-24.

Haynes, K. E. and Stough R. R. (1985). Investment in infrastructure for national scientific and technological research: policy considerations. Paper prepared for Sigma Xi, the National Scientific Research Society.

Haynes, K. E. and Stough R. R. (1988). Infrastructural investment for basic research: U.S. patterns in university science and technology. In Toonen T. and Stough R.R. (eds). *New Approaches to Infrastructure*. Leyden, the Netherlands: J.J. Groen.

Hill, C. T. (2006). *Where does science (and technology) fit in public policy?* [Online] Available at: http://www.aaas.org/programs/science_policy/ leadership/hill1106.pdf [Accessed March 16 2009].

Holt, M. (2008). *Congressional Research Service report for Congress: nuclear energy policy.* [Online] Available at: http://www.fas.org/sgp/crs/misc/RL33558.pdf [Accessed March 16 2009].

Kline, S. and Rosenberg N. (1986). An overview of innovation. In: Landau R. and Rosenberg N. (eds.). *The positive sum strategy: harnessing technology for economic growth.* Washington, DC: National Academy Press.

Lerner, J. (1999). The government as venture capitalist: the long-run impact of the SBIR program. *The Journal of Business*, 72(3), pp. 285-318.

Mowery, D. C. (1998). The changing structure of the US national innovation systems: implications for international conflict and cooperation in R&D policy. *Research Policy*, 27, pp. 639-54.

National Science Board (2008). *Science and engineering indicators 2008*. Arlington, VA: National Science Foundation.

National Science Foundation (2008). *Federal R&D funding by budget function: 2007-09*. [Online] Available at: http://www.nsf.gov/statistics/nsf08315/pdf/nsf08315.pdf [Accessed March 16 2009].

Rees, J. and Bradley R. (1988). State science policy and economic development in the United States: a critical perspective. *Environment and Planning A*, 20(8), pp. 999-1012.

Romer, P. M. (1990). Endogenous technological change. *Journal of Political Economy,* 98(5), pp. S71-S102.

Schmandt, J. and Wilson R. (1988). State science and technology policies: an assessment. *Economic Development Quarterly*, 2(2), pp. 124-37.

Smith, B. L. R. (1990). *American science policy since World War II.* Washington, DC: Brookings Institution.

Smith, P. W. (2006). Congressional Research Service report for Congress – the National Institutes of Health (NIH): organization, funding, and congressional issues. [Online] Available at: http://fas.org/sgp/crs/misc/RL33695.pdf [Accessed March 16 2009].

Stine, D. D. (2009). *Congressional Research Service report for Congress - science and technology policymaking: a primer.* [Online] Available at: www.fas.org/sgp/crs/misc/RL34454.pdf [Accessed March 16 2009].

10

Multinationals in the Knowledge Economy – a Case Study of AstraZeneca in Sweden

Martin Andersson, Börje Johansson, Charlie Karlsson and Hans Lööf

Introduction

Multinational companies play a large and growing role in the world economy. They contribute about 10 % to world GDP and about two thirds to global exports. In the vast majority of the countries in the world, the presence of multinationals has also been growing over time.

One defining characteristic of multinational companies is that they have high knowledge and technology intensity. For example, they have high ratios of Research and Development (R&D) expenditures relative to sales and a large fraction of their workforce is composed of scientific, technical and other 'white-collar' workers. Estimates show that their share of world-wide private R&D amounts to about 70 %. Research also demonstrates that multinational companies generate positive spillovers to the countries and regions they are located in. They provide channels for technology and knowledge transfers to domestic economies hosting them. From their dominating role in scientific, vertical and horizontal innovation systems in different parts of the world, they often function as nodes for the diffusion of knowledge and technology. Their linkages to suppliers, other firms, research teams in different research institutions and customers, etc., imply that knowledge and technology 'spills over' to different parts of the economies in which they are located. In view of this, multinational companies play a significant role in the 'knowledge economy'.

This paper presents key results from a large-scale case study of the role of a large multinational company, active in one of the most R&D and knowledge intensive industries of the world, with establishments in a small open economy. The case study examines the role of AstraZeneca in the Swedish economy, i.e. an economy dominated by multinational companies. They account for almost all of Sweden's aggregate investments in private R&D, over 90 % of the country's exports and imports as well as a significant share of the total number of employees in the private sector. The analyses in the paper make it possible to assess the importance of the local presence of such a large knowledge-intensive multinational for Sweden.

The paper focuses on the interaction of AstraZeneca's units in Sweden with the rest of the Swedish economy, and the Swedish innovation system in particular. The following questions are in focus:

- What role does a large knowledge-intensive MNE play for a small open economy like Sweden?
- What role does a large knowledge-intensive MNE play in a 'knowledge economy' and what is its importance for the Swedish innovation system?

These questions are assessed with AstraZeneca as a case from two major perspectives. The first concerns the company's role as an employer in the private sector, its transaction links with other Swedish firms and its role for Sweden's exports. The second perspective focuses on the company's role in the Swedish knowledge economy and innovation system. The paper analyses the company as a node for knowledge flows in the Swedish economy and innovation system, and its role as an employer of highly educated and skilled workers in Sweden. For example, the study examines the company's collaboration networks with links to researchers at universities and research institutes, collaborations with other firms as well as its importance for the Swedish labor market for PhDs and other research personnel. As for other global R&D intensive firms in Sweden, knowledge and ideas flow to the country through the company's extensive international networks.

The remainder of the paper is organized in the following way: Section 2 presents a literature review of the role of multinational companies in the global economy. Section 3 presents AstraZeneca and its activities in Sweden. Section 4 describes the company's interaction with the Swedish economy. Section 5 concludes and discusses policy issues and suggestions.

Multinational Companies in the Global Economy

The Growing Importance of Multinational Companies

During the second half of the 20th century multinationals have grown at a rapid rate and are today an important part of the global economic system. According to figures presented in McCann (2008a), which are based on a set of UNCTAD reports, the number of multinational companies in the world have increased from about 7 000 in the beginning of the 1970s to about 78 000 in 2005. Moreover, these multinationals comprise about 780 000 foreign affiliates and it has been estimated that they together employ about 73 million workers, i.e. around 3 % of the global workforce (McCann 2008a).

The value-added generated by multinational companies in 2006 amounted to almost 5 trillion $ US. This means that multinational companies account for about 10 % of the total value-added in the world, i.e. world GDP. Compared with the 1980s, the contribution of multinationals to world GDP has almost doubled. Moreover, trade flows of multinationals constitute about two thirds of global exports. The value of export flows by multinationals in 2006 amounted to about 4.7 trillion $ US. In recent decades both output, employment and trade of multinationals have grown faster than world trade and the largest component of the global stock of foreign investments is overseas investments by multinational firms (McCann and Mudambi 2004, 2005).

R&D investments are more often than not considered as the driving force in the 'knowledge economy'. Multinational companies are responsible for a significant share of the total R&D investments worldwide. Figure 1 presents estimates of total R&D expenditures by the

700 largest multinationals in the world in terms of R&D as well as figures for global total R&D expenditures.

Figure 1: Contribution of Multinational Companies to Global R&D Expenditures.

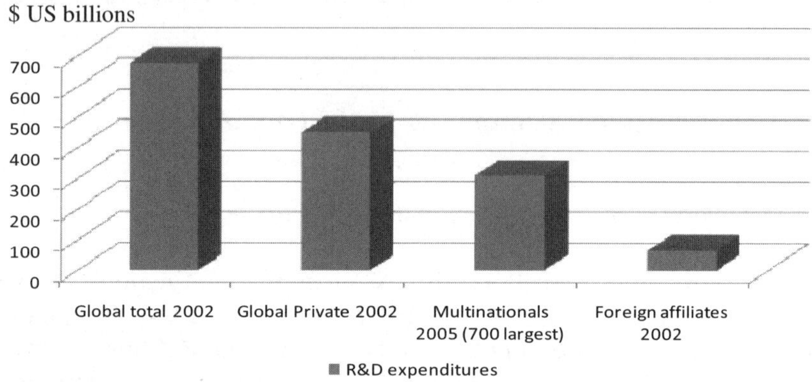

Source: McCann (2008a) based on figures presented in UNCTAD (2005).

The expenditures on R&D by the largest multinationals is calculated to be about 310 billion $ US in 2005. As a share of global R&D expenditures in 2002 it amounts to over 45 % and nearly 70 % of global private R&D. Global private R&D expenditures in 2002 was about 450 billion $ US. McCann (2008a) notes that more than half of the 700 largest multinationals in terms of R&D are active in three sectors: (1) pharmaceuticals and biotechnology, (2) IT hardware and (3) automotive.

Given the magnitude of these figures, it is clear that multinational companies can be of great importance for individual economies. McCann (2008b) refers for example to figures showing that over half of China's exports are internal trade within foreign-owned multinational firms and about two-thirds of India's ICT exports are controlled by foreign-owned multinationals.

Multinational firms are overrepresented in R&D and knowledge-intensive industries (Gustavsson 2004). The research literature shows that multinationals in general have a set of defining characteristics and many of these pertain to their knowledge and technology intensity (see e.g. Markusen 1995, 1998 and 2004). In addition to the fact that multinational firms constitute a significant fraction of trade, value-added, R&D, employment and other economic variables of economies across the world, there is a large literature on 'spillover effects' from activities of multinationals in a country or region. A review of the literature can be found in Blomström and Kokko (1998). One argument is that multinational firms play an important role for technology and knowledge transfers to the countries (or regions) they are located in, and that their local presence has positive effects on the local industry. From their dominating role in scientific, vertical and horizontal innovation systems in different parts of the world, they often function as nodes for the diffusion of knowledge and technology. Their linkages to suppliers, other firms, research teams in different research institutions and customers, etc., imply that knowledge and technology 'spills over' to different parts of the economies they are located in.[1]

In view of the aggregate figures reflecting the role of multinational companies in the global economy as well as in individual economies and the evidence on positive spillover effects associated with their local presence in a country or region, a natural conclusion is that national and regional growth and trade depend to a significant extent on the location decisions of multinational firms (cf. McCann 2008b). It is thus important that individual countries and regions are able to attract and retain activities of multinationals.

Location of R&D by Multinationals

Modern companies have to formulate business strategies, design organizational structures, and take operational decisions in a global context. Pharmaceutical companies are no exception. Actually, there are few industries so dominated by multinational companies as the pharmaceutical industry (Schweitzer 2007). However, what is typical for this industry is that all its major companies have substantial operations in several countries, and much production as well as R&D activities are performed in countries other than the home country of each corporation.

R&D activities of multinational firms have often been characterized as 'sticky in space' in the sense that their R&D tends take place primarily in their respective home countries (Patel and Pavitt 1995).

Indeed, the spatial fragmentation of multinationals' value chains have increased primarily because of changing localization patterns of production activities, in particular routine and less knowledge intensive activities. The globalization of the R&D activities of multinationals is a more recent phenomenon and has developed much slower (cf. Carlsson 2006).

No process has however been immune to the trend of globalization. Since the drive for more rapid and more effective product innovation has been a major factor behind the globalization of companies, it may be perceived as natural that also the R&D function has been strongly affected. Off-shore spending on R&D has increased among the large multinational companies and evidence suggests that the R&D activities of multinationals are increasingly distributed over several concentrations. Multinational companies tend to perform R&D at different locations in the world. It is also documented that over time, R&D activities of multinationals have grown rapidly outside the R&D-intensive 'triad', i.e. Europe, the US and Japan (UNCTAD 2004). Research has also demonstrated that the establishment of internal as well as external R&D networks by multinational companies has become more frequent during the last decades (see e.g. Cantwell 1989, Zander 1999).

The globalization of R&D is interesting, since it has happened in spite of the fact that companies theoretically have many reasons not to globalize their R&D operations. In particular, the spatial dispersion of R&D activities, which implies that R&D laboratories are located in a number of different locations in different countries, generates a number of demanding management problems (De Meyer 1993):

- It is well established that R&D activities are characterized by economies of scale and scope (see e.g. Teece 1987). Successful R&D depends upon a critical mass of scientific and other development competence.[2] Generically, R&D also builds upon the experience of the past, which implies that a dispersion of R&D makes it more troublesome to preserve the historical knowledge base, since much of the knowledge is embedded in people.
- It is a characteristic of R&D activities that they often tend to be abstract and demand a lot of frequent both planned and un-planned direct face-to-face interaction. The costs of direct face-to-face in-

teraction could bring about prohibitive frictions when the interaction has to take place between people localized thousands of kilometers from each other.

- The R&D activities are normally an integrated part of the strategic plans of companies, which they want to keep secret from competitors. It is normally easier to manage secrecy if the R&D activities are geographically concentrated. There is a general tendency among companies to locate R&D in the proximity to their head offices.
- The knowledge generated by the R&D activities is an important intellectual asset of companies. Strategic control of such intellectual assets may be more difficult with a decentralized R&D structure (Steele 1989).
- The control of global R&D networks potentially involves several game-like conflicts such as stimulation of creativity versus efficiency and cooperation versus competition between R&D units.

Given the above obstacles, why do companies globalize their R&D activities? And how do they manage their global networks for governance of their R&D activities in off-shore laboratories?

The literature dealing with R&D highlights three major factors behind the globalization of R&D activities and R&D laboratories within companies:[3]

- *Demand side factors.* Performing R&D activities in other countries can be an instrument to penetrate foreign markets by e.g. developing variants of the current generation of products that are tailored for the customers in strategic markets. R&D located in a foreign market can also be a measure to improve the image of the company in the actual market.
- *Supply side factors.* The location of R&D to other countries can be a mechanism to take advantage of knowledge spillovers from R&D already performed in that country at universities, research institutes and other companies. Another motivation for locating R&D to another country can be to get access to competencies and skills, which are scarce in the home country or to get access to low cost scientists and engineers.
- *Competition factors.* The location of R&D in another country can be a strategic reaction to similar location decisions made by com-

petitors or to options neglected by competitors. It can also be an attempt to create a balance between R&D, production, marketing and distribution in a multinational company's value chain.

There are several empirical analyses of foreign direct investment (FDI) in R&D. Kuemmerle (1999) analyzes the propensity of multinational companies to invest in home-base augmenting R&D subsidiaries. He finds that it "rises with the relative commitment to R&D of private and public entities in the target country, as well as with the quality of the human resource pool and with the level of scientific achievement in relevant sciences" (Kuemmerle 1999: 18). Also, the propensity to invest in off-shore R&D units to exploit existing firm-specific advantages in foreign markets, depend on the attractiveness of the target country's market. Gassmann and von Zedwitz (1999) report results from almost 200 interviews in 33 multinational companies. The authors identify five trends pertaining to the organization of international R&D in multinationals. These include stronger orientation towards international markets and knowledge centers and establishment of "tightly coordinated listening posts", increased integration of decentralized R&D units and strengthening and reinforcement of foreign R&D sites. Meyer-Krahmer and Reger (1999) present results from 120 interviews in 21 multinational companies. The authors find that the internationalization of R&D is still characterized by "Triadization", i.e. located in the EU, the US and Japan. As regards choice of location, the paper finds an increasingly selective focus on few locations and a concentration of innovation activities to worldwide centers of excellence. The motives for establishing R&D units abroad are maintained to be driven by learning from technological excellence, lead markets as well as interactions between R&D, marketing and advanced manufacturing. Pearce and Papanastassiou (1999) review the literature and indentify two increasingly important roles for overseas R&D in multinational companies. The first motive is to develop new products, or very distinctive variants, for key segments of the global marketplace. Labs with this function are closely associated to other subsidiary functions such as marketing and engineering. Secondly, labs may carry out specialized pieces of basic research that reflect particular areas of expertise within the host-country science-base. Both these roles are confirmed by an analysis of data on UK laboratories.

Kumar (2001) conducts an analysis at the country level. This paper finds that US and Japanese MNEs locate R&D in countries with large domestic markets, abundance of low cost R&D manpower and large "national technological efforts". The Science and Engineering (S&E) knowledge base of a nation (as measured by S&E articles) "critically determines the level and sophistication of US foreign subsidiaries' innovative activity" (Hegde and Hicks 2005: 1). They also find significant differences across industries.

In summary, recent literature put particular emphasis on supply side factors. While rationales related to markets and production certainly matter, knowledge augmenting motives have grown in importance over time (Narula 1999; Narula and Zanfei 2004; Criscuolo et al. 2005). An important motive underlying the globalization of multinationals' R&D activities is that the competitiveness of companies can be improved by having R&D laboratories located in proximity to foreign milieus in which frontier knowledge and technology are produced. Foreign R&D subsidiaries are viewed as important sources of new knowledge and technology (Florida 1997; Braunerhjelm and Svensson 1998; Zanfei 2000) and internationalization of R&D within multinational companies allow them to capitalize on host countries' knowledge and technology (Cantwell 1995, Le Bas and Sierra 2002). Strategic location of R&D in regions rich in knowledge and technology can hence be viewed as a means to augment a firm's competitive advantage(s).[1] Kuemmerle (1997) refers to this type of foreign knowledge and technology accumulation as 'Home Base Augmenting'.

Firms in the pharmaceutical industry are of course highly dependent on R&D. Studies of location of R&D in different industries find that pharmaceuticals is not only an industry in which R&D is highly internationalized, but also a product area where multinational pharmaceutical companies have a particularly high tendency of locating foreign R&D laboratories close to knowledge and technology sources (e.g. von Zedtwitz and Gassmann 2002, Gerybadze and Reger 1999).

AstraZeneca – Activities in Sweden and its Impact on the Swedish Economy

Section 2 described the role of multinational companies in the global economy. It also illustrated the overall importance of these firms for the Swedish economy. This Section presents an overview of AstraZeneca, a large knowledge-intensive multinational company, in the Swedish economy.

AstraZeneca employs close to 12 000 individuals in Sweden. The firm has both R&D and production activities in Sweden, where all major establishments are located in Sweden's three metropolitan areas, Stockholm, Göteborg (Gothenburg) and Malmö. The current location pattern in Sweden is due to several historical circumstances, of which proximity to university R&D in the pertinent areas has been decisive.

Table 1 presents the total number of employees in Sweden by region and activity. The majority of the employees is assigned to establishments in the Stockholm region. In particular, AstraZeneca's production facilities with over 3 800 employees are located in the Stockholm region. The same region hosts about 37 % of the firm's total R&D employment in Sweden. The largest fraction of the R&D workers is employed at AstraZeneca's R&D facility in the Göteborg region. The implant business, Astra Tech, is also located in Göteborg. The R&D facility in the Malmö region accounts for about 19 % of the R&D employment.

Table 1: AstraZeneca Employment in Swedish Establishments (January 2008)

	Total employment	*R&D*	*Production*	*Other*
Stockholm	7 199	1 651	3 829	1 719
Göteborg	2 417	2 005	0	412
Malmö	1 082	853	1	228
Other	1 146	-	-	-
Sum	11 844	4 509	3 830	2 359

AstraZeneca is the largest actor in the Swedish pharmaceutical industry and its role has grown over time. In the end of the 1990s the pharmaceutical industry in Sweden employed about 14 500 persons.[5] Ten years later the industry had grown to comprise about 16 500 employees. During the same period AstraZeneca's share of Sweden's pharmaceutical employment (excl. Astra Tech) expanded from about 50 to over 60 %. The firm accounts for about ¾ of the total turnover of the Swedish pharmaceutical industry. Today, between 17 and 18 % of the total employment of AstraZeneca Plc is located in Sweden.

The presence of AstraZeneca activities leaves considerable marks in the aggregate statistics. The total employment of the firm amounts to about 0.4 % of the total Swedish private employment. The firm's share of Sweden's exports is more than ten times as large.

There are two basic measures of a sector's role for aggregate exports. The first is the sector's share of total exports. The other is its share of the world export market. Sweden's exports of pharmaceuticals have increased substantially during the last 40 years. Figure 2 illustrates the development of Sweden's share of world exports of pharmaceuticals and it shows a steady increase since the beginning of the 1960s.

In relation to the size of the Swedish economy, Sweden's share of global export flows should fall in the interval 1-2 %. Paper, pulp and wood products are the largest Swedish export product groups in terms of their share of global exports during the 2000s. All these industries have however experienced a declining export market share for the last 40-50 years. *Other* product groups with relatively large export market share comprise (1) telecom products and (2) medical products and pharmaceuticals, and these product groups have continued to grow over the long term. During the last century Sweden's share of global exports in each of these two product groups amounts to around 5 %. This is about twice as large as the corresponding figure for road vehicles.

The strong Swedish position as an exporter of pharmaceuticals reflects that only a few countries develop new drugs and medicines at a larger scale. In this sense Sweden belongs to a small group of countries hosting large-scale pharmaceutical R&D, such as the US, Switzerland and the large countries in the EU.

Figure 2: Sweden's Share of Global Exports of Pharmaceuticals 1960-2002 (Average Share in each Period)

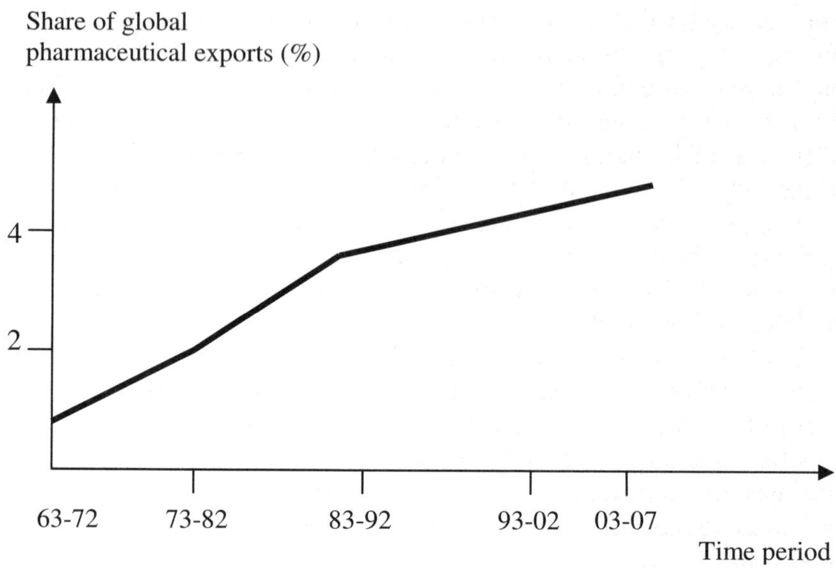

Source: Statistics Sweden

Comparable data for 2004 show that AstraZeneca accounts for about 80 % of Sweden's total exports of manufactures by firms in the pharmaceutical industry and about 5 % of the total exports of manufactures by firms in the manufacturing sector.[6] The total exports of manufactures by firms in the manufacturing sector in Sweden amounted to about 850 billion SEK in 2004. AstraZeneca's share of Sweden's total exports is significant and reflects how the countries' aggregate trade flows are affected by the location of MNEs, in particular for small economies like the Swedish one. In 2007, Sweden's total exports of manufactures (by all types of firms) amounted to about 1 114 billion SEK and the corresponding figure for total exports (including services) was about 1 610 billion SEK.

The majority of the product groups that constitute a large fraction of Sweden's total exports are based on natural resources. It is primarily three knowledge-based export product groups whose share is as large as or larger than pharmaceuticals, i.e. telecom products, road vehicles and machinery equipment.

AstraZeneca's importance for Swedish exports can be put in further perspective by calculating net exports, i.e. the export value minus the import value. In this way one can calculate a net export share:

– Net exports = exports – imports

– Net export share = $\dfrac{\text{Net exports}}{\text{Exports} + \text{Imports}}$

The net exports of the whole pharmaceutical sector in Sweden amounted in 1997 to about 15 billion SEK. A decade later this figure has more than doubled. The lion's share of this development can be attributed to AstraZeneca:

– In 1997 AstraZeneca's net exports from Sweden was approximately 8 billion SEK and seven years later this figure had increased to more than 30 billion SEK, that is, more than three times as large. The same figure in 2007 is estimated to be about 10 billion larger. Large net exporters like AstraZeneca provide Sweden with opportunities to be a net importer of other products.
– The net exports of AstraZeneca can be related to Sweden's total net exports. The firm's net export of manufactures is estimated to about 40 billion SEK in 2007. This corresponds to over 30 % of Swedish total net exports. Sweden's net exports of manufactures were about 120 billion SEK in 2007.

The net export share for the Swedish pharmaceutical industry was about 40 % in 2006 and 2007. The corresponding figure for AstraZeneca is somewhat higher. In this regard one can compare the pharmaceutical industry with the paper, pulp and wood products that are based on natural resources. As a comparison, Table 2 presents total exports and imports in 2007 for three product groups; (1) forest-based products, (2) engineering industry and (3) pharmaceuticals.

The large net export share for paper, pulp and wood products can primarily be attributed to domestic supply of forest-based inputs. For pharmaceuticals there is in essence only one fundamental factor of production; the knowledge, the creativity and the experiences of the pharmaceutical labor force in Sweden.

Table 2: Sweden's Exports and Imports of Goods in Three Large Product Groups 2007

	Exports (billion SEK)	*Imports (billion SEK)*	*Net export share(%)*
Forest-based	128	32	60
Engineering industry	502	399	11
Pharmaceuticals	59	25	40
Sweden (total for manufactures)	**1 140**	**1 020**	**6**

(Source: Statistics Sweden)*

*)Product groups are defined according to SITC 2: forest-based products (24,25,63,64), engineering industry (71-79), pharmaceuticals (54).

AstraZeneca has an evident importance for Sweden's aggregate exports. It is equally evident that Sweden is of minor importance as a market for AstraZeneca's products. Sweden accounts for a small fraction of the firm's total sales from Sweden. The firm's sales in Sweden and the other Nordic countries constitute about 1 % of total sales from Swedish units. The distribution of AstraZeneca's sales from Swedish units is presented in Figure 3.

Figure 3: Distribution of Exports from AstraZeneca Units in Sweden in 2007

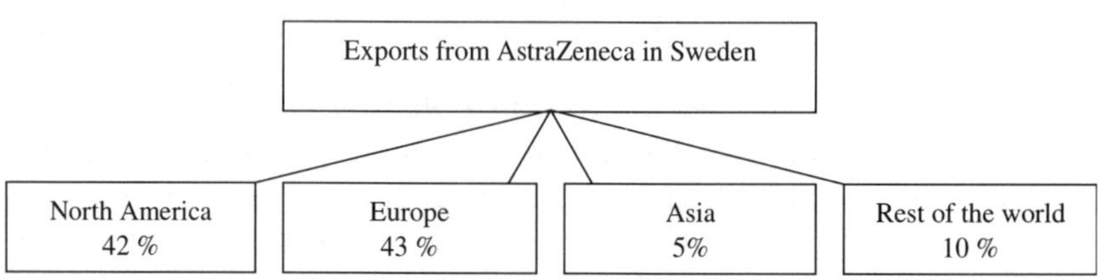

Source: Internal Figures from AstraZeneca

AstraZeneca in Sweden's Knowledge Economy – an Overview

AstraZeneca's establishments in Sweden form an R&D and knowledge-intensive multinational organization, which demands labor with a diversity of competence profiles. In this role it adds to the formation of the Swedish knowledge economy and contributes to a Swedish research competence of importance for healthcare as well as the life sciences.

R&D is the main activity in AstraZeneca. The firm's establishments in Sweden invested over 12 billion SEK in R&D in each year 2006 and 2007. This figure can be compared with the following figures for Sweden:

– The R&D investments in Swedish firms amounted in 2006 to about 81 billion SEK. The total R&D expenses in universities were about 22 billion.

The R&D investments of Swedish AstraZeneca units in 2006 amount to almost 15 % of the total R&D investments initiated in the Swedish private sector during the same year. The volume of AstraZeneca's R&D investments initiated by Swedish units can also be illustrated with figures on R&D man-years. Between 7 and 8 out of 100 man-years in R&D in the Swedish private sector can be attributed to AstraZeneca's units in Sweden. The magnitude of these numbers illustrate in itself that AstraZeneca constitutes a major player in Sweden's innovation systems.

AstraZeneca's global R&D activities take place in several different innovation milieus and comprise a large set of collaborations all over the world. Knowledge and information flow within the firm's internal network for knowledge and information exchange. Indirectly these knowledge flows provide the Swedish healthcare system as well as the medical and the pharmaceutical research milieu in Sweden with advantages that other small countries lack.

An important way in which researchers in Sweden can indirectly access the knowledge flows is by means of research collaborations with AstraZeneca. In 2007 AstraZeneca Plc had about 350 larger research collaborations with universities, research institutes and other firms across the globe. Over 20 % of these are with Swedish actors. One out of three research collaborations in Europe comprise Swedish partners.

Another measure of the magnitude of the R&D activities is R&D outputs in the form of patent applications and granted patents. Patenting is a global phenomenon for most pharmaceutical companies in the sense that they apply for patents in several countries. Between 2000 and 2007 AstraZeneca applied for over 20 000 patents, protection of designs, etc., in different parts of the world. The firm's yearly number of applications to the Swedish Patent and Registration Office (PRV), European Patent Office (EPO) and Patent Cooperation Treaty (PCT) amounted during the same period to about 600. This can be compared with the total number of applications to PRV that is about 3 000.

AstraZeneca's R&D activities in Sweden also generate royalties and incomes from licensing activities. Incomes of this kind from abroad amount to about 10 billion SEK, which corresponds to roughly a fourth of the total export incomes. This form of "knowledge sales" to foreign countries is typical for most R&D-intensive industries in Sweden, but for AstraZeneca they are especially large.

Interaction with the Swedish Economy

Input Delivery Networks in Production and R&D

Firms play a role in the economy as both suppliers of their output and customers who buy inputs from the market. More specifically, firms interact with the rest of the economy by purchasing inputs from other firms and by delivering goods and services to other firms. These transactions bring about a rather invariant pattern of deliveries, such that the pattern changes at a slow pace between years. The pattern of firms' interaction can be aggregated to a delivery pattern between sectors, forming an intersectoral delivery network. Such a network is recorded in most countries as a Social Accounting Matrix (SAM), in which the deliveries between sectors are a core component, represented by the Input-Output table (I/O table), depicting transaction links between all the sectors of an economy.[7] SAM also includes labor and capital inputs as well as export and import information. SAM can be constructed for regions, countries and entire groups of countries like the EU. In this chapter we employ SAM for the Swedish economy to provide a picture of the role that the company group AstraZeneca plays in the Swedish economy.

With the help of an I/O model it is possible to describe how the expansion of a firm's (and a sector's) output generate additional demand for inputs (goods and services) that the firm uses in its production. In a similar way the model describes how reduced production in a sector impacts the economy by demanding a lower amount of inputs. Such changes have thus repercussions on the activities in other parts of the economy. Expansion generates demand for increased input deliveries, which may originate from domestic or foreign firms. When most deliveries are domestic the feedback from a sector to the domestic economy may be considerable. The feedback becomes weaker as the share of deliveries from foreign suppliers increase.

As explained above, it matters how large the domestic share of inputs to a firm is. When the share is large the firm stimulates the rest of the domestic economy to a greater extent than when the share of imported inputs is large. In the former case domestic deliverers are stimulated to grow. However, if the domestic deliverers are not capable of offering the right inputs at competitive prices then the firm has to acquire its inputs from other parts of the world. Most large multinational firms are skillful in making use of the diversified specialization that the global economy offers. Obviously, this tendency will be larger for multinationals in a small economy – like the Swedish – than in a larger economy.

Figure 4: Inputs to and Output from AstraZeneca's Production Facilities

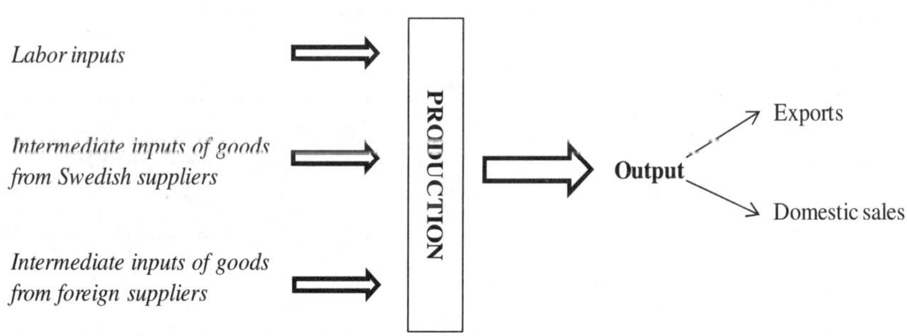

The task of the present section is to establish the links or couplings between AstraZeneca and the rest of the Swedish economy with regard to the firm's (1) production activities and (2) R&D activities. The analysis employs traditional techniques of computing multiplier effects, making use of SAM-information for Sweden and information from AstraZeneca's own accounts. Figure 4 presents the structure of inputs to and outputs from AstraZeneca's production facilities, upon which the calculations are made.

Transaction links between a firm and the set of sectors in the economy are reported in I/O tables also called transaction matrices. An I/O table informs for a sector about the sector's input coefficients, where each coefficient shows the input per unit output, in value terms, from each of the economy's different sectors. With the help of an I/O table it is possible to calculate the multiplier effects that a sector (or a firm in a sector) has on the total activity in the economy when the output from the sector increases by 1 %.

Figure 5: AstraZeneca's Production in Sweden, 2007

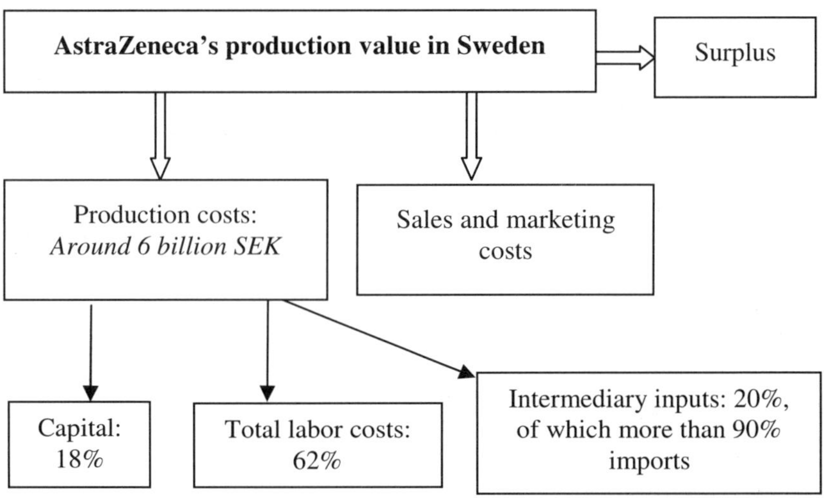

Source: Internal Figures from AstraZeneca

In this section the input coefficients of Astra Zeneca have been estimated for the firm's total production in Sweden and for the firm's total R&D-activities. On this basis the analysis provides answers to two different questions. First, how much is the Swedish economy stimulated when the production activities in Sweden increase? Second, how much is the Swedish economy stimulated when the R&D activities increase? These calculations also provide information about the impact from reduced production and R&D activities.

In order to provide an overall understanding of input deliveries, the inputs of labor, capital and intermediaries are presented as a share of the total costs of AstraZeneca's activities in Sweden. Such an overall picture is presented in Figure 5, where total costs are divided into production costs and sales costs, including marketing and contacts with buyers in different parts of the world. The surplus from production is calculated as sales value minus production and sales costs. This surplus can be used to finance R&D activities.

In AstraZeneca's annual accounts, the costs associated with sales, distribution and administration are reported together, as one compound part. The major share of these costs consists of sales and marketing costs. However, it should be recognized that the sales of AstraZeneca's products are managed by different sales units located in a large number of countries, and the sales operations cover the entire product mix of the company group. The Swedish share of the corresponding costs cannot easily be traced, and the important feature of the costs is that they, in all essence, occur abroad. Thus, sales costs do not stimulate production in other parts of the Swedish economy.

From a technical point of view, AstraZeneca's production value in Sweden is calculated according to the principles for establishing the Swedish national accounts (Statistics Sweden). We may then observe that when the production costs have been determined, we can subtract production costs from the production value to obtain the sum of (1) surplus and (2) sales costs. If this is done, sales costs have the same order of magnitude as production costs.

The figure shows that costs associated with production amount to about 6 billion SEK. The natural division of these costs is into labor costs (wage sum), capital costs, and intermediary deliveries. Labor costs comprise the major share of production costs, around 60 %. Intermediary deliveries correspond to about 20 % of production costs, and this is a small share, if a comparison is made with the average for the manufacturing industry. The basic observation is, however, that AstraZeneca's production in Sweden is labor intensive. As a consequence, changes in AstraZeneca's production affect other firms in the Swedish economy to a limited degree, since input deliveries from other firms are comparatively small and primarily originate from firms outside Sweden. Stimulation of the Swedish economy is generated via the labor market. These conclusions can be summarized as follows:

- Increased production in AstraZeneca generates very small stimulus to deliverers of inputs.
- Increased production in AstraZeneca stimulates primarily the rest of the economy via increased demand for labor inputs and thereby increased wage sums.

The two observations above indicate that AstraZeneca's Swedish production units have their location because of the available labor force, and that the accessibility to labor inputs outweighs the disadvantage of distant suppliers of intermediaries, including chemical materials. The latter are to a large extent imported, and this accentuates the conclusion about small upstream stimulation of Swedish firms. Rephrasing this into economic jargon, AstraZeneca's production units in Sweden have small multiplier effects on the Swedish economy. As a way to benchmark, the reader may observe that for chemical production in general, an increase in output of one million SEK stimulates the overall economy to grow 2.4 million SEK. This growth stimuli is a consequence of augmented input deliveries and employment increases. In the case of AstraZeneca the corresponding stimulation is not larger than 1.5 million SEK.

In this analysis of AstraZeneca's interaction with the rest of the economy, we have separated the R&D activities from the production activities. There are several reasons for that choice. For R&D activities, the nature of a pharmaceutical company's upstream and downstream linkages is quite different from the linkages of its production. In particular, since the middle of the 1960s large pharmaceutical companies have gradually allocated an increasing share of their R&D in sites outside the country of the head quarter (Kuemmerle 1990). Moreover, R&D efforts generate knowledge that is an output in its own right, and the created knowledge represents a property which can be sold or licensed to other firms, and which is often transferred between different units of each individual multinational company group.

Figure 6: AstraZeneca's R&D Expenditures in Sweden, 2007

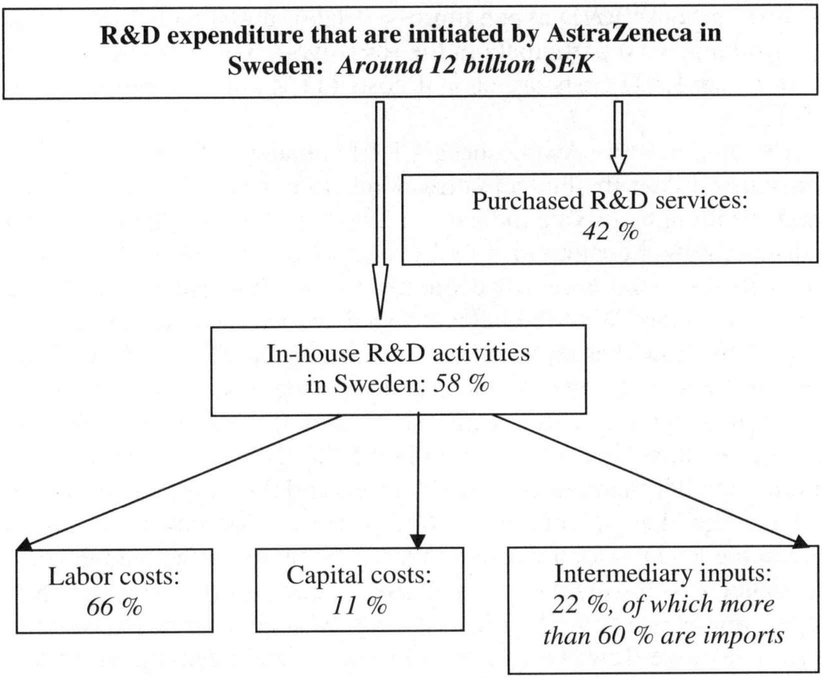

Source: Internal Figures from AstraZeneca

Figure 6 presents the costs of R&D activities that are initiated by AstraZeneca in Sweden. The figure shows that more than 40 % of the R&D investments are carried out with the help of purchases of R&D services, and these services add to the R&D efforts made by AstraZeneca's ca. 4 500 R&D workers in Sweden. A major part of the purchased R&D is imported from abroad, and these imported R&D services concern primarily clinical studies which are made on populations in several different countries. Hence, these studies have to be conducted globally. Currently, the company group AstraZeneca organizes clinical test programs that involve about 68 000 patients in different parts of the world. Around 3 000 of these patients are Swedish, i.e. about 4 %. Studies that take place in Sweden have a budget around 120 million SEK, and this budget corresponds to more than 2 % of the R&D services that are purchased by the company in Sweden.

AstraZeneca's R&D work is labor intensive. About 2/3 of the Swedish in-house R&D expenditures are labor costs, including a crew of consultants who participate in the R&D work. Other components of the in-house R&D costs are capital costs (11 %) and intermediate inputs (22 %).

How important is AstraZeneca's R&D budget in Sweden? As will be discussed later the budget corresponds to around 15 % of the total R&D spending by private industry in Sweden. However, here we want to discuss how a change in AstraZeneca's R&D investments in Sweden will affect the Swedish economy in the short run via different multiplier effects. With the help of social accounting calculations it is possible to show that an increase of AstraZeneca's Swedish R&D by 1 billion SEK will generate increased input deliveries, and increased employment with growing wage sums that together will make the Swedish economy grow by 750 million SEK. Thus, the overall stimulation is smaller than the increased budget, and this is primarily caused by the large share of imported R&D services. Moreover the inputs used in the R&D work are also to a large extent imported, and this circumstance also lowers the stimulation of the rest of the economy. In a longer time perspective the increased R&D budget can be expected to generate income flows in the form of royalties and license payments.

In summary, the traditional network analysis presented in this subsection demonstrates that AstraZeneca's links to other economic actors in the Swedish economy are thin in a similar way that one often finds for multinational companies in many industries. Like other multinational pharmaceutical companies, AstraZeneca in Sweden has instead well developed international networks – with regard to both its production and R&D activities. The AstraZeneca units in Sweden stimulate the rest of the surrounding economy primarily via the labor market. Growing production and increasing R&D generate expanding income, which stimulates demand in the economy.

Couplings to the Swedish Labor Market

In general, large multinational enterprises have an important role in the development of the Swedish labor market, by diversifying the demand for new types of skills and knowledge, and by learning on the job effects as people are employed in the pertinent firms. Of special importance is the international interface that many employees get when working in a multinational firm. Thus, the major influence from Swedish multinationals is their effects on knowledge growth and expansion of international trade.

International research recognizes the long-term impacts from large research-intensive firms and their influence as "anchor-tenants" for other small and medium-sized firms. According to this hypothesis, anchor-tenants support the evolution of knowledge and competencies which would not have developed without the presence of the research-intensive firms in each individual functional urban region. The message is that the anchor-tenants generate qualities to the economic milieu in which they are located, and that these qualities spill-over to other firms in the milieu, including firms that interact more persistently with the anchor firms. An article by Agrawal and Cockburn (2003: 1230) expresses this as follows:

"... large anchor-tenant firms thicken factor markets differently than many small firms that equal the size of the anchor tenant in the aggregate. Economies of scale and scope allow large firms to employ workers with highly specialized skills such as experience in large-scale manufacturing, taking firms publicly and entering foreign markets. The presence of workers with these skills and in local labor markets may make these skills available to smaller firms."

The different AstraZeneca sites in Sweden are themselves anchor-tenants in each of their locations. However, the AstraZeneca's establishments in the Stockholm region (Södertälje) have benefited considerable from a neighboring tenant, namely the Scania establishment in Södertälje. The multinational company Scania has a long tradition in developing *lean-production* techniques, and because of this the local labor market is an excellent fishing area for other companies which demand labor with lean-production experiences. The AstraZeneca management of the production sites in Södertälje recognizes this fact as an important regional milieu characteristic that has favored the company's process innovations over a long period of time.

At the same time, AstraZeneca also functions as an anchor-tenant itself, and it does so in a country-wide sense, with its locations in all three metropolitan regions of Sweden. In this context, the company has in a marked way been a driving force in the development of those knowledge and competence profiles that characterize R&D and production of the pharmaceutical industry. This influence is evident for Sweden's three large functional urban regions Stockholm, Göteborg and Malmö, in which the presence of the company has stimulated university research and the start-up of new firms in the biotechnology area.

It should not be a surprise that AstraZeneca's large R&D activities are knowledge dependent. Less well known is that the firm's manufacturing activities have high knowledge intensity, with a considerable amount of employees with at least three years of university education. Table 3 presents the composition of the labor force, divided into (1) PhDs, (2) engineers, and (3) other university educations extending three years or longer. AstraZeneca's R&D and production operations in Sweden can be described as follows:

- Close to 100 % of the employees occupied in R&D activities have three years or longer university education, when excluding some basic support activities
- In production, the share of employees with long university education (three years or longer) is about 20 %. This figure is around four times as large as the average for a typical manufacturing firm.

Table 3: Composition of the Employment in AstraZeneca's Swedish Units

	R&D	***Production***
PhDs	1 070	31
Engineers	495	325
Other employees with long university education	3 040	367
Share of total employment	***100%***	***about 20%***

AstraZeneca's R&D operations in Sweden had in 2007 a staff of more than 1 000 researchers with a PhD education. This figure could be assessed as follows:

- The total number of R&D workers with a PhD in Swedish firms was in 2005 about 5 000.
- At the same time, the medium-sized Jönköping University employed around 150 full time PhDs.
- Turning to the Royal Institute of Technology in Stockholm, we find that the number of PhDs amounted to 700, while the number of doctoral students was ca 1 500.
- In 2005, the number of full time R&D workers at Karolinska Institute was about 1 700.

The above comparisons illustrate that the size of AstraZeneca's R&D efforts can be compared with a technical university like the Royal Institute of Technology (KTH), when the input of PhDs is the benchmark variable. On top of this, AstraZeneca's R&D operations currently employ about 3 500 engineers and other employees with a long university education, comprising at least three years.

A conclusion from the preceding discussion is that AstraZeneca imposes demanding requirements on the Swedish supply of knowledge-intensive labor through its R&D activities as wells as its advanced production and logistics activities. The R&D operations generate a demand for a diversity of bio-medicine educations. From the perspective of the Swedish society, AstraZeneca in this way offers career tracks outside the university area for undergraduates and graduates from a wide set of university disciplines. Without these tracks the Swedish universities would not have the opportunity to maintain education programs at the current level. In a future perspective, the current interplay between the pharmaceutical industry and the university education in Sweden reproduces the knowledge base in areas such as bio chemistry, micro biology, pharmacology and research on "large" molecules, and these are areas with potential applications outside drug design and production.

Labor Mobility and Embodied Knowledge Flows

The evolution of R&D intensive firms in the pharmaceutical industry is to a large extent determined by two parallel ambitions of each individual firm. On the one hand a firm strives to control knowledge flows in such a way that knowledge does not diffuse – unintended – to competitors. On the other hand the firm will benefit from exchanging information with other actors whenever this will enhance the firm's own R&D processes. These aspects were discussed in the previous sub-section; here we shift the focus to illuminate knowledge flows that depend on labor market mechanisms.

Contributions to the international research literature on knowledge flows emphasize the importance of labor market mobility as an important vehicle in diffusing knowledge both between firms in the same industry and between firms in different industries (e.g. Almeida and Kogut 1999, Oetll and Agrawal 2008). This latter aspect is of course especially important when we study a large multinational firm as AstraZeneca and its influence on the relatively small Swedish economy.

Spread of knowledge occurs when a firm recruits a researcher from university as well as when it hires experienced persons who have previously worked in other firms. In a similar manner knowledge is transferred to the rest of the economy, when employees leave a firm for employment elsewhere in the economy (e.g. Zucker, Darby and Brewer 1998; Johansson and Karlsson 2008; Andersson and Thulin 2008). This phenomenon is recognized as an important stimulus to economic growth both in microeconomic and macroeconomic studies. These knowledge flow effects of labor mobility should be important for all types of employment, although the conscious deliberations of a firm are more systematic when it concerns recruitment of R&D workers and R&D managers.

During a normal year in recent time, the employment turnover of AstraZeneca in Sweden has been around 5-6 %. This means that approximately 600 persons annually leave the Swedish units to be replaced by about the same amount of new employees. In the company's R&D activities the turnover of personnel is clearly lower, with a figure varying between 2 and 4, which implies that the research team is renewed by at least 70-100 persons on a yearly basis. The corresponding inflow of new R&D workers is vital for the company's knowledge renewal, bringing in additional competencies and experiences as well as specialist skills.

The prime sources for attracting Swedish researchers are universities around the country, with the three metropolitan regions as the most important suppliers. But the company also recruits a smaller part of the R&D workers from other firms in Sweden. This latter recruitment pool refers to companies that are not competitors on the markets for drugs, although they compete for the same labor force.

Interviews with managers of AstraZeneca in Sweden reveal that recruitment from Swedish universities has to be an act of balance.[8] On the one hand the company wants to associate prominent researchers with its R&D activities. On the other hand there is also a clear cut need to ascertain that the very best researchers in the Swedish research community can remain in their positions of performing first class research and to continue to generate a sequence over the years of young competent researchers. The capacity of securing this reproduction process is equally important already for the medium-term demand for new researchers.

AstraZeneca's annual recruitment of researchers from abroad combines to much thinner flows of new competence into the company. This can be viewed in Table 4. The annual inflow of persons from the Nordic countries and the rest of Europe has in recent years been around 6-8 in number. A small amount comes from North America. However, it should be observed that there is a fair amount of researchers in AstraZeneca in Sweden where the inflow has its origin in places outside Europe and North America. The estimation of this report is that in 2007 the Swedish R&D units employed about 425 persons with forcign background.

Table 4: AstraZeneca's Annual Recruitment of Researchers from Abroad, 2005-2007.

Inflow of foreign researchers	*Annual recruitment*
From other Nordic countries	3-4
From the rest of Europe	3-4
From North America	0.2

Researchers who leave the R&D sites in Sweden find their way to new jobs outside Sweden, in other Swedish companies, and to some extent also to Swedish universities. Only a very small amount disappears to academic research in Sweden, and this is primarily caused by wage compensations that are limited compared to the wage level in the pharmaceutical industry. The largest share of persons who leave from AstraZeneca R&D units get employment in other companies in

Sweden, and this is evidently an important aspect of the company's knowledge diffusion to the rest of the Swedish economy. Today, a considerable number of former employees of AstraZeneca have leading positions in small and medium-sized pharmaceutical and biotechnology firms.

Experiences from the pharmaceutical industry tell us that the pertinent R&D activities are very dependent on a small number of key persons and researchers with edge competencies. Managers of AstraZeneca report that any loss in this category of persons has profound effects, because those who leave also attract skillful colleagues to follow them on their new endeavor.

Recruitment of new personnel to the company is the most decisive type of investment decisions that it has to do. The main source of information for these continuing investment choices is what can be retrieved from the company's broad and far-reaching informal networks. These networks play a role both when the company strives for staff renewal and when it searches for collaboration partners. More than 40 % of the recruitment events are based on person-to-person information and second-order information from the established channels of the company's communication network. As a consequence, the maintenance of this network is vital and crucial. The network is one of the company's most basic resources.

The networks that we are discussing are important not only for recruitment from the academy and other research units, with which the company has established research collaboration. The informal networks are equally important for recruiting persons who are employed by other companies. One additional argument put forward in interviews has to do with the smallness of the country, implying that it is possible to have an overview of recruitment options inside the country.

R&D Networks for Collaboration with External Actors

What determines a company's possibilities to organize successful R&D work? On the one hand, R&D activities require internal resources in the form of knowledge labor and the experiences and knowledge embodied in the firm's R&D workers, as well as the routines for knowledge creation that the firm has developed over time. On the other hand, the firm can make use of knowledge flows from external knowledge providers. Part of these flows are acquired through purchase, while other parts are the result of cooperation with external researchers, institutes and universities as well as other firms in the same and associated industries. The collaboration with universities has a particular importance. Persons responsible for R&D efforts in AstraZeneca estimate that up to 80 % of all research related to various forms of cancer are carried out as university research, whilst the remaining 20 % take place within the pharmaceutical industry.

Leading persons in the industry argue that currently there are so many eminent research milieus across the world that it becomes an impossible objective also for a large pharmaceutical company group to locate in all these environments of knowledge creation. In view of this, a favorable strategy must include the formation R&D networks with links to prominent knowledge producers in relevant fields. AstraZeneca has developed processes and technologies for orchestrating collaboration networks that facilitate knowledge interaction over distance. These links function as an infrastructure for research coordination, knowledge exchange, as well as trade with new research results.

AstraZeneca's global R&D is carried out in a set of R&D units in different parts of the world. Those R&D establishments are interlinked in a network which provides AstraZeneca's production and R&D units in Sweden with qualified knowledge flows from knowledge nodes over the world.

- The AstraZeneca group has organized a scheme for systematic information exchange between the nodes in the group, and this exchange ascertains that specialized information is made available for assessment across the entire internal network of the group.

The Swedish units of AstraZeneca employ collaboration strategies in a far reaching way. First and foremost cooperation takes place between R&D units inside the company group, AstraZeneca PLC, but the interaction with other pharmaceutical firms has increased over the years. Other external collaborators include universities and hospitals that are in charge of clinical studies.

AstraZeneca's R&D units in Sweden have a large international network for collaboration, but there is also a dense network of interaction links to actors inside the country. This is illustrated in Figure 7. With the help of interviews and other forms of information, it has been possible to estimate that the total number of collaboration and cooperation links amount to about 550, divided in the figure into agreements of collaboration and more well-specified joint research projects. A large share of the collaboration partners are found in Karolinska Institute, Chalmers Institute of Technology, and the universities in Göteborg, Uppsala and Lund.

- Considering the 550 links for collaboration and exchange of knowledge referred to in Figure 7, the estimated branching of direct and indirect contact links represents an area of interface with the Swedish research community in the order of 1 500 persons or more.
- The company's direct and indirect contact links for research interaction can be estimated to comprise 20-25 university research departments in Sweden.

AstraZeneca's collaboration links include various types of cooperation and collaboration such as agreements to carry out joint research, funding of research, sponsoring of students with research grants and other research support, especially in the form of so-called fee for service. Still another form of support is sponsoring of scientific events and meetings.

Figure 7. AstraZeneca's Collaboration with External Actors in Sweden, 2006.

AstraZeneca's Agreeements and Contracts with Universities
and Research Organizations in Sweden

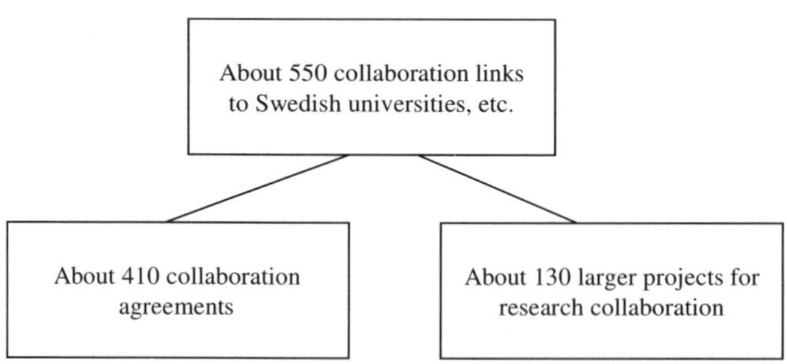

Figure 7 shows that around 25 % of the total amount of collaboration links comprise large research projects. In 2006 the resources set off for these 130 major projects is estimated to be 55-60 million SEK. The major part of these R&D expenditures has been classified as pure research cooperation. These figures imply that AstraZeneca supports research and education in Swedish universities and other research organization to an extent that exceeds the annual costs of a normal university department. To provide a benchmark figure, it is meaningful to observe that a typical research budget at a regional college university in recent years has amounted to around 150 million SEK.

From the information presented one may conclude:

– AstraZeneca's financial support to research and education at Swedish universities amounts to about 2/3 of the research volume at a representative regional university. The university in Jönköping with around 10 000 students has had a research volume of ca 150 million SEK.

In addition AstraZeneca works together with Swedish universities by supporting PhD projects, often combined with resources for tutoring and thesis advice allocated to adjunct professors. Moreover, PhDs can get so-called post-doc grants, and many persons who get this type of support are later recruited to take part in AstraZeneca's in-house research. The described forms of resources for young researchers provide support to around 30 persons annually.

Conclusions and Policy Suggestions

The location and capacity decisions of large research intensive multinational companies like AstraZeneca are based on the location conditions in different regions world-wide. Each region's location characteristics include the possibilities to recruit researchers, cooperate with leading research institutions, conduct clinical tests and collaborate with hospitals in a variety of other ways. The global perspective implies that locations in Boston, Montreal as well as regions in China and India are compared with Sweden, the Malmö, Göteborg and Stockholm regions in particular. As illustrated by recent research, proximity to markets as well as knowledge sources play a role in such comparisons, although the latter motive has grown in importance.

The data and analyses presented in this report illustrate that a large knowledge-intensive multinational firm like AstraZeneca may play an important role in small open economies, in particular for their 'knowledge economy'. Our case study illustrate that AstraZeneca appears as a significant part of the Swedish economy from different perspectives. This may motivate more than just general economic policy. The company accounts for example for a significant share of Sweden's exports, both in the form of exports of manufactures and services. The large export flows contribute substantially to the country's net exports.

Our analysis of the Swedish units' interaction with the rest of the Swedish economy shows that 'traditional' couplings in the form of transactions with Swedish suppliers are limited. It is instead the company's position in the 'knowledge economy' that makes its presence in Sweden important.

The strategic choices for pharmaceutical companies comprise a large set of factors. For Sweden, an important consequence is that the companies need to make location choices and build networks that secure accessibility to knowledge, embodied by universities, biotechnology firms and other pharmaceutical firms.

- Locations in Sweden must be attractive for firms as well as individuals. The possibilities to attract foreign researchers are important but problematic for the Swedish pharmaceutical industry. A critical question for research is to clarify which characteristics in a local milieu that make it attractive and stimulate foreign workers to remain in the milieu, while developing durable social networks.
- In a longer perspective, the density of pertinent firms in the Swedish environment is an important location characteristic. Biotechnology firms are for example becoming more important as knowledge sources and collaboration partners for the large multinational pharmaceutical companies (Rothaemel 2001, Gassman et al. 2008). There is a large international literature analyzing the role of clusters of biomedicine and biotechnology firms as well as the role of networks for R&D and knowledge transfers for pharmaceutical firms. This literature is however not systematized and structured in such a way that it can be used for the formulation and design of

economic policy in Sweden. In this perspective, there is a relevant Swedish research area. Existing knowledge suggests that there is role for economic policy to create an infrastructure and incentives for expansion and cluster formation among small biotechnology firms. Feldman and Francis (2003: 765) draw the following conclusion about the development of the biotechnology cluster in Washington DC in the US: "The Capitol region biotechnology cluster, in essence, is the result of three reinforcing sets of factors: pre-existing resources, entrepreneurship and the incentives and infrastructure provided by government".

For the pharmaceutical companies the possibilities to recruit highly qualified personnel is a critical location factor. This is affected by the education systems (including graduate studies), by the conditions for doctors and other employees within the healthcare system to conduct research as well as by the possibilities to recruit personnel from abroad.

The Swedish pharmaceutical industry's ability to compete for leading researchers is paramount for the industry's long-term future in the country. Such ability requires an administrative, economic and social environment which makes it possible to attract researchers with work and research experience from any of the world's leading research milieus.

The milieus that have developed in Boston, Washington DC, San Francisco and Southern California generate a cluster of researchers that benefit from each other despite disparate disciplines. These research milieus attract talents form all over the world. The ventures in Malmö and Lund in collaboration with Copenhagen and Odense are an attempt to imitate the development in the US regions. A corresponding venture currently takes place in Mälardalen, i.e. the Stockholm-Uppsala Bioregion.

The triangle Stockholm/Uppsala-Göteborg-Malmö/Copenhagen corresponds to many of the US regions and some of the EU regions when it comes to R&D networks and interaction. There are thus two layers of the region concept:

- The first type of region should be a base for frequent interaction between researchers at universities, healthcare institutions within the biomedicine and biotechnology areas firms. Such an R&D region can comprise that whole Swedish "pharmaceutical triangle".

- The second type of region is much more local in nature and relates to its attractiveness as a place of settlement for Swedish and foreign researchers.

The following statement by Malecki (2004) illustrates that importance of attributes and amenities that make regions attractive for highly educated and skilled individuals:

"The latest priority is being placed on attracting mobile workers and mobile investments. Creative workers are the core of the knowledge economy [....] Lists or league tables of 'the best place' to live, to retire and to visit are key features of economies or societies whose factors of success are highly mobile [....] Competition among places involves more than marketing or attempting to sell them. It involves the enhancement or improvements in the attributes that make it possible to attract and keep investments and migrants – that is, to become 'sticky places'." (Malecki, 2004: 1101 and 1103).

It is of course a long way before anything that corresponds to the large US research milieus is developed. It is also unclear to what extent milieus of this type can be planned. However, initiatives to develop competitive research milieus can be critical for the long-term future of the Swedish pharmaceutical industry.

At a general level, policy suggestions point to an increase in the faculty allowances for pertinent research areas, the conditions for clinical research, adjustments in the expert tax subsidy, the planning of functional regions as attractive places of settlements, etc. Other conclusions for pharmaceutical firms include:

- Swedish industrial and R&D policies should contemplate developing conditions that can facilitate the formation of R&D networks for the discovery and development phases of the pharmaceutical industry. An important issue is the collaboration opportunities between pharmaceutical companies and the healthcare system, including university and other hospitals. A related issue is communication at early stages about which treatments, for which the healthcare system is willing to pay.

- Health economic cost-benefit assessments should be developed to cover the whole value chain. This may require a standardized and sanctioned method of analysis – where priority should be given to completeness and transparency.
- The legal conditions for stem cell research in Sweden are considered to be favorable from a research perspective. In combination with Swedish rules for bio banks the favorable conditions is a typical example where there is an option for developing an industrial policy.

Endnotes

[1] There are several other potential effects. Blomström and Kokko (1998, p.2) writes that "local firms may be able to improve their productivity as a result of forward or backward linkages with MNC affiliates, they may imitate MNC technologies, or hire workers trained by MNCs." Other potential mechanisms that they discuss are (i) increased competition that may force local firms to introduce new technology and (ii) spillovers of knowledge and information about foreign markets to local firms, which can make it easier for the latter firms to enter foreign markets. See also Markusen and Trofimenko (2007) who analyze the impact of foreign experts' training of domestic workers on knowledge transfers.

[2] Early studies of multinational R&D emphasized precisely that economies of scale created a drift towards concentrating R&D to the home country, which only in some cases could be outweighed by specific advantages of locating R&D in a "foreign" country (Broström 2008). In this simplified view, an MNE was perceived as determining "the location of its R&D by reconciling centripetal and centrifugal forces" (Hirschey and Caves 1981, cited in Pearce 1999).

[3] These general factors apply in principle to all industries. In addition, there are industry-specific characteristics, which govern the decisions to globalize R&D in specific industries. One such specific factor for the pharmaceutical industry is the critical role of the US market for almost all medicines. Since the US market is by far the largest market for drugs in the world, an early approval of a new drug by the Federal Drug Administration (FDA) is critical for securing a rapid growth of sales and profits.

[4] Cantwell and Piscitello (2005) maintain that this strategy is distinct from the internationalization strategies in the early post-war period. According to

the authors, the internationalization strategy of firms was in this period based on the view that foreign markets should be entered by adjusting product attributes to local consumer preferences, i.e. demand side factors.

[5] The pharmaceutical industry is here defined as NACE 24420, Manufacturing of Pharmaceuticals.

[6] The manufacturing sector is defined as NACE 15-37. Pharmaceutical exports are defined as the total export of manufactures by firms belonging to NACE 24420, Manufacturing of Pharmaceuticals.

[7] Transaction links provide an overall image of how different sectors of the economy buy and sell goods and services to and from each other.

[8] The AstraZeneca individuals interviewed for this report were executive leaders of the company´s operation in Sweden:

- Head of Sweden Operations
- Head of Sourcing and Supply Management
- Executive Vice President, Head of Global Discovery Research
- Head of Turbuhaler and API
- Vice President Human Recourses
- Assistant General Counsel, Legal Department
- Vice President, Global Safety Assessment
- Director Clinical Project Coordination
- Vice President and Global Product Director, CVGI Therapy Area
- Global Vice President Research Area CV/GI
- Vice President PA R&D
- Vice President Global Discovery Research Area CNS/Pain
- Marketing Company President Sweden
- Head of Sweden Purchasing
- Business Analyst R&D Operations Finance
- Vice President Clinical Sweden
- Chief Financial Officer
- Vice President Discovery Information
- Regional Director Medical Science

Additional interviews were done with former executives of AstraZeneca, individuals now in new positions outside the company, and with external experts in relevant fields.

References

Allen, T. J. (1977). *Managing the Flow of Technology*, MIT Press, Cambridge, MA.

Almeida, P. and Kogut B. (1999). "Localization of Knowledge and the Mobility of Engineers in Regional Networks," *Management Science*, 45, 905-917.

Andersson, M and Thulin P. (2008). *Globalisering, Arbetskraftens Rörlighet och Produktivitet,* Globaliseringsrådet, kommande.

Andersson, M., Lööf H. and Johansson S. (2008). "Productivity and International Trade – firm-level evidence from a small open economy", *Review of World Economics*, 144, forthcoming.

Antonelli, C. et al. (eds.) (2006). New Frontiers in the Economics of Innovation and New Technology, Edward Elgar, Cheltenham.

Arvidsson, G., Bergström H., Edquist C., Högberg D. and Jönsson B. (2007). *Medicin för Sverige – nytt liv i en framtidsbransch*, SNS Förlag, Stockholm.

Blomström, M. and Kokko A. (1998). "Multinational Corporations and Spillovers", *Journal of Economic Surveys*, 12, 1-31.

Braunerhjelm, P. and Ekholm. K. (eds.) (1998). *The Geography of Multinational Firms*, Kluwer, Dordrecht.

Braunerhjelm P. and Svensson R. (1998). "Agglomeration in the Geographical Location of Swedish MNEs", in Braunerhjelm, P and Ekholm. K. (eds.) (1998), *The Geography of Multinational Firms*, Kluwer, Dordrecht, 99-115.

Broström, A. (2008). "How can we Study Innovation Systems?", CESIS WP 124, Royal Institute of Technology.

Cantwell J. A. (1989). Technological Innovation and Multinational Corporations. Basil Blackwell, Oxford.

Cantwell J. A. (1995). "The Globalization of Technology: what remains of the product cycle model?", *Cambridge Journal of Economics*, 19, 155-174.

Cantwell, J. A and Piscitello L. (2005). "Recent Location of Foreign-Owned Research and Development Activities by Large Multinational Corporations in European Regions: the role of spillovers and externalities", *Regional Studies*, 39, 1-16.

Carlsson, B. (2006). "Internationalization of Innovation Systems: a survey of the literature," *Research Policy*, 35, 56-67.

Cockburn, I. M. (2006). "Blurred Boundaries: Tensions Between Open Scientific Resources and Commercial Exploitation of Knowledge in Biomedical Research", in Kahin, B. and Foray D. (2006) (Eds.), *Advancing Knowledge and the Knowledge Economy*, The MIT Press, Cambridge, MA, 351-368.

Cockburn, I. M. et al. (1999)."Pharmaceuticals and Biotechnology", in Mowery, D. (1999), *U.S. Industry in 2000: Studies in Competitive Performance*, National Research Council, Washington, D.C, p. 363-398.

Criscuolo, P., Narula R. and Verspagen B. (2005). "Role of Home and Host Country Innovation Systems in R&D Internationalisation: a patent citation analysis," *Economics of Innovation and New Technology*, 14, 417-433.

De Meyer, A. (1993). "Management of an International Network of Industrial R&D Laboratories", *R&D Management*, 23, 109-120.

Deiaco, E and Melin G. *Hur mår klinisk forskning*?, SISTER arbetsrapport 2006:50.

DiMasi, J. A.., Hansen R. W. and Gabrowski H. (2003). "The Price of Innovation: new estimates of drug development costs", *Journal of Health Economics*, 22, 151-185.

Feldman, M and Francis J. (2003). "Fortune Favors the Prepared Region – the case of entrepreneurship and the capitol region Biotechnology cluster", *European Planning Studies*, 11, 765-788.

Florida, R. (1997). "The Globalization of R&D: results of a survey of foreign-affiliated R&D laboratories in the US", *Research Policy,* 26, 85-103.

Furman, J. et al. (2005). "Knowledge Spillovers, Geographic Location, and the Productivity of Pharmaceutical Research", *Annales d´Economie et de Statistique*.

Gabrowski, H. J and Vernon J. (1990). "A New Look at the Returns and Risks to Pharmaceutical R&D", *Management Science*, 36, 804-821.

Gabrowski, H., Vernon J. and Dimasi J. A. (2002). "Returns on Research and Development for 1990s New Drug Introductions", *Pharmacoeconomics*, 20 (supp 3), 11-29.

Gambardella, A. (1995). Science and Innovation: The U.S. Pharmaceutical Industry During the 1980s, Cambridge University Press, Cambridge.

Gassman O., Reepmeyer G. and von Zedtwitz M. (2008). *Leading Pharmaceutical Innovation*, Springer, Berlin.

Gassman, O. and von Zedtwitz M. (1999). "New Concepts and Trends in International R&D Organization," *Research Policy*, 28, 231-250.

Gerybadze, A. and Reger G. (1999). "Globalization of R&D: recent changes in the management of innovation in transnational corporations," *Research Policy*, 28, 251-274.

Gustavsson, P. (2004). "Effekten av Näringslivets Internationalisering på Forskning och Utveckling", in ITPS (2004). *Näringslivets Internationalisering*, ITPS A 2004:014: 135-154.

Hegde, D. and Hicks D. (2005)."The Maturation of Global Corporate R&D: Theory and evidence," Ivan Allen College Working paper series #3, Georgia Tech.

Hirschey, R. C. and Caves R. E. (1981). "Internationalization of Research and Transfer of Technology by Multinational Enterprises," *Oxford Bulletin of Economics and Statistics*, 42, 115-130.

ITPS (2004). Näringslivets Internationalisering, ITPS A 2004.014.

Johansson, B and Lööf H. (2006). "Globala FoU-företag i Sverige – vilken betydelse har de för ekonomins utvecklingskraft?", in D. Johansson och N. Karlsson (red.), *Svensk Utvecklingskraft*, Ratio, Stockholm.

Johansson, D. and Karlsson N. (red.). *Svensk Utvecklingskraft*, Ratio, Stockholm.

Kahin, B. and Foray D. (2006) (eds.). *Advancing Knowledge and the Knowledge Economy*, The MIT Press, Cambridge MA.

Koretz, S. and Lee G. (1998). "Knowledge Management and Drug Development", *Journal of Knowledge Management*, 2, 53-58.

Kuemmerle W. (1997). Building effective R&D capabilities abroad. *Harvard Business Review* March-April, 61-70.

Kuemmerle, W. (1999). "The Drivers of Foreign Direct Investment into Research and Development: an empirical investigation," *Journal of International Business Studies*, 30, 1-24.

Kumar, N. (2001). "Determinants of Location of Overseas R&D Activity of Multinational Enterprises: The Case of US and Japanese Corporations," *Research Policy*, 30, 159-174.

LeBas, C. and Sierra C. (2002). "Location versus Home Country Advantages in R&D Activities: some further results on multinationals' locational strategies," *Research Policy*, 31, 589-609.

Lichtenberg, F. (1996). "The Effect of Pharmaceutical Utilization and Innovation on Hospitalization and Mortality", *NBER Working Paper.*

Lichtenberg, F. (2000). "Are the Benefits of Newer Drugs worth their Costs?", *Health Affairs*, 20, 242-251.

Malecki, E. (2004). "Jockeying for Position: what it means and why it matters to regional development policy when places compete", *Regional Studies*, 38, 1101-1120.

Malerba, F. and Orsenigo L. (2006). "A History-Friendly Model of Innovation, Market Structure and Regulation in the Age of Random Screening of the Pharmaceutical Industry", in Antonelli, C et al. (eds) (2006). *New Frontiers in the Economics of Innovation and New Technology*, Edward Elgar, Cheltenham: 70-118.

Markusen, J. R (1995). "The Boundaries of Multinational Enterprises and the Theory of International Trade", *Journal of Economic Perspectives*, 9, 169-189.

Markusen, J. R (1998). "Multinational Firms, Location and Trade", *World Economy*, 21, 733-756.

Markusen, J. R (2004). Multinational Firms and the Theory of International Trade, The MIT Press, Cambridge.

Markusen, J. R. and Trofimenko N. (2007). "Teaching Locals New Tricks: foreign experts as a channel of knowledge transfers", NBER WP 12872.

McCann, P. (2008a). "Globalization, Multinationals and the BRIICS Countries", *Mimeograph.*

McCann, P. (2008b). "The Economic Geography of Globalization: technology, institutions and multinationals", Keynote speech at the congress of the European Regional Science Association (ERSA), Liverpool, UK, August 2008.

McCann, P. and Mudambi R. (2004). "The Location Decision of the Multinational Enterprise: Some Theoretical and Empirical Issues", *Growth and Change*, 35, 491-524.

McCann, P. and Mudambi R. (2005). "Analytical Differences in the Economics of Geography: The Case of the Multinational Firm", *Environment and Planning A*, 37, 1857-1876.

Meyer-Krahmer, F. and Reger G. (1999). "New Perspectives on the Innovation Strategies of Multinational Enterprises: lessons for technology policy in Europe," *Research Policy*, 28, 751-776.

Mowery, D. (1999). *U.S. Industry in 2000: Studies in Competitive Performance*, National Research Council, Washington, D.C.

Mowery, D. et al. (2001). "The Growth of Patenting and Licensing by U.S. Universities – an assessment of the effects of the Bay-Dole act", *Research Policy*, 30, 99-119.

Narula, R. (1999). "Explaining the Growth of Strategic R&D Alliances by European Firms", *Journal of Common Market Studies*, 37, 711-723.

Narula, R. and Zanfei A. (2004). "Globalization of Innovation: The Role of Multinational Enterprises," in Fagerberg, J., Mowery D., Nelson R.R. (ed.), *Handbook of Innovation*, Oxford University Press, 2004.

Oettl, A. and Agrawal A. (2008). "International Labor Mobility and Knowledge Flow Externalities", *Journal of International Business Studies*, Online February 2008.

Patel, P. and Pavitt K. (1995). "Patterns of Technological Activity: their measurement and interpretation", in Stoneman, P (ed.) (1995). *Handbook of the Economics of Innovation and Technological Change*, Blackwell, London: 14-51.

Pearce, R. and Papanastassiou M. (1999). "Overseas R&D and the Strategic Evolution of MNEs: evidence from laboratories in the UK," *Research Policy*, 28, 23-41.

Pearce, R. D (1999). "Decentralized R&D and Strategic Competitiveness: globalised approaches to generation and use of technology in multinational enterprises (MNEs)," *Research Policy*, 28, 157-178.

Pharmaceutical Research and Manufacturers of America, Industry Profile 2004.

Pisano, G. P. (1997). The Development Factory: Unlocking the Potential of Process Innovation, Harvard Business School Press, Boston, MA.

Ramirez, P. (2003). *Globalization, Technology and Organizational Change in the Pharmaceutical Industry*, Institute of Science and Technology, University of Manchester (diss.).

Ramirez, P. and Tylecote A. (2004). "Hybrid Corporate Governance and its Effects on Innovation: a case study of AstraZeneca", *Technology Analysis and Strategic Management*, 16: 97-119

Randles, S. (2002). "Complex Systems Applied? The merger that made GlaxoSmithKline", *Technological Analysis and Strategic Management*, 14: 331-354.

Roberts, P. W. (1999). "Product Innovation, Product-Market Competition and Persistent Profitability in the US Pharmaceutical Industry", *Strategic Management Journal*, 20: 655-670.

Rothaermel, F. T (2001). "Complementary Assets, Strategic Alliances and the Incumbent's Advantage: an empirical study of industry and firm effects in the biopharmaceutical industry", *Research Policy*, 30: 1235-1251.

Scherer, F. M. (1993). "Pricing, Profits and Technological Progress in the Pharmaceuticals Industry", *Journal of Economic Perspectives 7*, 97-115.

Scherer, F. M. (1999). New Perspectives on Economic Growth and Technological Innovation, Brookings Institutions Press, Washington.

Schweitzer, S. O. (2007). *Pharmaceutical Economics and Policy*, 2nd ed., Oxford University Press, Oxford.

Socialdepartementet (2003). *Högspecialiserad sjukvård - kartläggning och förslag*, Regeringskansliet, DS 2003:56 .

SOU (2008). Åtgärdsplan för den kliniska forskningen, SOU 2008:7.

Steele, H. W. (1989). *Managing Technology: The Strategic View*, McGraw-Hill, New York.

Stoneman, P. (ed.) (1995). Handbook of the Economics of Innovation and Technological Change, Blackwell, London.

Teece, D. (1987). "Profiting from Technological Innovation: Implications for Integration, Elaboration, Licensing and Public Policy", *Research Policy*, 15, 285-305.

UNCTAD (2004). *The Impact of FDI on Development: Globalization of R&D by Transnational Corporations and Implications for Developing Countries*, Note by the UNCTAD secretariat, December 7. Prepared for the expert meeting on the impact of FDI on development, Geneva, January 24-26, 2005.

UNCTAD (2005). *World Investment Report: Transnational Corporations and the Internationalization of R&D*, United Nations Conference on Trade and Development, United Nations, New York and Geneva.

UNCTAD (2007). *World Investment Report: Transnational Corporations, Extractive Industries and Development*, United Nations Conference on Trade and Development, United Nations, New York and Geneva.

von Zedtwitz, M. and Gasssman O. (2002). "Market versus technology drive in R&D internationalization: four different patterns of managing research and development", *Research Policy*, 31, 569-588.

Walsh, V. and Lodorfos G. (2002). "Technological and Organizational Innovation in Chemicals and Related Industries", *Technological Analysis and Strategic Management*, 14, 273-297.

World Bank (2007). *2007 World Development Indicators*, Washington DC.

Yeoh, P.-L. and Roth K. (1999). "An Empirical Analysis of Sustained Advantage in the US Pharmaceutical Industry: Impact of Firm Resources and Capabilities", *Strategic Management Journal 20*, 637-653.

Zander I. (1999). "How do you mean Global? A taxonomy of innovation networks in the multinational corporation", *Research Policy*, 28, 195-213.

Zanfei A. (2000). "Transnational Firms and the Changing Organization of Innovative Activities", *Cambridge Journal of Economics*, 24, 515-542.

Zucker, L., Darby M. and Brewer M. (1998). "Intellectual Human Capital and the Birth of U.S. Biotechnology Enterprises", *American Economic Review 88*, 290-306.

The Future of Public and Private Health Systems and Retirement Systems in Aging Societies

11

Collaborative Governance and the US Healthcare and Retirement Systems

Siona Listokin

Introduction

Taken as a whole, the US healthcare and retirement systems display many of the key characteristics of collaborative governance: a mix of public and private funding, co-regulation and both government and industry provision of services. While the public/private mix in the US is frequently deemphasized in comparisons to other developed countries (which generally rely more heavily on public resources), there is little denying that whole portions of these social services are vastly influenced by government. Indeed, analysis of spending on healthcare and retirement illustrates the combination of resources. 40 % of retirement expenditures in the US is publicly funded (Hacker 2002); likewise 45 % of healthcare expenditures are likewise provided by the government.

Despite the raw numbers, however, neither retirement nor healthcare systems in the US constitute cases of collaborative governance. Rather, these systems' public/private mix illustrates a destructive co-dependency that is path dependent, and not structured purposefully in the pursuit of social welfare goals.[1] In addition, while there are significant differences between the provision and design of retirement and healthcare systems – most significantly, publicly provided retirement programs are universal while healthcare is not – both display similar ad-hoc and ultimately inefficient government and private elements.

This study will examine the retirement and health care systems in the United States, and show that while both use a mix of public and private funding and delivery, they do not meet the criteria of collaborative governance. An analysis of the development of each system will show that the private aspects of these systems were frequently at odds with state social welfare goals, and the result of political economy concerns.

The article will proceed as follows. Section 2 will define collaborative governance and review the literature on co-regulation. Section 3 will describe the healthcare and retirement systems in the United States, including development and current practices. Section 4 will demonstrate the lack of collaborative governance within these systems, and section 5 concludes.

Literature Review: Collaborative Governance

While there is no universally agreed upon definition of collaborative governance, there is consensus about its necessary conditions. At a minimum, collaborative governance requires "broad participation" of public and private stakeholders (Koch 2008). More expansive requirements explicitly include a public/private mix in responsibility and provision of services (see, for example, Freeman 1997). Consensus appears to end, however, with these necessary conditions. For example, Koch (2008) suggests that collaborative governance must be conducted in a non-adversarial manner, and "based on positive problem solving." Freeman (1997) goes further, and gives five characteristics of collaborative governance: (1) a problem-solving orientation; (2) participation by interested and affected persons at all stages of the decision making process; (3) solutions that are provisional and subject to revision; (4) accountability; and (5) flexible, engaged government institutions.

Other discussions of collaborative governance shift focus to local participation and multi-level policymaking (Newman et al. 2004). Here again, broad stakeholder involvement is emphasized, but the sufficient conditions center on civic engagement. Implicit in this consideration is the hierarchical impetus of governance – in Freeman's discussion there is a horizontal structure that drives decision making, while Newman et al. suggests a more top-down organization. This distinction gets to a key issue about whether government policies with private industry participation qualifies as collaborative government (top-down), or if a more fundamental role is necessary by private actors. The former definition would include traditional governance with private contracting and outsourcing as collaborative governance, while the latter requires additional conditions. See (Huxham 2000) for similar arguments.

Additional elements of collaborative governance are relevant. Huxham (2000) discusses the organizational complexity that frequently occurs with broad participation in decision making. A related point concerns the ability of participants to consider themselves as part of a particular organization – if stakeholders are disparate to the point of not being identifiably part of a collaborative organization, the title may not apply (Vangen and Huxham 2003).

This paper will apply Freeman's (1997) five characteristics of collaborative governance, with the condition that decisions are not entirely hierarchical. In addition, following Huxham (2000), participants in policymaking and deliverance should be identifiably part of an organization (or a more informal stakeholder group). These narrowing conditions will allow for a distinction between social systems that involve public and private elements by design from those that are ad hoc or contract-based. The US retirement and health care systems clearly include a mix of public and private stakeholder participation; an analysis of the systems' development will consider whether they have the additional conditions necessary for collaborative governance.

Development of US Retirement and Healthcare Systems

A close look at the current state and development of both the US retirement and healthcare systems is necessary to determine if they are examples of collaborative governance. This review will emphasize that while health care and retirement appear to have fundamentally different mixes of private and public participation, they share important characteristics; both fail to meet the necessary conditions of collaboration.

Retirement in the US

The retirement system in the US appears to be an outlier in the country's social services provision in that there is a robust public retirement program with widespread availability, along the lines of many other developed countries, though less dependent on government transfers (Brown and Prus 2004). The federal Social Security program paid out $516.2 billion in retirement benefits (Old Age and Survivors Insurance) in 2009 to 41.6 million people (Social Security and Medicare Boards of Trustees 2009), and it is the largest public program in the country (Office of Management and Budget 2009). Most Americans over the age of 65 rely on their Social Security benefits for the majority of their income. At the same time, however, most Americans also receive retirement benefits from a private investment source, such as retirement accounts through their employer or independently (Beland and Gran 2008).

On its face, then, retirement in the US for over half of Americans is a joint endeavor between government provided benefits and privately saved or compensated benefits (though the mix is different than in many other developed countries). Table 1 shows the sources of income for those overage 65 in the US and selected countries. The mix between public and private elements goes beyond provision of retirement income and extends to the structure of many American's plans for retirement. Private pensions and investments are part of a system that responds to a number of public incentives and structures. For example, employers can avoid taxes on retirement benefit compensation; in fiscal year 2009 this amounted to $96.6 billion in uncollected taxes (Copeland 2008). Favorable tax treatment on capital gains and IRA accounts through the Employee Retirement Investment Security Act (ERISA) represents another public subsidy (Disney and Johnson 2001).

The current retirement system is based in large part on a series of government decisions in the first half of the twentieth century. In the

1910s - 1920s, a number of tax incentives were created for employer-based retirement benefits (Beland and Gran 2008).

Table 1: Percentage Distribution of Adjusted Household Income by Source, Selected Countries, Household Heads Aged 65+

	Sweden	Denmark	Germany	Norway	Canada	U.K.	Netherlands	Australia	U.S.
Earnings*	7.2	11.0	14.9	20.9	19.6	15.9	8.6	29.3	28.2
Investments**	7.2	8.7	4.9	10.1	14.0	14.1	9.4	16.8	15.8
Pensions***	16.0	20.1	13.9	15.3	20.0	25.1	29.9	10.7	17.0
Government Transfers	69.6	60.2	66.3	53.7	46.3	44.9	52.1	43.3	39.1

Note: Percentages are based on before-tax household income adjusted for household and may not total to 100 % due to rounding
* Includes self-employment income
** Includes other income from private sources
*** Private (occupational) pension income
Source: Luxembourg Income Study, via Brown and Prus (2004)

At the same time, state employee pensions were growing, as were other systems based on state citizenship (Mitchell and Husead 2000). Following the Great Depression, as the need for a stable and wide-spread social safety net became clear, the federal government created Social Security in 1935. The Social Security Act changed the face of retirement in the US for both public and private parties, and the incidence of private pensions grew after 1935 (Beland and Gran 2008). Since the 1930s, both public retirement benefits (via Social Security) and private pensions have grown. The combined effects of organized labor's ability to use retirement benefits favorably in wage negotiations and the tax incentives caused employer-based pensions to grow in importance for middle and upper-class workers (Disney and Johnson 2001). While employer-based pension plans have largely shifted from guaranteed levels of retirement income (defined benefit) to blocks of employer contributions that are managed by the retiree (defined contribution), the model of private and public retirement elements remains (Disney and Johnson 2001).

A major issue in the retirement system today is the uneven conditions between lower-to middle class retirees and the rest of the population (Bernheim, Skinner, and Weinberg 2001). In addition, funding for Social Security is set up as pay-as-you-go, which sets up a generational entitlement where today's workers contribute to today's retirees with the expectation that the same will occur in the future. Demographic trends – a higher retiree to worker ratio – has created a condition where payouts are higher than contributions to the system; Social Security is expected to run out of reserve assets money in 2037 (Social Security and Medicare Boards of Trustees 2009).

Healthcare in the United States

While there are many similarities between the US retirement and healthcare systems, the divide between the US and other developed countries in the percentage of government funding is significantly greater in healthcare. Total healthcare spending also takes up a greater percentage of GDP in the US, and portions of the population have poor access to care.

Because of the high cost and rarity of medical emergencies, healthcare is often covered by insurance. This is true for most Americans, and there is a mix of private and public insurance programs (most of the actual provision of health care is private, including not-for-profit organizations). On the public side, the elderly and the poor, as well as a number of more specific categories of groups, are covered under the federal Medicare and Medicaid programs; over 25 % of Americans are covered by government programs (Gallup Inc. 2009). On the private side, employer-based insurance covered 58 % households in 2008 and there are a number of nationwide insurance companies that offer a range of coverage services (US Census Bureau 2009). Figures 1 and 2 give a comparative view of public and private healthcare expenditures across selected OECD countries in 1970 and 2007. The figures show the growth in spending as a percent of GDP and the greater reliance on private expenditures in the US.

Figure 1: Total Health Expenditures as a % of GDP, 1970

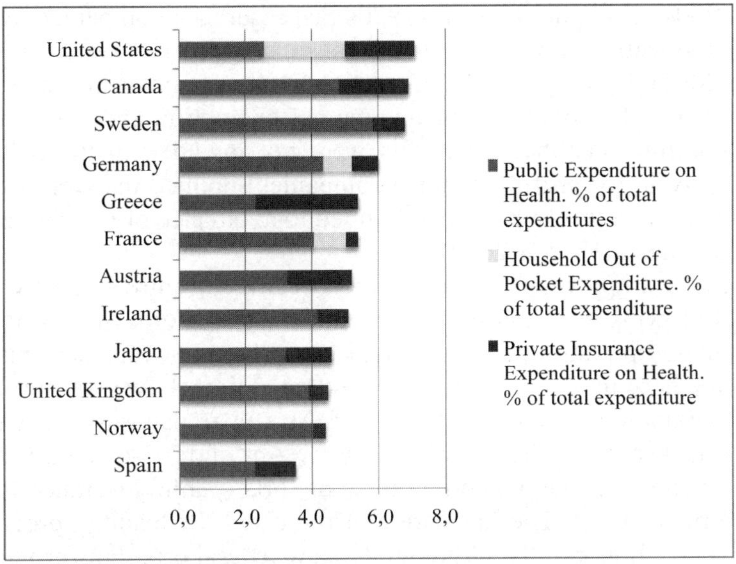

Figure 2: Total Health Expenditures as a % of GDP, 2007

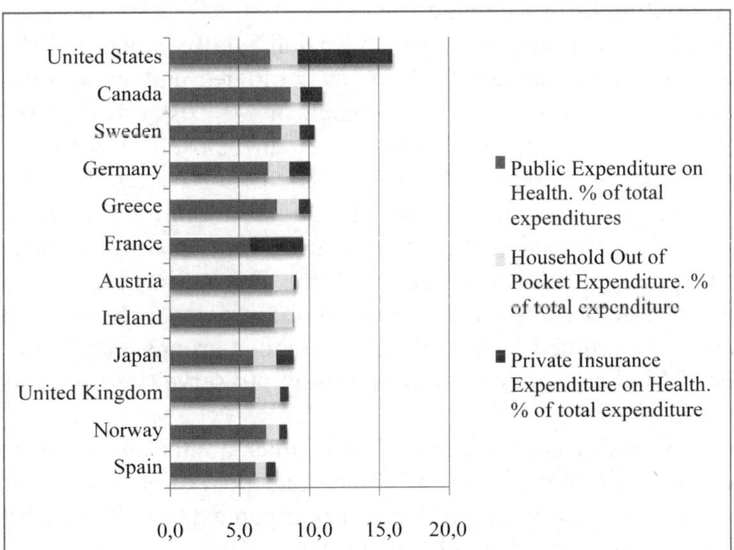

Source: OECD Health Data, 2009
Note: OECD expenditure categories aggregated for presentation

While there were patchwork insurance programs in the 1800s and early 1900s, it was not until the 1920s that insurance companies really grew, frequently representing local physician and/or hospital groups (Cohn 2007). Employer-based insurance became popular in the 1940s as a way to take advantage of income tax exemption and get around wage controls (healthcare benefits were not included in the restrictions). Private for-profit insurance companies supplied the employers' plans; over time, profit maximization led to avoidance of risky, expensive, customers (Hacker 2002).

Because employer-based coverage became so entrenched by the 1950s following an expansion in incentives after World War II, there were enough private interests to fight broad-based government insurance like those in other countries. At the same time, however, portions of the population – such as retired workers – were naturally left uninsured (Hacker 2002). The Social Security Act of 1965 created Medicare, which represented a compromise of sorts (public insurance for a limited population). The legislation also created Medicaid, a program for the poor. Importantly, although the new federal programs provided funding for insurance, provision for services was largely handled through existing insurance plans.

Healthcare spending has grown exponentially since the 1960s (Baltagi and Moscone 2009). New technologies and expansions in government programs have driven much of the costs. Today, public and private funded insurance plans remain closely linked (Cohn 2007). For example, gaps in Medicare's medical coverage have led to private insurance company growth (Beland and Gran 2008). In addition, as Medicare reimbursement rates are set, the private medical industry responds (Cutler and Gruber 1996). Private insurance companies may charge their customers more in order to cover the lower rates set by the government; alternatively, provider groups may limit the number of Medicare patients they are willing to serve (Perloff, Kletke, and Fossett 1995).

The US healthcare system today is thus a mix of government funded insurance and private insurance and provision, with parts of the industry operating as not-for-profit organizations (Cohn 2007). Healthcare spending accounts for 16 % of GDP, with government spending taking up 7% in 2006 (Jensen 2008). These numbers are expected to rise, and the Centers for Medicare and Medicaid Services projected in March 2009 that healthcare expenditures is estimated to account for 20.3 % of GDP in 2018. In addition, 46.3 million people did not have health insurance in 2008 (US Census Bureau 2009).

In response to these realities, healthcare reform has been proposed (and failed) in 1994 and was vigorously debated in 2009. At the time of this writing, the fate of healthcare legislation is uncertain. The outlines of possible reform in any realistic bill in 2010 are clear, however. The broad structure of a private/public mix will remain for the foreseeable future (Kaiser Family Foundation 2010). Individuals without insurance, however, may have expanded options for coverage, through a government-run insurance option, increased regulation on existing insurance providers or an expansion of the existing government programs. Various ideas to "bend the cost curve" of increasing healthcare spending may also be included (Kaiser Family Foundation 2010). It is clear that whatever legislation passes (and it not certain that anything will pass), reform will very much be tied to the historical development and events that have created the current state; major changes are currently not being considered.

Collaborative Governance in Retirement and Healthcare

Given the current state and development of the retirement and healthcare systems, it is unclear if the relationship between government and private parties is collaborative, or an instance of coregulation. This section considers each condition necessary for collaborative governance in the context of retirement and healthcare.

Problem-solving Orientation

The demographic and funding issues facing both private and public provision of retirement benefits represents the system's biggest challenges. Yet the private and public actors do not appear to work together to solve this issue. For example, in the Pension Protection Act of 2006, federal legislation attempted to deal with the growing risks in corporate pension funds; fiduciary funds were being used for corporate capital and frequently fell below adequate funding levels. The legislation passed against the wishes of corporations, and essentially mandated proper funding ratios for the private pensions (Williams Walsh 2008).

In healthcare, the mix of entrenched interest groups – both public and private – makes the system difficult to improve collaboratively. Physician and private insurance interests repeatedly resisted federal programs, until concessions were made to protect or improve their financial conditions (Relman 2009). Public interests, such as state administrative responsibilities over federal programs, have likewise been wary of expanding eligibility.[2] The 2009 healthcare reform debate crystallizes the lack of problem-solving collaboration. Individual negotiations with special interests, such as pharmaceutical companies, major insurance groups and hospital providers, were oriented to lessen resistance rather than work towards solutions. At the same time, state leaders expressed concern with the proposals, and key parties wavered in their support (or lack of active resistance) throughout the process.

Participation by Interested and Affected Persons at all Stages of the Decision making Process

On one hand, retirement in the US appears to enjoy broad and mixed participation: public programs (Social Security), employer pensions and individual investments. However, this multi-tiered retirement system commands very little collaborative planning or organization. In fact, this lack of coordination may be the reason for the severe demographic differences in retirement income. Retirement benefits are not entirely protected by law (outside of those contracted in the employment agreement), and many individuals lack the means and/or the knowledge to create individual savings accounts. The 2008 presidential campaign offered a direct alternative to this disparate system when Hillary Clinton, a candidate for the Democratic Party nomination, highlighted a proposal to create private savings accounts through government funds. These accounts would introduce many to private investments and would engage private retirement managers through public moneys (Clinton 2007).

The policy making process in healthcare is unique in that there is only occasional reform debates despite its looming problems. Compare the attempts at reform of healthcare to Social Security, which has been tried more frequently and until recently was considered a bigger problem. Between 1994 and 2009 (the two most recent attempts at major reform), the healthcare system has largely reacted to market conditions rather than driven the system through policy decisions. For example, as managed care through HMOs decreased and medical costs increased, insurance companies prudently cut costs – frequently through denied coverage (Beland and Gran 2008).

Solutions that are Provisional and Subject to Revision

This condition for collaborative governance is connected to the idea that system participants are collectively thinking through problems. This has not been the case in retirement, though legislation can be changed over time. Within the separate private and public spheres, there is room for revision. For example, many employer pension funds have experimented with (and generally switched to) defined contribution systems from defined benefit (Disney and Johnson 2001). A number of state pension plans have followed suite, as this shifts risks from the employer to the employee (Mitchell and Hustead 2000). Following strong resistance from organized labor, state pension plans have largely stopped the exodus to defined contribution – and many states that had switched over actually returned to defined benefit.

Given the political difficulties in reforming healthcare, it is somewhat unreasonable to require provisional solutions. However, there are elements of the current system that do allow for corrections. For example, Medicare reimbursement rates are constant reevaluated – and institutional pressure frequently plays a role in rate setting Pear 2008). In addition, coverage for certain populations under federal programs has fluctuated in recent years (for example, SCHIP coverage for children). The 2009 healthcare bills that passed through the House and Senate both included ideas to lower overall healthcare costs with the thought that the unsuccessful components would be phased out (Kaiser Family Foundation 2010).

Accountability

While there is no central organization with broad stakeholder participation considering retirement issues, there is a fair measure of accountability within the major public programs and private spheres. The Social Security Administration is the most visibly accountable public actor; they issue annual reports and have been vocal about funding issues. At the private level, there is less accountability for each employer. Moreover, the governmental organization that helps protect private pensions – the Pension Benefit Guaranty Corporation – is frequently unable to fully fund those pensions from bankrupt companies (Hawthorne 2006).

There appears to be consensus about the two major problems with the current healthcare system: rising costs and the uninsured (Cohn 2007). Yet the major participants disagree over what or who is responsible for these issues. For example, hospitals complain that they are frequently left with unpaid bills from services provided to uninsured patients. As a result, they charge insured patients more to cover costs. Pharmaceutical companies, physician groups, insurance companies, public providers and hospital groups are each blamed for the rising costs even as they are reacting to the circumstances created by the status quo (Cohn 2007).

Flexible, Engaged Government Institution

Followers of the US retirement system quickly become aware of the difficulty of reforming the system. Social Security reform is oft-discussed but rarely acted on, perhaps due to the politics of benefit rules. For the first forty years of Social Security, benefit adjustments required a federal legislation (even to adjust to cost of living) (Disney and Johnson 2001). The attempt at fairly major reform (private accounts) in 2004 was not successful, and more minor fixes are frequently difficult to pass.

As discussed previously, the political realities of healthcare reform do not seem to allow for flexibility. In addition, government engagement in finding solutions is sporadic. As healthcare spending increases as a portion of GDP, however, it may no longer be possible for legislators to ignore healthcare reform.

Conclusion

Like most major social policy issues in developed countries, the retirement and healthcare systems in the US are products of their historical development. However, US retirement and healthcare are uniquely path-dependent. This reality has created an ad hoc mix of government funding and private services, a necessary condition for collaboration and "co-regulation." The systems do not show the sufficient characteristics of collaborative governance, which include participation, flexibility, accountability, and a problem-solving orientation.

Given the entrenched systems, is it possible for a collaborative governance system to emerge with reform? For retirement policy and distribution, there is some consensus that the retirement age will need to be raised, which will have consequences for employers with large populations of older workers. These employees are expensive, yet have valuable reputation and skills. Government and industry will have to work together to determine the terms of an employment extension – for example, will salaries need to be maintained at their high level? Critically, though, this situation represents opportunities for public and private stakeholders, which will enable collaboration.

A collaborative healthcare system is harder to envision in the near future. Eventually, nearly every interested party will be forced to reduce costs and/or maximize efficiency. It is not certain that reform will result from cooperative problem solving or incremental fixes that necessarily creates winners and losers. Ultimately, healthcare reform in the US will require cultural consensus; is healthcare a right? Should everyone get the same level of care? Is there a minimum value required from healthcare expenditures? Until these questions are addressed (let alone answered), special interests will continue to negotiate, not collaborate.

As with many industry analyses of collaborative governance, it is hard to generalize the conclusions of this study. It would be useful to take a comparative perspective of other countries' retirement and healthcare systems, where either public or private actors dominate funding or provision. American exceptionalism in these particular social policy areas makes comparative studies difficult. US state level reforms (such as the expansion of Massachusetts healthcare coverage) may offer empirical options. All studies will need to distinguish between broad public and private participation and true collaborative governance; the retirement and healthcare systems in the US are acute examples of non-cooperative participation badly in need of reform.

Endnotes

[1] Other research has analyzed the historical development of social policy in the US. In his book, "The Divided Welfare State," Jacob Hacker details the path dependency/policy feedback (Hacker 2002).

[2] For example, the National Governors Association website (accessed 1/06/10) homepage for healthcare reform expresses support for general reform, and adds "Nevertheless, governors are cautious about moving forward…"

http://www.nga.org/portal/site/nga/menuitem.1f41d49be2d3d33eacdcbeeb501010a0/?vgnextoid=2012e313c90d3110VgnVCM1000001a01010aRCRD

References

Baltagi, B. H. and Moscone F. (2009). Health Care Expenditure and Income in the OECD Reconsidered: Evidence from Panel Data. *University of Leicester, Department of Economics wp* 9, no. 05.

Beland, D. and Gran B. (2008). Public and Private Social Policy: Health and Pension Policies in a New Era. Palgrave Macmillan, November 15.

Bernheim, B. D., Skinner J. and Weinberg S. (2001). What accounts for the variation in retirement wealth among US households? *The American Economic Review* 91, no. 4: 832-857.

Brown, R. L. and Prus S. G. (2004). Social transfers and income inequality in old age: A multinational perspective. *North American Actuarial Journal* 8, no. 4: 30-36.

Clinton, H. (2007). Remarks in Webster City Iowa. The American Presidency Project, October 9.

Cohn, J. (2007). Sick: the untold story of America's health care crisis–and the people who pay the price. HarperCollins Publishers.

Copeland, C. (2008). Labor force participation: The population age 55 and older. *EBRI Notes* 28, no. 6: 2-8.

Cutler, D. M, and Gruber J. (1996). Does public insurance crowd out private insurance. *The Quarterly Journal of Economics* 111, no. 2: 391-430.

Disney, R. and Johnson P. (2001). *Pension systems and retirement incomes across OECD countries*. Edward Elgar Publishing.

Freeman, J. (1997). Collaborative Governance in the Administrative State. *UCLA Law Review* 45, no. 1.

Gallup Inc. (2009). Gallup-Healthways Well-Being Index. July 30.

Hacker, J. S. (2002). The divided welfare state: The battle over public and private social benefits in the United States. Cambridge University Press.

Hawthorne, F. (2006). If Company Goes Bankrupt, Don't Count on Your Pension, October 24, sec. Business.

Huxham, C. (2000). The challenge of collaborative governance. *Public management* 2, no. 3: 337-357.

Jensen, J. (2008). Government spending on healthcare benefits and programs: A Data Brief. Congressional Research Service, June 16.

Kaiser Family Foundation (2010). Side-by-side Comparison of Major Health Care Reform Proposals. January 13. http://www.kff.org/healthreform/sidebyside.cfm.

Koch, Ch. (2008). Collaborative Governance: Lessons for Europe from U.S. Electricity Restructuring. *SSRN eLibrary* (May 30).

Mitchell, O. S and Hustead E. C. (2000). *Pensions in the public sector*. University of Pennsylvania Press.

Newman, J.; Barnes M.; Sullivan H. and Knops A. (2004). Public participation and collaborative governance. *Journal of Social Policy* 33, no. 02: 203-223.

Office of Management and Budget (2009). Mid-Session Review, Budget of the US Government 2009.

Pear, R. (2008). Doctors press Senate to undo Medicare cuts. *NY Times* 7:7.

Perloff, J. D., Kletke P. and Fossett J. W. (1995). Which physicians limit their Medicaid participation, and why. *Health Services Research* 30, no. 1 Pt 1: 7.

Relman, A. S. (2009). Doctors as the Key to Health Care Reform. *The New England Journal of Medicine* 361, no. 13: 1225.

Social Security and Medicare Boards of Trustees (2009). Summary: Reports from the Board of Trustees.

US Census Bureau (2009). Income, Poverty and Health Insurance Coverage in the United States: 2008. September 10.

Vangen, S. and Huxham C. (2003). Enacting leadership for collaborative advantage: Dilemmas of ideology and pragmatism in the activities of partnership managers. *British Journal of Management* 14: 61-76.

Williams W. and Mary (2008). Trying to Clear Fog from Pension Plans. *The New York Times*, February 3, sec. Business.

12

The Economics of Frailty: Disability and Long-Term Care Systems in OECD Countries

Martin Karlsson

Introduction

Most developed countries' populations are ageing rapidly with consequent implications for public spending on long-term care (LTC), pensions and health care. The UK dependency ratio (the number of retired people per 100 people of working age) is projected to increase from 24 today to 40 in 2040. Although substantial, the increase is lower than in many other countries. In Japan, for instance, the ratio is projected to increase from 30 today to 65 in 2040 (United Nations 2006). The main driver of these changes is of course the increasing life expectancy.

Such demographic changes are expected to have a significant impact on the demand for LTC. Most consumers of LTC are over age 80; for example, in England, almost 80 % of care home inhabitants belong to this age group (Bajekal 2002). Since increasing life expectancy causes this group to grow at a faster rate than the general retired population, there is concern that the demographic burden could make the current system of financing LTC unsustainable. Indeed, in the many countries, there is already a trend towards concentrating resources only on individuals with severe disability (Karlsson et al. 2004).

Figure 1: Life Expectancies at 50 in some Countries

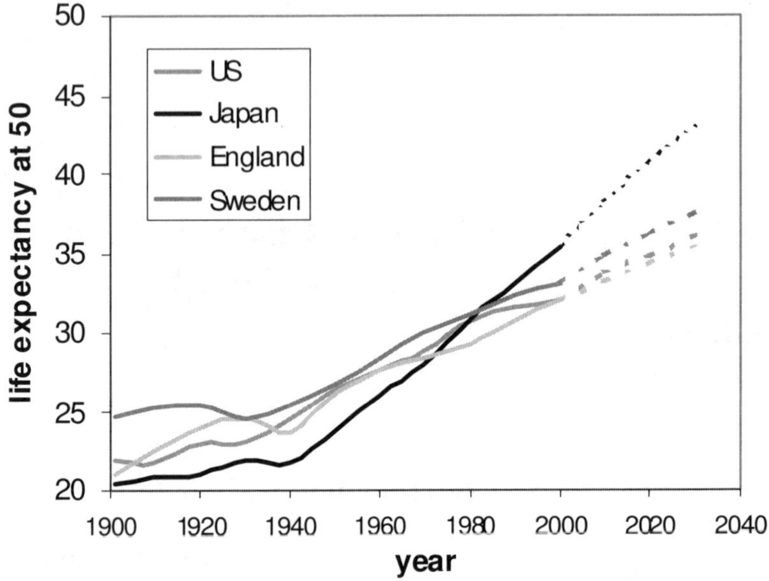

Source: Mayhew (2000)

It is the purpose of this chapter to discuss different models for governance within the LTC sector, by drawing on the experiences from some OECD countries. Our starting point will be a conceptual discussion of definitions and the different options available to policy-makers responsible for LTC. Then we will compare the experiences made in countries practicing different models for LTC. These models range from the relatively free-market oriented models in America and Britain, where the state fills a residual role once other possibilities have been exhausted – to the social democratic model of Scandinavia, where the state is almost exclusively responsible for the funding and, to a slightly lesser degree, provision of long-term care services.

Our analysis will show that the public policies pursued concerning LTC are strikingly different in otherwise relatively similar countries. It appears that national traditions in the areas of social policy and health care have been much more important for the design of LTC systems, than the social and demographic challenges that are common, to some extent, to all of these countries. This is an important observation, since public policies in this area have very strong implications for the redistribution of resources – between young and old, between rich and poor, or between males and females. We will also see that the systems appear to be comparable in terms of their sensitivity to demographic changes – but they can still be expected to diverge over time since the demographic outlook of the countries involved is so different.

The chapter is organized as follows. In the next section, we define concepts and discuss the various options for public policy in this area. After that, we provide a description of the LTC systems in different countries, and analyze their implications for public finances. The last section concludes and discusses how the funding of LTC could be reformed to achieve a system that is economically efficient and yet offers good financial security to older people.

Long-Term Care: Definitions and Policy Options

Long-Term Care (LTC) is a complex matter and it may be defined in a variety of ways. The American Institute of Medicine gives one such definition as "a variety of ongoing health and social services provided for individuals who need assistance on a continuing basis because of physical or mental disability"; thus, this definition is mainly based on the particular *needs* of the recipient (Karlsson et al. 2004). The characteristics of long-term care might become clearer if compared with medical care, as Norton (2000) does. He points out that LTC a) is care for chronic illness or disability for which hospital care is no longer deemed appropriate and b) is often provided by unpaid care workers, instead of professionals.

LTC Systems

One of the difficulties involved when analyzing LTC is the wide array of services that the concept includes. The most important divide is between *institutional* and *domiciliary* care. However, these categories are very broad and incorporate a vast diversity of services themselves. Concerning institutional care, in most countries a distinction is made between nursing homes and residential homes – where nursing homes generally entail more intensive care. Domiciliary care includes services such as personal care, meals and home adaptations. Finally, as a separate category one could distinguish community care services with, for instance, day care centers.

On top of the wide variety in services, a complicating factor when comparing LTC systems in different countries is that definitions differ – this goes for the definition of LTC itself (e.g. the boundary with mainstream health care) as well as for the definitions of different kinds of services. Furthermore, the assessment of need and the mapping from severity into a particular service will typically differ between countries.

To summarize, there are several policy dimensions in which national LTC systems may differ from each other (cf. Wittenberg et al. 2002):

- the boundary between LTC and health care
- the role of the family in provision and financing of LTC
- the balance between residential and home-based services
- the provider roles of public and private bodies
- the form of the public subsidy

In this chapter, the main focus will be the last of these points: i.e. the design and implications of the public subsidy. In order to circumvent the difficulties implied by the other dimensions listed above, we will generally work with UK definitions and UK standards, unless otherwise stated.

Public and Private Roles in Long-Term Care

Designing a national LTC system basically involves distributing roles of provision and financing between the family, the market and the private sector, in a way that is perceived as equitable as well as economically efficient. How different countries do this in practice varies a lot more than for other public programs such as pensions or health care – as Figure 2 illustrates.

Figure 2: Public and Private Spending on LTC as Proportion of GDP in Various OECD Countries

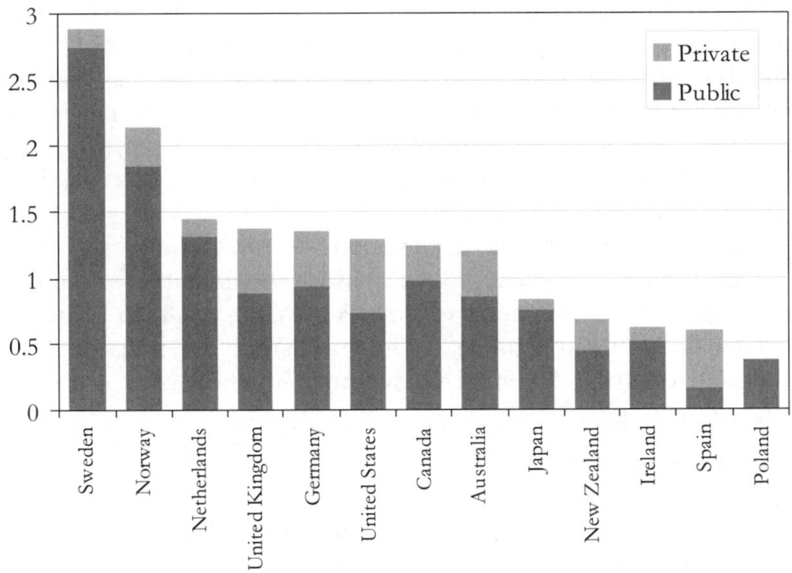

Source: OECD, 2005

Important criteria against which to evaluate a LTC system have been suggested by Glendinning et al. (2004):

- equity
- promotion of dignity (stigma, exclusion)
- choice and independence
- efficiency (resource economy)
- effectiveness (achievement of objectives)
- economic and political sustainability.

The objective to promote equity is particularly delicate for LTC, since there are so many different dimensions of equity that need to be taken into consideration. Hence, an equitable LTC system should strike the right balance between those who need care and those who do not; between young and old (since otherwise the political sustainability of the system might be in peril); between poor and rich – which is a greater challenge than for income taxes in general, since there are important differences between rich and poor not only concerning resources available, but also in terms of care needs and life expectancy. Furthermore, equity between men and women has often been overlooked in discussions concerning LTC, but this issue is of tremendous importance, considering the fact that women provide the bulk of informal (i.e. unpaid) care to frail spouses or parents, whereas men tend to contribute more to the funding of public LTC services, but get less back from the system in terms of care. Thus, the design of an LTC system will inevitably have strong implications for discussions of gender equality (Karlsson 2007).

Now, concerning the role of the public sector, the degree of public involvement can – for illustrative purposes – be imagined as a continuum ranging from a situation of no risk pooling at all, to a situation where the government assumes the role of insuring the individual LTC risk completely for everyone. Drawing on Wittenberg et al. (2002), we get the following list:

1. private savings
2. private insurance
3. private insurance with public-sector support (USA)
4. public sector tax-based support (Britain, Scandinavia)
5. social insurance (Japan, Germany).

We will now briefly comment on some of the most important differences between these different models in theory and practice.

Private Savings

Starting at the top, we imagine an LTC system where everyone is expected to save for their own future LTC needs. This model has at least two crucial weaknesses. Firstly, it requires everybody to build up a considerable net wealth in liquid assets, to draw one once need for LTC possibly arises. From an economic point of view, this system is highly inefficient, since a) the majority of individuals will not require costly LTC services; and b) there is a great amount of uncertainty concerning the *timing* of the LTC need occurrence, the *intensity* of the need and the *duration* of the need. Thus, there is scope for insurance – be it private or public or some mixture of the two – to pool the risks concerning all these uncertainties. A second weakness of a savings-based system is the *free-rider problem*: i.e., that there is a high probability that the government will step in and help those who are unable or unwilling to save for their future LTC needs – thus removing the incentives to do so.

It should further be noticed that a vast majority of the population does not have liquid assets in the magnitude required to meet normal LTC costs. In *Figure 3*, we show how many years of nursing home care different types of elderly households can afford based on their combined resources from incomes and savings. Apparently, a vast majority can afford less than one year of care. The picture is likely to be similar in other OECD countries.

Figure 3: Ability to Pay Nursing Home Care out of Income and Savings, United Kingdom

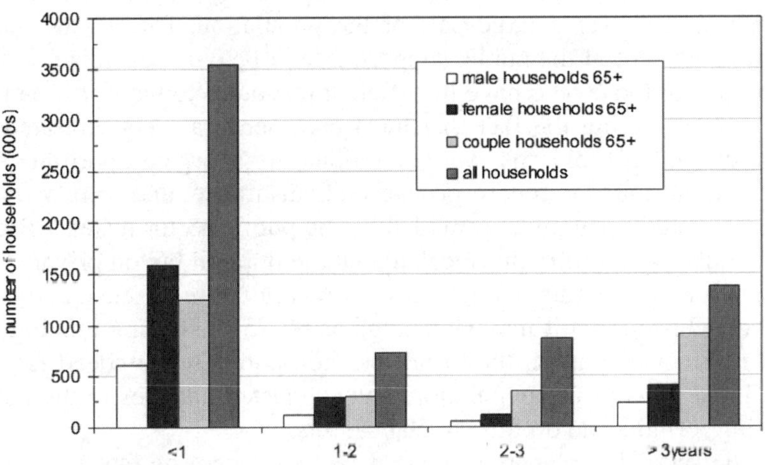

Source: Mayhew 2009

Private Insurance

Long-Term Care risk represents one of the most significant risks in life. According to one survey, an average American 65-year old woman faces a 44 % risk of ever entering a nursing home. On average, she will spend around two years in that care setting, which is associated with a cost of around USD 100,000. For males, the risk is slightly lower (27 %) and the average duration as well (1.3 years); but the risk is nevertheless considerable (Brown and Finkelstein 2007). According to the standard economic textbook model, risk-averse individuals should desire to insure this risk, so as to undo most of the financial consequences of needing LTC.

Nevertheless, only 4 % of American LTC costs are paid from insurance policies, and roughly one third is paid out of pocket. This is clearly at odds with the standard model of rational consumer behavior, and many explanations to this puzzle have been suggested. The explanations can roughly be divided into three categories: public sector crowding out, market failure, and limited consumer rationality.

The public sector crowding out argument relies on the fact that the public sector provides a safety net, which removes the incentives to purchase LTC for a large part of the population. Due to the means testing element of the public support, free or heavily subsidized care is provided to those who have insufficient resources to pay for it on their own. Considering the fact that most care needs are concentrated before the end of life, it may well be rational for a large proportion of the population not to purchase private LTC insurance, and to rely on the means-tested 'insurance' provided by the public sector instead. Brown and Finkelstein (2008) have calculated the implicit tax on private LTC insurances which this public sector crowding out represents, and reach the conclusion that it may be as high as 60-75 %. Taking this implicit tax into consideration, they find that non-purchase is indeed rational for large parts of the population, and suggested changes to the means testing formula can do little to change this.

The second explanation, market failures, suggests that the private market is unable to handle the risks associated with long-term care. This may have a wide range of reasons: for instance, unpredictable cost inflation in the LTC sector may in fact be uninsurable, considering the long time perspectives involved (assuming, for example, that a policy is purchased at retirement whereas LTC need materializes after the age of 80). Furthermore, there may be asymmetric information between insurance companies and their customers, leading to an adverse selection problem, where those that know they are 'bad risks' are more likely to purchase insurance. If the insurance companies are unable to distinguish different risk types, this may lead to very poor outcomes for the 'good risks', or even to a situation where the market collapses entirely (Rothschild and Stiglitz 1976).

There are many indications that there are indeed market failures present in the market for LTC insurance. Firstly, premium rates tend to be highly overpriced compared with the actuarially fair rate – or compared with premium rates in health insurance. Furthermore, the policies actually offered in the market tend to have very strong limitations in the benefits that they offer, so that in practice, they offer only marginal improvements compared with the situation of not having any insurance. Thus, benefits are typically not indexed to inflation (which, again, considering the long time perspectives involved is a serious weakness), and there are often also certain other restrictions: a qualifying period (typically 30-100 days) once the policy holder has become needy; a maximum benefit period (typically 5 years) after which the consumers are again left on their own; and a maximum daily benefit (typically $ 100) above which the care recipient has to pay the full cost (Brown and Finkelstein 2007).

As an illustration of these indications of market failure, in *Figure 4*, we provide an overview of four types of insurance policies offered on the American market. The bars show the degrees of *comprehensiveness* of these policies – defined as the proportion of a policy holder's total LTC costs which can be covered by the insurance policy – for males and females. Clearly, adding inflation protection to the policy (the index-linked variant) increases the comprehensiveness significantly: from 30-50 per cent to over 60 per cent. The lines in the figure, on the other hand, show the *loading factor* (i.e. the markup in per cent over the actuarially fair premium). In a perfect market, this loading factor would be close to zero. In the LTC insurance market, however, it varies between 20 and 60 per cent for men, whereas, quite remarkably, females appear to be offered *subsidized* policies.

Thus, there is ample evidence that the private insurance market has some difficulties in handling the risks associated with LTC need, and the graphs in *Figure 4* make clear why purchasing private insurance may not seem very attractive to consumers. However, it has also been suggested that the small size of the market is related to demand side factors. Explanations range from *limited rationality* (i.e., consumers have difficulties handling significant but low-probability risks) to *state-dependent utility* (i.e. that the marginal utility from consumption decreases significantly once LTC need arises). However, since very little research has been performed to formally test these hypotheses, it should be noted that there is no a priori reason to think these factors *reduce* the demand for private insurance, as they might just as well have the opposite effect.

Figure 4: Typical LTC Insurance Policies, US Market

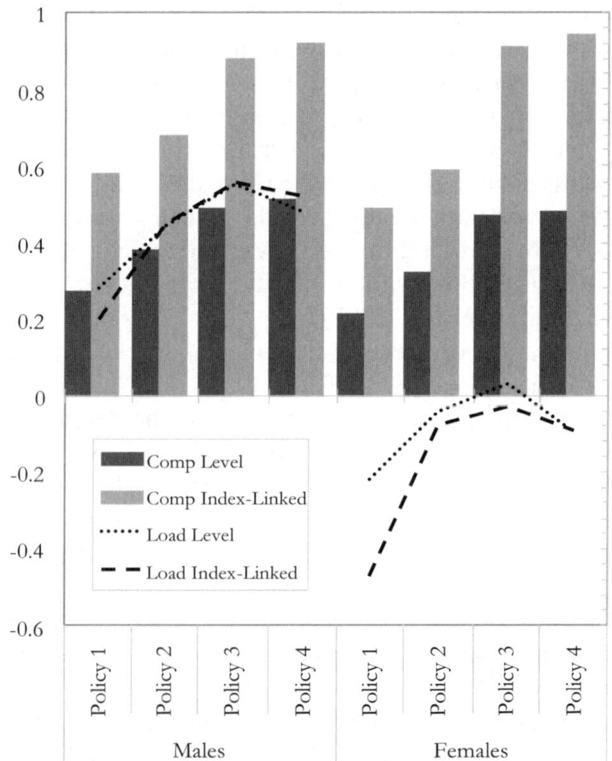

Source: Adaptation from Brown & Finkelstein 2007

Taxes Versus Social Insurance

Before we turn to a systematic assessment of various LTC systems in the next section, the distinction between the funding regimes "general taxes" and "social insurance" merits some further discussion. There are four main differences which distinguish a social insurance scheme from a tax-based regime (such as the Scandinavian model) and a social insurance regime (such as the German and Japanese models): firstly, revenues are *hypothecated* and thus not available for spending in other parts of the public sector; secondly, there is a link between contributions and benefits (although this link may be very weak, such as having paid contributions for a minimum number of years); thirdly, there are national, enforceable eligibility criteria; and fourthly, there is no *means test* and hence the financial situation of the individual does not matter for eligibility.

LTC in Four OECD Countries

In this section, we give a brief overview of the LTC financing systems used in the four OECD countries. Focus is put on financial eligibility, reliance on taxes or social insurance, the role of out-of pocket payments and the public benefits attached to different care settings.

Germany

In Germany, a social insurance scheme for LTC was introduced in 1995. The introduction of the scheme followed several years of increasing costs of income support related to LTC, and so one of the main objectives of the insurance was to reduce the dependency on social assistance among the elderly (Evers 1998).

German insurance shares many traits with the older social insurances in Germany. Thus, all low earners who earn income below a certain threshold are covered by the compulsory scheme, whereas high earners can choose to opt out of the system and purchase private insurance instead. Workers covered by social insurance pay a contribution proportional to their income (currently 1.7 %) that is shared between them and their employer. Family members who are not working are also covered by the insurance. Insurance is provided by semi-public care funds that are all affiliated to corresponding sickness funds (currently there are 400 of them). The scheme is run on a "pay as you go" basis, and only accumulates a small balance, corresponding to 1.5 months' expenditure (Bundesministerium für Gesundheit (2005)).

German LTC insurance offers three kinds of benefits, depending on the severity of the need; a cash benefit (to be used at the recipient's discretion), domiciliary care and institutional care. Benefits in kind are also denominated in monetary terms and normally cover roughly half of the actual charges. There is outlier compensation for particularly severe cases, but for these benefits there is a spending limit. In any event they are not allowed to comprise more than 3 % of any care fund's budget. Since the social insurance benefits are insufficient for many elderly to cover actual LTC costs, income support still accounts for somewhere between 5 and 10 % of total LTC costs.

The mandatory (but not universal) scheme covers approximately 90 % of the German population. Most of the rest of the population have signed up for voluntary private insurance. According to the ministry responsible, some 300,000-500,000 people (who are mainly small business owners and people dependent on income support), do not have insurance coverage. The mandatory scheme has a yearly turnover of around € 16 bn. which represents slightly less than 1 % of GDP (Bundesministerium für Gesundheit (2005)).

Japan

In Japan, a social LTC insurance scheme was launched in 2000. This mandatory LTC insurance, which is comprehensive and relatively generous, represents a distinct break with the Japanese tradition of having a quite limited welfare state.

The new social insurance scheme covers the entire population. Half of the revenues are raised from general taxation, and half through insurance contributions from people aged 40 and over. Insurance contributions are income related – for the working population they amount to 0.6 % of income (up to a certain ceiling) and retired people pay a certain multiple (depending on their income) of the so-called 'standard premium'. The insurance also covers family members (Campbell and Ikegami 2001).

People aged 65 and older can apply for benefits in respect of any kind of disability, whereas people between 40 and 65 are only entitled to care related to cognitive impairments. Eligibility for benefits is based solely on need. Thus, there is no means testing and the availability of informal carers does not change the entitlement to formal care. The assessment of need follows a quite complex procedure which ultimately divides needy persons into seven different severity categories. All but the lowest level of severity are allowed to choose between different care settings (all benefits are in kind); but an out-of-pocket payment of 10 % of the costs is charged (Karlsson et al. 2007).

Even after the introduction of the mandatory LTC insurance, there is a substantial proportion of elderly in long-term care who are cared for in hospitals, paid for by public health insurance. The transition to the LTC system has not happened as quickly as expected, which reduces the comparability of the figures with other countries. The Japanese LTC market had a turnover of ¥ 8.4 trillion (£ 46 billion) in the year 2000. This corresponds to around 1.5 % of GDP. The bulk of this is financed by public institutions. The public insurance in itself comprised around 1.0 % of GDP (Karlsson et al. 2007).

Sweden

In Sweden, the provision and financing of long-term care is the responsibility of the municipalities. The national government takes on a regulatory role in order to impose national standards.

Since 1992, the provision and financing of long-term care has been almost entirely the responsibility of local authorities (LAs). LTC costs are financed out of general income taxation; most of it local income taxes, but the national government also transfers some resources targeted at LTC for the elderly. To compensate for regional differences, there is a risk adjustment system that redistributes revenues among LAs.

A local authority has to offer appropriate care to all inhabitants in need. Furthermore, the law stipulates that LAs should actively investigate the needs within the elderly population. Services provided are mainly domiciliary and institutional care, but there is a great variation across municipalities in the procedures for assessment of need and the care provided for given conditions. Care is partly financed by income-related out-of-pocket charges which are also determined locally. To reduce the risk of impoverishment of the elderly, the central government has recently introduced national standards for personal needs allowances and caps on the out-of-pocket payments.

In the last twenty years, there has been an ongoing trend towards concentrating care on the most severe cases. Nevertheless, the total cost for publicly financed long-term care was SEK 91.7 billion (€ 8 billion) in 2007 (3.0 % of GDP). Out of this, the bulk came from institution-based care (61 %); home-based care accounted for 37 % and community care 1.5 % (Socialstyrelsen (2009)).

The United Kingdom

The United Kingdom has a dual system in place, where different principles apply to health care services – provided by the National Health Service (NHS) – and social services – financed by local authorities.

The majority of public LTC spending in the U.K. is financed by local authorities. LAs raise revenues through the council tax and also receive a grant from the central government. The grant is not earmarked, but there are recommendations on how to spend the money. The NHS is responsible for funding some nursing home places and also financing nursing care in all care settings. The NHS is financed by the constituent countries and is largely financed out of income taxation (Karlsson et al. 2007). Apart from the public payers, there is a small and stagnant market for private long-term care insurance. In total, fewer than 40,000 policies have been sold. Thus, private insurance currently accounts for a negligible share of total LTC expenditure in the UK.

Benefits are primarily provided in the form of institutional and domiciliary care. Local authorities are obliged to appoint a care manager to assess the needs of the clients. Furthermore, services provided by local authorities are subject to means testing, where the individual's income and assets are taken into account. There is, however, a personal needs allowance ensuring that every person has sufficient income left to cover essential needs. The NHS, on the other hand, generally provides services free of charge (Karlsson et al. 2007).

Currently the UK spends around £ 19 billion (€ 21 billion) a year on long-term care of which £ 13.4 billion (70 %) is in institutional care and £ 5.7 billion (30 %) in home care. The public sector accounts for 65 % of all expenditure and the private sector 35 %. Of private expenditure around 80 % is spent on institutional care and 20 % on home care (Mayhew 2009).

Discussion

The exposition above has demonstrated that these countries have chosen quite different models to finance LTC. This is characterized first and foremost by the degree of state intervention; in this respect we can distinguish three different types. At one extreme we have the British approach, which largely assigns to the state a residual role once other sources have been exhausted. In an intermediate position we have Germany, where the state offers supplementary coverage to all, but still expects individuals to bear a large share of LTC costs. At the other extreme, we have Sweden and Japan, where the state takes on a comprehensive role and the individual pays a minor out-of-pocket charge only. A short summary of some characteristic facts is provided in Table 1.

Table 1: LTC System Characteristics

Country	Financing	Predominant Provider Type	Means-Testing	Level of Responsibility	Benefits	Costs (GDP)
Germany	Social Insurance, Taxes	Private, non-profit	No	National	In-kind, Cash	~1.0
Japan	Social Insurance & Taxes	Private, non-profit	No	Local	In-kind	~1.5
Sweden	Taxes	Public	No	Local	In-kind	~3
United Kingdom	Taxes	-	Yes	Local (National)	In-kind	~1 %

Source: Karlsson et al. (2007)

Another dimension where the countries differ is in how revenues are raised to cover public LTC costs. In Japan, the new social insurance system places a greater share of the burden on those who are eligible for services (i.e. age 40+). In Sweden, by contrast, the risk adjustment system and income-related charges almost completely cuts the link between contributions and expected services.

Sustainability

Karlsson et al. (2007) analyze the economic sustainability of the four LTC systems discussed here. To avoid having the quantitative analysis confounded by national differences in definitions, we based our comparisons on the thought experiment of importing the systems from Germany, Japan and Sweden to the United Kingdom. Thus, the results presented here and in the original article use British demographics and a British model for projection of demography, to compare the long-term performance of the different systems.

An overview of the implied overall costs to the public sector is given in Figure 5. The top curve represents the total of tax and social insurance contributions that an individual would have to pay over the age of forty if the Japanese social insurance were introduced in the United Kingdom. The next curve is the portion of the income tax necessary for LTC if a Swedish system were introduced. Below that, starting from a point of around 2 %, we have the total contribution which would result with a German system – for an individual who does not earn enough to opt out of the social insurance scheme. The dotted line below that shows the contributions paid by individuals aged less than forty in a Japanese-style system. The line below that indicates the status quo option of keeping the current UK system. Finally, the curve at the bottom represents an individual who has opted out of the German social insurance scheme and only contributes to the general costs of LTC through income taxes.

Figure 5: Implied Tax or Contribution Rates for Different LTC Systems

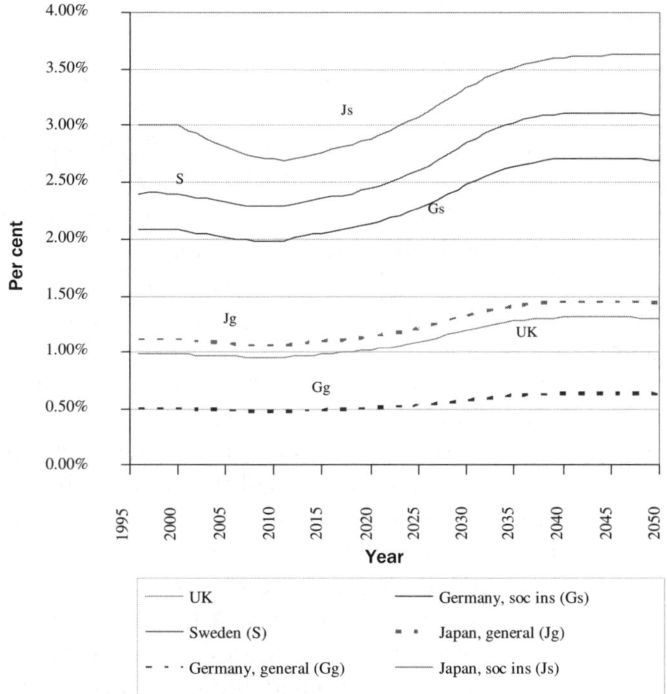

Three main observations can be made in the figure. Firstly, the different systems exhibit substantial differences in terms of public finances, even if they are implemented in the same country. Thus, the differences in aggregate spending which we have observed are indeed mainly attributable to differences in system parameters, and not differences in need. Secondly, the impact of demographic ageing appears to be similar in the different countries – the curves apparently move in parallel – and thus it is not possible to rank them according to their 'economic sustainability'. Nevertheless, there is, thirdly, one notable exception: since Japan puts a disproportionate share of the funding burden on the 40+ population – a group that will keep on growing for several decades – they do indeed insulate the social insurance scheme from some of the demographic impact. However, the difference, although important in principle, is so small that it is hardly discernible in the figure.

Conclusions

The purpose of this chapter has been to discuss different models of governance in the long-term care sector. We have seen that otherwise relatively similar countries differ considerably in their approaches to long-term care – and the respective roles of the family, the market and the state vary accordingly. These differences have significant implications for the degree of redistribution in the system and hence for the perceived equity.

Our main conclusion from the discussion above is that the different LTC systems have strong implications for the level of public and private spending, but their sensitivity to demographic changes do not vary much. However, the analysis was based on the thought experiment of importing three countries' systems into the United Kingdom. It is very likely that the systems considered here evolve very differently in the future, due to the demographic differences between them. Thus, the United Kingdom and Sweden can look forward to rclatively modest increases in LTC needs, thanks to immigration and high birth rates. Germany and Japan, on the other hand, are very likely to experience major changes to their age structures over the next few decades, and the consequences for LTC are likely to be vast.

We have also found that older people generally have insufficient resources to cover the actual LTC costs on their own. Furthermore, we have found that the private market appears to be unable to provide satisfactory insurance policies – even if we abstract from the crowding out problem caused by the public means tested system. These two observations open for discussions of how the state intervention in this sector can be designed so as to achieve an efficient and sustainable distribution of the costs related to LTC. In these concluding remarks, we would like to point out three possibilities which have received scant attention in the literature.

The first possibility concerns the priority between public and private insurance. Today, in the United Kingdom as well as in the United States, the individual consumer gets access to the public subsidy only after other options – including private insurance – have been exhausted. However, it would not affect the public finances a lot if an exception were made for private insurance, so that the insurance policy tops up the public sector, instead of vice versa.

A second option would be to bundle LTC insurance and pensions. From the insurance company's point of view, a frail person represents a good risk in their pension insurance, but a bad risk for LTC insurance. Thus, if a package of annuity coupled with a 'disability bonus' were offered, it would even out these differences. Since the risks cancel out, the risk of adverse selection would be reduced, and the insurance companies could spend fewer resources on screening out bad risks. Furthermore, forecasts of future costs could become more precise, since mistakes in assumptions concerning future trends also cancel out.

Finally, another option which merits further attention is a more direct interaction between government policies and the private market. We have seen that insurance companies tend to limit the risk they insure on several margins. Clearly, the government is able to handle the risk also beyond these margins – as the Scandinavian experience of heavy state intervention shows. Thus, a hybrid system could be envisioned, where the government steps in and insures exactly the risks that the private sector is unable to handle. Thus, the government would insure the risk of high care intensity and of long durations (and possibly inflation risk), and the individual would then be left to choose whether they insure the remaining risk on the private market. Such a system would probably need some degree of copayment to avoid overutilization of services. In any case, it appears that such a hybrid model would provide older people with security at a reasonable cost to the public purse.

References

Bajekal, M. (2002). *Care Homes and their Residents*, London: The Stationery Office.

Brown, J. and Finkelstein, A. (2007). "Why Is the Market for Long-Term Care Insurance so Small?", *Journal of Public Economics* 91(10): 1967-1991.

Brown, J. and Finkelstein A. (2008). "The Interaction of Public and Private Insurance: Medicaid and the Long-Term Insurance Market", *American Economic Review* 98(3): 1083-1102.

Bundesministerium für Gesundheit (2003). *Zahlen und Fakten zur Pflegeversicherung*, Berlin: Bundesregierung.

Campbell, J. and Ikegami N. (2001). Designing an Independent LTC System: In General and in Japan. Discussion Paper.

Glendinning, C; Davies, B; Pickard, L. and Comas-Herrera, A. (2004). *Funding for Long-term Care for Older People: Lessons from other countries*, Joseph Rowntree Foundation, York.

Evers, A. (1998). "The new long-term care insurance program in Germany", *Journal of Ageing & Social Policy*, vol. 10(1).

Karlsson, M.; Mayhew L.; Plumb R. and Rickayzen B. (2004). An international comparison of LTC Arrangements. An investigation into the equity, efficiency and sustainability of Long-Term Care Systems in Germany, Japan, Sweden, the United Kingdom and the United States. Actuarial Research Paper No. 156, Cass Business School.

Karlsson M.; Mayhew L.; Plumb R. and Rickayzen. B (2007). "Long-term care financing in four OECD countries: Fiscal burden and distributive effects". *Health Policy*, 80, 107-134.

Karlsson, M. (2007). "Distributional Effects of Reform in Long-Term Care", *Ageing Horizons* No. 6, pp. 133-41.

Mayhew, L. (2000). *Health and Elderly Care Expenditure in an Aging World.* IIASA Research Report RR-00-21, International Institute for Applied Systems Analysis, Laxenburg, Austria.

Mayhew, L. (2009). *The market potential for privately funded long-term care products in the UK*, Actuarial Research Paper No. 188, Cass Business School.

Norton, E. C. (2000). "Long-Term Care", in: Culyer and Newhouse (ed.), *Handbook of Health Economics, Volume Ib,* pp. 955-94. Amsterdam: Elsevier.

OECD (2005). Long-term Care for Older People, Paris: OECD.

Rothschild, M. and Stiglitz J. (1976). "An Essay on the Economics of Imperfect Information", *Quarterly Journal of Economics* 90: 629-649.

Socialstyrelsen (2009). *Jämförelsetal för socialtjänsten år 2008*, Stockholm: Socialstyrelsen.

United Nations, Population Division of the Department of Economic and Social Affairs (2006). *World Population Prospects: The 2006 Revision*.

Wittenberg, R., Sandhu B. and Knapp M. (2002). "Funding long-term care: the public and private options", in Mossialos, E., A. Dixon, J. Figueras and Kutzin J.: *Funding health care: options for Europe*. London: The European Observatory on Health Care Systems.

13

Different Approaches to Providing Intergenerational Transfers in Aging Societies

Thomas Lindh

Intergenerational transfer systems that provide consumption for dependents are an integral and fundamental part of every society. These transfers can be mediated through capital markets, intra-family transfers and inter-family transfers, or by public transfers. The intention of this text is to illustrate the constraints which different approaches to the mediation of these transfers put on an aging society and its economy.

What is the problem with aging? At an individual level increasing longevity is overall a benefit for mankind and from that viewpoint hardly something to worry about. Aging in society, i.e. when the mean and median age increases or the elderly dependency rate is increasing is another matter since it puts pressure on the arrangements involving intergenerational transfers. Aging in the age distribution of the population in the industrialized countries has been going on for a very long time and currently almost the whole world (except in sub-Saharan Africa) is aging. It is a phenomenon with roots in the demographic transition.

Sweden will be used as a concrete example throughout to illustrate the discussion. There are two reasons for that. Sweden is a fairly typical example of the demographic transition and more importantly has been early in its aging process.

Therefore we start by looking at the Swedish demographic transition in the next section. Then we move on to a closer look at how intergenerational redistribution of resources is institutionalized and the overall budget restrictions this creates for any society. Finally the sustainability of the systems is discussed against the background of the general macroeconomic repercussions that aging will create.

Background: Demographic Transition and Economic Development

The demographic transition is the process whereby human societies have developed from a regime of high death rates and high birth rates to a regime with low mortality and low fertility. For many European countries the beginning of this process started already in the 19th century and in England even in the 18th century. The pace and details of the demographic transition differ across countries but by now it has proven to be a world-wide process with revolutionary consequences for social and economic development. In Asia, Japan had a very fast transition in the 1950s, South Korea a little later, and China and India have at different paces entered into the transition as have many other Asian countries.

This demographic transition is illustrated in Figure 1 for the Swedish population. Since the middle of the 18th century vital statistics have been collected for the whole population. Initially this collection of population statistics was organized through the clergy of the Swedish Church and compiled at a central authority (Tabellverket, later to become Statistics Sweden) but since the 1990s the records have been kept by the Tax Authorities. The Swedish demographic transition is often considered typical although both England and France for example were earlier.

In the beginning of the 19th century death rates in Sweden started to decrease and around the middle of the century birth rates started to follow suit. Around 1900 the birth rates then started to decrease faster and in the 1930s closed in on the death rates. In the 1950s death rates reached a minimum as the elderly population started to increase faster.

Figure 1: Death and Birth Rates in Sweden per 1000

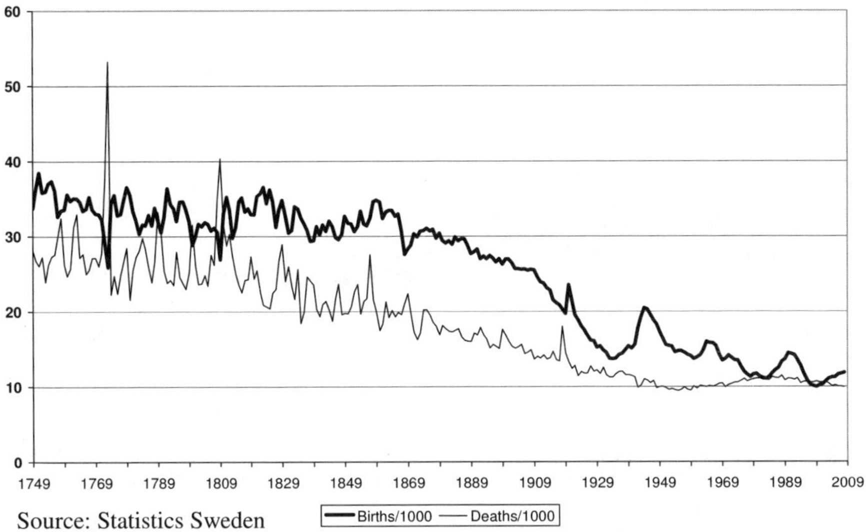

Source: Statistics Sweden

In the birth rates we can see a cyclical trend where the gap between birth rates and death rates narrow down and in 1999 for the first time since the Napoleonic wars the number of deaths became greater than the number of births in Sweden making the natural rate of population growth negative.

It is important to note that the mortality decrease initially was mainly driven by increasing survival of children who generally had a higher mortality than those aged 80 in the 18th century, see Figure 2. A quarter of all Swedish children in the 18th century died before their first birthday and another quarter before their 10th birthday.

For people who live in high GDP per capita welfare states this demographic regime is emotionally almost incomprehensible, although there are countries in the world where similar conditions of life still rule. During the 18th and 19th century infant mortality in Sweden decreased by a factor of 100 and is today in the Swedish population only 0,2 %, among the lowest in the world. The decrease in mortality of 80-84 years old is on the other hand quite moderate until the 1950s when especially medicines against infectious diseases became more effective.

Figure 2: Mortality Rates for Below 1 Year Old and in the Group 80-84 Years Old

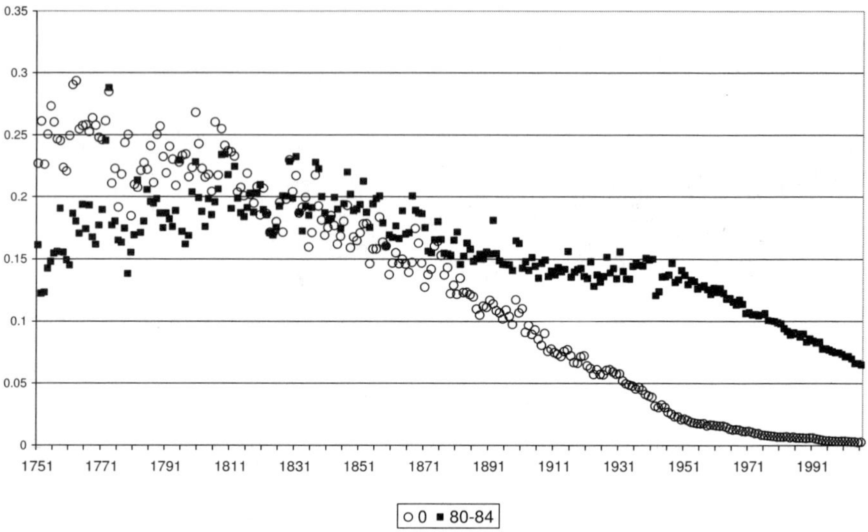

Source: Human Mortality Data Base

The aging of the Swedish population has therefore been driven mostly by fertility decreases, and only recently decreases in old age mortality have started to play a substantial role. The reason why Japan, Italy and Germany among others are aging much faster today than Sweden is due to lower fertility and not any substantial differences in mortality.

In Figure 3 we see the consequences of the demographic transition on the Swedish age pyramids of 1800, 1900, 1950 and 2008. The 1900 pyramid differs from the 1800 pyramid mainly by a broader base. This shape is essentially the same that we can observe in, for example, Africa today. If one studies the evolution of the Swedish age pyramid closer one can note that the young adults and especially the males have been thinned out by the previous migration trends. This is not immediately apparent though since such culling also decreases the fertile population and therefore the number of children born domestically.

In the second stage when fertility starts to decrease faster than mortality the pyramid form starts disappearing. There is a pronounced aging in the population already in 1950 and in 2008 the pyramid has undergone a substantial rectangularization as it is called by demographers. Due to the cyclical fertility behavior that is rather peculiar to Sweden, the shape is rather more like a bush with baby boom branches sticking out at regular intervals.

Figure 3: Age Pyramids in Sweden 1800-2008

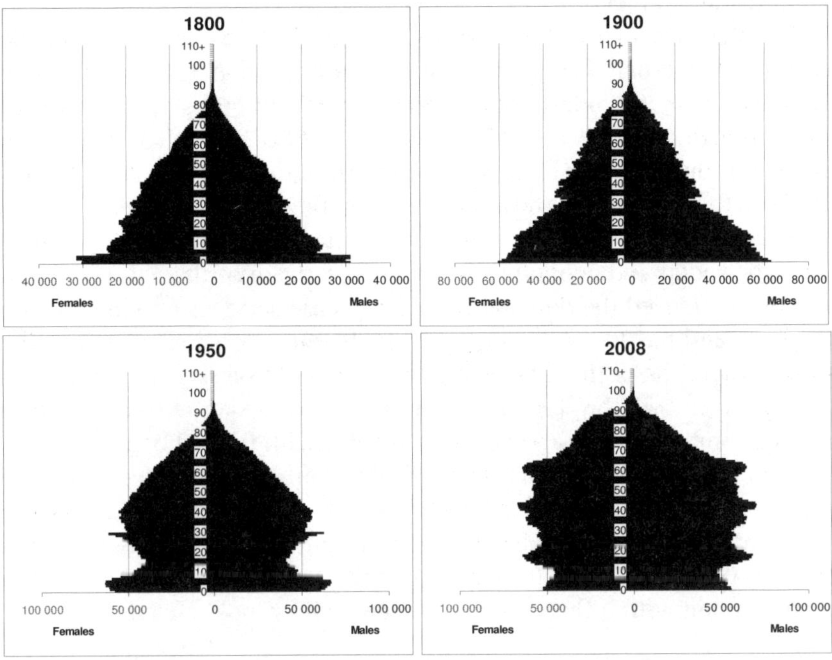

Source: Human Mortality Data Base

Economically the demographic transition in Sweden, during the late 19th century, created overpopulation, scarcity of resources, even starvation when harvests failed. This gave rise to a very substantial emigration flow where roughly a quarter of the population left Sweden. This period was also characterized by rapid industrialization and urbanization that was at least partly driven by an abundance of cheap labor. But the period also sees increasing and universal education, political and liberal reforms and the emergence of the first traces of the modern welfare systems. The demographic transition in combination with these processes transformed a traditional monarchy with guilds and trade associations and aristocratic privileges to a capitalist parliamentary democracy (although still with some restrictions on voting rights). In the following phase in the 20th century the demographic gift of (Bloom et al. 2003) a growing (and better educated) adult population and decreasing support burdens for children strongly helped to lift Sweden from the position of one of Europe's poorest nations to a top welfare state in the 1960s.

But because of the low fertility in the 1930s Sweden was in the 1970s aging much faster than other countries and for almost three decades it was the oldest country in the world in terms of the share of the population above age 65. Since the 1990s several nations have overtaken this position. But Sweden is still aging and the baby boomers from the 1940s are now again swelling the ranks of retirees.

The aging of Sweden has already substantially changed the conditions for social and economic welfare. The strain of the aging population has increased the demand for elderly care services and health care services, and has led to the comparatively early pension reform in the 1990s where the defined benefit pension system on pay-as-you-go basis introduced in the 1960s was replaced by a defined contribution system combining pay-as-you-go financing with funded benefits.

This brief recount of the demographic transition in Sweden and its accompanying economic and social development shows that society can adapt to aging but also that this requires and has, as a consequence, extensive social and economic change, bringing further change along with it that also affects the aging process itself.

Intergenerational Redistribution – a Basic Aspect of Human Life

Intergenerational redistribution patterns have been observed in all human societies and differ in crucial aspects from the patterns observed in, for example, other primates who spend much less resources in raising their offspring than humans do. In fact the burden of raising children is so large that humans have the rather unusual trait to survive their reproductive period and to help providing for their grandchildren (Kaplan and Robson 2003). The substantial surplus production of the active population has led to a capacity in human societies to provide also for those that happen to outlive their physical and mental capacity. Before the advent of industrialization and the demographic transition, these elderly dependents were very few and in general only had a marginal impact on the dependency burden on the economically active population.

With the rise of capitalist economies a new medium for transferring means to old age dependency opened up that until then had been reserved only for the wealthy. People could save in capital assets and property by abstaining from some consumption during their active life. Financial markets became part of the intergenerational transfer system. By enabling capital investment and faster technological change this further promoted economic development and gave rise to urbanization and increased division of labor. Still another mediation mechanism for intergenerational transfers became important for the many people that were too poor or impatient to save for themselves or simply had bad luck in their life course. Public pension systems, health care and elderly care started to evolve in response both to increasing numbers of elderly and to the severance of family ties that was a consequence of the extensive migration increase that followed in the wake of fast population increase and urbanization in the early stages of the demographic transition.

These processes developed quite differently in different countries due to shifting initial conditions in terms of traditions, institutions and the pace of economic and social development. In continental Europe public redistribution became more dominant than the market oriented redistribution in the Anglo-Saxon countries. In the Asian countries with fast demographic transition family redistribution has retained a strong position up until recently but is now increasingly coming under stress.

While demographers previously have taken for granted that fertility rates should stabilize around reproduction levels many are now contemplating whether there could be low-fertility traps leading to age pyramids standing on their peaks (e.g. Lutz et al. 2006). Lately some evidence (Myrskylä et al. 2009) points to a relation with Human Development Indexes (HDI) where fertility actually does stabilize at a threshold level. But the issue is still very much undetermined.

The word demographic transition suggests that the population should be on its way to a new equilibrium but in fact we do not know whether there is such a new stable population configuration or how it would look. In the case of Sweden the fertility swings means that a stable population cannot arise anywhere near in time. It certainly cannot be achieved in this century.

Our knowledge of the intergenerational flows of resources within modern economies is still very incomplete. How they are adapting to the unstoppable change of the age structure that follows the still not completed demographic transition we are living in is even more unknown. We know rather little about how the different mechanisms for intergenerational transfers are adapting to the population pressures. Other aspects of the processes have been much more emphasized and investigated by researchers. In the last decades some progress has been made in the study of intergenerational transfers (e.g. Albertini et al. 2007) but systematic mapping of the intergenerational resource flows at a macroeconomic level has only just begun.

Recently an international project was started in order to construct internationally comparable accounts of the intergenerational transfers within the National Accounts framework (Mason et al. 2006). This National Transfer Accounts (NTA) approach distinguishes the economic form for these flows and their different mechanisms through asset reallocation, family based transfers and public transfers in kind and cash. There is now a well-developed theoretical framework using overlapping generations modeling (Samuelson 1958; Diamond 1965; Willis 1988; Bommier and Lee 2003) to interpret and make use of such data, but the data themselves and the methodology to produce them are still experimental and preliminary, although a growing number of countries and researchers have joined the project.

Some elements of theory are helpful to understand the issues arising in the adaptation of intergenerational transfer systems to aging. I will take my departure in Willis (1988) and very briefly and simplified describe the constraints that age structure places on the economy. Let us consider a closed economy where saving and consumption has been chosen in order to maximize consumption for all generations, i.e. a Golden Rule equilibrium (Samuelson 1958). This presumes a stable population growing at a rate n and a stable growth process of per capita production assumed to grow at some exogenously given rate g. The optimization conditions for a Golden Rule path require that the rate of return on savings $r = n + g$. At such a path a lower rate of population growth will decrease the rate of interest and if population starts decreasing the rate of interest may even become negative.

Now, let us assume that babies go into debt in order to finance their consumption. Let $c(x) > y_l(x)$ and let the first term in the inequality stand for consumption at age x and the second term stands for labor income at the same age. Obviously babies have zero labor income but as they grow older they will start to earn some income, and at some point the inequality reverses. Provided they survive long enough they will at some point retire, and again the original inequality will hold. An intergenerational transfer has to take place no matter whether consumption in retirement comes from capital assets or public or private transfers. Either an asset reallocation has to take place where somebody with a surplus labor income buys or pays interest on the capital in order to finance the consumption of the retiree or someone with a surplus in the family (or other private agent, be it charity or relatives or friends) pays, or the state taxes labor income in order to pay public benefits.

If we keep an account of these future surpluses and deficits over the life cycle discounted to age 0 the credit lost or gained at age x will be $e^{-rx}l(x)(y_l(x) - c(x))$ where $l(x)$ is the survival probability from age 0 to x. Cumulated up to age x we get life cycle wealth up to this age given that r is the interest rate

$$W(x) = \int_0^x e^{-rx} l(x)[y_l(x) - c(x)]dx$$

At the age when $l(x)$ reaches zero this expresses the total life cycle wealth. In the Golden Rule steady state this expression will hold not only for one individual but also across the individuals in the population at a given point in time. One can then deduce (Willis 1988) that $W = c(A_c - A_y)$ where c is average per capita consumption, A_c is the average age of consumption and A_y is the average age of earning labor income. If the average age of consumption is higher than the average age of labor income then the average individual in the population needs to have positive net savings in order to sustain future consumption and average wealth is positive. In the opposite case individuals on average need to go into debt.

When the population is aging A_c will tend to increase faster than A_y unless retirement is postponed to the same extent as longevity increases. Theoretically this will be the case only if individuals do not value leisure and retain the same labor supply as always. Empirically the trend since World War II has been the opposite, i.e. we have observed how retirement ages have decreased. Only in the last decades do we, in Sweden for example, observe increasing labor supply above age 55. An aging population thus sooner or later must amass a positive wealth. Before drawing too strong conclusions from this it should be observed that wealth in this context include claims on future private or public transfers. Obviously actual savings in productive capital will yield tangible returns.

However, it is important to note that part of the transfer wealth is actually financing the costs of breeding, raising and educating new generations of workers and thus constitute an investment into human capital that also may yield a return either through family bonds or the public sector. A PAYG pension system yields return from the contributions of current workers.

Without going further into formal details we can note that positive average wealth means that future consumption can be increased by raising fertility since this increases the rate of return. Immigration has the same effect. But nota bene that if average wealth is negative you would instead want to decrease fertility and encourage emigration.

Of course, these results hold strictly only in the simplified setting of a Golden Rule steady state, but since it is derived from the basic budget restriction needed to satisfy intergenerational transfer needs similar results will also hold although in more complex ways also for our destabilized aging populations. Thus we expect to see a tendency that positive average wealth will be more and more necessary to maintain the older the population gets and that overall consumption can be increased by increasing population growth and the rate of return on savings. But again note that this transfer wealth concept does not imply that wealth needs to be held in the form of capital assets.

Sustainable Transfers in Aging Economies

One lesson from the theory is that saving for the future is not only a question of putting money into capital but also to sustain transfer systems by enabling the young population to support the elderly through family or taxes. The crucial question boils down to which of these alternative investments that will yield the higher return and thus which alternative that can sustain a higher level of welfare. We have fairly good estimates of average returns over extended time periods from capital assets. Occasional crises will require some insurance arrangements to actually insure a reasonably smooth flow of returns for old age consumption.

However, whether constantly increasing capital intensity can sustain sufficient capital returns for the long term even for a decreasing active population is much more uncertain. There are several reasons for that. First, there may be decreasing marginal returns to capital. Nobody can know that for sure, but for example empirical estimates imply that the Solow growth model may be a good fit to country data and thus indirectly do imply decreasing returns (Mankiw et al 1992). Technological innovations driven by capital investment may foil that conclusion, but our evidence on this issue is not very strong. Second, capital and skilled labor are likely to be complements and thus scarcity of skilled labor may drive down the demand for capital and contribute further to decreasing returns. Third, decreasing numbers of net savers may further diminish the demand for assets as implied by the life cycle theory of saving. In a decreasing population housing demand would also tend to drive down demand for real estate investment. There may be counteracting forces to these tendencies, but since we lack observations of very old societies we have little empirical evidence to use for predicting the macro outcomes of these forces. A temporary escape route is, of course, foreign investment into countries with more favorable age structures. But as these countries also will be aging it is not long-term sustainable.

When it comes to the returns of human capital we know even less about this than about future capital returns. Although Mincer type equations fairly consistently imply that in cross-section data an additional year of education will yield positive returns relative to those who lack that education, the actual figures vary widely and cannot be interpreted as evidence of a social return to education. In fact longitudinal data imply that average returns to education have been decreasing quite substantially for the cohorts we can observe over longer time spans. In country cross-section data returns to education were long difficult to observe but due to better data and techniques (Krueger and Lindahl 2001, Lutz et al. 2008) we now feel pretty confident that a higher educated population actually do yield a return in terms of higher GDP growth, but it is still very hard to relate this directly to the actual expenditure on education.

Research over the last two decades have revealed that age structure is linked to economic development in many more ways than analytic theory can handle. There are links to economic growth, to the balance of investment and saving (and thus to external balances). There are even links to inflation and financial markets that interact in many different ways in the economy. New evidence has been presented that politics and civil conflicts have strong links to age structure, etc. Space does not permit any comprehensive discussion of these links. The basic insight is that both economic and social behavior as well as the access to resources (financial as well as human capabilities) varies over the life cycle in roughly predictive ways. Changing age structure thus disrupts all equilibria and force new adaptations in all areas of social and economic life. Although there is room for stretching the different life cycle phases over age to some extent, the basic patterns derive from innate evolutionary based traits in the human genome and thus cannot be ignored as random variations (as is often implicitly assumed by the use of terminology like age shocks and so forth).

In order to give some impression of what age structure change may mean, and how planning ahead can ameliorate the consequences of age structure change, a quick description of how events may evolve in Sweden in the next decade will serve as illustration.

The current age structure in Sweden is illustrated for the end of 2008 in Figure 4. There are two crucial features. Firstly, the baby boomers from the 1940s are now going into retirement and the cohorts who are next in turn to replace them are substantially smaller. Empirical research by Lindh and Malmberg (1998, 1999, 2000, 2007, 2008, 2009 and others cited by them) indicates that this will lead to a rather gloomy macroeconomic scenario. This is not due to any decrease in the active population per se because the second important feature is that large young cohorts are now starting to enter the labor market so the workforce will actually be rejuvenating at the same time that the population is aging, see Figure 5.

Figure 4: Age Pyramid in 2008

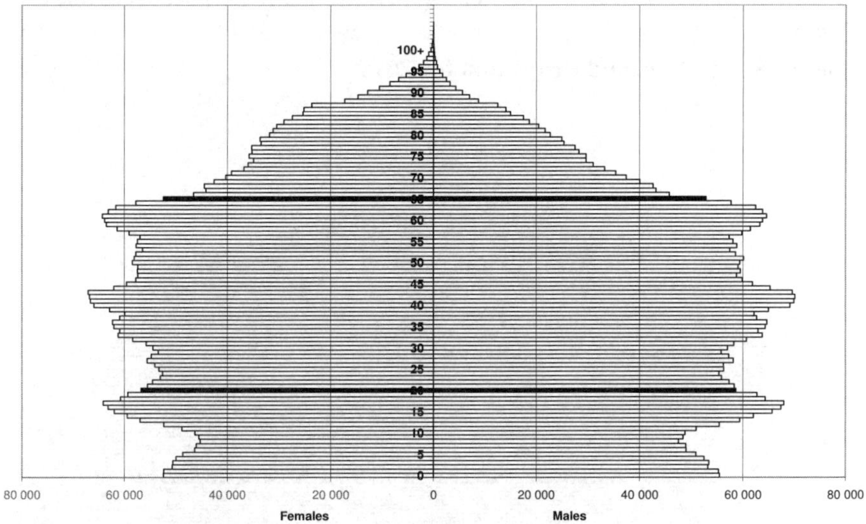

Source: Statistics Sweden

Very few of these will be able to directly step into the vacancies left by the boomers since they will lack the experience and specialized education required for these positions. Most of the low-skill vacancies are also likely not to be filled anyway due to global low-wage competition. The young adults will need further education (and thus further expenditure) and will be in a phase of life where they are still seeking for good job matches. The financial crisis will be hitting these youngsters extremely hard with increasing youth unemployment rates, difficulties to find and afford housing, form families etc.

Since there will be a decrease of the number of high earners, tax revenue will decrease at the same time that public expenditure starts to increase, heralding a long period of strained public budgets. The retirees increase total consumption demand as their share in the population increases but supply will tend to lag behind causing inflationary pressures in the economy (Lindh and Malmberg 1998). External balances also deteriorate as import demand increases and national savings trend downward (Higgins 1998).

In Figure 5 we see that the active population is rejuvenated as the inflow of young adults increase and the oldest active cohorts become smaller. That will only reinforce the trends caused by the retiring cohorts.

Figure 5: Age Pyramid Projection for 2015

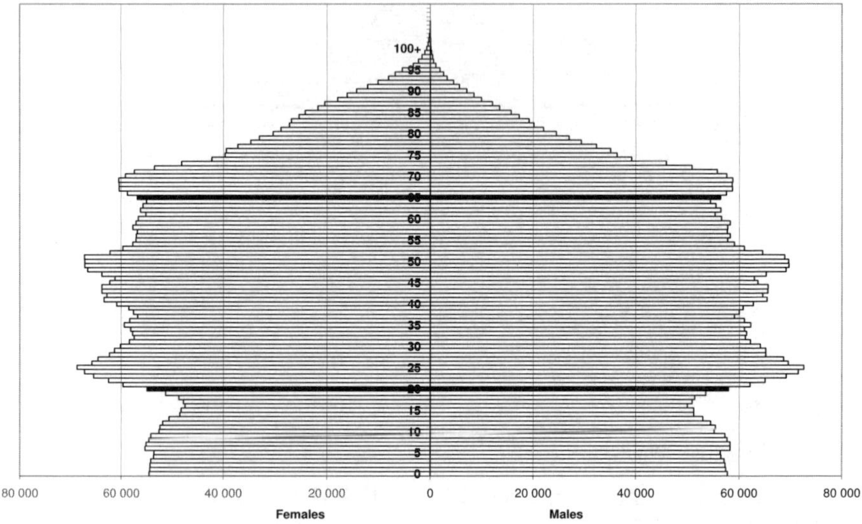

Source: Statistics Sweden.

So why does it not help that the workforce is rejuvenated? Young people earn considerably less and are also liable to remain to some extent in education, increasing public expenditure further. Estimation also shows that they are considerably less productive than the more mature population partly because of inexperience, partly because they are not yet well matched to the labor market. As they get into more fertile ages it is also likely that the number of children increases. On average they will be needing consumption and housing credit in order to form a family and for higher education. Thus they will be competing on tighter financial markets with capital formation needs, further tightening the already tightening markets for credit. In the wake of the financial crisis unemployment benefits and expenditure on active labor market policies will grow.

This situation in connection with increasing elderly voter shares creates a risk situation where politicians may neglect supporting investment in the future tax base, i.e. family support, education support and expenditure to achieve early establishment in the labor market, as well as expenditure aimed at immigrant integration. Short sighted budget balance policies – appropriate in the 1990s crisis – have been inherited and made into social norms that hinders adaptation to a situation where borrowing for investment in the future tax base although economically sound is viewed as dangerous. When the baby boomers from the 1940s reach their eighties and care expenditure has to swell in the 2020s, the tax base may prove insufficient.

In Figure 6 we see the distribution of tax revenue over age in the Swedish National Transfer Accounts for 2003.

Figure 6: Age Structure of Swedish Tax Payments in 2003

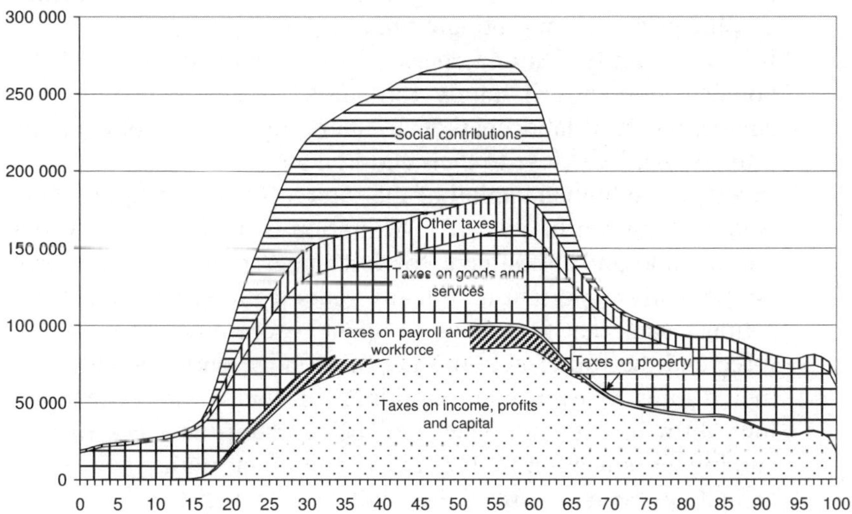

Source: Swedish NTA

Comparing this to the age pyramids it is evident that the public budget is in for a hard time. Increasing public expenditure as revenues are decreasing demands either raising taxes or increasing public debt. Alternatively expenditure has to be cut. Politically none of these options will be particularly popular. In particular it is risky to cut expenditure on elderly care and health care when the electorate is aging.

It has been shown that unemployment experiences as well as dragging out on education have substantial consequences for life cycle earnings well up into the ages 40-50 (Holmlund et al. 2008).

Summary: What Can Be Done?

There is thus a need to invest in the sustainability of the intergenerational transfer systems. There are essentially three ways to do that.

1. Invest in capital assets that will be yielding returns when the elderly dependence increases. For the reasons explained previously capital investment should preferably take place in international markets and countries that will be enjoying a demographic gift at the appropriate time.
2. Invest in family ties and charity. This is hard to sustain if the young cannot afford family formation. Due to education and concentration of labor markets to metropolitan areas old parents often do not live close to their children any more.
3. Invest in the human capital of the future. Such investment must be very long run in character. Migration is the quickest fix, but due to time and investment for full integration its effects may not be really important until many years from initial entry. Education means that time must be spent before entering the work force and the full effect does not materialize until people are in their forties or even later. Children, of course, are even more long term investment. They will be entering the labor market and higher education in their twenties but before the investment capital has been amortized they will be in their fifties.

There are quicker fixes though, which are more of a one-shot nature that we cannot keep repeating in the future. We can increase work intensity and participation rates and thus increase the degree of human capital utilization. Given the current situation where large parts of the population are already suffering from stress symptoms the scope of this fix have generally been strongly exaggerated in the current debate. Sweden already has the highest participation rates among the elderly in Europe and female participation is already almost as high as male participation.

The most efficient fix is to increase the length of work life since it has the double effect to decrease dependency and increase the active population. It is, however, even if we live longer, a biological fact that our cognitive and physiological abilities will be starting to deteriorate at some point so the scope of this fix is highly uncertain at the present stage of knowledge. It is most probable that career ways and workplace stresses will have to adapt substantially for this to be of any high importance.

The systems for intergenerational transfers will have to adapt and this adaptation will affect all aspects of social and economic life. It is problematic that political horizons often are too short to really weigh in all factors since many of the necessary adaptations have effects only at very long horizons.

One strong conclusion I draw from research on the possible approaches to adapt the transfer systems is that the highest risk for those of us who are active today will be to ignore investment in the young today. It is possible to overspend on the elderly and that might be preferred by the electorate today. But that would undermine the future welfare of our children as well as the elderly care for ourselves and the life opportunities for our children. *Après nous le déluge!*

References

Albertini, M., Kohli M. and Vogel C. (2007). Intergenerational transfers of time and money in European families: common patterns different regimes? *Journal of European Social Policy* 17, 319-334.

Bloom, D. E., Canning D. and Sevilla J. (2003). *The Demographic Dividend: A New Perspective on the Economic Consequences of Population Change*. MR-1274, RAND Population Matters Monograph, Santa Monica.

Bommier, A. and Lee R. D. (2003). Overlapping generations models with realistic demography. *Journal of Population Economics*, 16(1), 135-160.

Diamond, P. A. (1965). National Debt in a Neo-Classical Growth Model. *American Economic Review* 55, 1126-1150.

Higgins, M. (1998). Demography, National Savings, and International Capital Flows. *International Economic Review* 39(2), 343-369.

Holmlund, B., Liu Q. and Nordström Skans O. (2008). Mind the gap? Estimating the effects of postponing higher education. *Oxford Economic Papers* 60, 683-710.

Krueger, A. B. and Lindahl M. (2001). Education for Growth: Why and for Whom?. *Journal of Economic Literature* 39(4), 1101-1136.

Lindh, T. and Malmberg B. (1998). Age structure and inflation – A Wicksellian interpretation of the OECD data. *Journal of Economic Behavior and Organization* 36(1), 19-37.

Lindh, T. and Malmberg B. (1999). Age structure effects and growth in the OECD, 1950-90, *Journal of Population Economics*, 12(3), 431-449.

Lindh, T. and Malmberg B. (2000). Can age structure forecast inflation trends? *Journal of Economics and Business*, January/April, 52(1/2), 31-49.

Lindh, T. and Malmberg B. (2007). Demographically based global income forecasts up to the year 2050. *International Journal of Forecasting* 23(4), 553-567.

Lindh, T. and Malmberg B. (2008). Demography and housing demand – What can we learn from residential construction data? *Journal of Population Economics* 21(3), 521-539.

Lindh, T. and Malmberg B. (2009). EU Economic Growth and the Age Structure of the Population. *Economic Change and Restructuring*, 42(3), 159-187.

Lutz, W., Skirbekk V. and Testa M. R. (2006). The low fertility trap hypothesis: Forces that may lead to further postponement and fewer births in Europe. In *Vienna Yearbook of Population Research 2006*, Austrian Academy of Sciences, Vienna.

Lutz, W., Crespo Cuaresma J. and Sanderson W. (2008). The Demography of Educational Attainment and Economic Growth. *Science* 319(5866), 1047-1048.

Mankiw, N. G., Romer D. and Weil D. N. (1992). A Contribution to the Empirics of Economic Growth. *Quarterly Journal of Economics* 107 (2), 407-437.

Mason, A., Lee R., Tung A.-C., Lai M.-S. and Miller T. (2006). Population Aging and Intergenerational Transfers: Introducing Age into

National Account. NBER Working Paper No. 12770, Cambridge, Massachusetts.

Myrskylä, M., Kohler H-P. and Billari F. C. (2009). Advances in development reverse fertility declines. *Nature* 460(6), 741-743.

Robson, A. and Kaplan H. (2003). The evolution of human life expectancy and intelligence in huntergatherer economies. *American Economic Review* 93, 150-169.

Samuelson, P. A. (1958). An Exact Consumption-Loan Model of Interest with or Without the Social Contrivance of Money. *Journal of Political Economy* 66, 467-482.

Willis, R. J. (1988). Life Cycles, Institutions and Population Growth: A Theory of the Equilibrium Interest Rate in an Overlapping-Generations Model. In Lee, R.D., Arthur W.B. and Rodgers G., *Economics of Changing Age Distributions in Developed Countries*. Oxford University Press, 106-138.

14

Conclusions on Hierarchical versus Collaborative Governance in Health and Retirement Systems

Anthony M. Bertelli (discussant)

To collectively understand the contributions of these papers, it is useful to develop a clear understanding of what collaborative governance means in political-economic terms. Governance refers to the mechanisms – formal and informal institutions – for producing policy outcomes. Substantive policy problems such as the health and retirement systems examined by the panelists are aggregated into a variety of structures. The key contrast made in these papers is between hierarchical organizations and collaborations between the state and civil society. Legal scholar Jody Freeman (1997) claims that collaborations – what this volume refers to as collaborative governance – promises substantial benefits of institutional innovation and legitimacy. The key, she claims, to these benefits lies in the involvement of interest groups in the process; expert perspectives achieve innovation in substantively focused micro-marketplaces of ideas and legitimacy is achieved in a quasi-corporatist sense from the involvement of key constituents and interests in the creation of public policies. Consequently, we should be interested in collaborative governance, and many scholars of public policy and administration actively advocate for its use (e.g. Bardach 1998).

For all the good feeling it produces in the academic community, we must deal with two realities. First, as Bovaird reminds us in this volume, most services are already co-produced. It is rather nonsensical to think of the production of public policy outcomes without the involvement – desired or not by public officials – of stakeholders in the process of policymaking. Second, as portrayed in the literature, collaborative governance seems rather iconic. Collaboration is new, sensible, and good; top-down, hierarchical governance is outmoded, theoretically rigid, and bad (e.g., Sirianni 2009).

What are the benefits and costs of collaboration? A primary benefit to bureaucrats and politicians is that described by Freeman (1997). These groups gain innovations and some kind of quasi-corporatist legitimacy for the means of implementing policies. The organizations in civil society gain some degree of input over those means. The level of input depends on what Donahue and Zeckhauser (2006) call the "focus" of the collaboration. If the focus is broader, organizations have input into more aspects of the relevant substantive policy. Consequently, the interest of each state and civil society actors in collaborating on process is induced by their preferences over policy outcomes.

Collaboration has significant costs. Bureaucrats must commit not to unilaterally veto policy using their formal or informal means to do so. Politicians must commit not to add veto players, such as the mass public (through direct democracy), additional organized interests that change the extant quasi-corporatist balance, and additional bureaucrats or politicians at other levels of government. Regulated business and civil society organizations must commit their members to the means selected via collaboration rather than engage in venue shopping. Moreover, these commitments must be intertemporal to ensure that the collaboration will survive the dynamics of policy outcomes.

Given their benefits and costs, when do collaborations occur? Without additional political incentives, an argument may be made that collaboration on the means of producing policies in the form advocates describe occurs only in the knife-edge scenario where the actors agree on the outcomes. Collaborations are more or less likely as the policy domain moves away from that condition and when political incentives are introduced. These incentives are strongest when actors in the collaboration become effective veto players who can unilaterally stop changes in the status quo of the collaboration (Tsebelis 2002).

When do collaborations dissolve? One expectation is that they are sullied when short-term incentives on the actors to breach commitments to improve outcomes are too strong to justify the benefits of involvement. Dissolution may also be expected when longer-term incentives to sustain commitments are too weak to justify the costs of involvement. Finally, collaborations may end because different actors have contradictory incentives that overwhelm the benefits of collaboration. For instance, politicians have short-term electoral motivations while interest groups are focused on longer-term policy outcomes.

What kinds of outcomes does collaboration produce? We may expect that such outcomes are stable when there are many effective vetoes in the scheme, producing an outcome consistent with path (North 1991) or alternative set (Page 2006) dependence. Outcomes can be anticipated to be more responsive when there are few effective vetoes from bureaucrats, stakeholders and politicians at multiple levels.

These expectations can be used to better understand the claims and evidence presented in the papers on this panel. I take the papers in terms of the substantive areas on which they focus and begin with health care. Listokin's analysis of the U.S. healthcare system identifies a variety of actors with effective vetoes. Politicians at the federal and state levels, labor unions, business interests, insurance companies, physicians groups, and other health interests are all involved in the collaboration and must weigh its costs and benefits in determining whether to continue their participation. The substantive policy problem is risk assignment, namely, the degree to which the employer or employee bears the risk of the employee's health conditions. Listokin astutely observes that the status quo policy in the U.S. is a private-public mix that looks like collaboration, but with each actor dealing with its own incentives. She discusses two shocks that may have changed the incentive balance and threatened the dissolution of the "collaboration" – rapidly rising healthcare costs and the worldwide financial crisis. Because of the many effective vetoes, the collaboration remained stable with an observable path-dependent shifting mix of public-private involvement.

Karlsson examines disability and long-term care in OECD nations. He identifies various actors with effective vetoes as well. While some local politicians are stronger than others, multiple levels of actors with electoral connections are involved. Insurance companies and business interests are also effective veto players in the collaboration. Gender imbalances in the system also shape the mix of political interests. The policy problem is to define the core terms in the policy domain – long-term care, disability – and to develop a risk assignment mechanism as in the U.S. healthcare case. The status quo is again essentially a collaborative outcome in which employers and employees contribute and insurance covers between half and all costs of care. He identifies two shocks that may have impacts on the collaboration, namely, rising costs as noted above and demographic changes. The collaborative has also remained relatively stable with formal (long-term care providers) and informal (children) provision financed by a mix of savings, insurance, taxpayer support, and social insurance.

Both Listokin and Lindh discuss the domain of intergenerational transfers. They identify effective vetoes from politicians at multiple levels, labor and business organizations, insurance companies, as well as physicians and taxpayer groups. The basic policy problem is income redistribution and the dissemination of investment information. In both the U.S. and Sweden, the status quo is, again, a private-public mix which looks like collaboration. The shocks with potential to change the status quo have been the aging of the population as well as the impact of the financial crisis. While these countries have systems that emerged from very different initial conditions, as in the foregoing cases, policies display path dependence with shifting degrees of public-private involvement.

From the political-economic perspective I have taken in reading these papers, the similarity of trajectory of outcomes in these policy domains is indicative of what might be seen as a surprisingly conservative pressure exerted through collaborative governance regimes. In broad and salient policy domains such as these, the involvement of actors with political longevity and gravitas raises their status to effective veto players in the collaboration. On the one hand, this makes it difficult for any actor to unilaterally act to dissolve the collaboration, thereby sustaining its benefits. On the other hand, these veto players engender a status quo bias that makes collaborative outcomes sticky. In this way, these case studies provide a new and important lens through which to view the collaboration question.

References

Bardach, E. (1998). *Getting Agencies to Work Together*. Washington, DC: Brookings Institution Press.

Donahue, John D. and Zeckhauser R. (2006). "Public-Private Collaboration." In *Oxford Handbook of Public Policy*, Michael Moran, Martin Rein, and Robert E. Goodin, eds. New York: Oxford University Press.

Freeman, J. (1997). "Collaborative Governance in the Administrative State." *UCLA Law Review* 45:1-84.

North, Douglas. C. (1991). "Institutions, institutional change, and economic performance." New York: Cambridge University Press.

Page, Scott E. (2006). "Path Dependence." *Quarterly Journal of Political Science* 1: 87-115.

Sirianni, C. (2009). *Investing in democracy: Engaging Citizens in Collaborative Governance*. Washington, DC: Brookings Institution Press.

Tsebelis, G. (2002). *Veto Players: How Political Institutions Work*. Princeton: Princeton University Press.

Lessons from the Colloquium: Observations on Governance Approaches

15

Observations from the United States

Suzanne J. Piotrowski (rapporteur)

This book, and the conference from which it flowed, focus on the topic of collaboration in the transatlantic context. The papers presented at this conference, and included in this volume, highlight a range of organizational relationships. Some of these chapters clearly describe collaborative relationships, while others show more nebulous organizational structures. To frame my discussion, I first present an established theory on collaboration. With this framework of collaboration as a guide, I then review each of the topical sections in this volume.

What is Collaboration?

In their 1991 article, Donna Wood and Barbara Gray, systematically review the collaboration literature and identify a series of competing definitions. After looking for common elements in these definitions, they settle on a definition of collaboration:

> "Collaboration occurs when a group of autonomous stakeholders of a problem domain engage in an interactive process, using shared rules, norms, and structures, to act or decide on issues related to that domain" (Wood and Gray 1991: 146).

Wood and Gray note that while the stakeholders may have differing interests at the beginning of the collaborative process, these interests can change over the life of the collaboration. Some scholars have described collaborations as a series of continuum stages. Building upon the work of Wood and Gray, Ann Marie Thomson and James L. Perry (2006), describe an antecedent-process-outcome framework for collaboration. This framework is represented in Figure 1.

Figure 1. The Antecedent-Process-Outcome Framework (adopted from Thomson and Perry 2006)

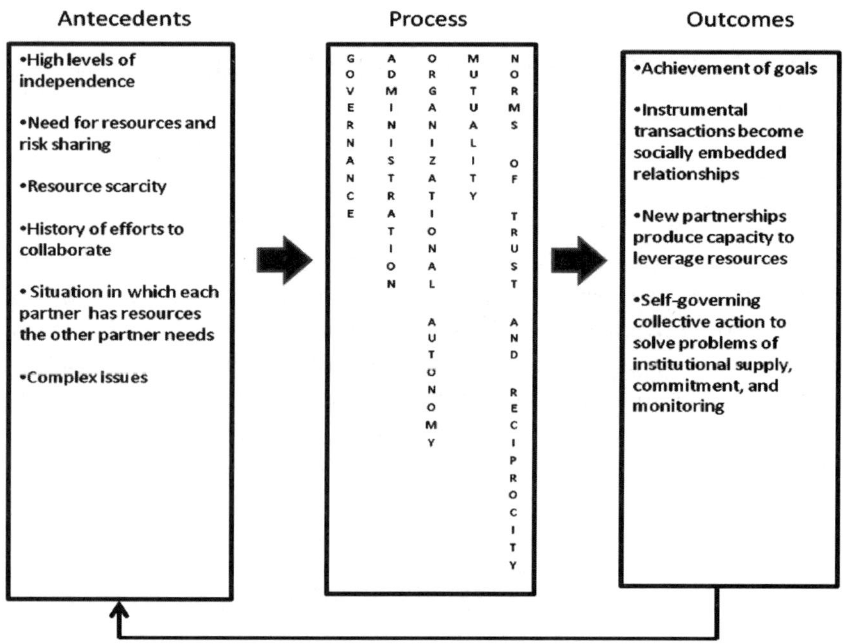

Thomson and Perry argue that a "process framework for collaboration suggests that collaboration occurs over time as organizations interact formally and informally through repetitive sequences of negotiations, development of commitments, and execution of those commitments" (Thomson and Perry 2006: 21). This repetitive nature of collaboration is included in the Thomson and Perry model. They push the reader to consider the "black box" of collaboration and spend more time reflecting on what goes on inside of the process stage. Public managers should systematically assess and analyze the five dimensions of collaboration. Two of these dimensions are structural (governing and administering), two are dimensions of social capital (mutuality and norms), and the last is an agency dimension (organizational autonomy) (Thomson and Perry 2006: 24).

The Collaboration Spectrum

The chapters in this volume illustrate different types and levels of collaboration. While not all cases meet the Wood and Gray definition of collaboration, they all contribute to our understanding of the ways in which organizations try to meet their goals within their contextual constraints. The first section of the book, *Co-production of Public Services and Collaborative Governance*, consists of a piece written by Tony Bovaird and Jörgen Tholstrup. The Bovaird and Tholstrup chapter centers on one specific type of collaborative relationship – co-production. Co-production has a number of distinctive qualities, including having service users actively participate in the collaborative process and a focus on outcomes, not simply services. This chapter addresses every stage of the antecedent-process-outcome model presented previously, and ends with a case study of a Swedish hospital. The variety of ways co-production can add value is a central theme of this chapter.

The second section of this volume, *Preventing and Resolving International Financial Crises through Regulation or Collaborative Arrangements*, explores the roles both of these tools (regulation and collaboration) have to play in producing and responding to financial crises. José Ramon Salelles' piece, *Responses to the Financial Crisis by the European Union and Member States*, discusses how both individual actors (member states), as well as a collaboration, the European Union, addressed the most recent financial crisis. Alasdair Roberts in *The Failure of the Guardians* approaches the financial crisis from the perspective of regulation and organizational arrangements. In his discussion of the changing nature of central banks, we gain a picture of technocratic administrators removed from political control. In *Reforming the International Financial System by Regulation or Collaborative Arrangements?*, Hubert Fromlet highlights five institutions that should, in concert, have ongoing responsibility for the financial crisis: central banks, supervision, government, rating agencies, and banks. Jörg Werner reviews the issue generally and summarizes the section's readings. He concludes that in the area of financial regulation neither collaborative governance, nor hierarchical solutions, are ideal but a combined approach is the wisest.

The third section of this book deals with energy markets and the same overarching theme as the previous section – hierarchal arrangements versus collaborative agreements. The first chapter in this section, authored by Richard Green, gives an in-depth look at how the gas and electricity utilities in Great Britain function. Green concludes that they have functioned reasonably well under a collaborative governance structure. The described arrangements regarding energy in the U.K. fit the definition of collaboration put forth by Wood and Gray. Eberhard Bohne gives the reader an overview of different approaches to regulating energy and ends with the idea the E.U. (again, itself a collaborative arrangement) should allow member states to pursue regulatory solutions of collaborative governance in the energy market provided that national measures meet the conditions of stakeholder inclusiveness and transparency. Caution is suggested by Sylvia Veit. Veit, echoing some of Bohne's themes, recommends more transparency of collaborative governance structures in the energy markets in order to avoid problems around less democratic control, sectoral "tunnel vision", and sub-optimal policy solutions that may arise in the long-term.

Policy Framework for Technology and Innovation through Markets or Regulation, the fourth section in this volume, consists of two excellent case studies. The first, by Kingsley Haynes and Haifeng Qian, describes research and development policies and practices in the United States. The authors conclude that in the U.S., research and development policymaking integrates both hierarchical and collaborative governance structures. The second case – AstraZeneca in Sweden – is presented by Martin Andersson, Börje Johansson, Charlie Karlsson, and Hans Lööf. These authors explain how AstraZeneca has a unique relationship with its host country because of the central and critical role it plays with respect to research and development in Sweden.

The final policy section in this volume addresses the issues of health care and retirement systems. Siona Listokin presents an overview of the U.S. healthcare and retirement systems and concludes that there is a "destructive co-dependence" in the present public-private mix, not collaboration. *The Economics of Frailty: Disability and Long Term Care Systems in OECD Countries* by Martin Karlsson looks at different possible long-term care solutions. He presents the U.K, U.S., Japan, Sweden, and Germany cases and highlights key characteristics. Thomas Lindh's piece on intergenerational transfers is an excellent companion to the Karlsson piece. Lindh explains how the issue of an aging society relates to intergenerational wealth transfers. Anthony Bertelli concludes the section by presenting a theoretical approach to collaboration, different from Thomson and Perry, and reviews the papers in this section from a rational choice perspective.

Conclusions

This volume presents a range of relationships forms. Some of these arrangements are clearly collaborative, while others are less well defined. In addition to the tensions between collaborative and hierarchical arrangements, there were some common threads throughout the volume. What should be the proper role of government and the desired level of regulation was a theme that came up in many of the chapters. What the papers by and large did not address was the role democracy played, and should play, in making these decisions. The book included examples from a range of countries with some being well represented, including the U.S., Sweden, England, and Germany. The rest of North America – Canada and Mexico – were not represented in the volume; neither were a many other European countries, particularly those in Eastern Europe. Taken as a whole, this volume pushes and expands the discussion on collaborative governance and addresses a range of policy issues relevant on both sides of the Atlantic.

References

Thomson, A. M., and Perry J. L. (2006). Collaboration Processes: Inside the Black Box. *Public Administration Review* (Special Issue): 20-32.

Wood, D. J., and Gray B. (1991). Toward a Comprehensive Theory of Collaboration. *Journal of Applied Behavioral Science, 27*(2): 139-162.

16

Observations from Germany

Margrit Seckelmann (rapporteur)

Collaborative Governance is a topic recently discussed on both sides of the Atlantic Ocean.[1] Whilst the American debate gained momentum by the "open government initiative" of President Barack Obama,[2] the German discussion focuses on the concept of the "ensuring state"("*Gewährleistungsstaat*") that gives the state the role of the "lender of last resort", when public private partnerships fail.[3]

But how can those discussions be exemplified? The presentations held in the course of the annual TPC colloquium at Jönköping International Business School, Sweden, in 2009 can highlight some of the aspects of the discussions not only in the United States and Germany but in the United Kingdom and a few Scandinavian countries. In doing so, all the "national" debates can be enriched by the foreign example.

The essay by Tony Bovaird and Jörgen Tholstrup, entitled *Collaborative Governance Between the Public Sector, Service Users, and their Communities*, deals with the joint production of collective goods by citizens and public sector entities as a means of creating value. The authors show that the benefits of well-designed collaborative processes are likely to include enhanced financial efficiency and a higher degree of satisfaction among recipients and wider groups. Moreover, they argue that this way of proceeding may also advance the attainment of environmental, political, social and environmental goals appreciated by the public. This line of thought is conclusively supported by a case study from the gastroenterology unit of a Swedish hospital, where the improved involvement of patients in their care not only brought about substantial cost savings and fewer supply shortfalls, but also enhanced the patients' sense of responsibility and overall satisfaction. However, the authors also warn that there may be areas of public service provision where co-production may not be beneficially applicable, and postulate that in cases where some individuals are unable or unwilling to use co-production possibilities, they must not suffer undue disadvantages.

Understandably, the recent financial crisis and the challenges it poses with regard to the international coordination of financial and monetary policies, regulatory standards and capital market supervision takes up much space in this volume. In his paper on the *Responses to the Financial Crisis by the European Union and Member States*, José Ramon Salelles delivers a conclusive analysis of the causes of the crisis, argues the rationale for interventions by governments and monetary authorities directed at the containment of the financial market emergency, gives a thorough account of the related policy reactions by the European Union and individual member states, and discusses the conclusions to be drawn with regard to regulatory provisions required to restore and maintain the stability of financial markets in future.

The behavior of central banks in the run-up and the course of the crisis is the centerpiece of Alasdair S. Roberts's article on *The Failure of the Guardians: Central Banking Reform and the Financial Crisis*. The author traces the failure of central bankers and supervisory authorities to detect and counteract the looming financial crisis in a timely and factually appropriate manner to the preceding transfer of authority from entities subject to constraints on democratic choice (like, e.g., government ministries) to "technocrat-guardians" effectively detached from democratic control. He contends that this transfer of authority may have led to a momentous underestimation of the contingent propensity of financial markets to exhibit "wild swings, driven by short term profit seeking and herd behavior", and therefore estimates that wariness and the stability of unregulated markets will foster a reassertion of political influence in policy domains currently dominated by technocratic governance.

Hubert Fromlet, in his contribution headed *Reforming the International Financial System by Regulation or Collaborative Arrange-*

ments?, emphatically rejects the theoretical concept of the *homo oeconomicus* and calls for its dismissal in favor of the behavioral model of bounded rationality, which explicitly accounts for the human susceptibility to sentiments like greed, hubris, historical amnesia, rashness and panic. As a key challenge to future regulatory provisions, Fromlet identifies the need to remove (or prohibitively discourage) "perverse" economic incentives which encourage rather than dampen excessive risk-taking and habitual short-sightedness of financial decision makers. As a means of attaining this goal, the author recommends an enhanced consideration of corporate governance issues in collaborative agreements between banks and public institutions, and calls for a substantially higher transparency of the asset holdings and trading operations, and instruments of financial institutions.

Jörg R. Werner's paper *Conclusions on Hierarchical versus Collaborative Governance in the Finance Sector* relates past changes in the mode of financial market regulation and supervision to globalisation, international financial market integration, and market-oriented policy reforms. He argues that, in the financial sector, these phenomena were a severe challenge to national modes of regulation and, particularly, to hierarchical governance arrangements, in which agents legitimised by democratic majority decision create binding rules by means of law. According to Werner, these developments led to the emergence of collaborative arrangements, in which coordination efforts are exerted by institutionalized arrangements or organizations in which public and private actors jointly participate. Noting that these forms of governance were subjected to harsh criticism in the course of the recent financial market turbulences, the author nevertheless remains cognisant of the weaknesses of national, hierarchical attempts at a solution. Instead, he calls for a combination of hierarchical and collaborative mechanisms in which their respective merits and shortcomings are accounted for.

The next two papers draw the attention to collaborative governance arrangements in the 'knowledge economy'. The paper by Kinsley E. Haynes and Haifeng Qian on *The Structure of US R&D Policymaking: An Overview* deals with the main characteristics of U.S. R&D policymaking. Drawing on examples from the fields of IT, nuclear power, biomedical research, and small business innovation, it examines the interaction between public sector entities on both federal and state levels, government-associated advisory groups and institutions, and private sector entities including not only inventors, entrepreneurs, and venture capitalists but also labor unions, trade and industry associations, and not-for-profit organisations. Haynes and Qian find that the role of the private sector entities in this process is not confined to the commercialization of new knowledge and the introduction of new products and processes, but can also include an active participation in allocation decisions regarding federal and state resources. The authors therefore conclude R&D policy is a process with highly interactive and recursive characteristics.

In their paper on *Multinationals in the Knowledge Economy*, Martin Andersson, Börje Johansson, Charlie Karlsson and Hans Lööf examine the interplay between the actions of large, knowledge-intensive multinational corporations and the economic development of their seat countries, using the pharmaceuticals firm AstraZeneca as an example. The authors contend that the geographical location decisions of such companies are strongly influenced by the perceived need to be close both to the relevant markets and the centers of related technical knowledge. Moreover, they find that the economic importance of such corporations for their seat countries exceeds the extent mirrored by their share in macroeconomic aggregates like GDP or export revenues by far. In this context, the paper places particular emphasis on the substantial contributions that multinational corporations can make to the attainment and diffusion of technological and economic knowledge, e.g. by directly supporting academic research and teaching efforts or by providing opportunities for on-the-job training. The authors conclude that public policy can contribute significantly to economic prosperity by furthering the attainment of key qualifications through the domestic educational system, promoting the interaction between business, state institutions, and academia, and rendering the target regions an attractive place of settlement for knowledge-intensive firms as well as highly skilled, internationally mobile individuals.

The challenge posed by the expected demographic transition processes to the stability of pension systems in most of Europe and North America is the overall subject of the three following essays. The contribution by Siona Listokin (*Private Versus Government-based Health Systems and Retirement Systems in the US*) examines closely the retirement and public health systems in the U.S., and deals with the question whether the workings of these systems meet the criteria of collaborative governance. To this end, the author reviews the literature on the subject co-regulation and provides instructive information on the historical development of these systems. She concludes that both the U.S. healthcare and retirement systems use a mix of public and private funding and delivery, but nevertheless fail to comply with key characteristics of collaborative governance, which include the principles of participation, flexibility, participation, and problem solving orientation.

Martin Karlsson conducts in his study on *The Economics of Frailty: Disability and Long-Term Care Systems in OECD Countries* a comparative analysis of the disability and long term care systems of the OECD member countries. He finds that, in particular, the national approaches to long-term care services diverge considerably even among countries which closely resemble each other in many other aspects. According to Karlsson, these variations are accompanied by disparities with regard to the roles assigned to governments, markets, and families. The author also warns that in countries with protractedly low birth and immigration rates, the burden of long-term care expenses might very well turn out to be unsustainable for citizens and governments in the decades to come. Based on these considerations, he suggests that governments should confine their role to dealing with the risk of high-intensity, long-term care (and, possibly, of inflation), while leaving the insurance against all other healthcare and age-related risks to the private market.

Thomas Lindh's essay on *Different Approaches to Providing Intergenerational Transfers in Aging Societies* examines closely a case study for Sweden. In doing so, the author demonstrates that the predicted shifts in the age structure of the population can be expected to put the public finances in the countries affected under considerable strain. The paper discusses several policy options aiming at a stabilization of intergenerational transfer systems, including lowering pension benefit levels, capital investments in countries with favorable demographic structures, increasing the effective labor supply via higher participation rates, longer work lives, and increased work intensity, and promoting immigration. Lindh comprehensively assesses each of these policy proposals with regard to their possible economic consequences, their socio-political side effects, and the likelihood of their public acceptance. On the grounds of the results obtained, he reckons that any attempt to deal with the demographic challenge which ignores the need to invest massively in the human capital of the younger generations is bound to fail.

Richard Green's contribution, *Energy Regulation in Great Britain: Lessons Learned for Collaborative Governance,* describes how the partitioning of decision making competencies between the government, its agencies (regulators and competition authorities), and private sector companies has affected the operations of the utilities of gas and electricity in the U.K. in recent years. According to Green, the conjoint approach applied in this field led to a higher level of transparency of regulatory actions under consideration, thus significantly diminishing the uncertainty for the companies involved, and creating favorable conditions for corporate investments. The author also points out that this mode of operation, along with the competency of the Monopolies and Mergers Commission to step in against restraints of trade, has led to an increased intensity of competition among market participants for the benefit of end users. He concludes that while some controversy among participants is inescapable, collaborative governance procedures can be a highly effective means of setting rules that promote secure and economically efficient supply energy.

Eberhard Bohne's contribution, *Clash of Regulatory Cultures in the EU: The Liberalization of Energy Markets*, comprises a critical account of the policy measures aiming at the establishment of truly competitive and integrated electricity and gas markets. Based on an instructive overview of the succession of related regulatory actions, the author establishes that the attainment of this central goal has eventually not been achieved to an extent that could justify the substantial implementation and enforcement costs incurred. Bohne attributes this unsatisfactory outcome to the fact that EU regulations somewhat exclusively follow the UK model of restructuring energy markets which, in turn, has been strongly shaped by neo-classical economic theory and a command-and-control nature of regulatory action. As a workable alternative to this way of proceeding, he advocates the concept of collaborative governance, where public agencies engage private stakeholders in a consensus-oriented decision process, thus allowing for a higher degree of consideration for the particularities of different national regulatory cultures.

In her comments on the issue of *Liberalization of Energy Markets in the European Union,* Sylvia Veit concurs with Eberhard Bohne's sceptical view of the "command-and-control" approach to regulation, and supports co-operative approaches to policy formulation and implementation, in which public actors and representatives of virtually all private stakeholders join forces "at eye level". In spite of the perceived advantages of this model, which may include a higher degree legitimacy of decision outcomes and an improved utilisation of expert knowledge, Veit warns that cooperative governance is not a self-acting automatism necessarily leading to higher stakeholder contentment: based on experience gathered in the context of restructuring processes in the U.S. electricity sector, she points out that decision makers must be aware that ill-conceived attempts to introduce collaborative, "open access" regulations might lead to unintended detrimental side effects ("negative externalities") in parts of society not included in the decision processes, bring about an attrition of democratic control processes, and lead to a decline in democratic participation by the general public. Decision makers aiming at a good balance between sector-specific requirements and the needs of society as a whole will have to be aware of these risks and respond to them adequately.

Anthony M. Bertelli's discussion essay focuses on the common themes of the individual contributions to this volume from a political-economic perspective. He points out that some of the main possible benefits of collaborative governance processes may accrue to bureau crats and politicians, who can utilize such schemes to gather new information and obtain a quasi-corporatist appearance of legitimacy for their actions. Moreover, Bertelli warns that collaborative governance procedures can entail significant costs if their outcomes are to be sustainable for long time periods. The balance of power between government actors and delegates from different (and potentially antagonistic) stakeholder groups may prove to be difficult to maintain when private sector entities not directly involved in the decision making process call for more influence, and discontent grows among the general public. Moreover, in cases where only a general consensus (rather than an absolute majority of votes) among the groups involved is regarded a sufficient condition for a certain rule to come into effect, collective governance procedures can introduce a significant bias in favor of the status quo into the decision making process. Bertelli concludes that the choice between hierarchical and collaborative patterns of public sector decision making, the design of the related information and negotiation procedures, and the granting of adequate representation to different, potentially heterogeneous stakeholder groups involve complex cost-benefit balancing processes of which the outcomes may very well differ from case to case.

Interestingly, Bertelli's comments from an American perspective almost sum up the German discussion concerning the "ensuring state" ("*Gewährleistungsstaat*"). His comments demonstrate the close interlinkage between the multinational discussions which are joint in the 2009 conference of the TPC.

Endnotes

[1] Thanks to *Sikandar Siddiqui* and *Christian Bauer* for their helpful comments.

[2] Barack *Obama* (2009): Transparency and Open Government, Memorandum of January 21, 2009. Federal Register, Vol. 74, No. 15, p. 4685.

[3] *Folke Schuppert* (2003), The Ensuring State, in: Anthony Giddens (ed.): The progressive manifesto: new ideas for the centre-left, Oxford: Blackwell, pp. 54-72.

Index

List of Authors

Martin Andersson, Associate Professor of Economics and CESIS research coordinator, Jönköping International Business School (JIBS), Jönköping and the Centre of Excellence for Science and Innovation Studies (CESIS), Royal Institute of Technology, Stockholm, Sweden

Anthony M. Bertelli, C. C. Crawford Chair in Management and Performance, University of Southern California, USA

Eberhard Bohne, Professor of Public Administration, Policy and Law for Environmental Protection and Energy, German University of Administrative Sciences Speyer, Speyer, Germany

Tony Bovaird, Professor of Public Management and Policy INLOGOV, School of Government and Society; and Third Sector Research Centre University of Birmingham, Birmingham, UK

Hubert Fromlet, Adjunct Professor Economics, Jönköping International Business School, Jönköping, Sweden and Visiting Professor, Linnaeus University, Kalmar/Växjö, Sweden

Richard Green, Professor, Director, Institute for Energy Research and Policy, University of Birmingham, Birmingham, UK

Kingsley E. Haynes, University Professor Director, State Economic Development Center, Professor of Public Policy, Decision Sciences, Geography and Public Affairs, Ruth D. and John T. Hazel, MD Endowed Chari and Eminent Scholar School of Public Policy, George Mason University, Fairfax, USA

Börje Johansson, Professor of Economics and director of CESIS, Jönköping International Business School (JIBS), Jönköping and the Centre of Excellence for Science and Innovation Studies (CESIS), Royal Institute of Technology, Stockholm, Sweden

Charlie Karlsson, Professor of Economics, Associate Dean of Education and Director of CISEG and INA, Jönköping International Business School (JIBS), Jönköping University, Jönköping, Sweden

Martin Karlsson, Assistant Professor at the Chair of Applied Econometrics of the Technische Universität Darmstadt, Darmstadt, Germany

Thomas Lindh, Professor of Economics at Linnaeus University in Växjö and Research Director at the Institute for Future Studies, Stockholm, Sweden

Siona Listokin, Assistant Professor, School of Public Policy, George Mason University, Fairfax, Virginia, USA

Hans Lööf, Professor of Economics and project leader at CESIS Royal Institute of Technology, Stockholm, Sweden

Suzanne J. Piotrowski, Associate Professor, School of Public Affairs and Administration, Rutgers University-Newark, Newark, USA

Haifeng Qian, Assistant Professor of Public Affairs, Levin School of Public and Urban Affairs, Cleveland State University, Cleveland, Ohio, USA

Alasdair S. Roberts, Jerome L. Rappaport Professor of Law and Public Policy, Suffolk University Law School, Boston MA, USA

José Ramón Salelles, Professor of Commercial Law, Universidad Pompeu Fabra, Barcelona, Spain

Margrit Seckelmann, Head of Administration, German Research Institute for Public Administration Speyer, Speyer, Germany

Jörgen Tholstrup, Head of the Unit of Gastroenterology, Medical Department, Eksjo, Sweden

Sylvia Veit, Faculty of Economics and Social Sciences, University of Potsdam, Potsdam, Germany

Jörg R. Werner, Dipl.-Kfm. Dr. rer. pol., Senior Researcher, Faculty of Business Studies and Economics, University of Bremen, Bremen, Germany

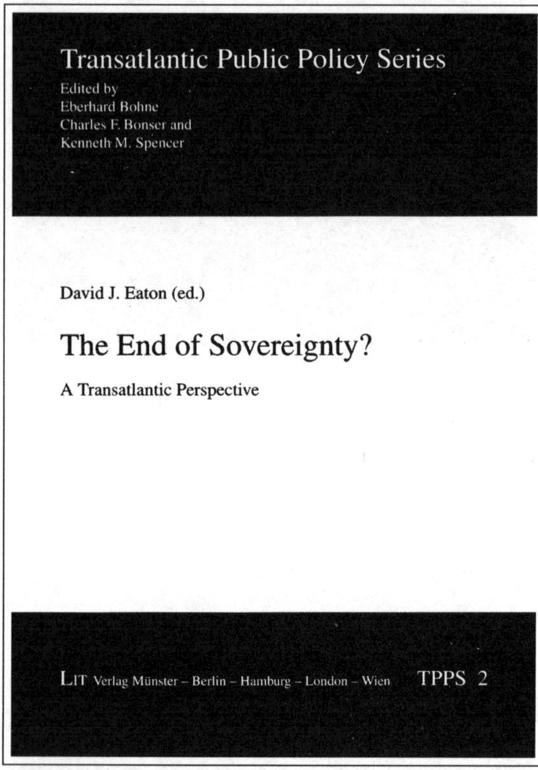

David J. Eaton (Ed.)
The End of Sovereignty?
A Transatlantic Perspective

The second volume of the Transatlantic Public Policy Series comprises contributions by members of the Transatlantic Policy Consortium (TPC). The 17 provocative contributions focus on the concept of internal and external sovereignty which is critical on both sides of the Atlantic. It is not easy to articulate the domain and limits of the state's control of its resources, its capacity to coerce activities within its borders, its powers to treat other states as co-equals across a border, or even implement its own defense, trade or regulatory policies. The volume provides a unique insight into these problems from a European and US perspective.

Bd. 2, 2006, 480 S., 39,90 €, br., ISBN 3-8258-9285-9

LIT Verlag Berlin – Münster – Wien – Zürich – London
Auslieferung Deutschland / Österreich / Schweiz: siehe Impressumsseite

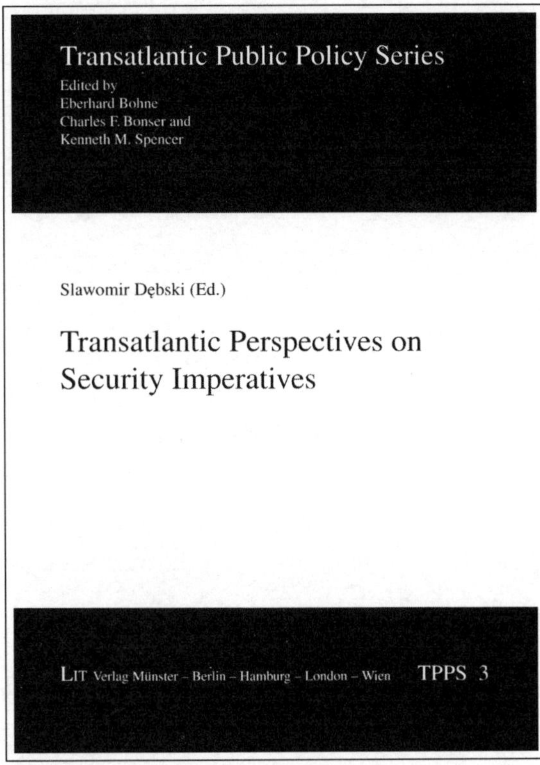

Slawomir Debski (Ed.)
Transatlantic Perspectives on Security Imperatives
The third volume of the Transatlantic Public Policy Series contains papers prepared by members of the Transatlantic Policy Consortium (TPC), representing American and European universities and institutions. The 13 contributions focus on the future of NATO, the possibilities of transatlantic cooperation in the Middle East problems, and the challenges to human security. The collection serves as an illustration of the state of the debate on security problems in transatlantic relations at this specific time. It will contribute to greater synergies of thinking and studies of global security pursued in American and European institutions.
Bd. 3, 2007, 296 S., 34,90 €, br., ISBN 978-3-8258-0655-2

Wirtschaft: Forschung und Wissenschaft

Eberhard Bohne (Hg.)
Neubestimmung ordnungspolitischer Aufgaben des Staates im Strommarkt
Die Liberalisierung des Strommarktes ist Ausdruck eines generellen Wandels im Verhältnis von Staat und Wirtschaft. Ausgelöst durch europarechtliche Vorgaben, führten Änderungen des Energiewirtschaftsgesetzes und des Gesetzes gegen Wettbewerbsbeschränkungen zu einem ordnungspolitischen Paradigmenwechsel für die Stromwirtschaft in Deutschland. Der Wettbewerb, der 100 Jahre lang im Strommarkt als schädlich galt, wurde zum Leitprinzip des neuen Ordnungsrahmens. Die in einem Tagungsband zusammengefassten Referate und Diskussionsbeiträge betreffen Probleme und Folgen dieses Paradigmenwechsels aus Sicht der Marktteilnehmer und der für die Sicherstellung des Ordnungsrahmens verantwortlichen staatlichen Akteure. Der Band zeigt Schwierigkeiten und Lösungsansätze bei der Einführung eines wirksamen Wettbewerbs auf, insbesondere bei der Gewährleistung des diskriminierungsfreien Netzzugangs, dem Handel mit Strom und strombasierten Finanzkontrakten und der Neustrukturierung staatlicher Aufgaben.
Bd. 4, 2003, 216 S., 34,90 €, br., ISBN 3-8258-7072-3